Shojo Beat

Tail of the Moon

10

Story & Art by

Rinko Ueda

Volume 10

**C
O
N
T
E
N
T
S**

Story Thus Far...

It is the Era of the Warring States. Usagi is a failure as a ninja, but she is a skilled herbalist. She is working hard to qualify as a ninja so she can be the bride of Hattori Hanzo (aka "Shimo no Hanzo")!

Usagi is happily living together with Hanzo in a secret hideout after escaping from Honnoji. Unfortunately, she is unable to go outside freely since their adversary Ranmaru has begun hunting the Iga ninja.

One day, after succeeding in creating a medicine for Mitsuhide (who is against the attack on Iga), Usagi is reunited with her childhood friend Kame. Seeing that the once-slow Kame has become a fine ninja, Usagi vows to work hard and receives an assignment from Hanzo. But during the assignment, she finds out that Kame and Ranmaru are lovers! Thinking that Kame has betrayed Iga, Usagi goes to confront her. Usagi is discovered by Ranmaru, who grabs her and...?!

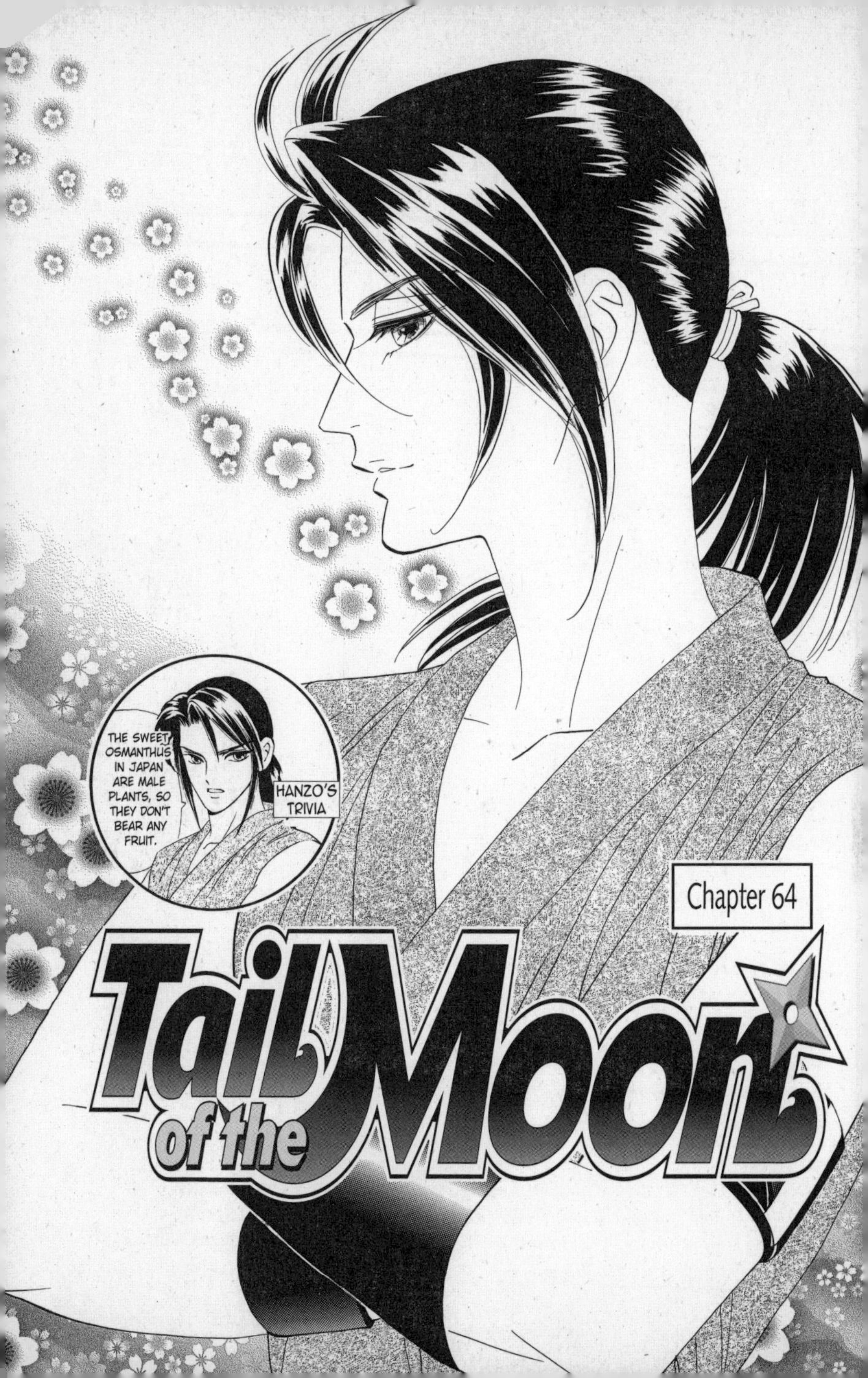
THE SWEET OSMANTHUS IN JAPAN ARE MALE PLANTS, SO THEY DON'T BEAR ANY FRUIT.
HANZO'S TRIVIA
Chapter 64
Tail of the Moon

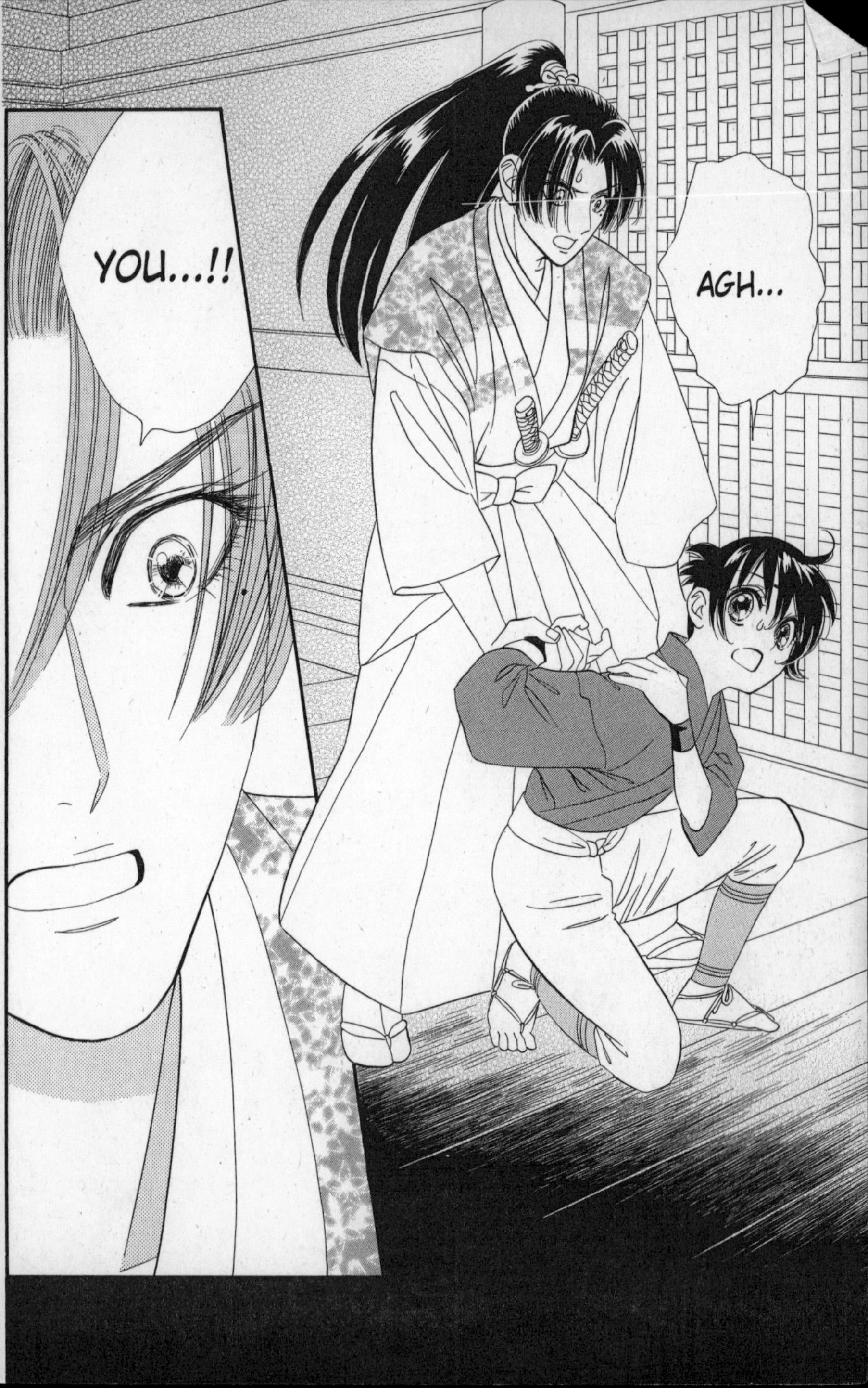
AGH...
YOU...!!

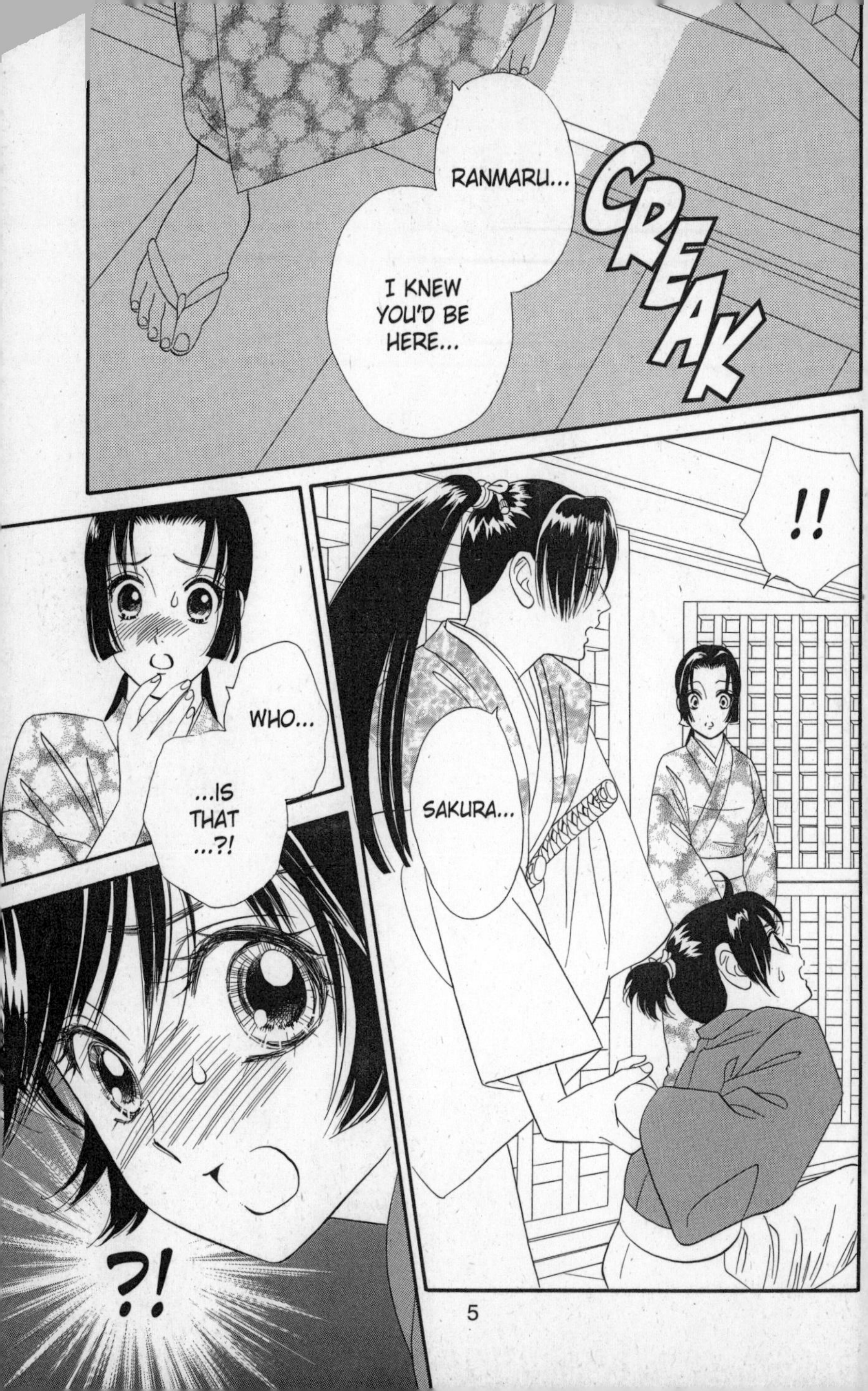
CREAK
RANMARU...
I KNEW YOU'D BE HERE...
!!
SAKURA...
WHO...
...IS THAT ...?!
?!

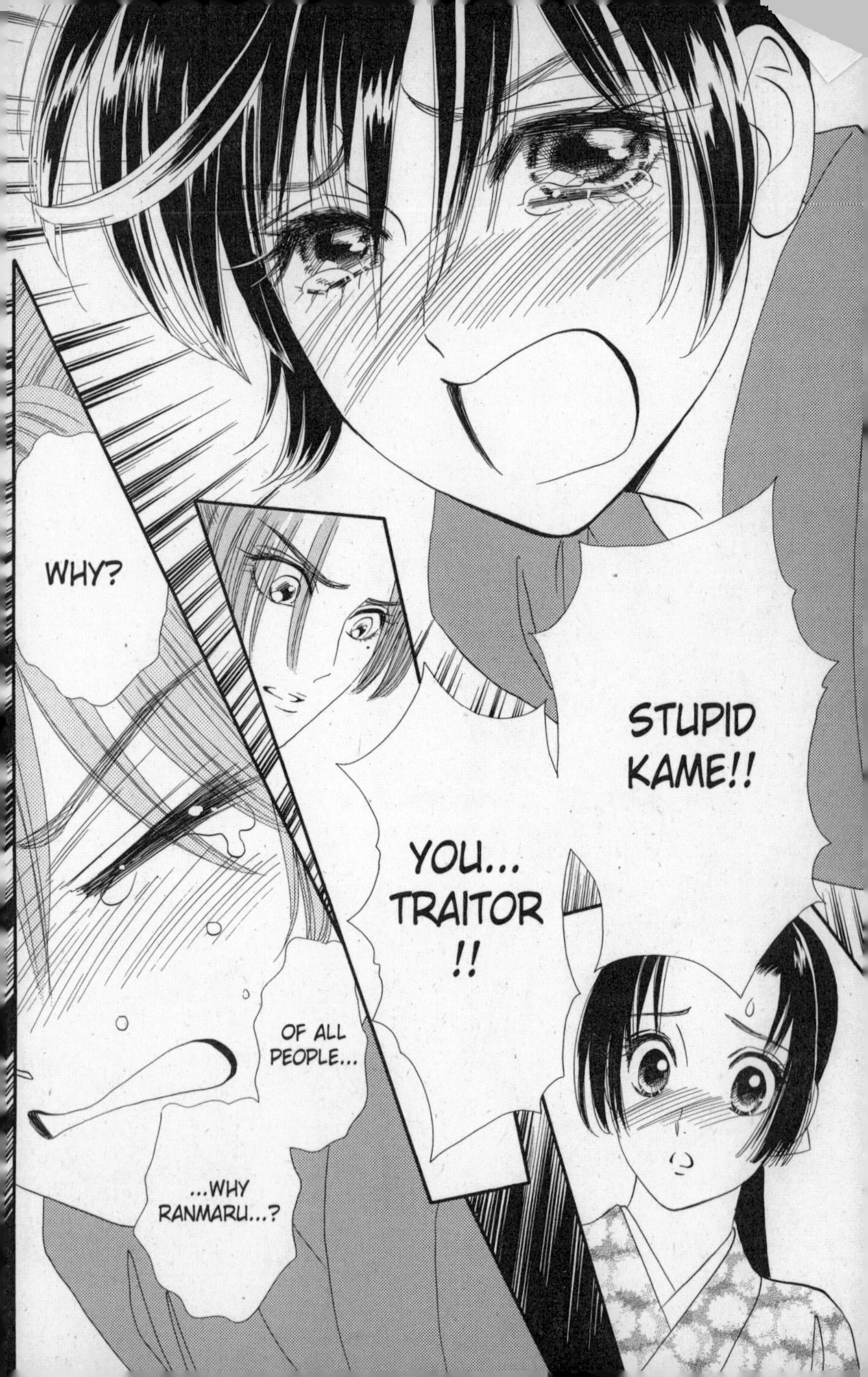
STUPID KAME!!
YOU... TRAITOR !!
WHY?
OF ALL PEOPLE...
...WHY RANMARU...?

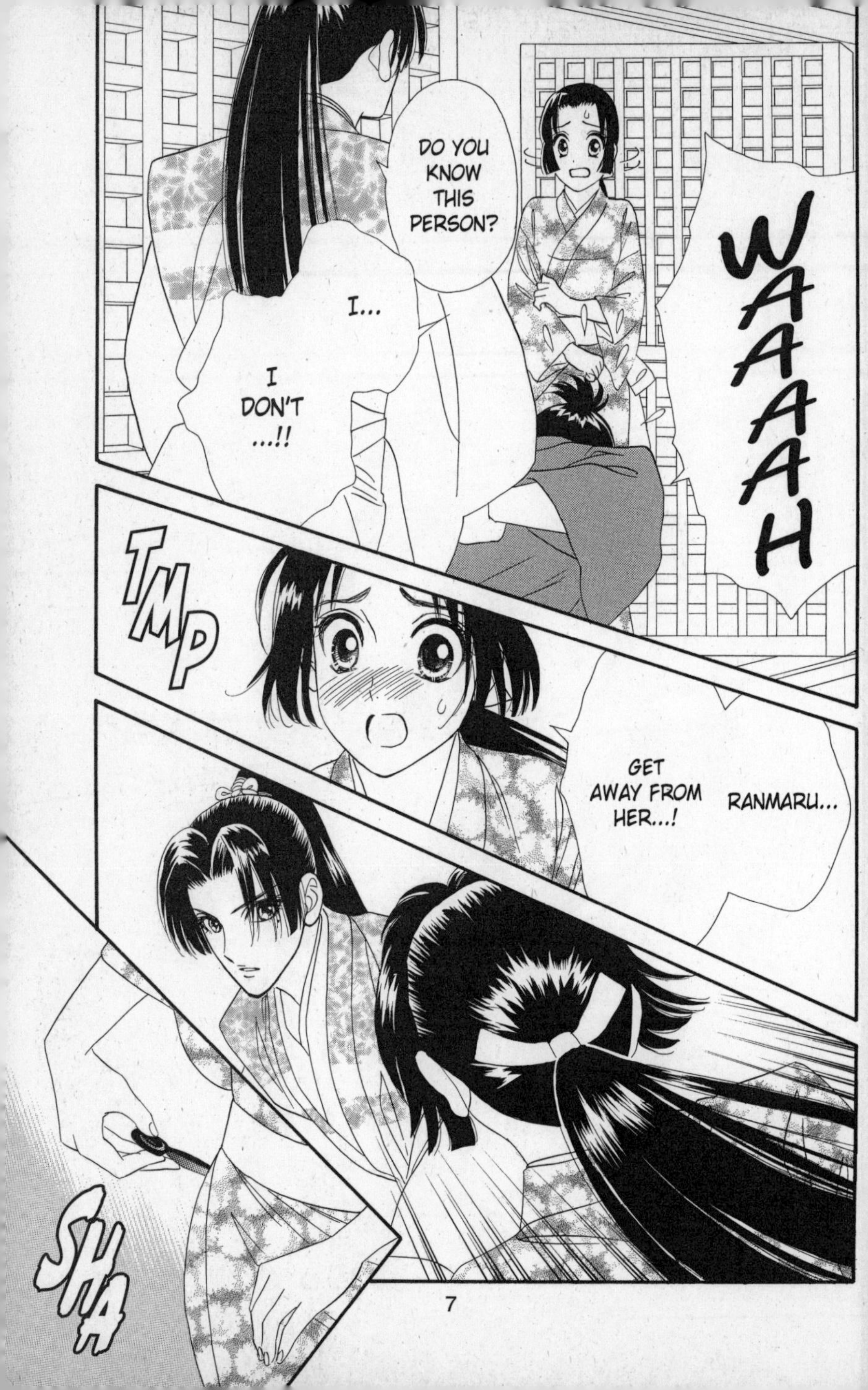
WAAAAH
DO YOU KNOW THIS PERSON?
I...
I DON'T ...!!
TMP
RANMARU...
GET AWAY FROM HER...!
SHA

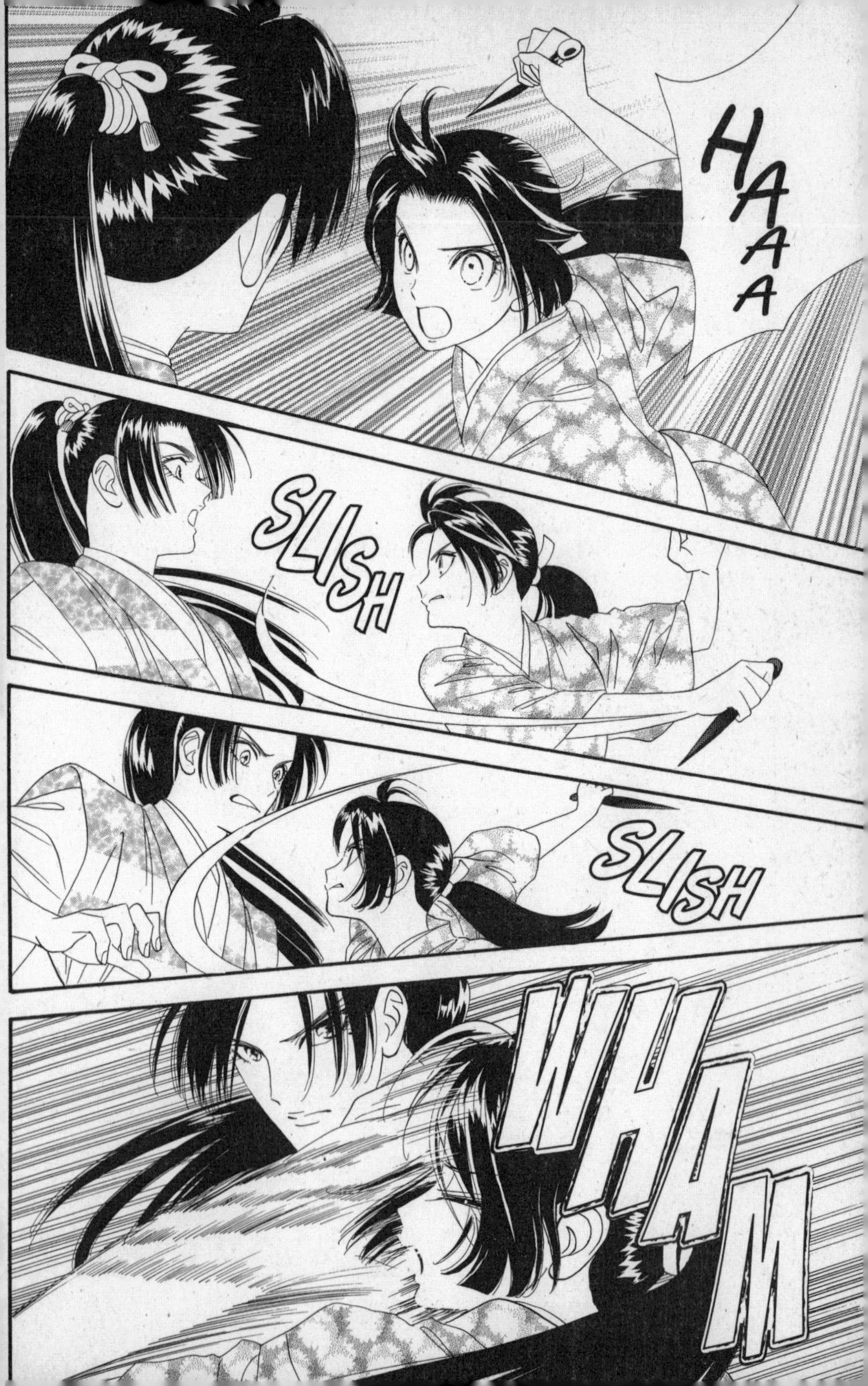
HAAAA
SLISH
SLISH
WHAM

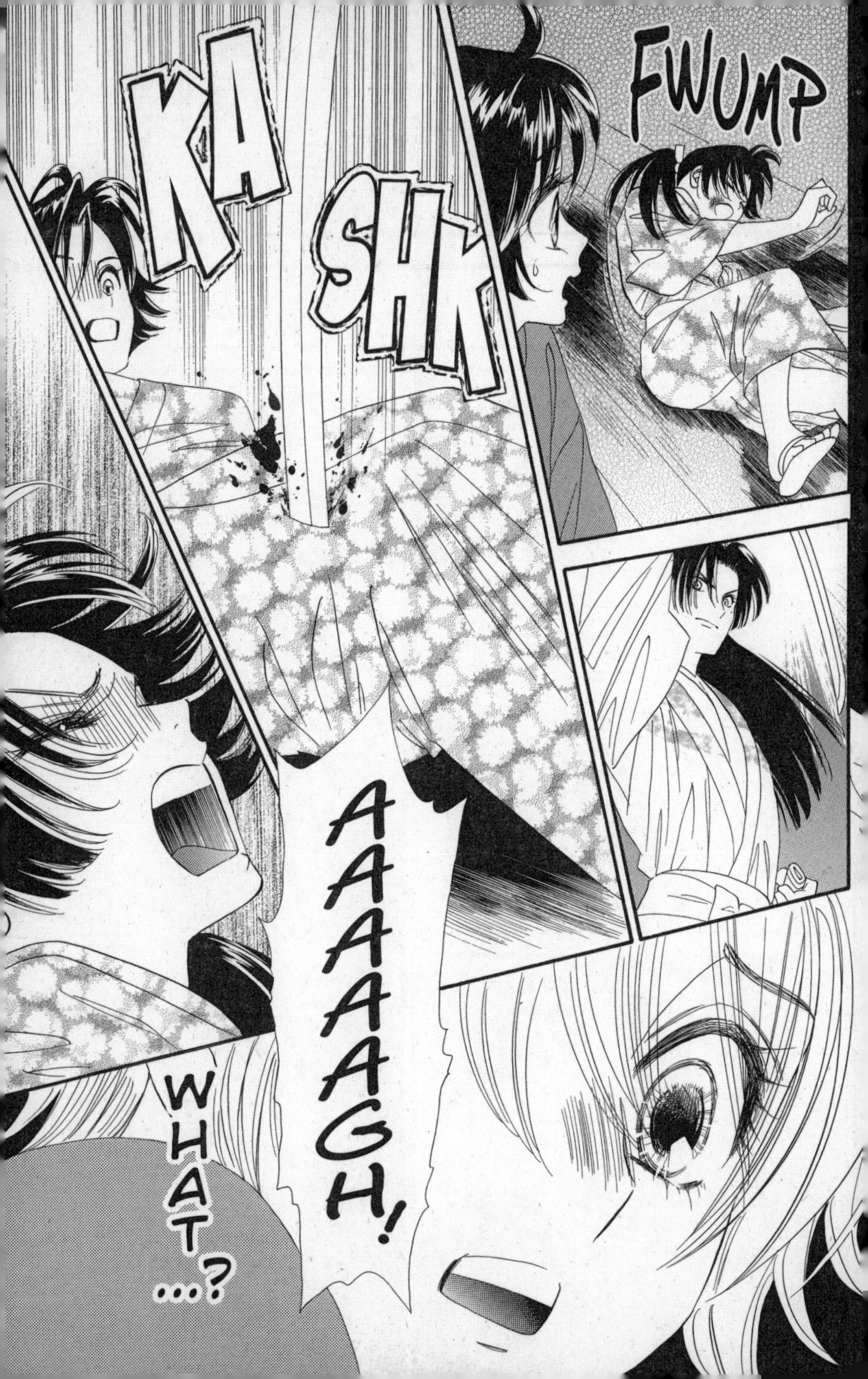
FWUMP
KA
SHK
AAAAAGH!
WHAT...?

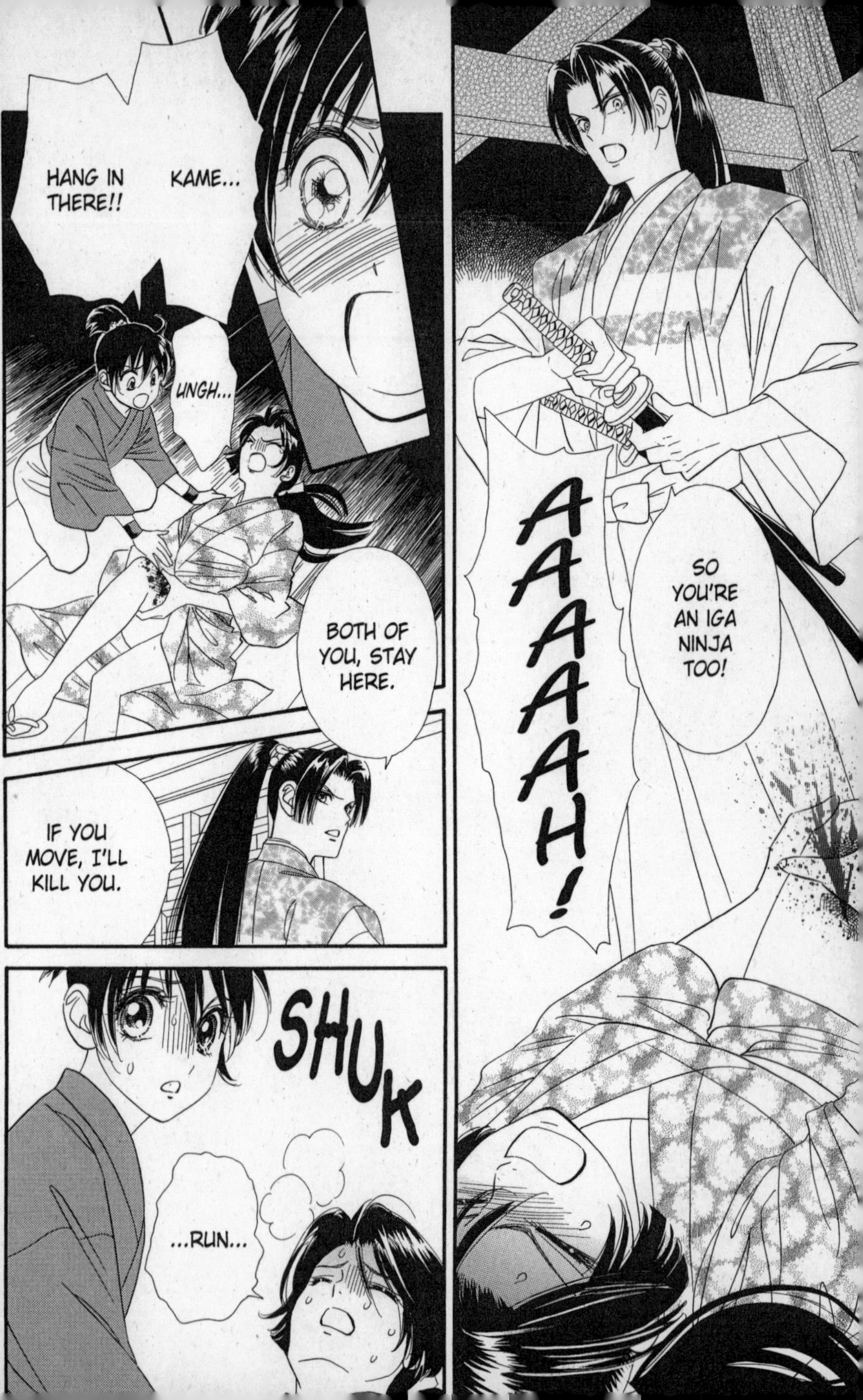
SO YOU'RE AN IGA NINJA TOO!
AAAAAH!
KAME...
HANG IN THERE!!
UNGH...
BOTH OF YOU, STAY HERE.
IF YOU MOVE, I'LL KILL YOU.
SHUK
...RUN...

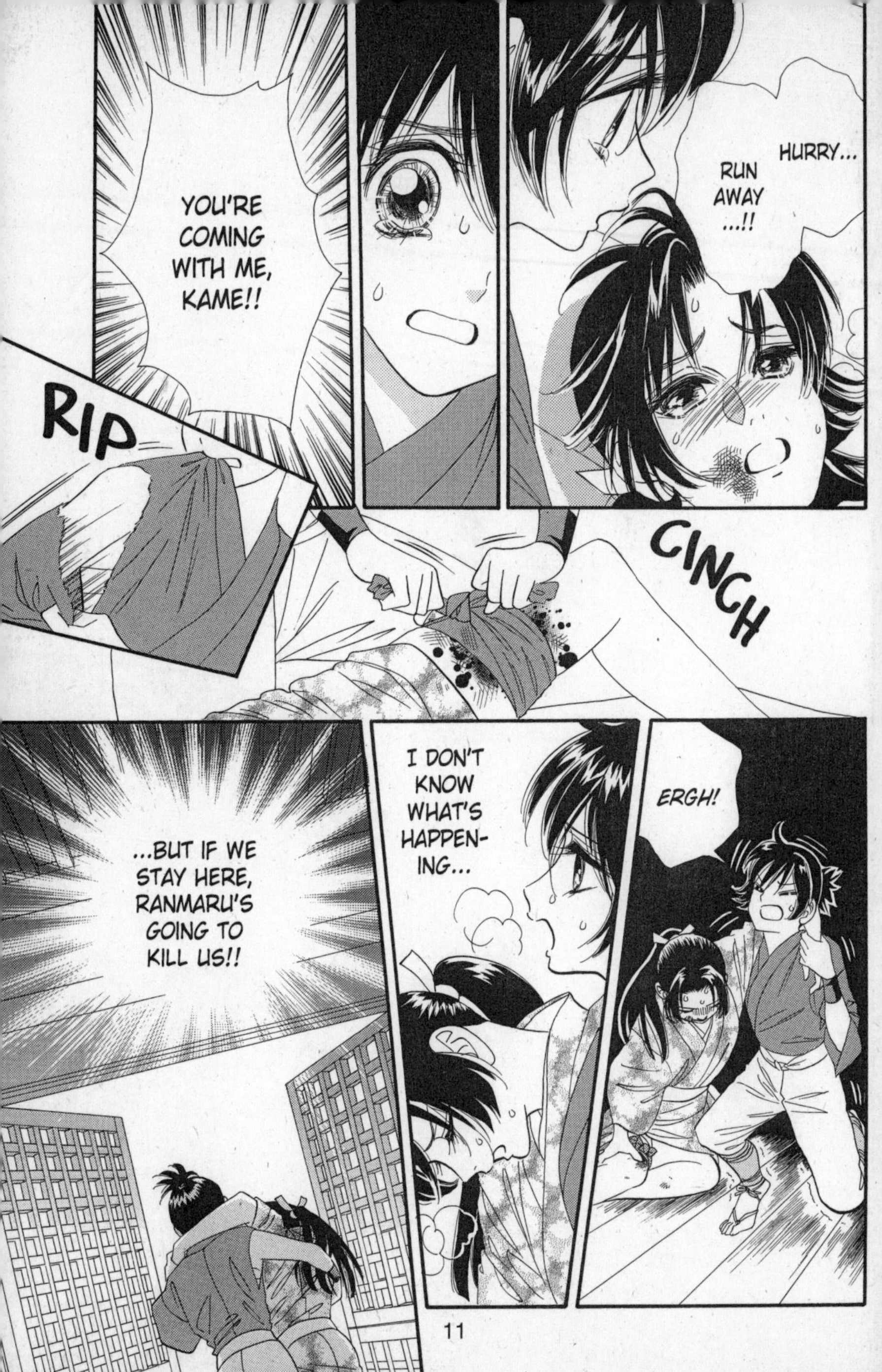
HURRY...
RUN AWAY ...!!
YOU'RE COMING WITH ME, KAME!!
RIP
CINCH
ERGH!
I DON'T KNOW WHAT'S HAPPEN-ING...
...BUT IF WE STAY HERE, RANMARU'S GOING TO KILL US!!

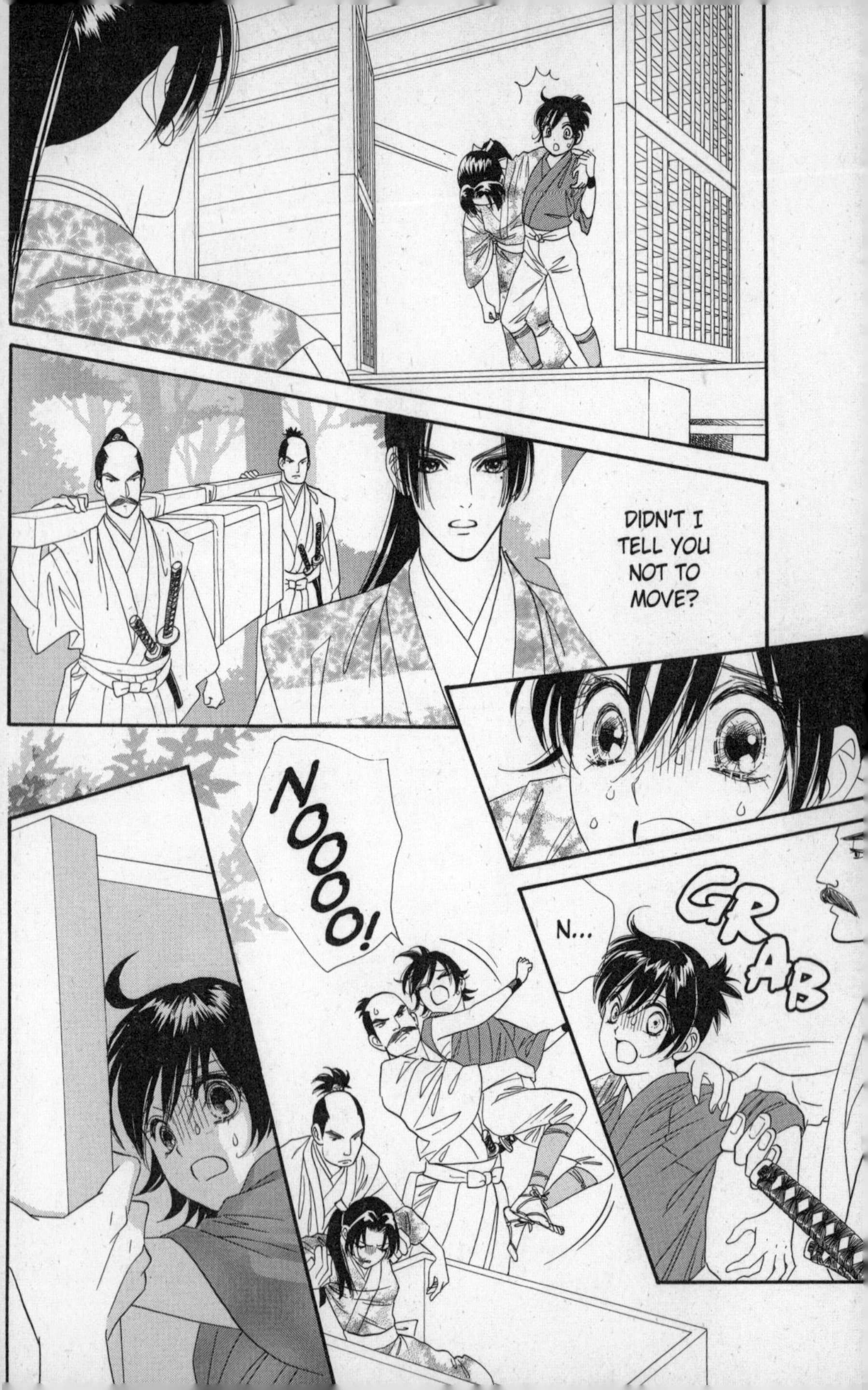
DIDN'T I TELL YOU NOT TO MOVE?
N...
GRAB
NOOOO!

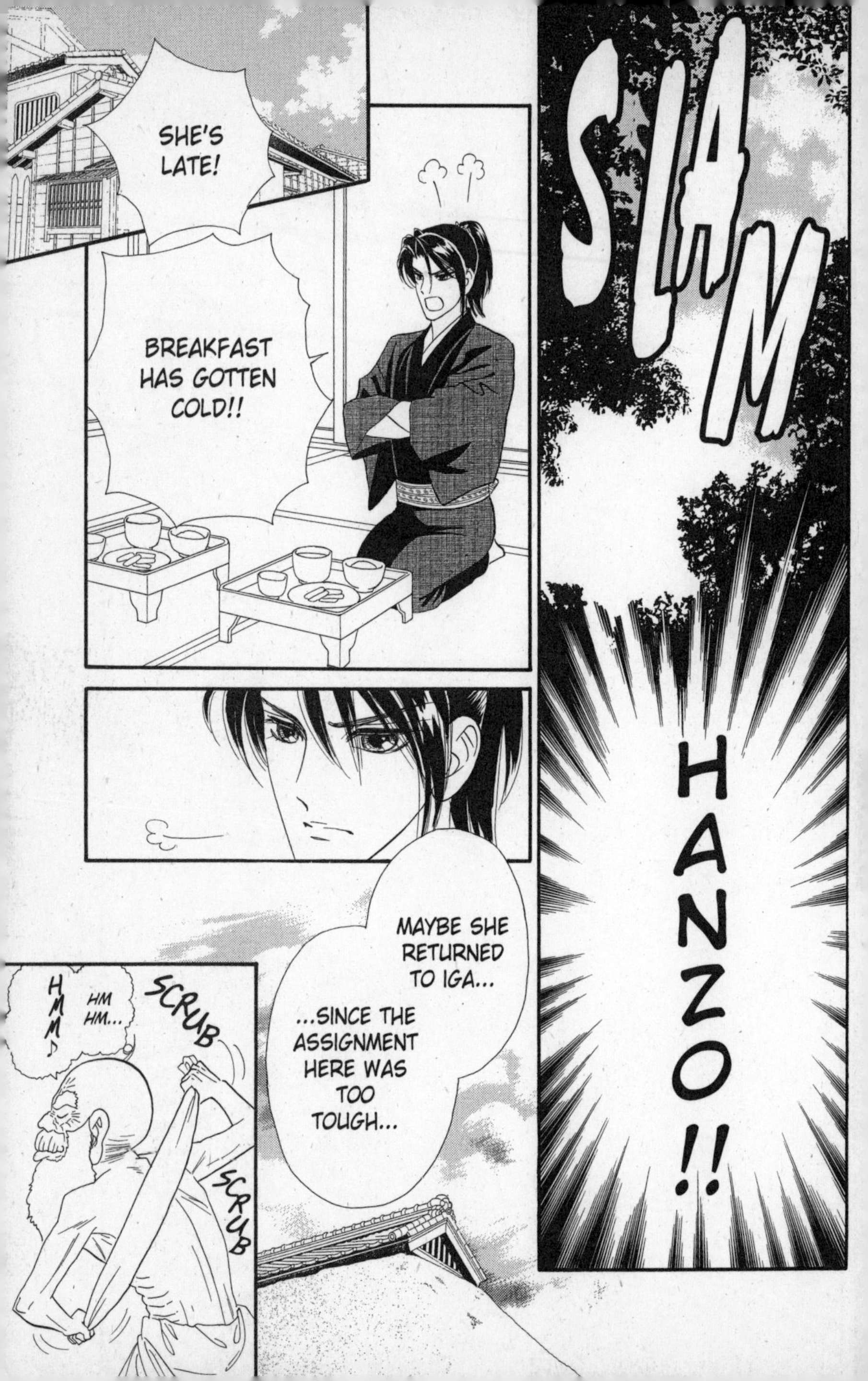
SLAM
HANZO!!
SHE'S LATE!
BREAKFAST HAS GOTTEN COLD!!
MAYBE SHE RETURNED TO IGA...
...SINCE THE ASSIGNMENT HERE WAS TOO TOUGH...
HMM♪
HM HM...
SCRUB
SCRUB

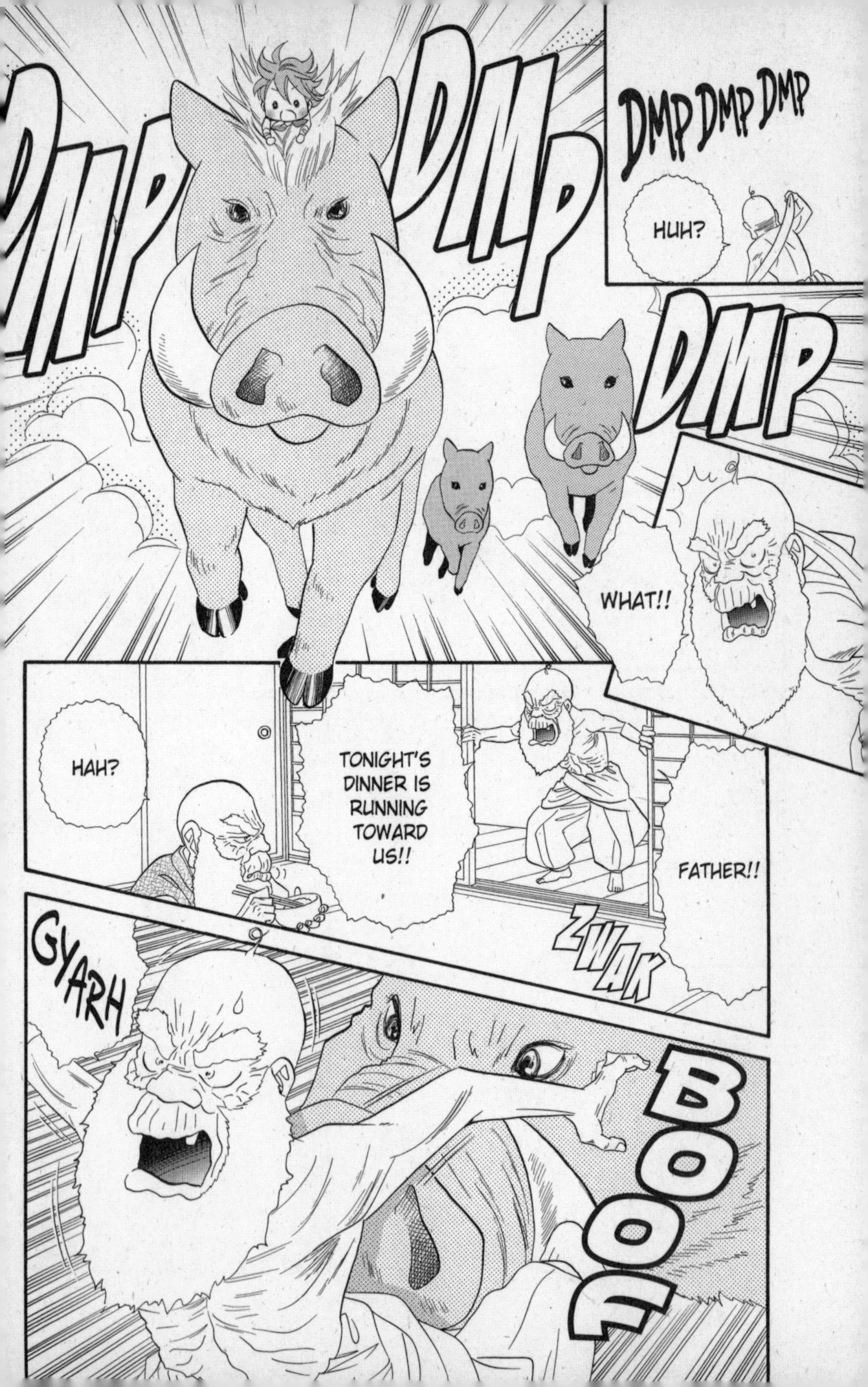
DMP DMP DMP
HUH?
WHAT!!
DMP
DMP
DMP
FATHER!!
TONIGHT'S DINNER IS RUNNING TOWARD US!!
HAH?
ZWAK
BOOF
GYARH

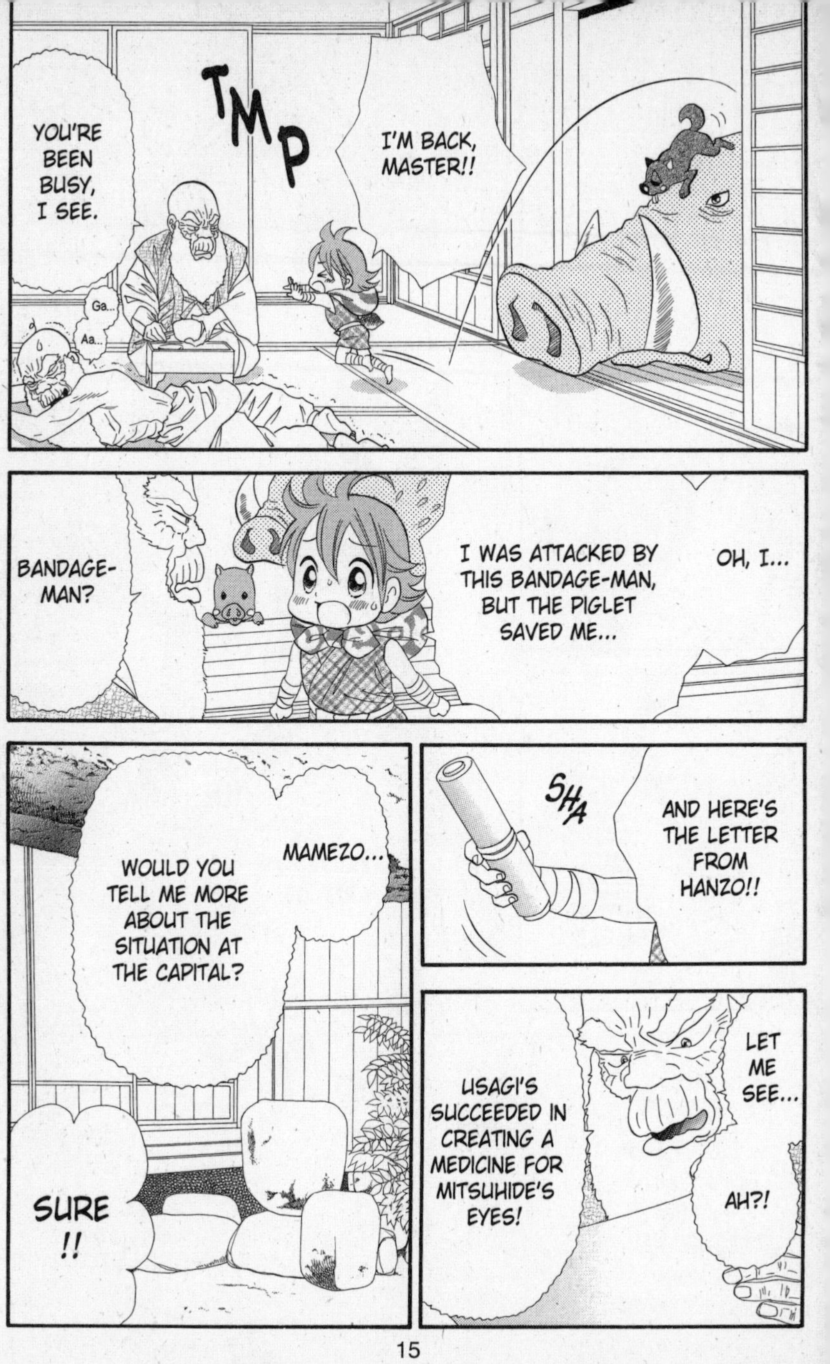
I'M BACK, MASTER!!
TMP
YOU'RE BEEN BUSY, I SEE.
Ga...
Aa...
OH, I...
I WAS ATTACKED BY THIS BANDAGE-MAN, BUT THE PIGLET SAVED ME...
BANDAGE-MAN?
AND HERE'S THE LETTER FROM HANZO!!
SHA
LET ME SEE...
USAGI'S SUCCEEDED IN CREATING A MEDICINE FOR MITSUHIDE'S EYES!
AH?!
MAMEZO...
WOULD YOU TELL ME MORE ABOUT THE SITUATION AT THE CAPITAL?
SURE!!

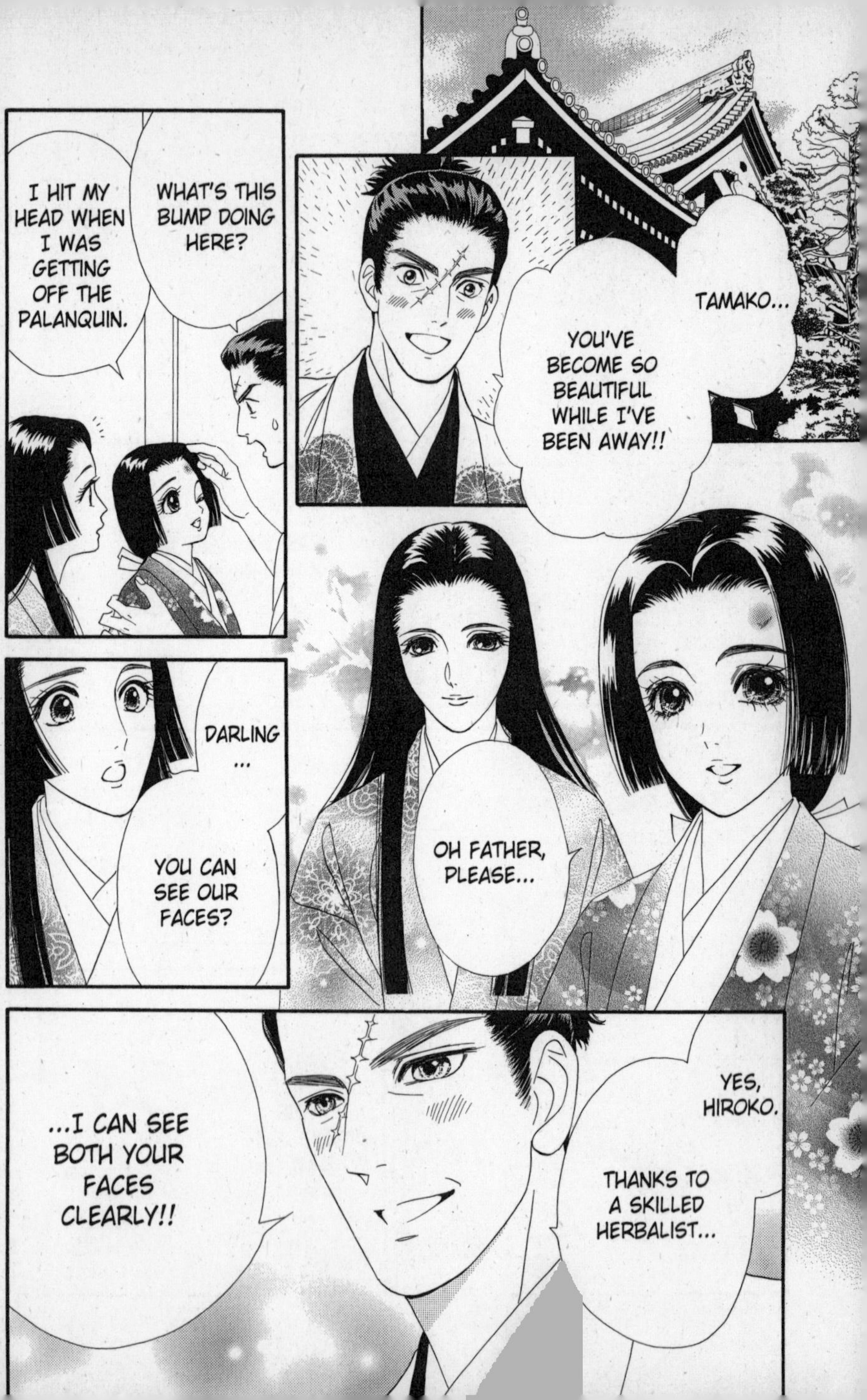
TAMAKO...
YOU'VE BECOME SO BEAUTIFUL WHILE I'VE BEEN AWAY!!
WHAT'S THIS BUMP DOING HERE?
I HIT MY HEAD WHEN I WAS GETTING OFF THE PALANQUIN.
OH FATHER, PLEASE...
DARLING ...
YOU CAN SEE OUR FACES?
YES, HIROKO.
THANKS TO A SKILLED HERBALIST...
...I CAN SEE BOTH YOUR FACES CLEARLY!!

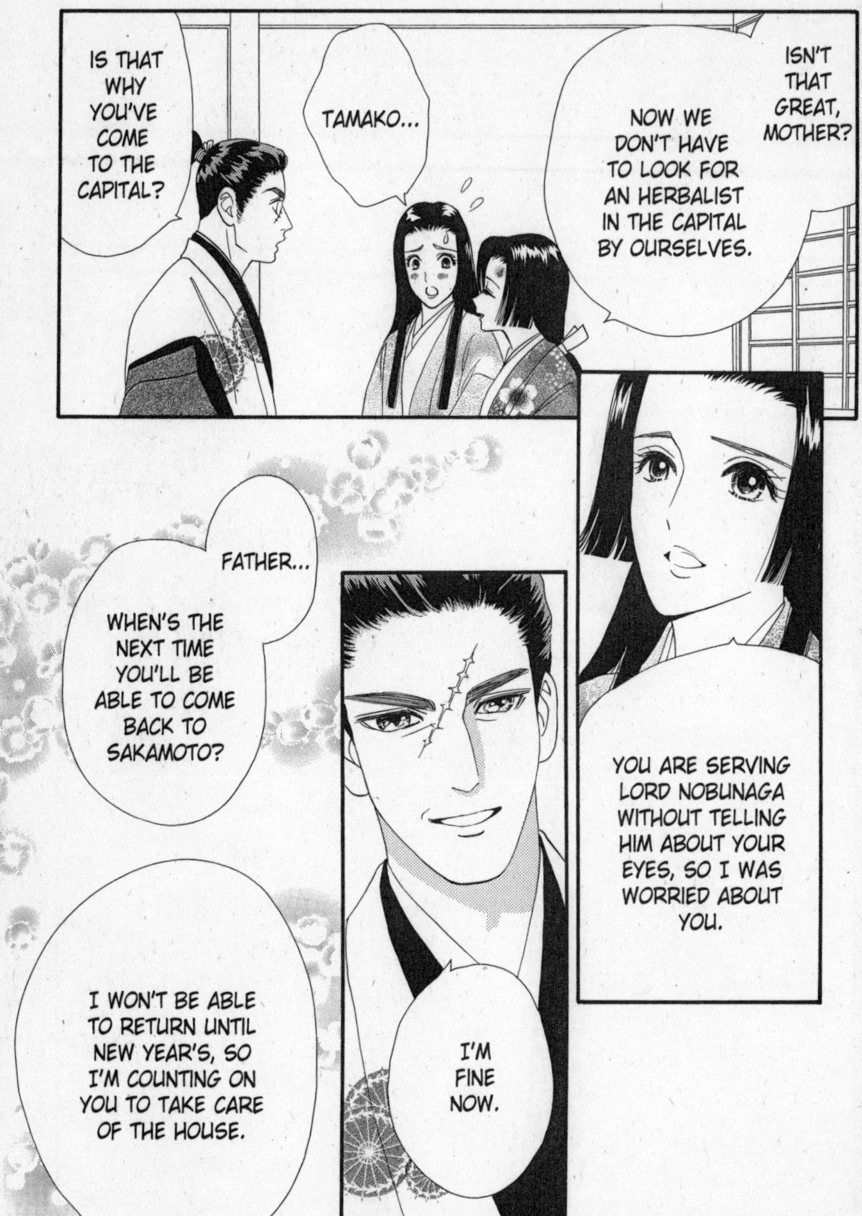
ISN'T THAT GREAT, MOTHER?
NOW WE DON'T HAVE TO LOOK FOR AN HERBALIST IN THE CAPITAL BY OURSELVES.
TAMAKO...
IS THAT WHY YOU'VE COME TO THE CAPITAL?
YOU ARE SERVING LORD NOBUNAGA WITHOUT TELLING HIM ABOUT YOUR EYES, SO I WAS WORRIED ABOUT YOU.
I'M FINE NOW.
FATHER...
WHEN'S THE NEXT TIME YOU'LL BE ABLE TO COME BACK TO SAKAMOTO?
I WON'T BE ABLE TO RETURN UNTIL NEW YEAR'S, SO I'M COUNTING ON YOU TO TAKE CARE OF THE HOUSE.

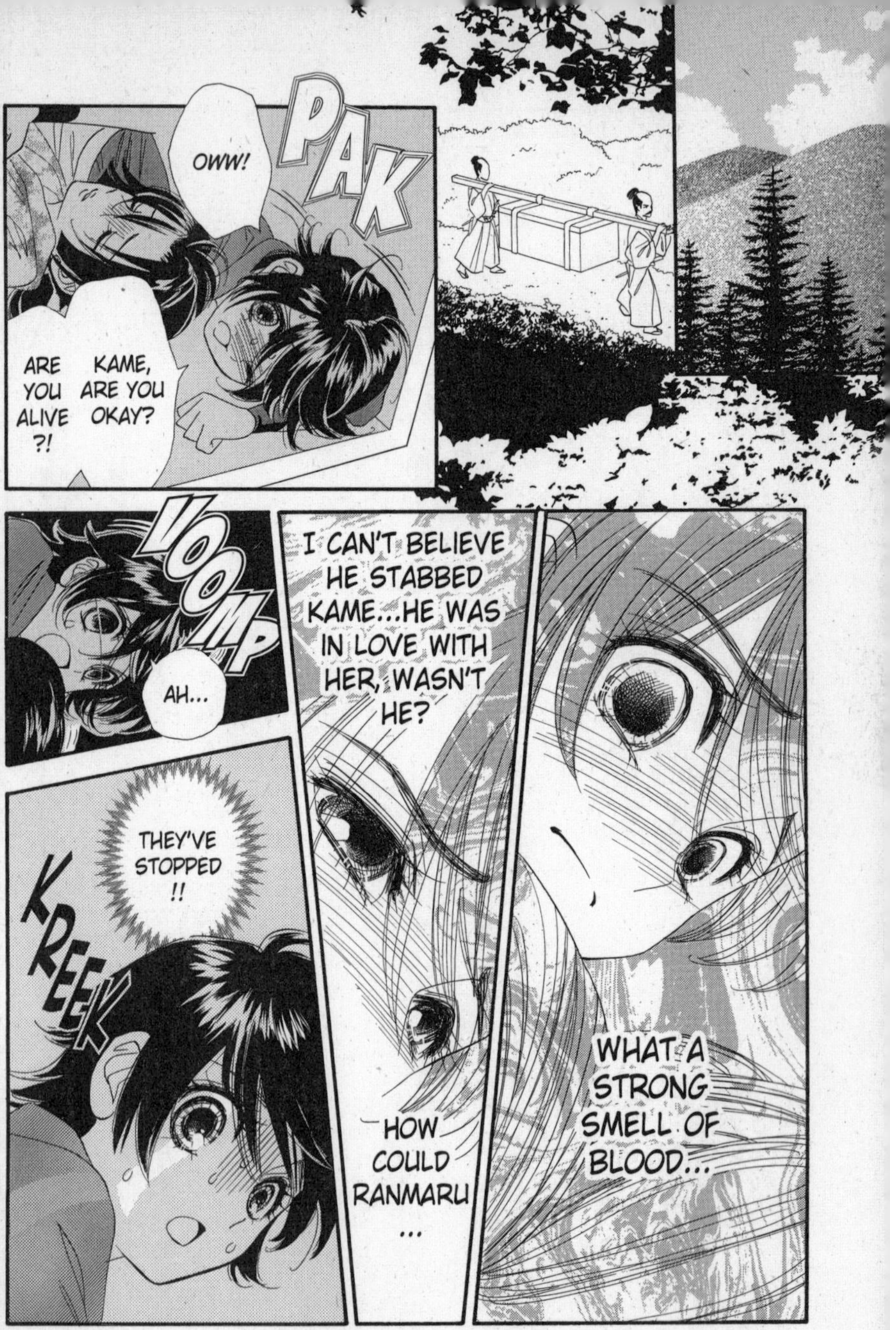
PAK
OWW!
KAME, ARE YOU OKAY?
ARE YOU ALIVE ?!
WHAT A STRONG SMELL OF BLOOD...
I CAN'T BELIEVE HE STABBED KAME...HE WAS IN LOVE WITH HER, WASN'T HE?
HOW COULD RANMARU ...
VOOMP
AH...
THEY'VE STOPPED !!
KREEK

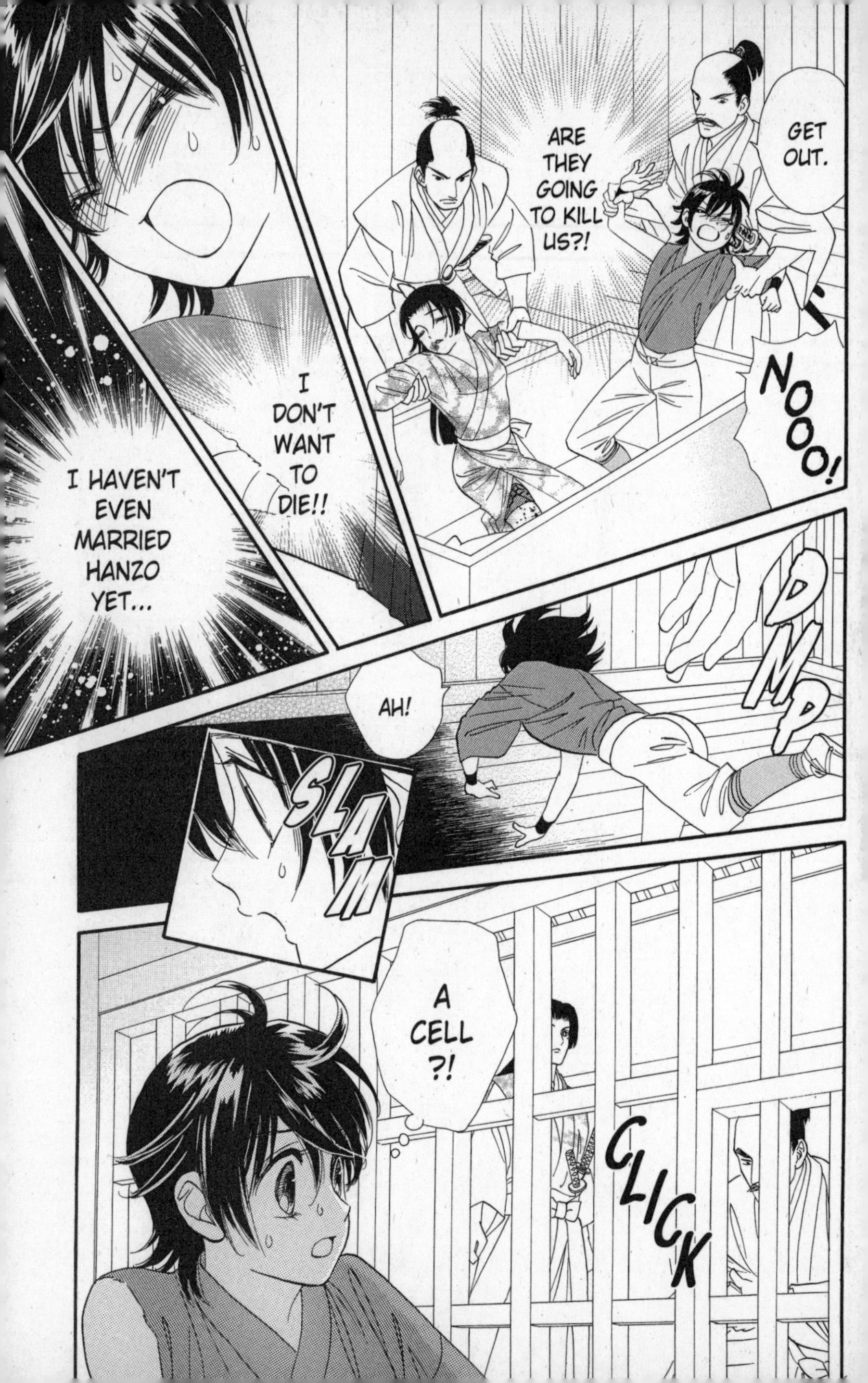
GET OUT.
ARE THEY GOING TO KILL US?!
NOOOO!
I DON'T WANT TO DIE!!
I HAVEN'T EVEN MARRIED HANZO YET...
DMP
AH!
SLAM
A CELL ?!
CLICK

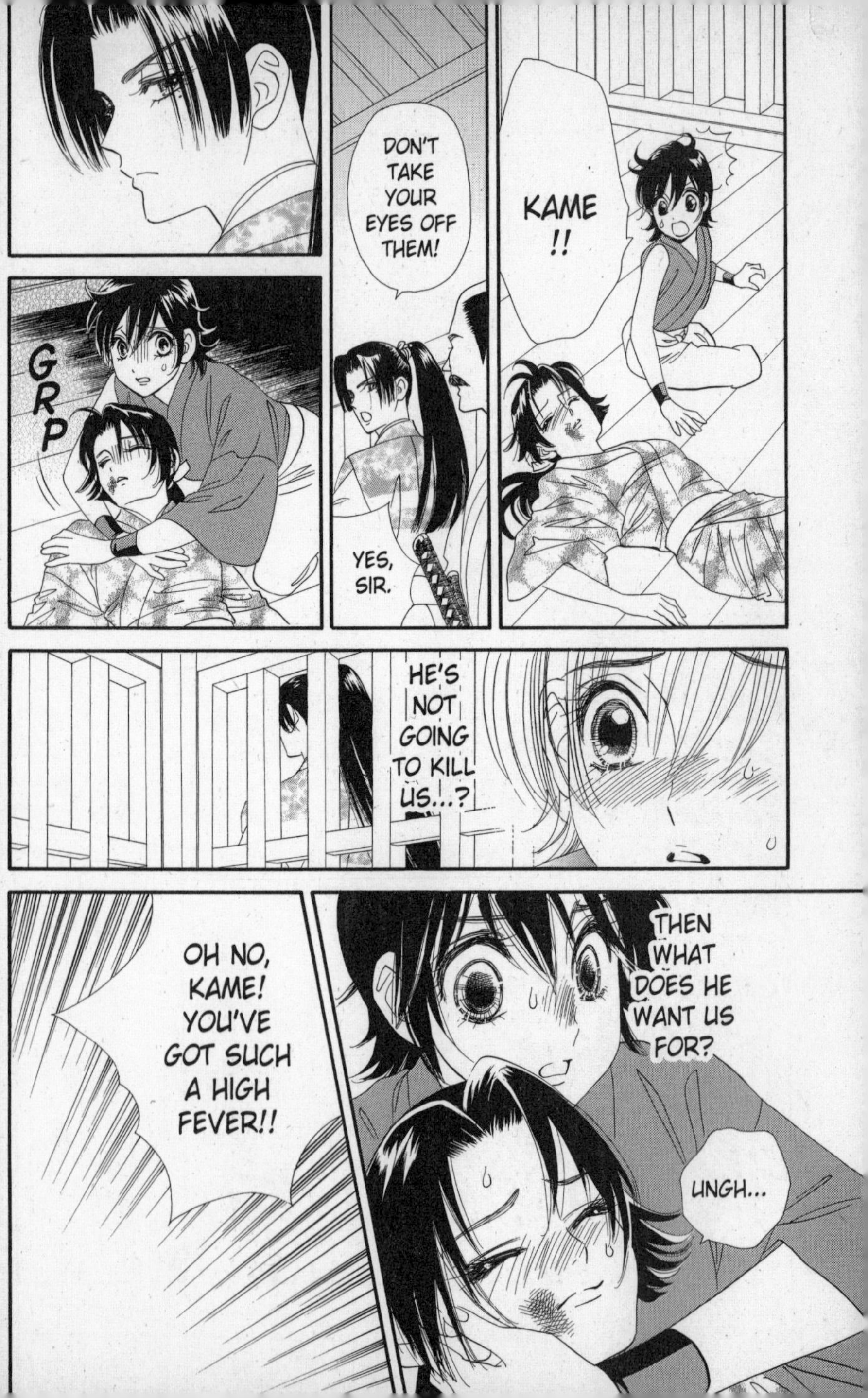
KAME!!
DON'T TAKE YOUR EYES OFF THEM!
YES, SIR.
GRP
HE'S NOT GOING TO KILL US...?
THEN WHAT DOES HE WANT US FOR?
UNGH...
OH NO, KAME! YOU'VE GOT SUCH A HIGH FEVER!!

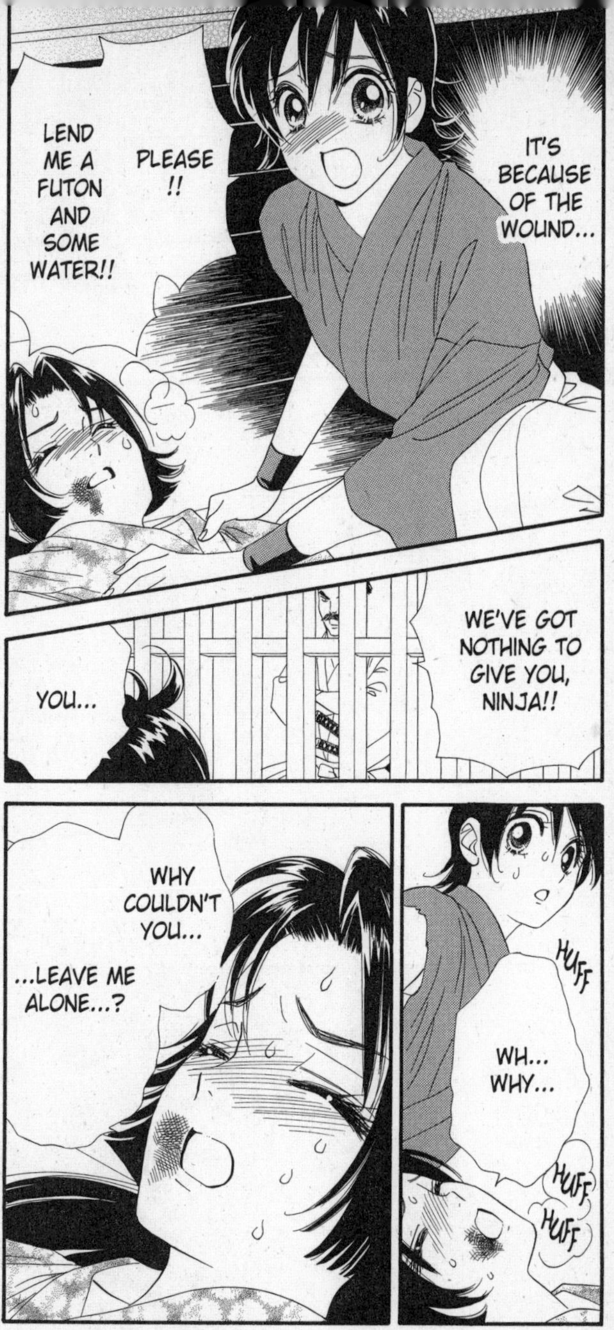
IT'S BECAUSE OF THE WOUND...
PLEASE!!
LEND ME A FUTON AND SOME WATER!!
WE'VE GOT NOTHING TO GIVE YOU, NINJA!!
YOU...
HUFF
WH... WHY...
HUFF HUFF
WHY COULDN'T YOU...
...LEAVE ME ALONE...?

NEWS FROM UE-RIN !!

"Ue-Rin's Manga School" (which was serialized in *Margaret's* "New Manga Seminar" section from volume 2 of 2004 through volume 5 of 2005) has now become a small booklet and is being handed out to people who send in their work to "Manga Seminar." It turned out to be a tough piece of work (?) since I needed to write about how to draw manga in 1-2 pages and include a story with an introduction, development, climax, and conclusion...all that in addition to my work on *Tail of the Moon*! I'd like everybody who's interested in becoming a manga artist to read it. Please check out *Margaret* for more details.

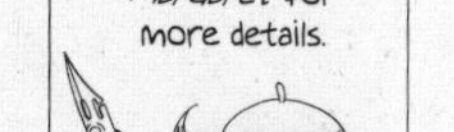

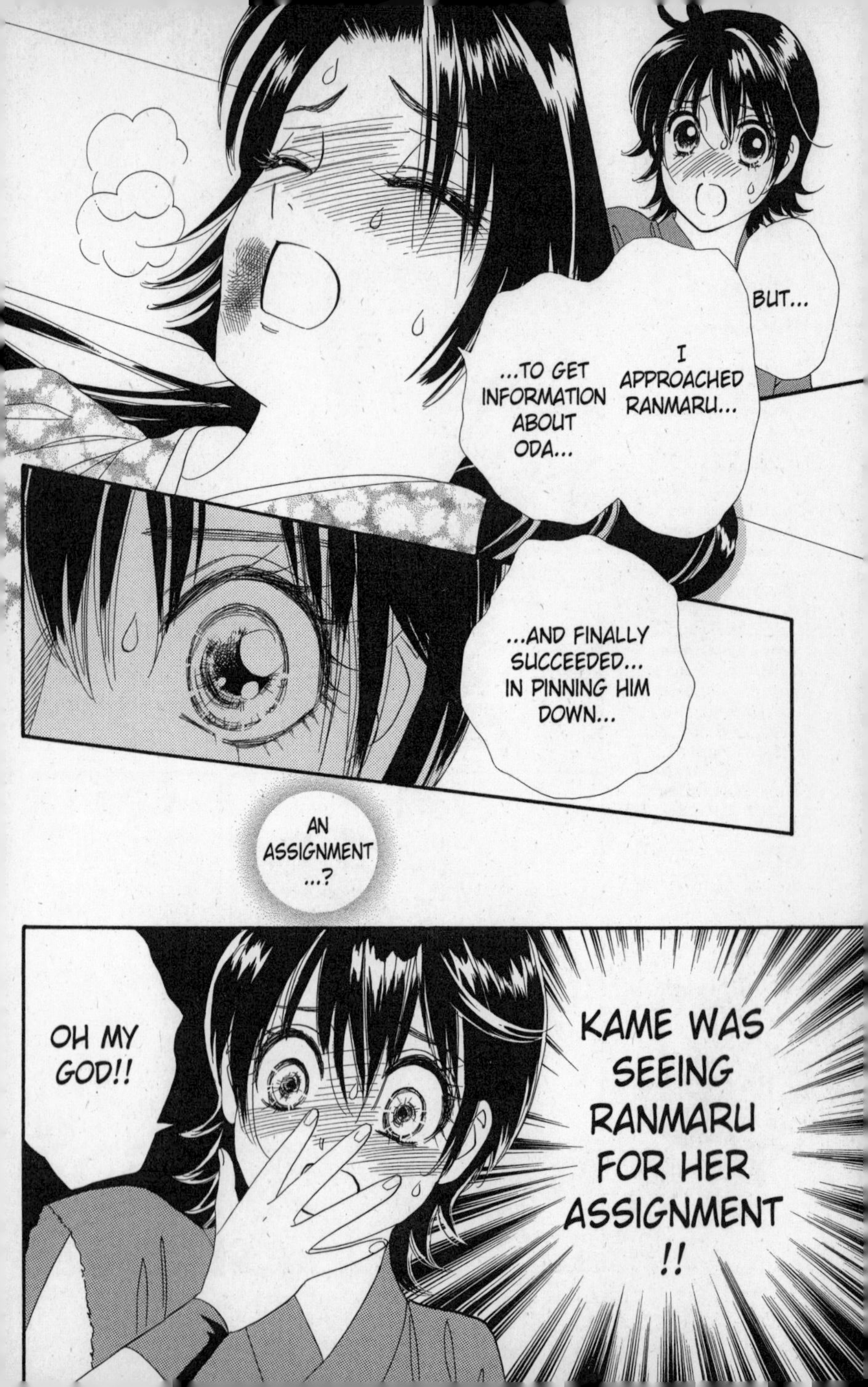
BUT...
I APPROACHED RANMARU...
...TO GET INFORMATION ABOUT ODA...
...AND FINALLY SUCCEEDED... IN PINNING HIM DOWN...
AN ASSIGNMENT ...?
KAME WAS SEEING RANMARU FOR HER ASSIGNMENT !!
OH MY GOD!!

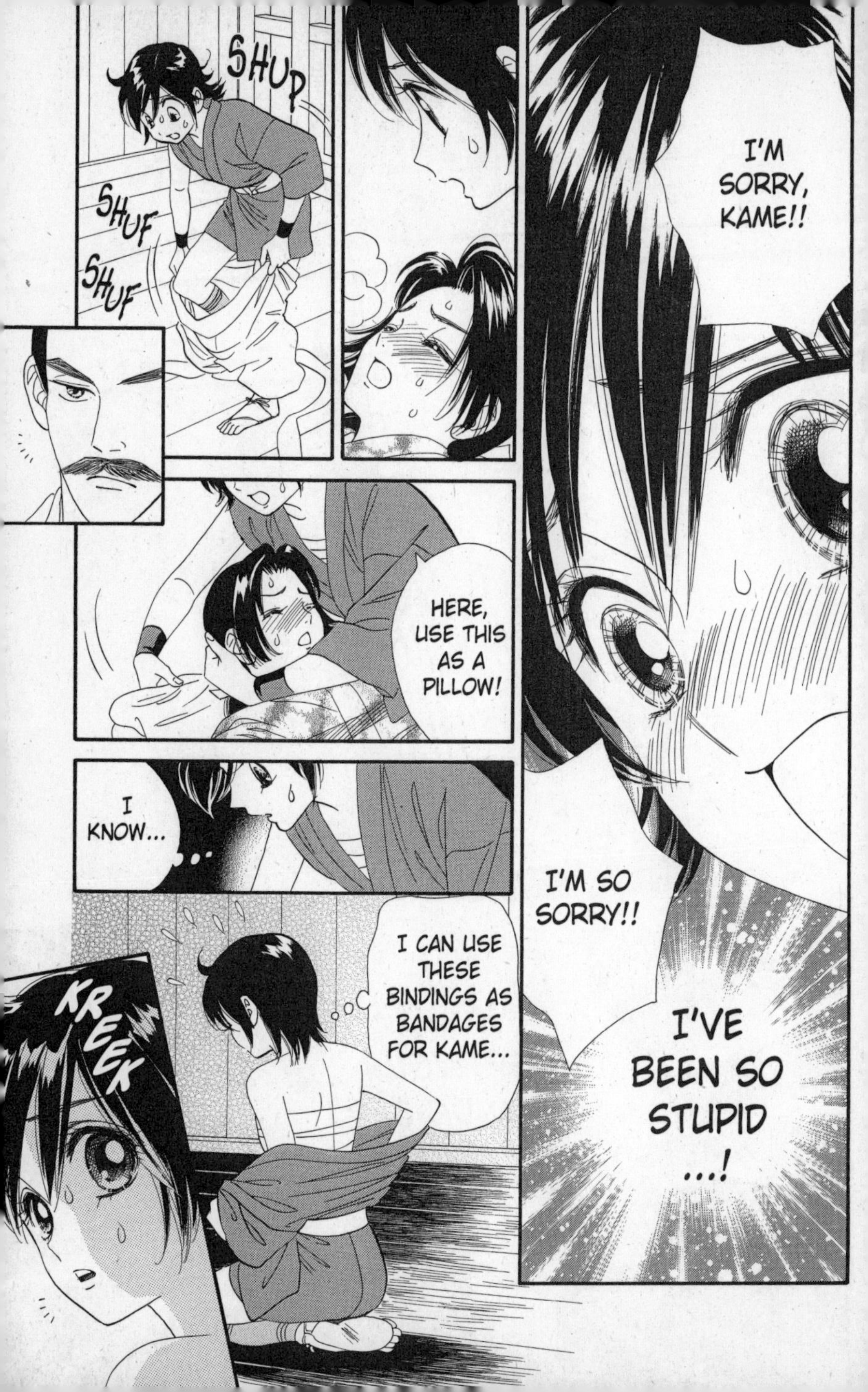
I'M SORRY, KAME!!
I'M SO SORRY!!
I'VE BEEN SO STUPID ...!
SHUP
SHUF
SHUF
HERE, USE THIS AS A PILLOW!
I KNOW...
I CAN USE THESE BINDINGS AS BANDAGES FOR KAME...
KREEK

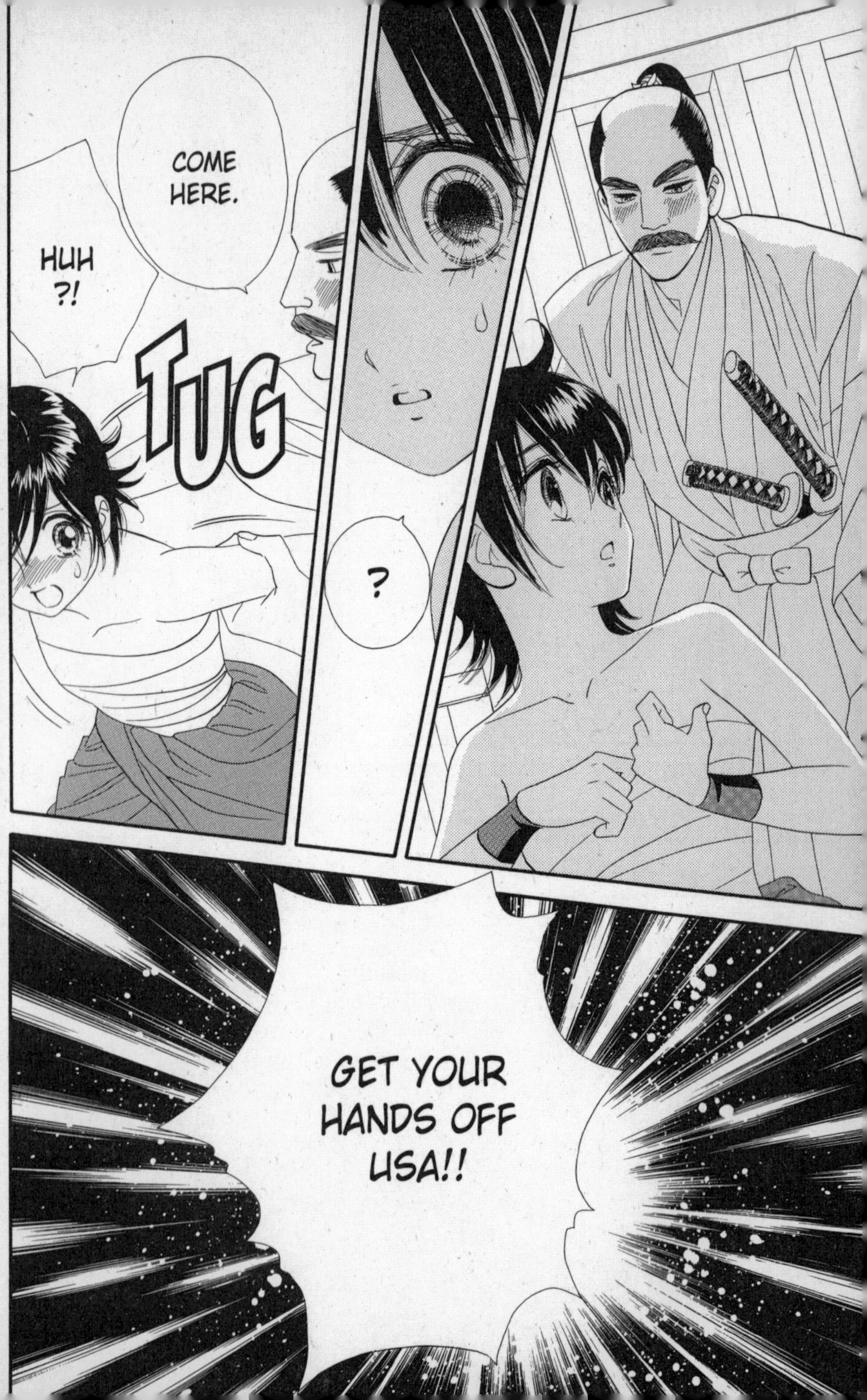
?
COME HERE.
HUH ?!
TUG
GET YOUR HANDS OFF USA!!

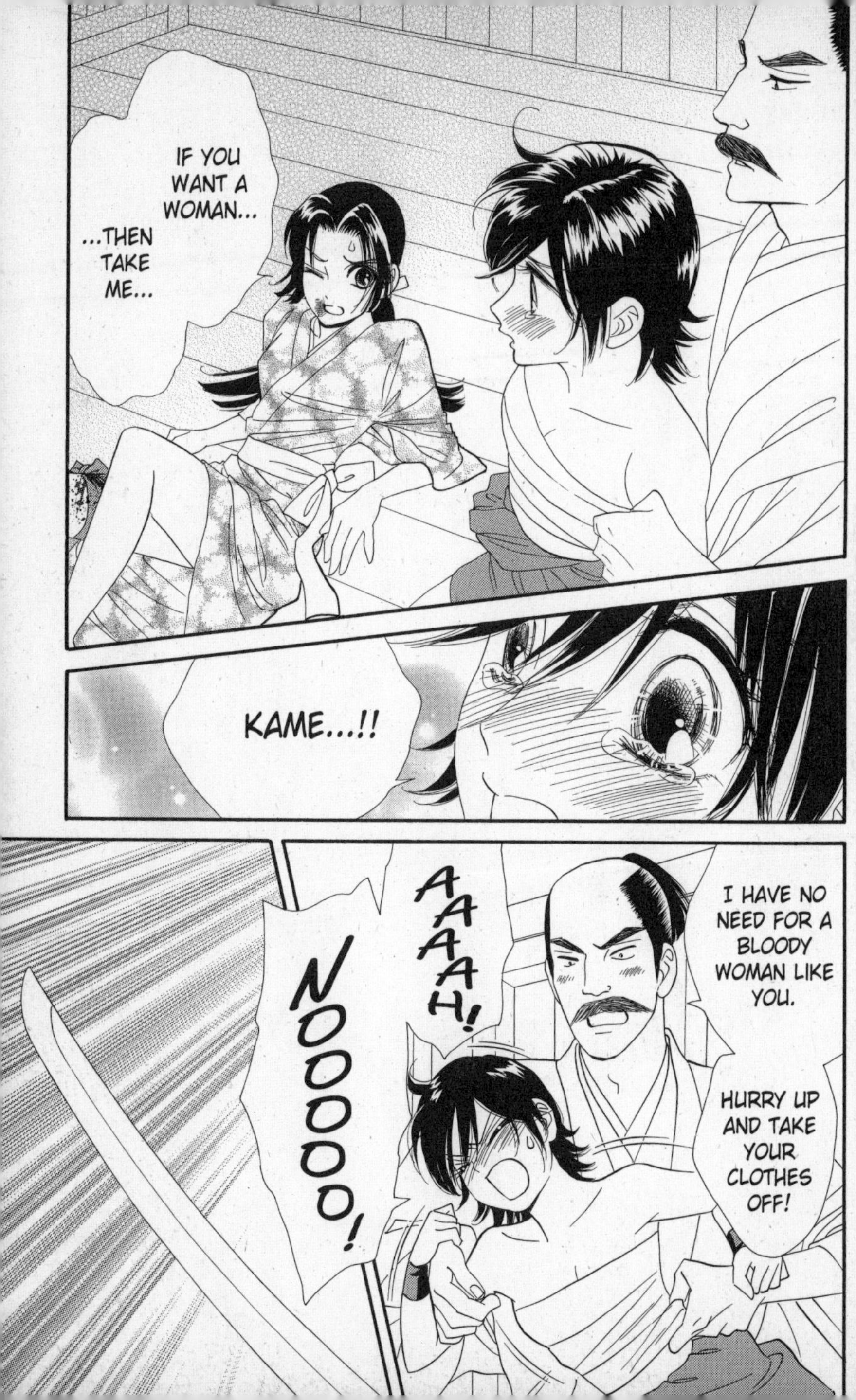
IF YOU WANT A WOMAN...
...THEN TAKE ME...
KAME...!!
I HAVE NO NEED FOR A BLOODY WOMAN LIKE YOU.
HURRY UP AND TAKE YOUR CLOTHES OFF!
AAAAH!
NOOOOOO!

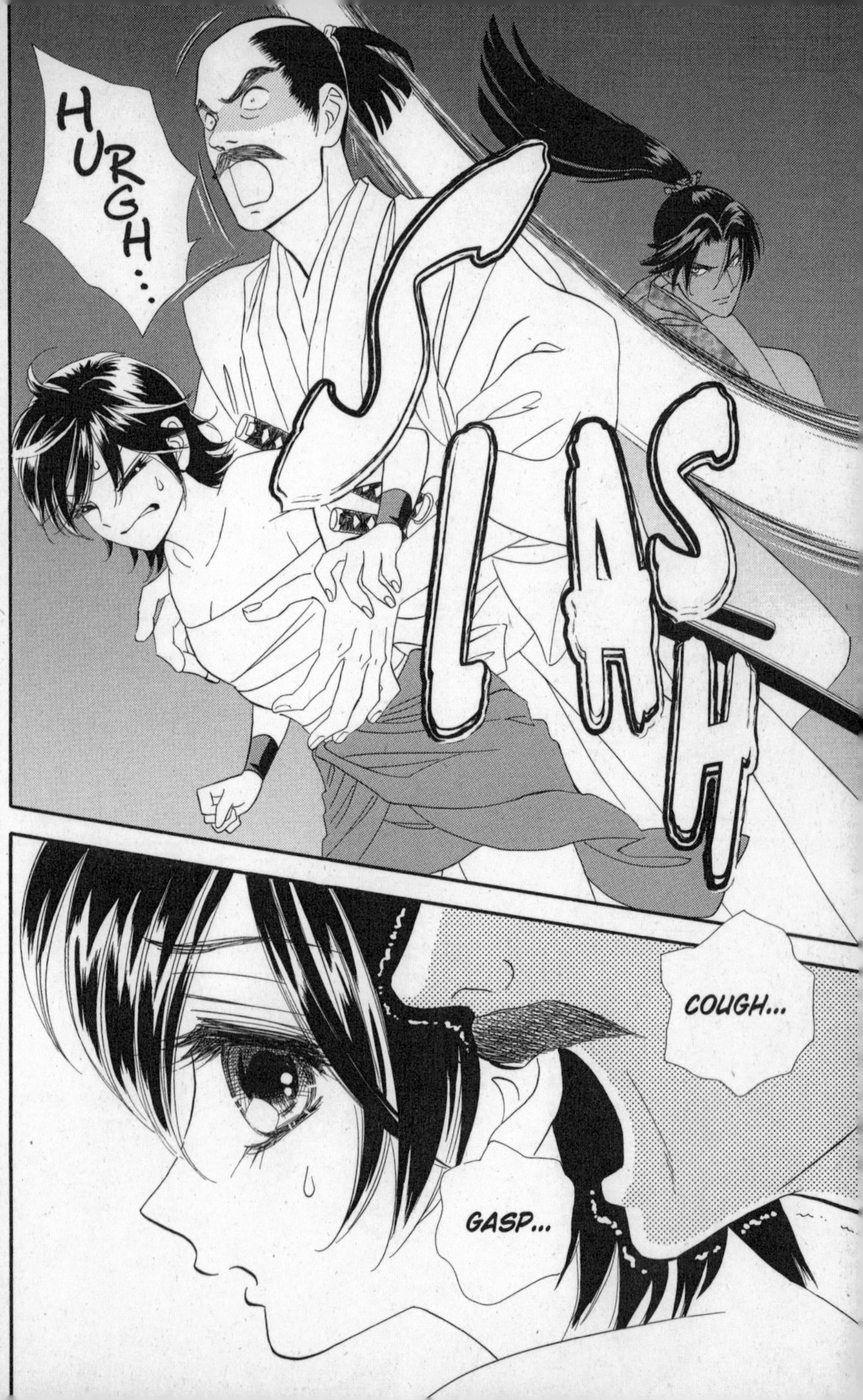
SLASH
HURGH...
COUGH...
GASP...

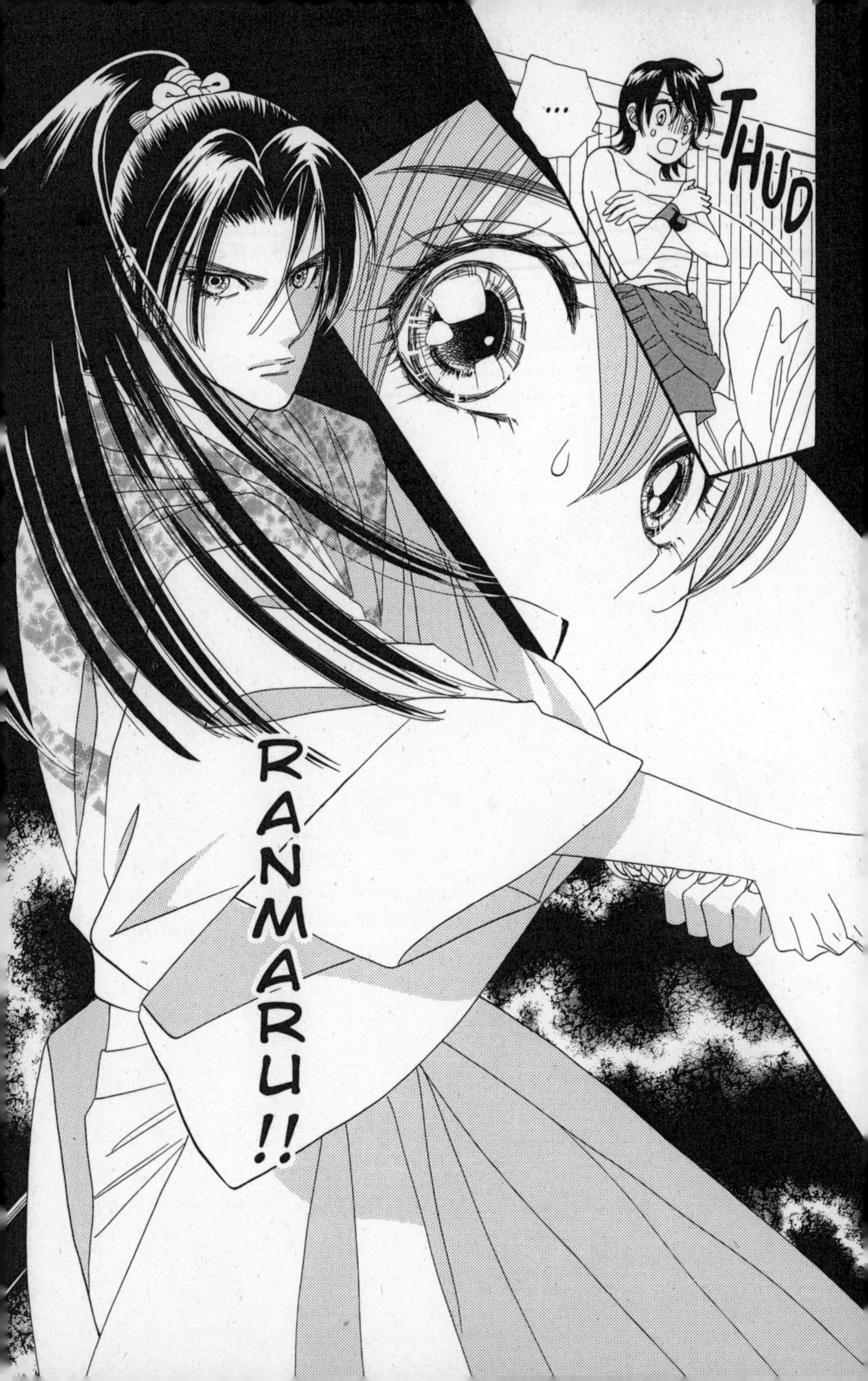
THUD
...
RANMARU!!

TAIL OF THE MOON EXTRA: TODAY'S MISSION

"I WANT TO SEE USAGI AS A DOLPHIN TRAINER!"

-MICHIRU, SHIGA PREFECTURE

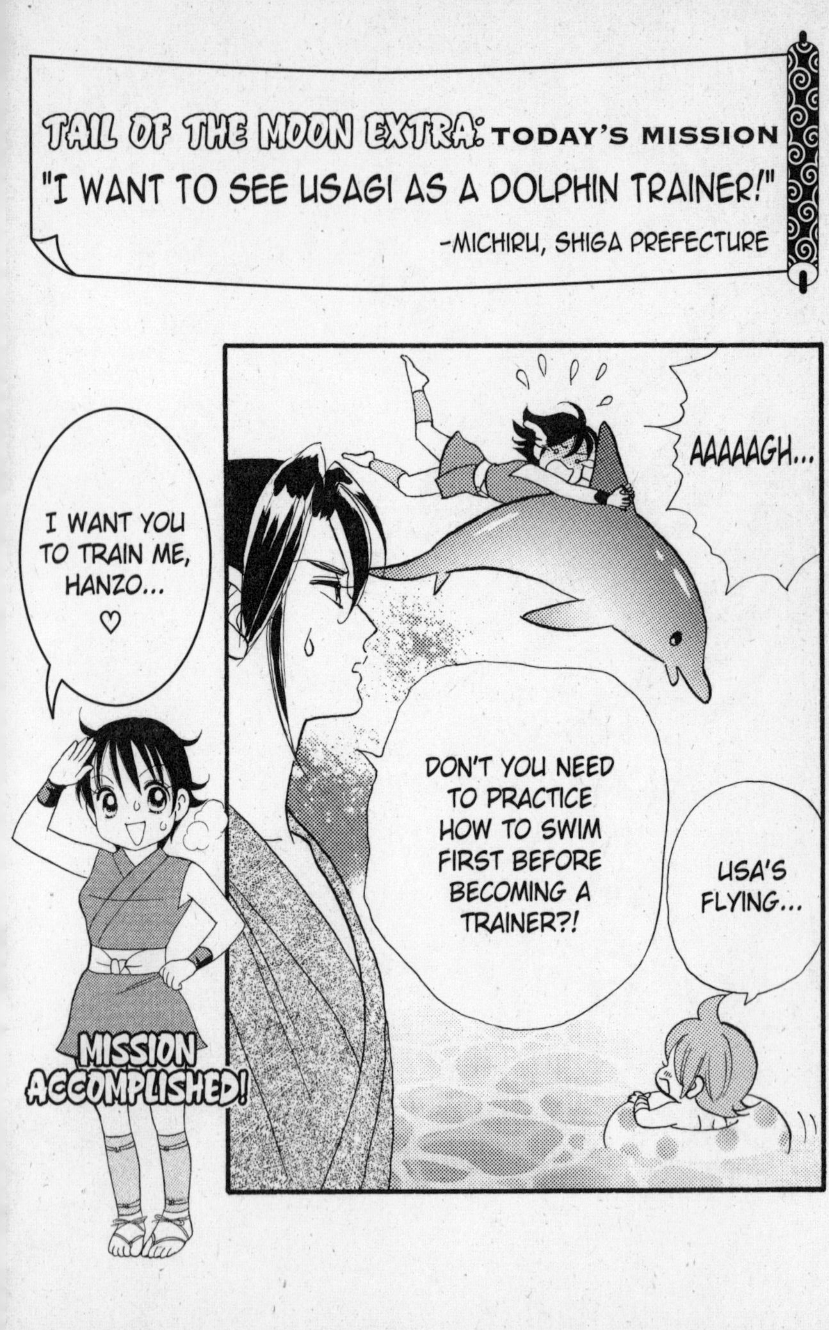
AAAAAGH...
DON'T YOU NEED TO PRACTICE HOW TO SWIM FIRST BEFORE BECOMING A TRAINER?!
USA'S FLYING...
I WANT YOU TO TRAIN ME, HANZO... ♡
MISSION ACCOMPLISHED!

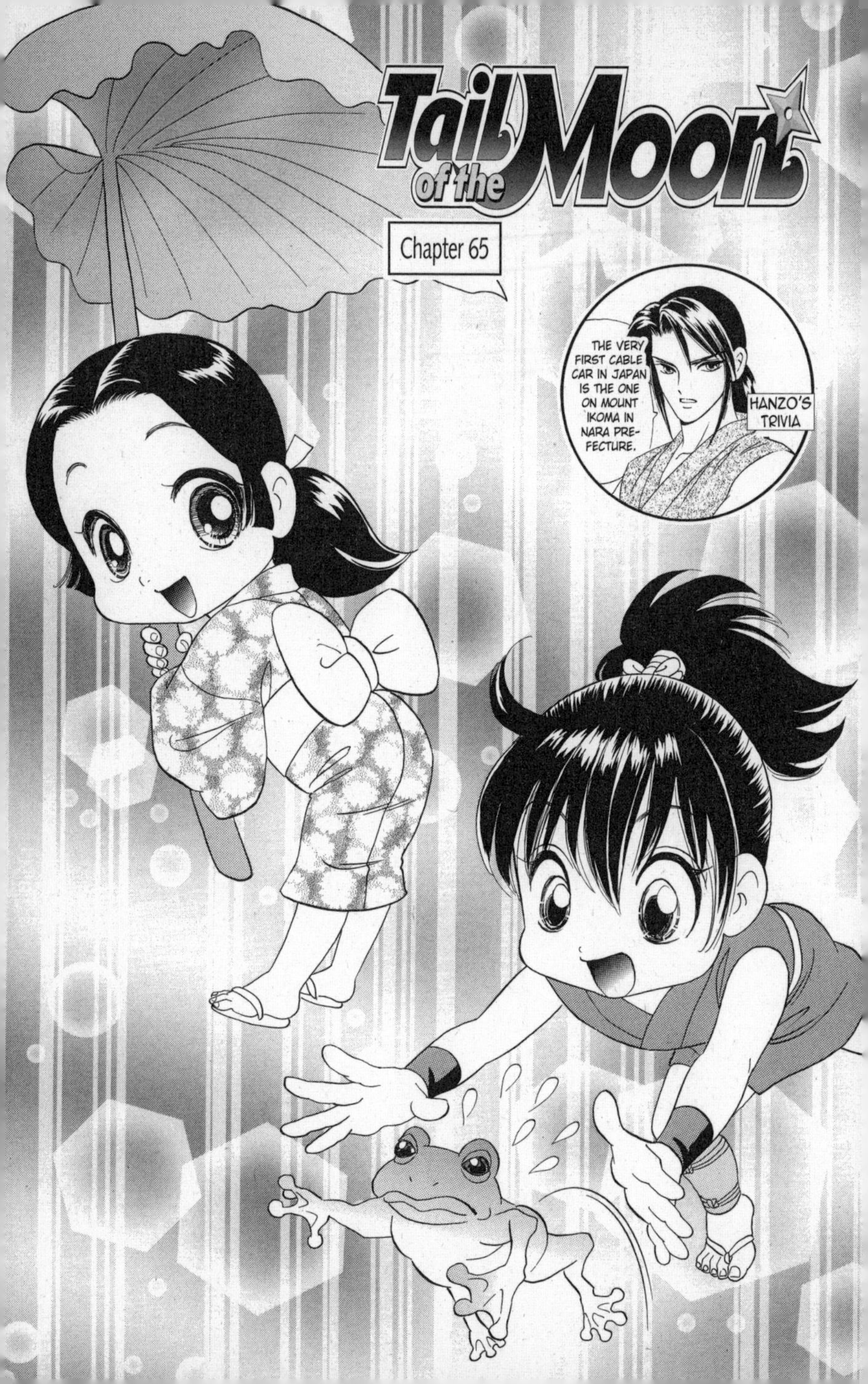
Tail of the Moon
Chapter 65
HANZO'S TRIVIA
THE VERY FIRST CABLE CAR IN JAPAN IS THE ONE ON MOUNT IKOMA IN NARA PREFECTURE.

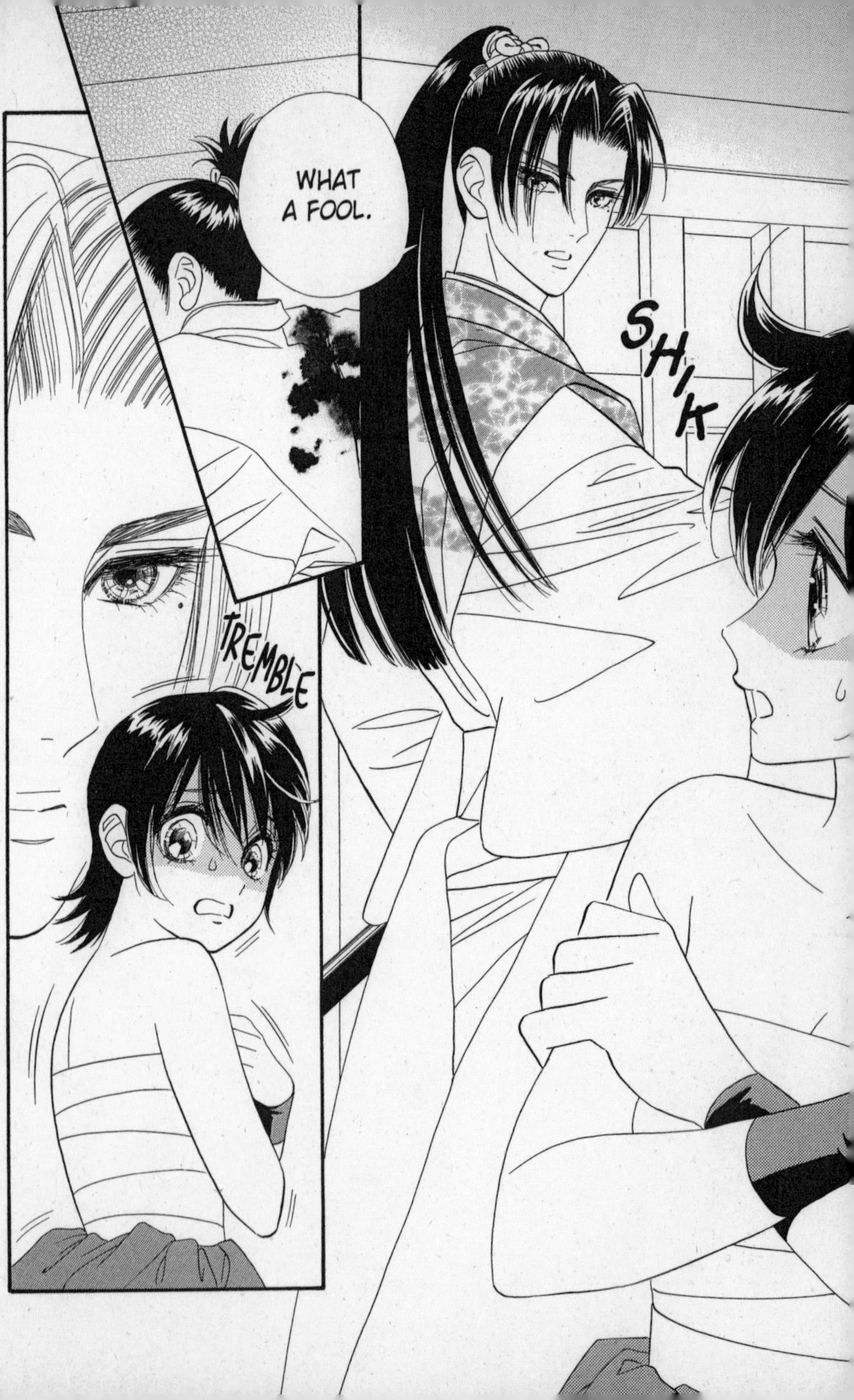
WHAT A FOOL.
SHIK
TREMBLE

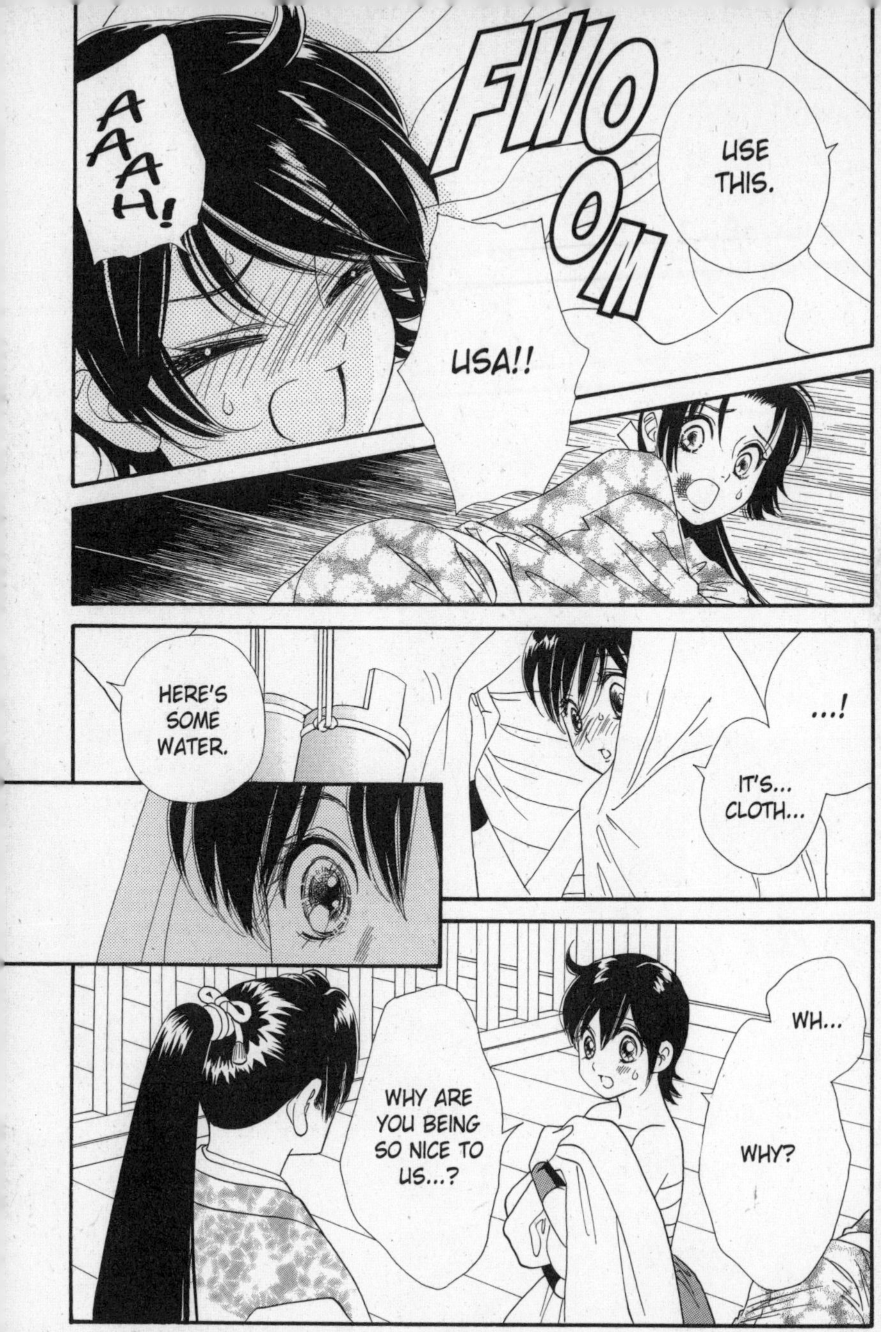
USE THIS.
FWOOM
AAAH!
USA!!
...!
IT'S... CLOTH...
HERE'S SOME WATER.
WH...
WHY?
WHY ARE YOU BEING SO NICE TO US...?

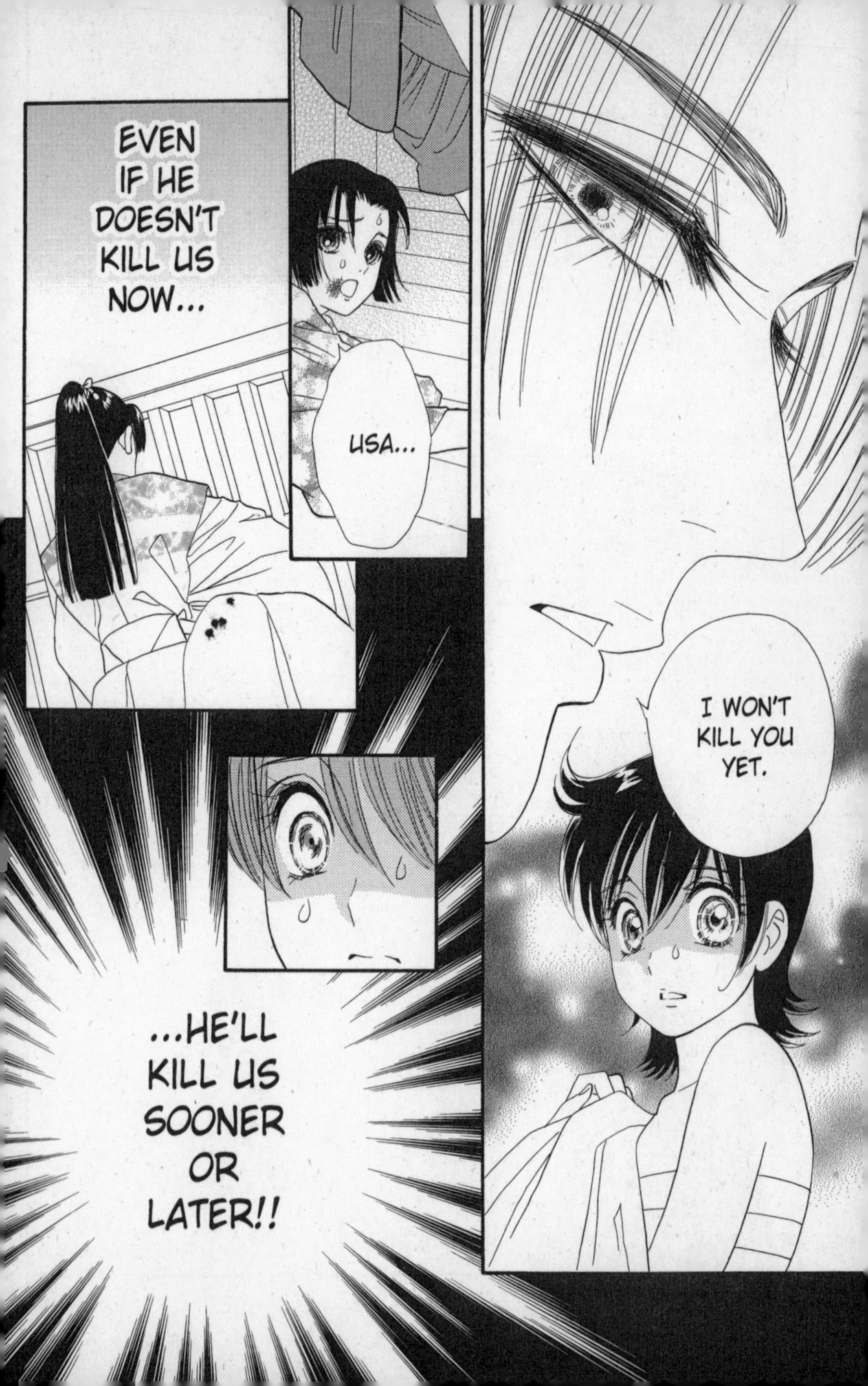
I WON'T KILL YOU YET.
USA...
EVEN IF HE DOESN'T KILL US NOW...
...HE'LL KILL US SOONER OR LATER!!

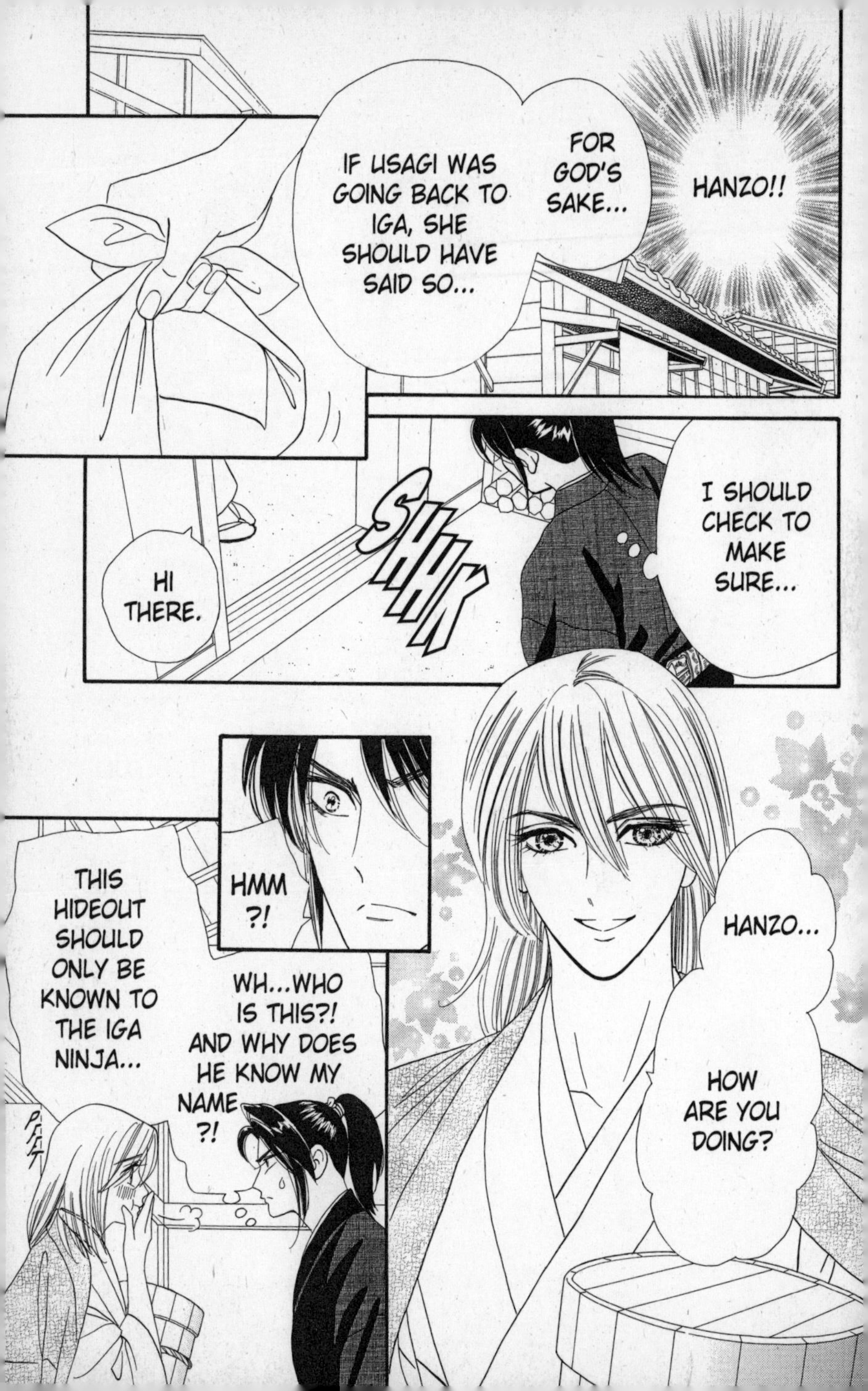
HANZO!!
FOR GOD'S SAKE...
IF USAGI WAS GOING BACK TO IGA, SHE SHOULD HAVE SAID SO...
I SHOULD CHECK TO MAKE SURE...
SHHK
HI THERE.
HANZO...
HOW ARE YOU DOING?
HMM ?!
WH...WHO IS THIS?! AND WHY DOES HE KNOW MY NAME ?!
THIS HIDEOUT SHOULD ONLY BE KNOWN TO THE IGA NINJA...
PFFT

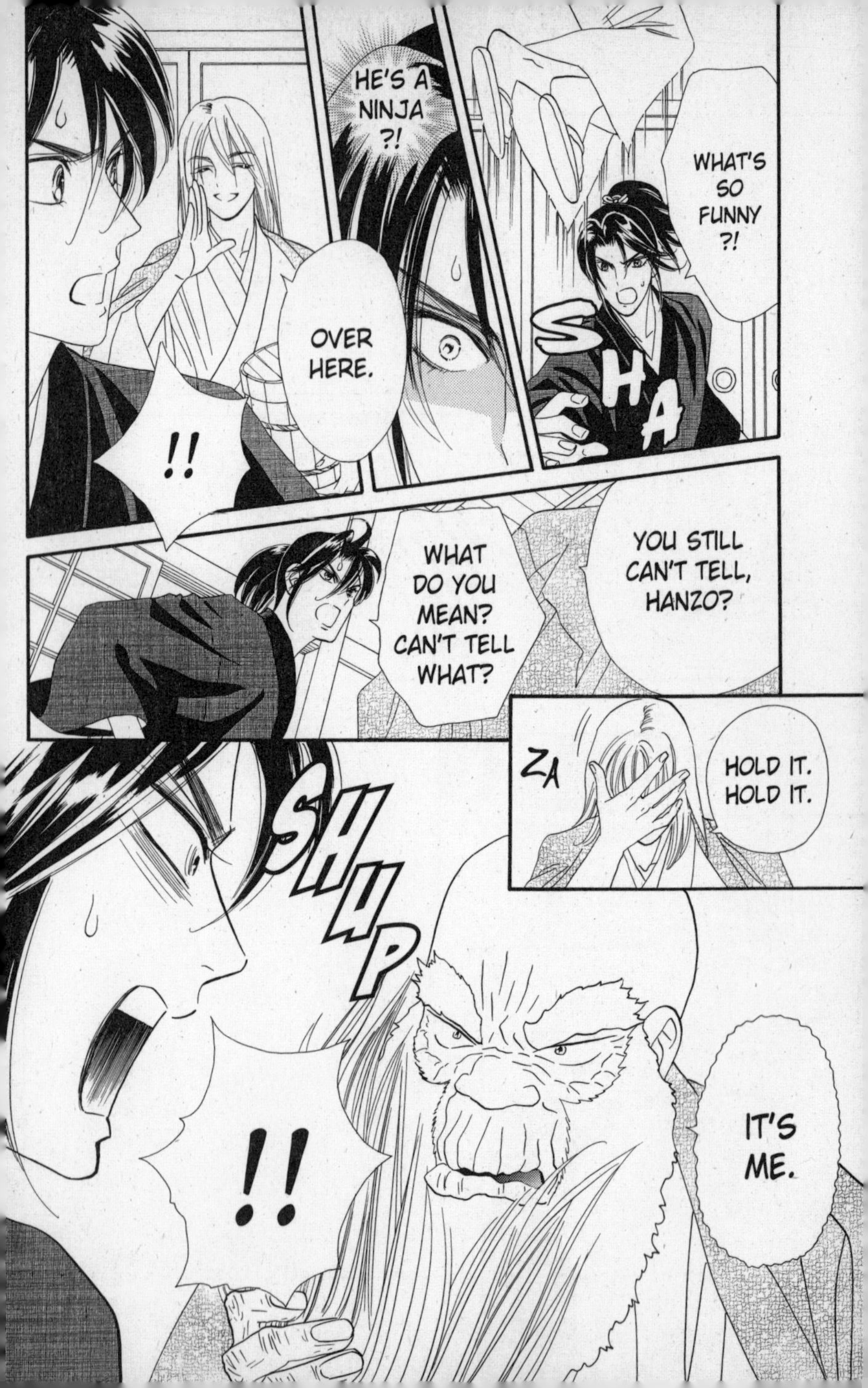
WHAT'S SO FUNNY ?!
SHA
HE'S A NINJA ?!
OVER HERE.
!!
YOU STILL CAN'T TELL, HANZO?
WHAT DO YOU MEAN? CAN'T TELL WHAT?
HOLD IT. HOLD IT.
ZA
SHUP
IT'S ME.
!!

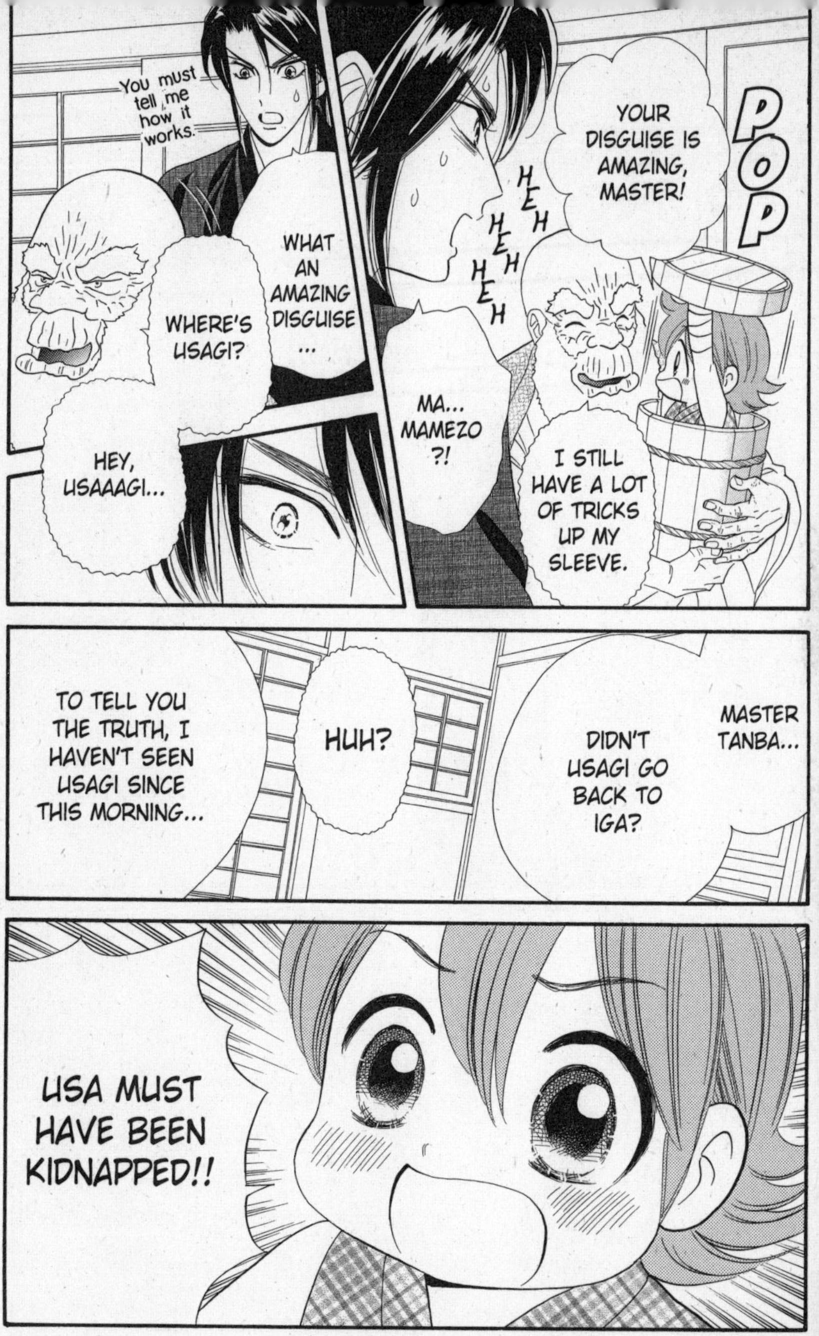
POP
YOUR DISGUISE IS AMAZING, MASTER!
HEH HEH HEH HEH
I STILL HAVE A LOT OF TRICKS UP MY SLEEVE.
MA... MAMEZO ?!
WHAT AN AMAZING DISGUISE ...
You must tell me how it works.
WHERE'S USAGI?
HEY, USAAAGI...
MASTER TANBA...
DIDN'T USAGI GO BACK TO IGA?
HUH?
TO TELL YOU THE TRUTH, I HAVEN'T SEEN USAGI SINCE THIS MORNING...
USA MUST HAVE BEEN KIDNAPPED!!

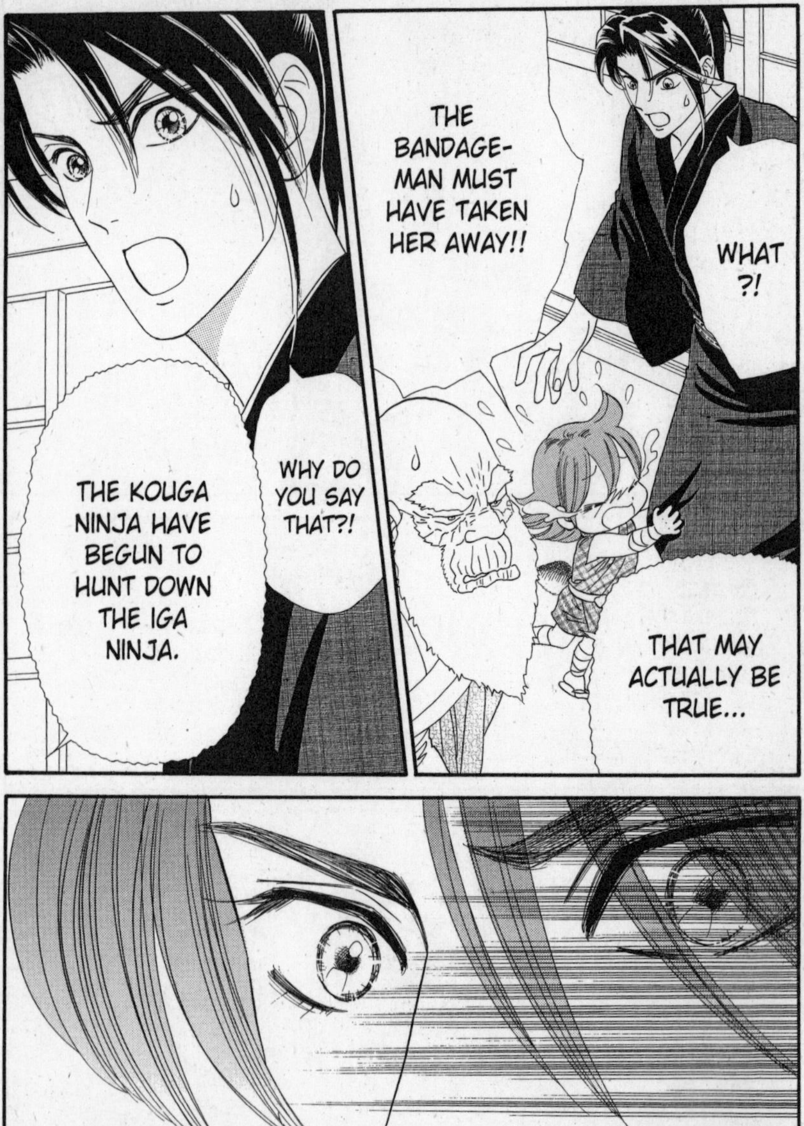
THE BANDAGE-MAN MUST HAVE TAKEN HER AWAY!!
WHAT ?!
THAT MAY ACTUALLY BE TRUE...
WHY DO YOU SAY THAT?!
THE KOUGA NINJA HAVE BEGUN TO HUNT DOWN THE IGA NINJA.

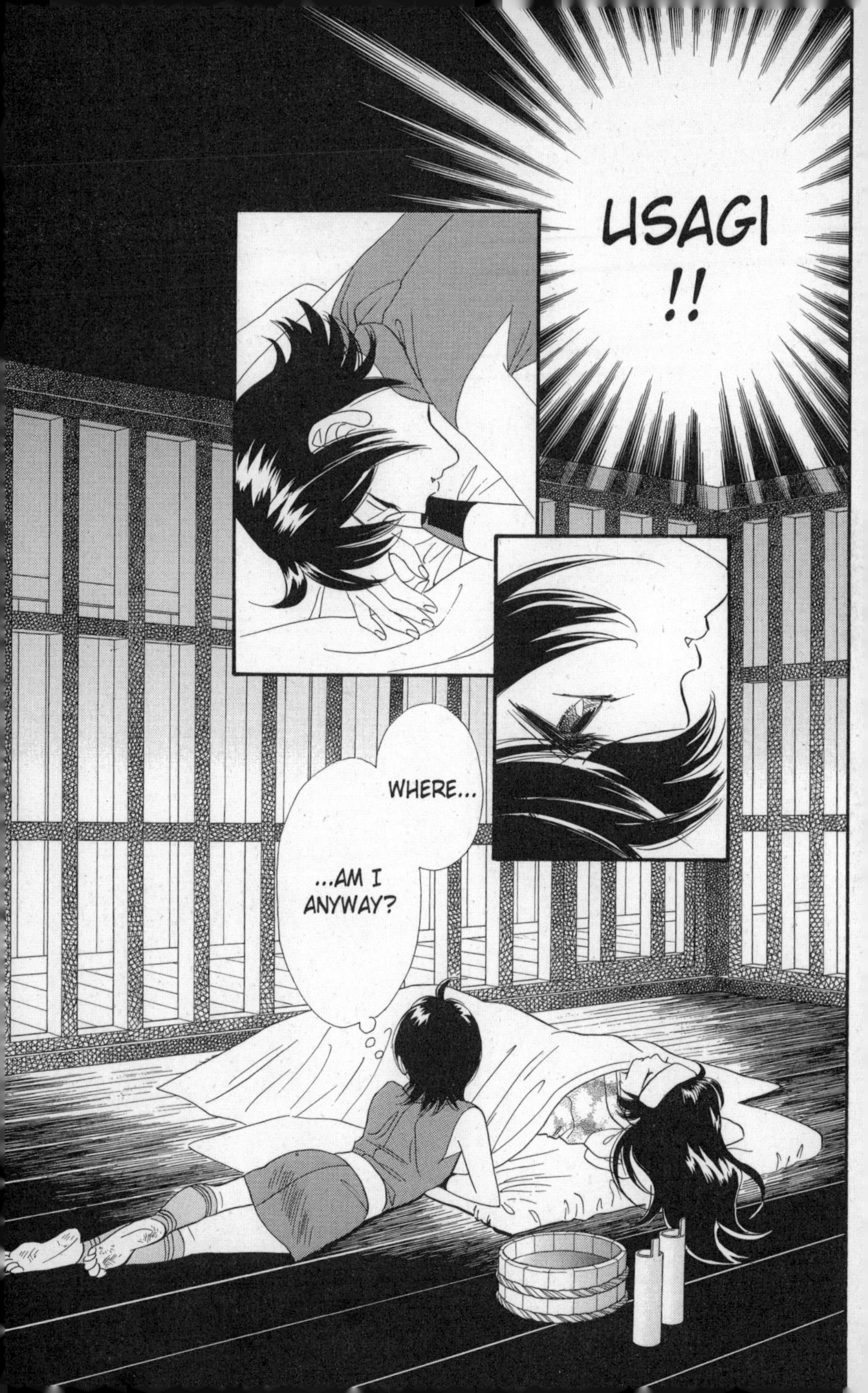
USAGI !!
WHERE...
...AM I ANYWAY?

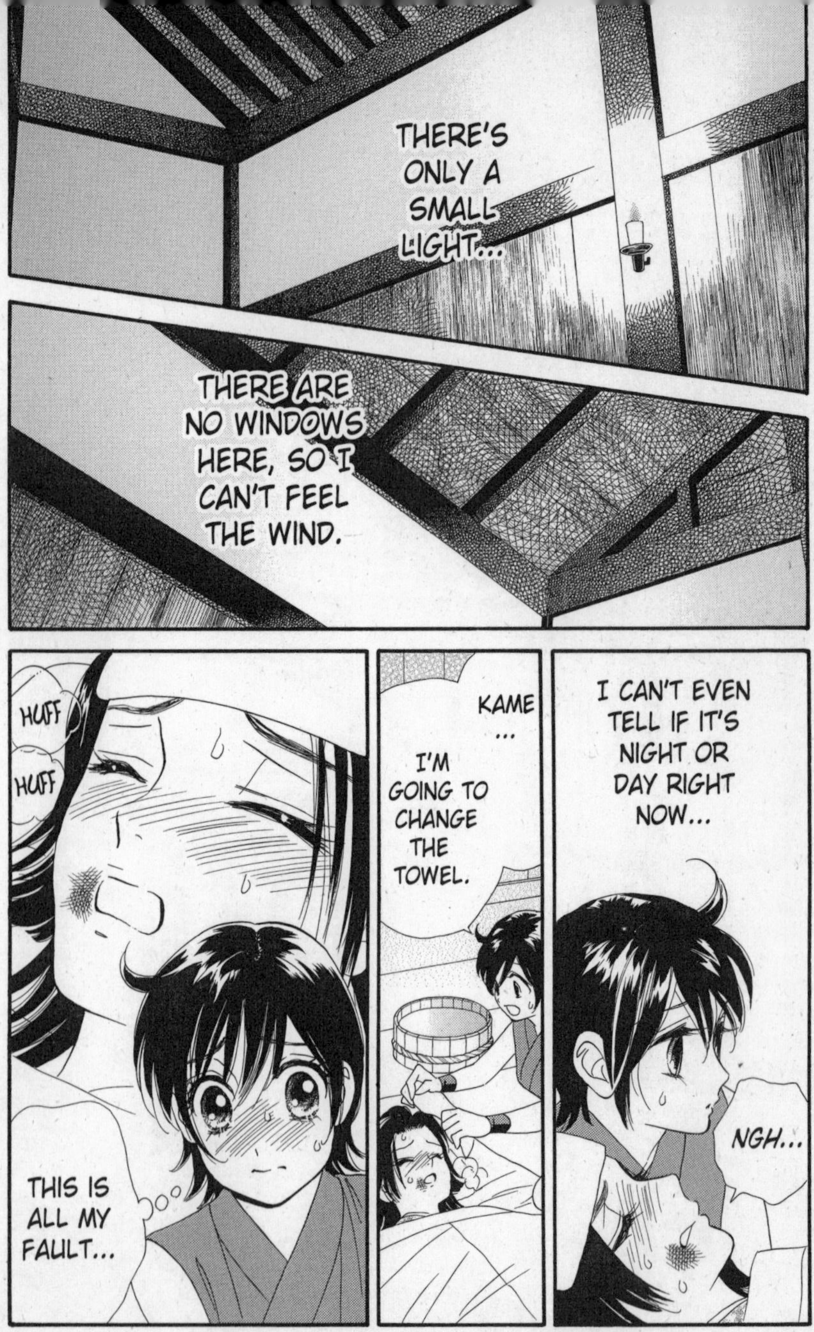
THERE'S ONLY A SMALL LIGHT...
THERE ARE NO WINDOWS HERE, SO I CAN'T FEEL THE WIND.
I CAN'T EVEN TELL IF IT'S NIGHT OR DAY RIGHT NOW...
NGH...
KAME ...
I'M GOING TO CHANGE THE TOWEL.
HUFF
HUFF
THIS IS ALL MY FAULT...

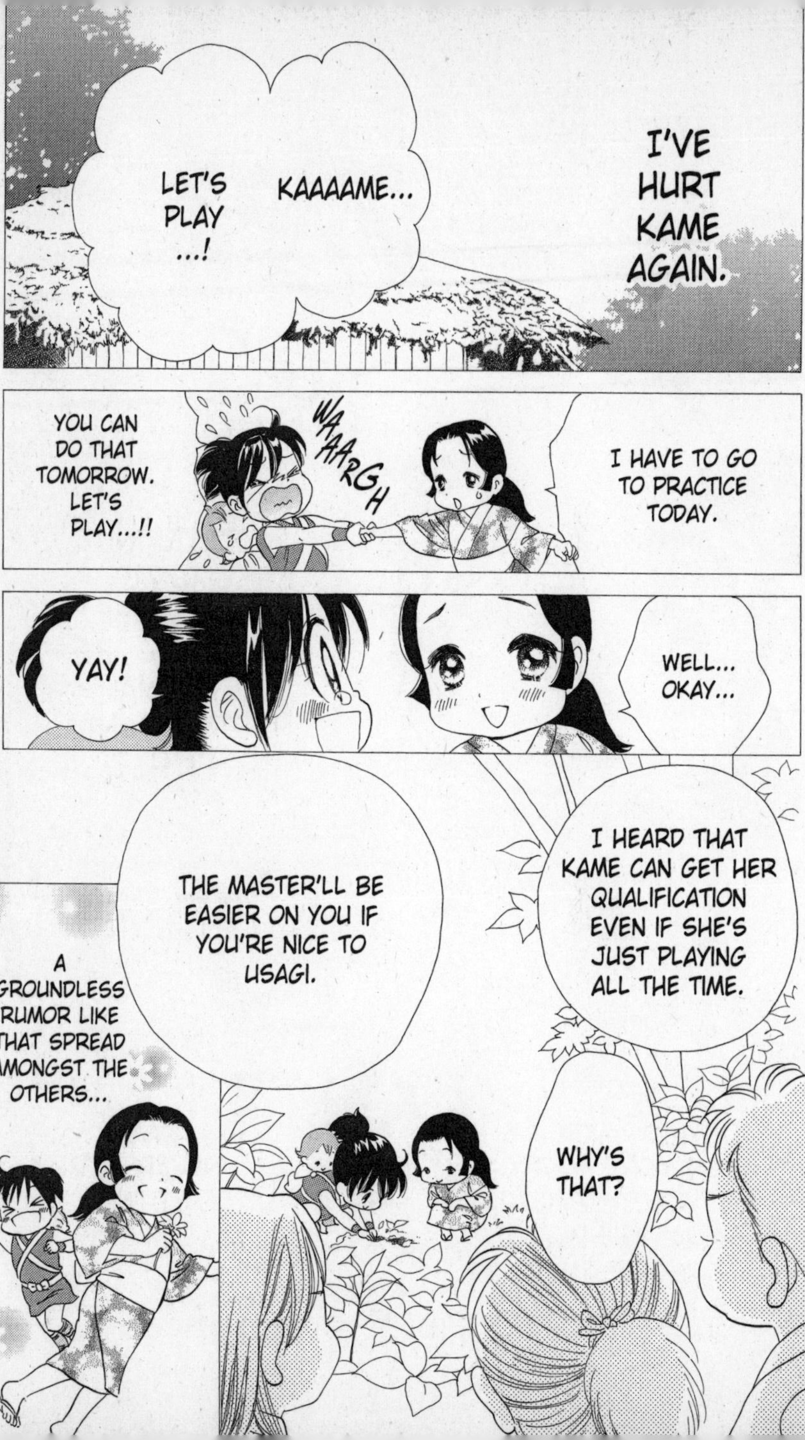
I'VE HURT KAME AGAIN.
KAAAAME...
LET'S PLAY ...!
I HAVE TO GO TO PRACTICE TODAY.
WAAARGH
YOU CAN DO THAT TOMORROW. LET'S PLAY...!!
WELL... OKAY...
YAY!
I HEARD THAT KAME CAN GET HER QUALIFICATION EVEN IF SHE'S JUST PLAYING ALL THE TIME.
WHY'S THAT?
THE MASTER'LL BE EASIER ON YOU IF YOU'RE NICE TO USAGI.
A GROUNDLESS RUMOR LIKE THAT SPREAD AMONGST THE OTHERS...

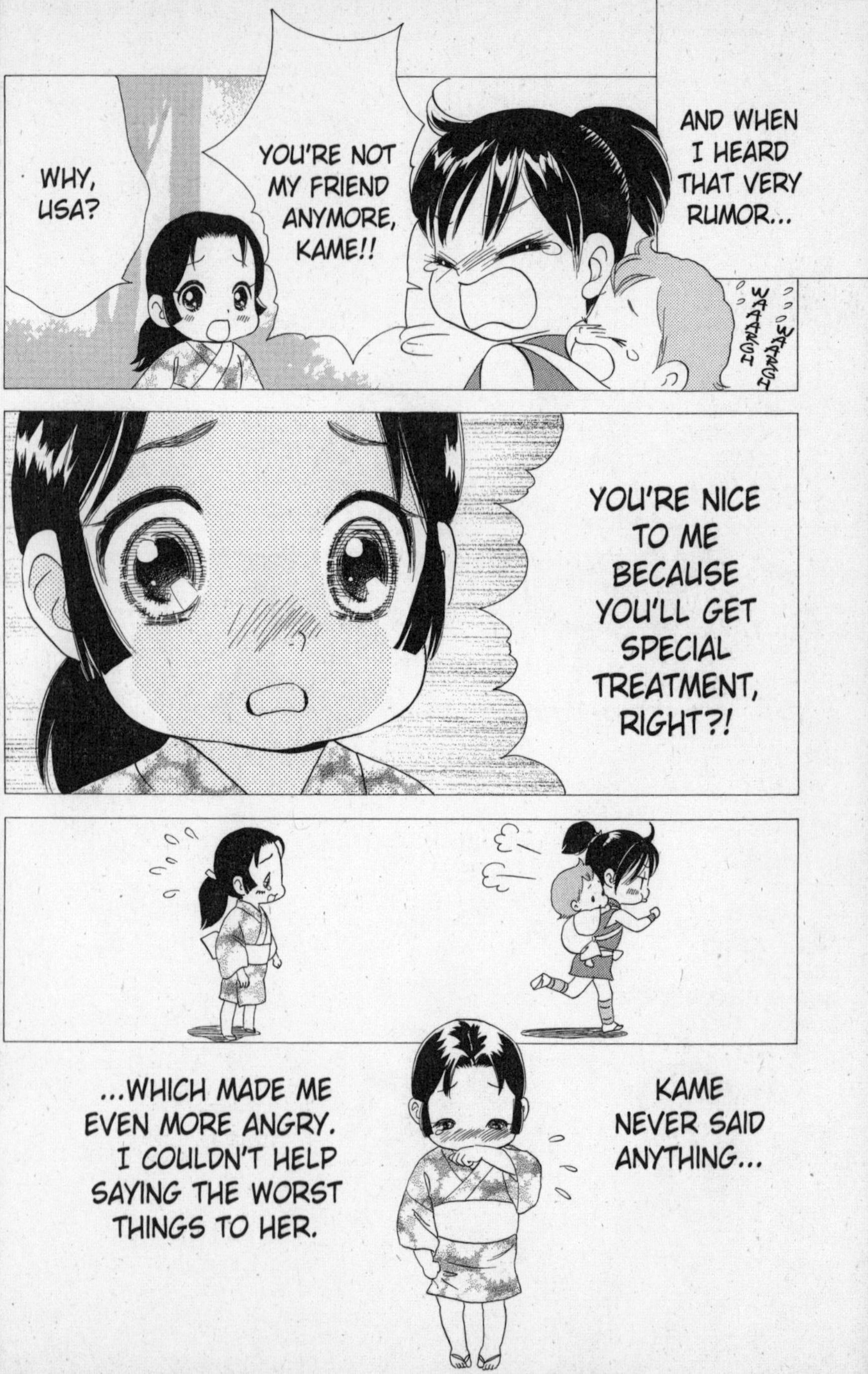
AND WHEN I HEARD THAT VERY RUMOR...
WAAARGH WAAARGH
YOU'RE NOT MY FRIEND ANYMORE, KAME!!
WHY, USA?
YOU'RE NICE TO ME BECAUSE YOU'LL GET SPECIAL TREATMENT, RIGHT?!
KAME NEVER SAID ANYTHING...
...WHICH MADE ME EVEN MORE ANGRY. I COULDN'T HELP SAYING THE WORST THINGS TO HER.

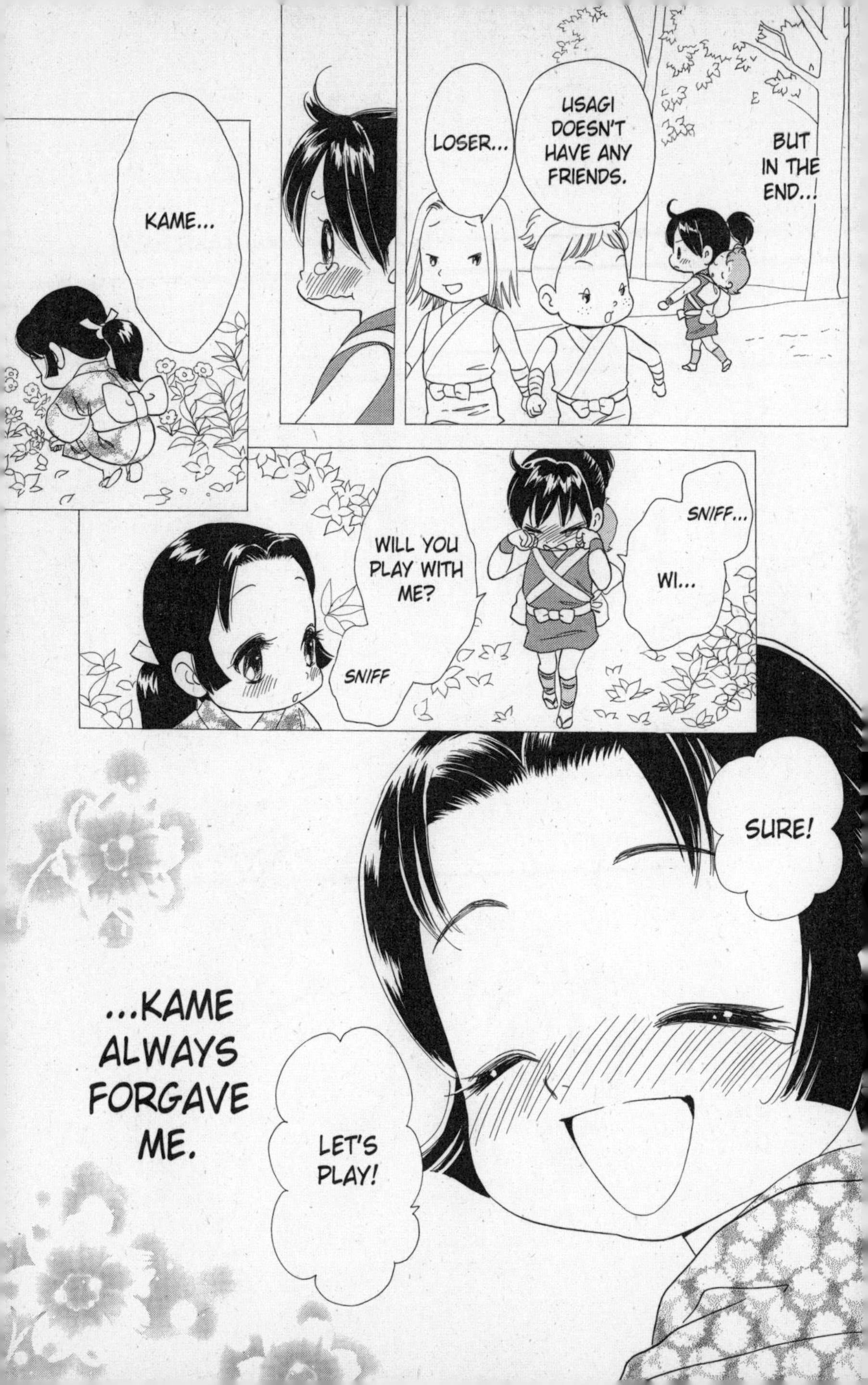
BUT IN THE END...
USAGI DOESN'T HAVE ANY FRIENDS.
LOSER...
KAME...
SNIFF...
WI...
WILL YOU PLAY WITH ME?
SNIFF
SURE!
LET'S PLAY!
...KAME ALWAYS FORGAVE ME.

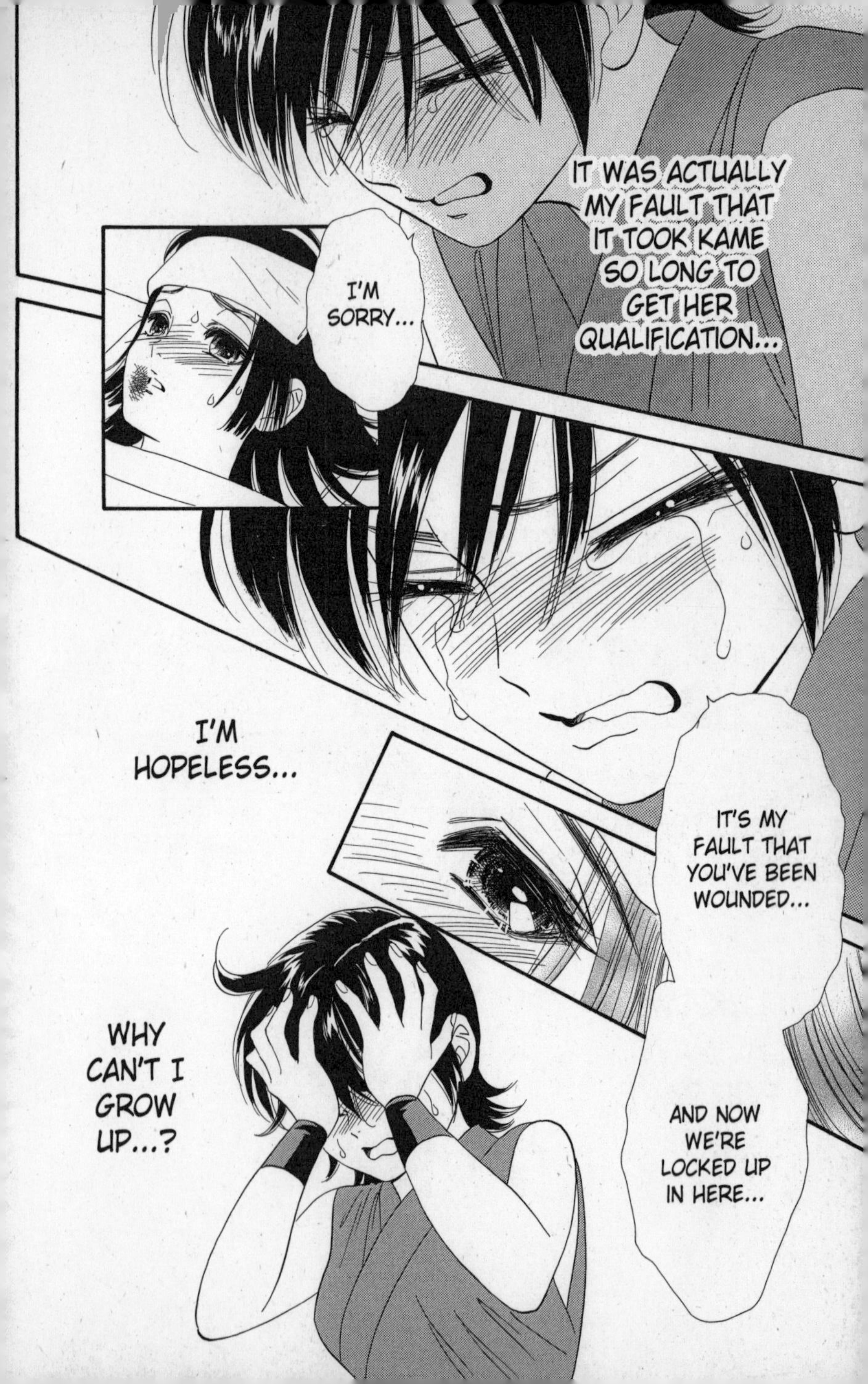
IT WAS ACTUALLY MY FAULT THAT IT TOOK KAME SO LONG TO GET HER QUALIFICATION...
I'M SORRY...
IT'S MY FAULT THAT YOU'VE BEEN WOUNDED...
AND NOW WE'RE LOCKED UP IN HERE...
I'M HOPELESS...
WHY CAN'T I GROW UP...?

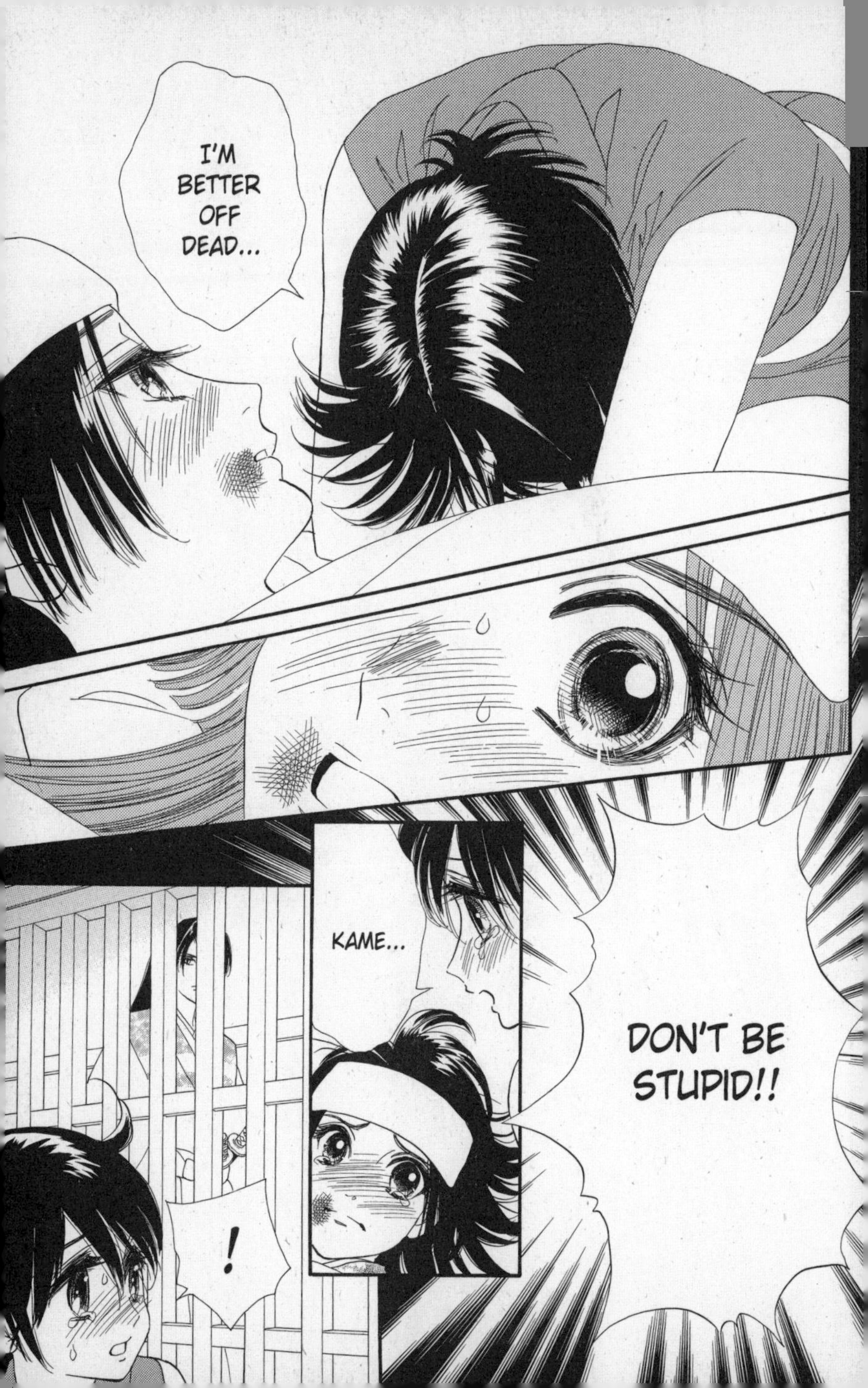
I'M BETTER OFF DEAD...
DON'T BE STUPID!!
KAME...
!

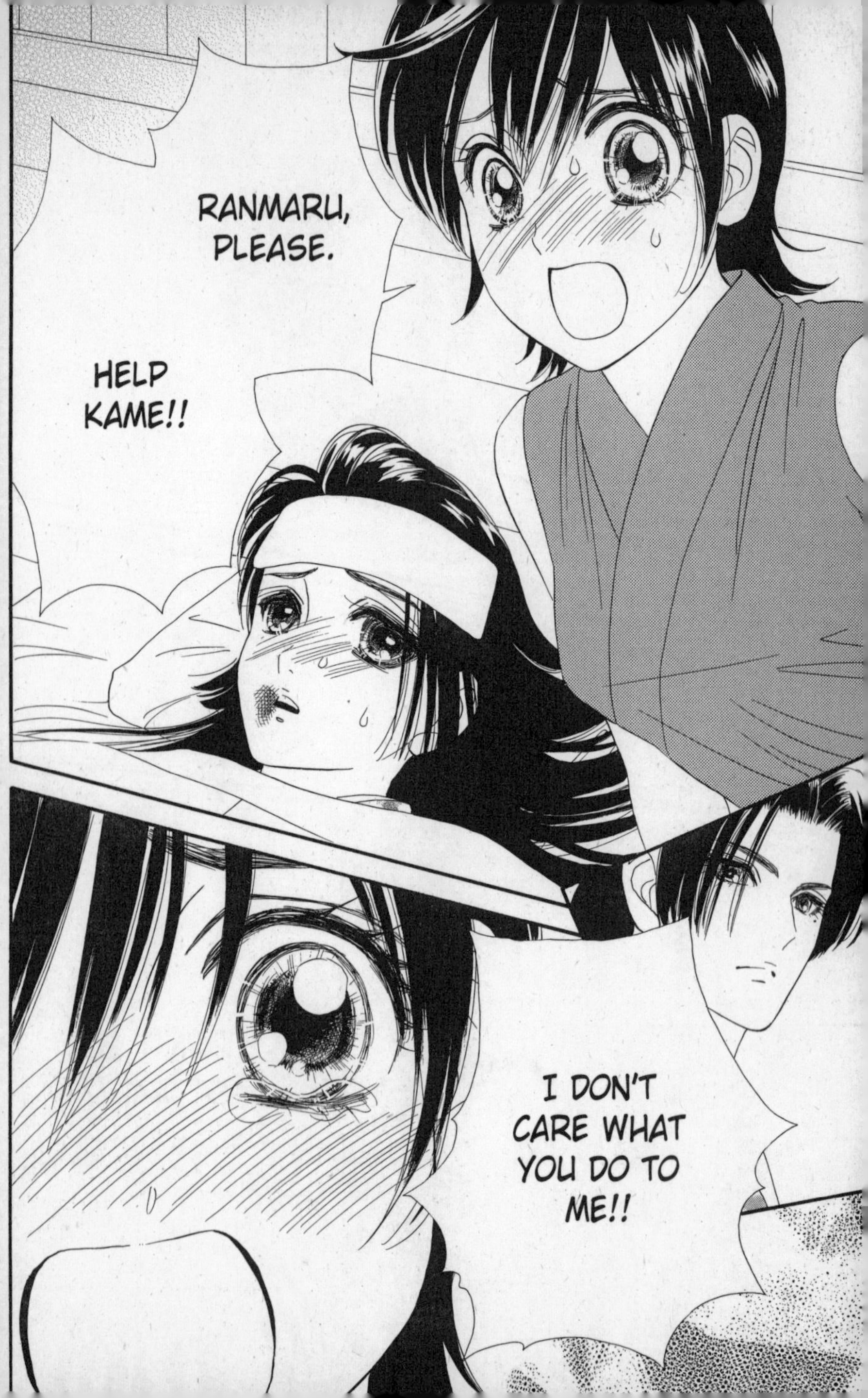
RANMARU, PLEASE.
HELP KAME!!
I DON'T CARE WHAT YOU DO TO ME!!

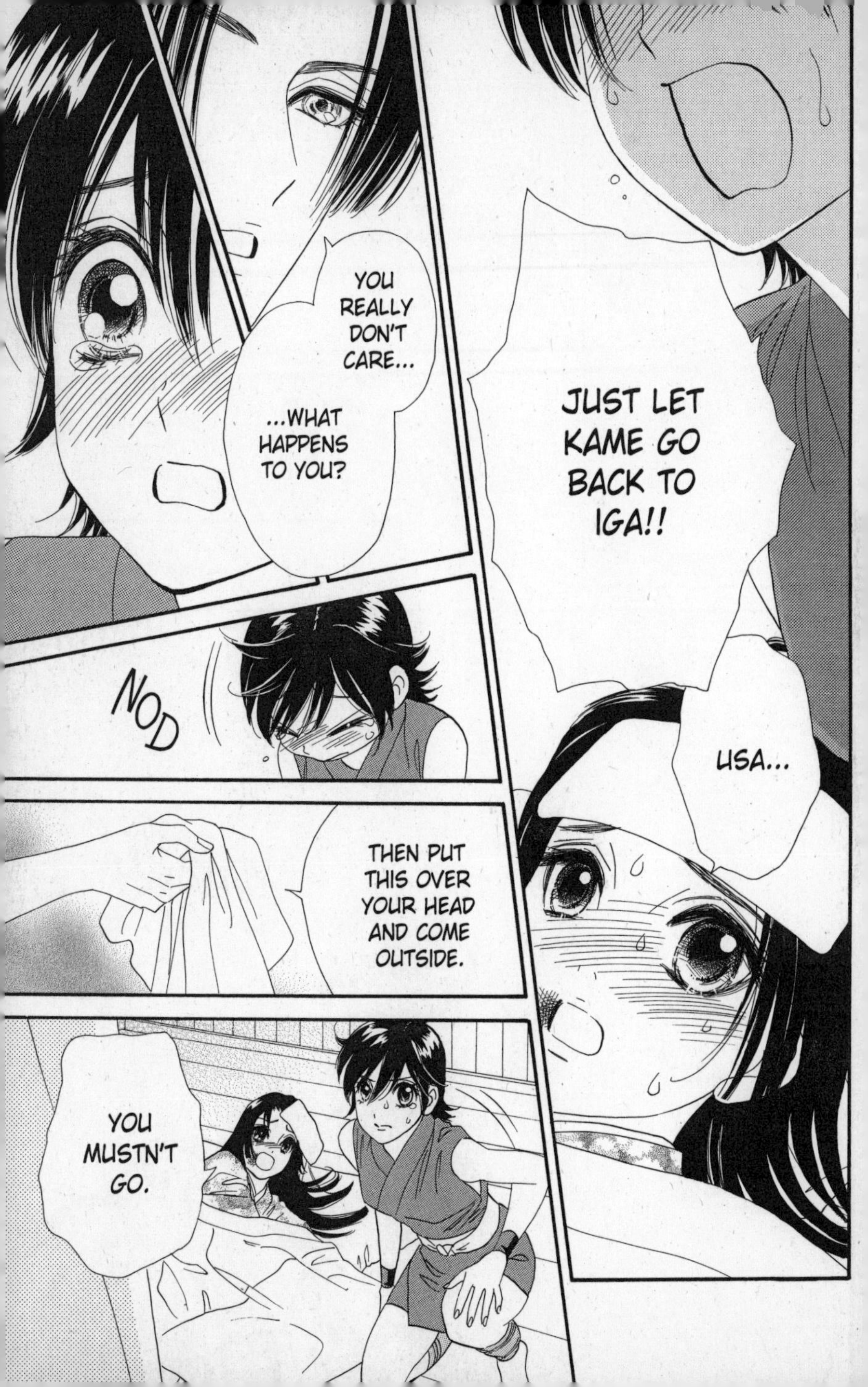
JUST LET KAME GO BACK TO IGA!!
YOU REALLY DON'T CARE...
...WHAT HAPPENS TO YOU?
USA...
NOD
THEN PUT THIS OVER YOUR HEAD AND COME OUTSIDE.
YOU MUSTN'T GO.

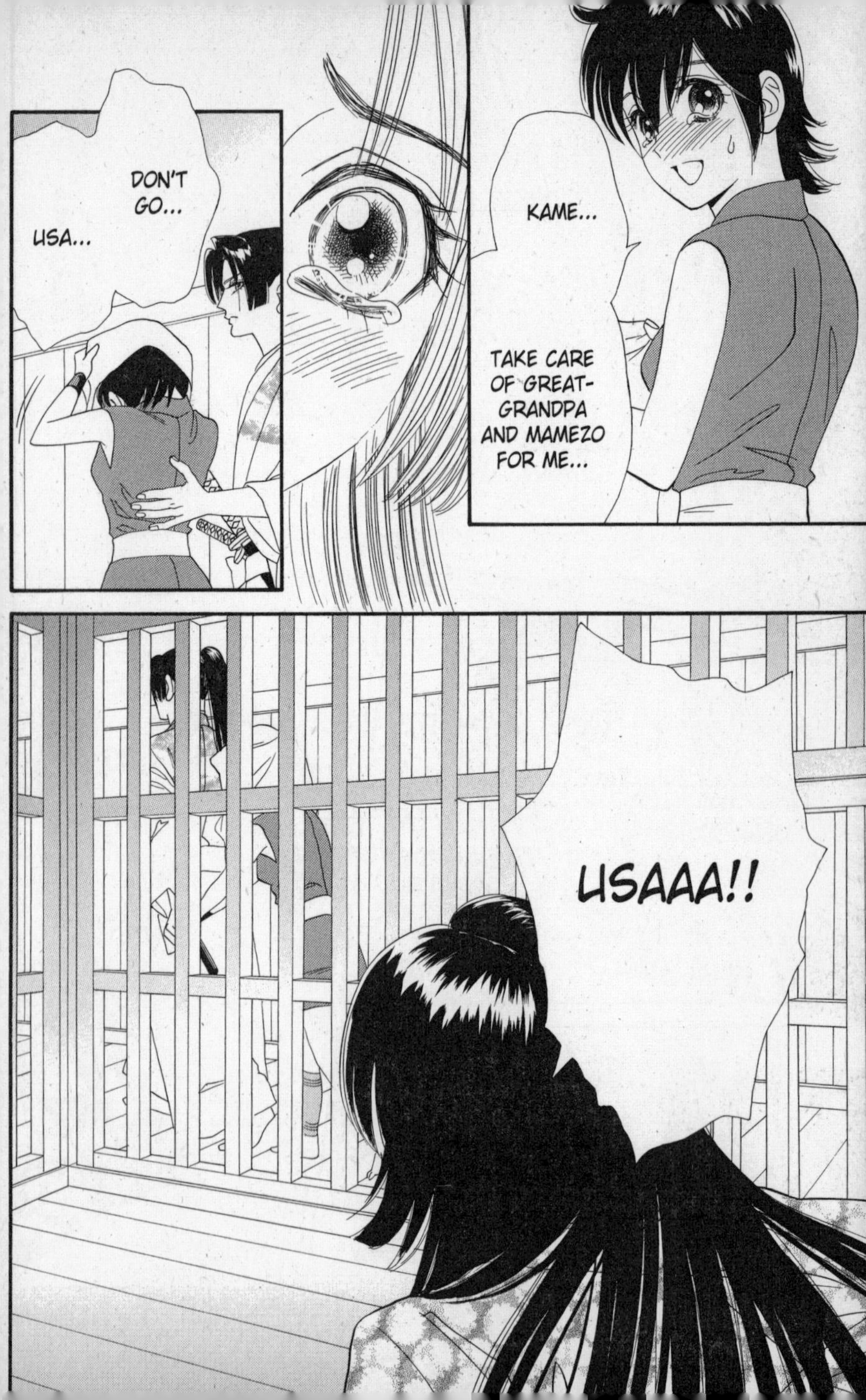
KAME...
TAKE CARE OF GREAT-GRANDPA AND MAMEZO FOR ME...
DON'T GO...
USA...
USAAA!!

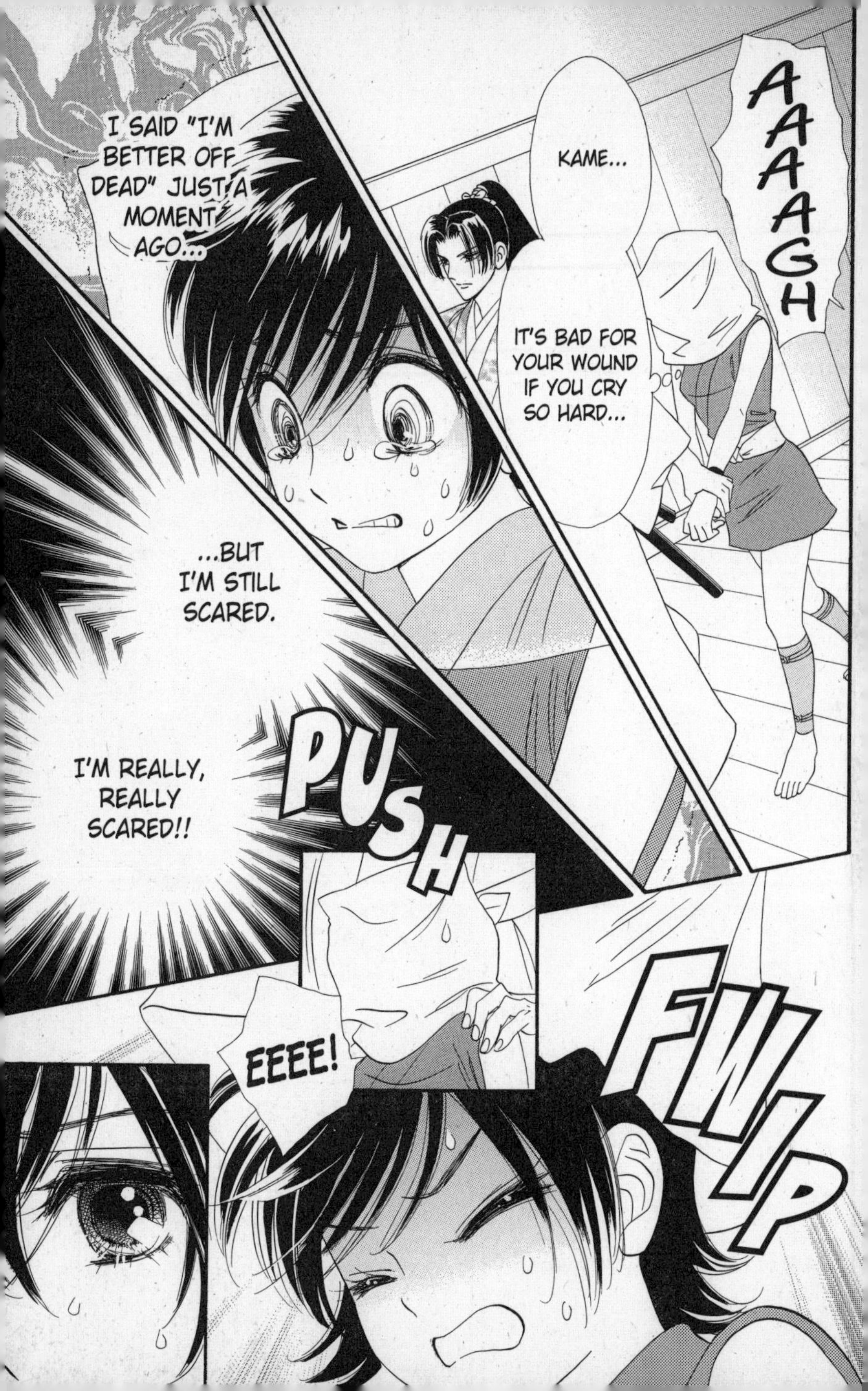
AAAAAGH
KAME...
IT'S BAD FOR YOUR WOUND IF YOU CRY SO HARD...
I SAID "I'M BETTER OFF DEAD" JUST A MOMENT AGO...
...BUT I'M STILL SCARED.
I'M REALLY, REALLY SCARED!!
PUSH
FLIP
EEEE!

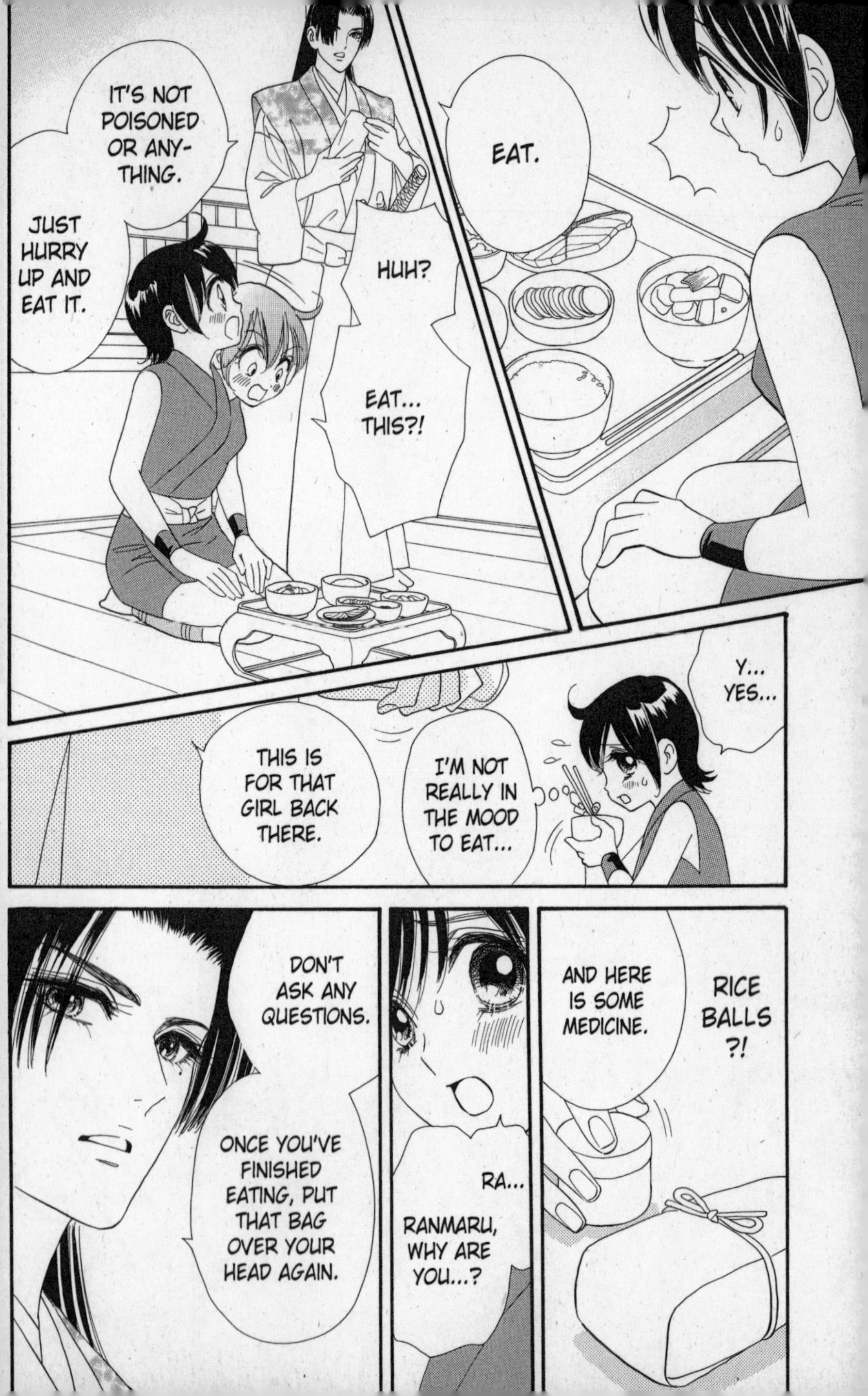
EAT.
HUH?
EAT... THIS?!
IT'S NOT POISONED OR ANY-THING.
JUST HURRY UP AND EAT IT.
Y... YES...
I'M NOT REALLY IN THE MOOD TO EAT...
THIS IS FOR THAT GIRL BACK THERE.
RICE BALLS ?!
AND HERE IS SOME MEDICINE.
RA...
RANMARU, WHY ARE YOU...?
DON'T ASK ANY QUESTIONS.
ONCE YOU'VE FINISHED EATING, PUT THAT BAG OVER YOUR HEAD AGAIN.

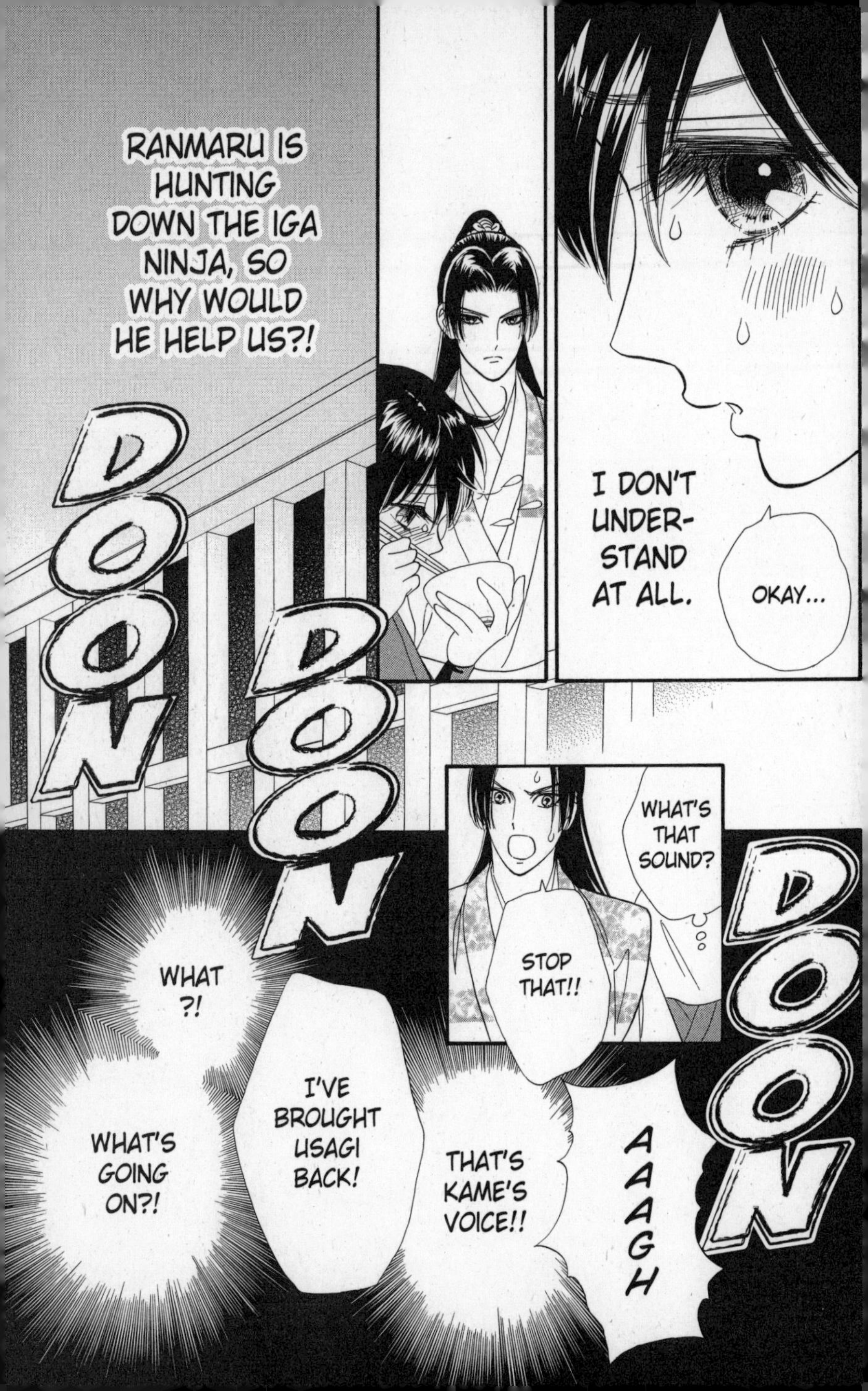
OKAY...
I DON'T UNDER-STAND AT ALL.
RANMARU IS HUNTING DOWN THE IGA NINJA, SO WHY WOULD HE HELP US?!
DOON
DOON
WHAT'S THAT SOUND?
STOP THAT!!
DOON
AAAAGH
THAT'S KAME'S VOICE!!
I'VE BROUGHT USAGI BACK!
WHAT ?!
WHAT'S GOING ON?!

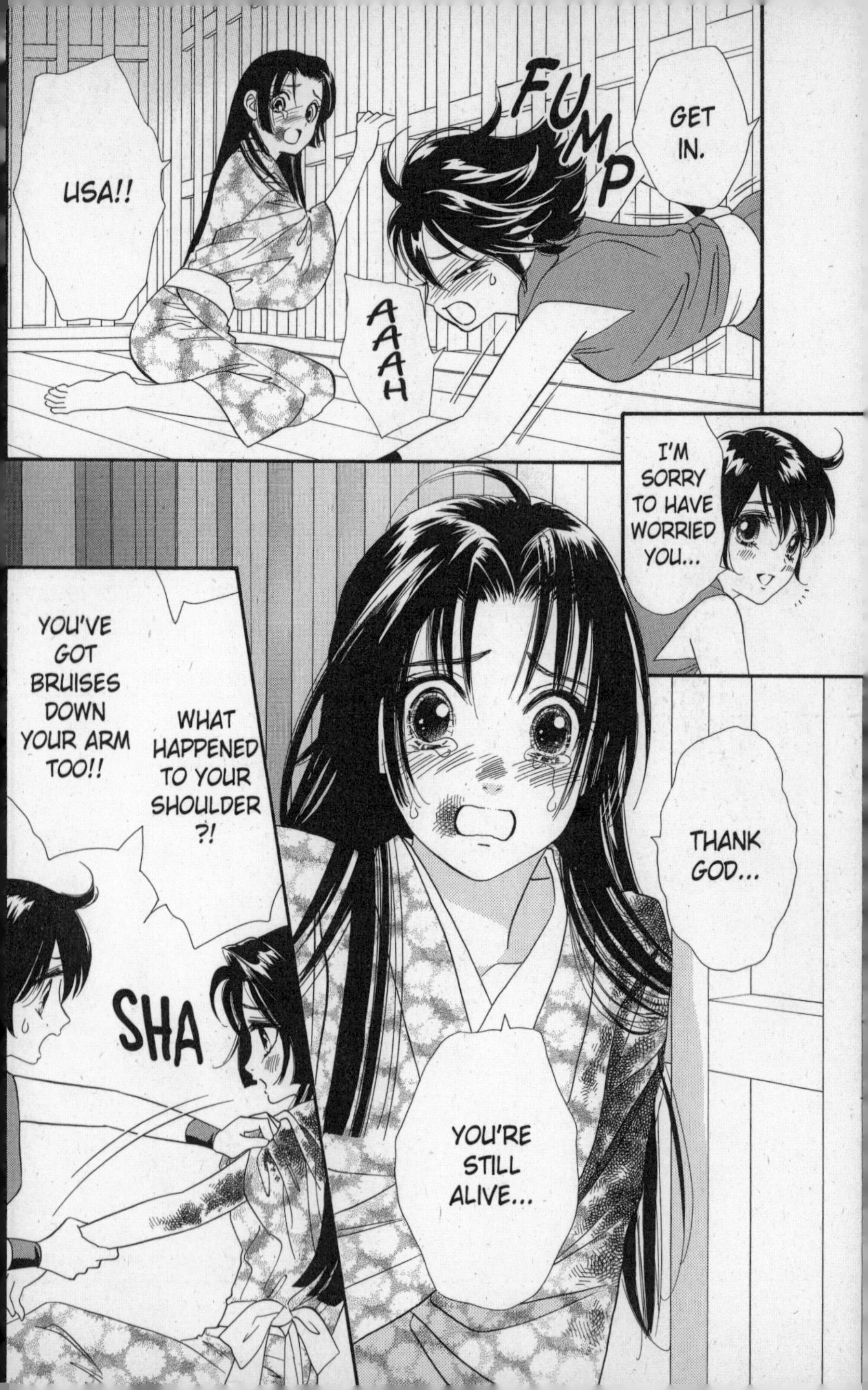
GET IN.
FUMP
AAAH
USA!!
I'M SORRY TO HAVE WORRIED YOU...
THANK GOD...
YOU'RE STILL ALIVE...
WHAT HAPPENED TO YOUR SHOULDER ?!
YOU'VE GOT BRUISES DOWN YOUR ARM TOO!!
SHA

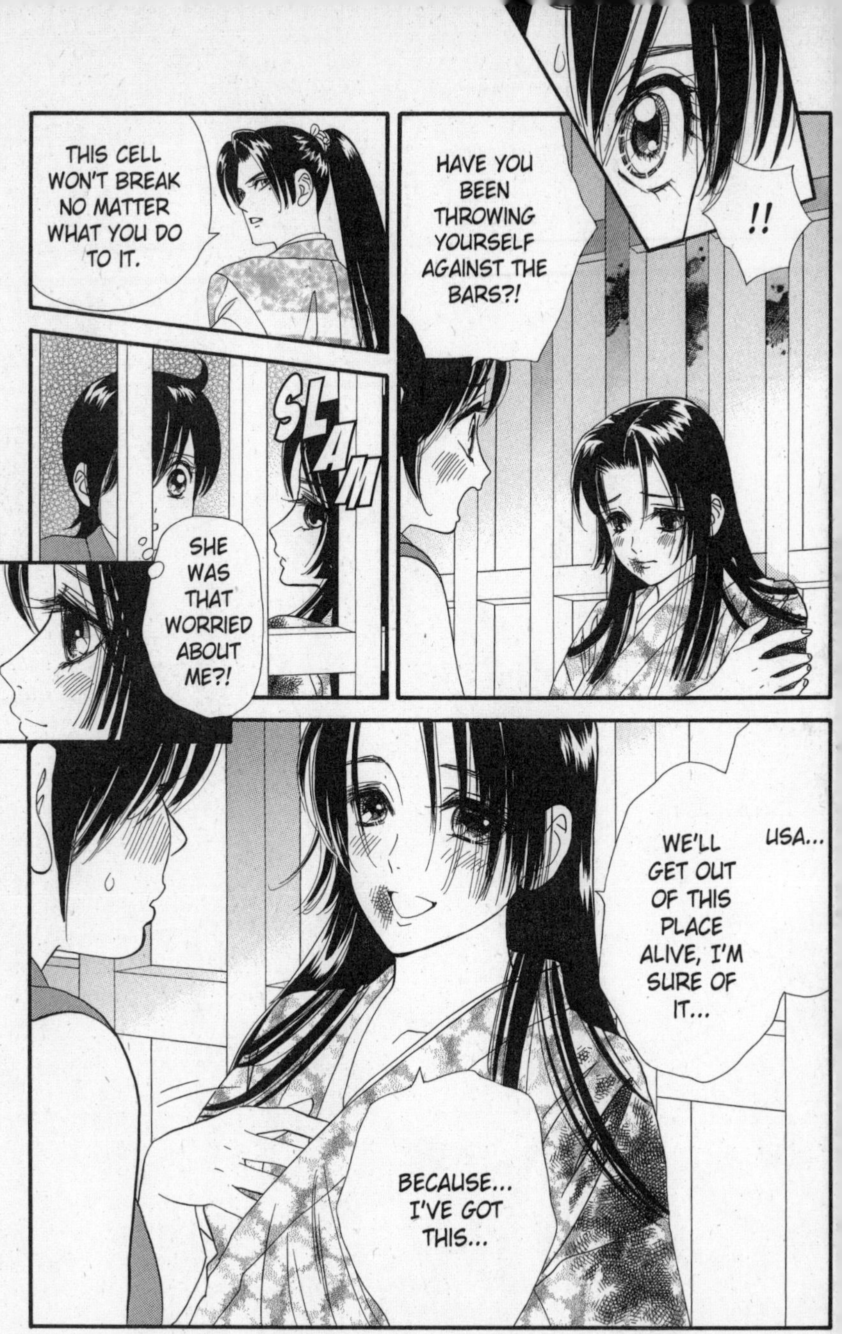
!!
HAVE YOU BEEN THROWING YOURSELF AGAINST THE BARS?!
THIS CELL WON'T BREAK NO MATTER WHAT YOU DO TO IT.
SLAM
SHE WAS THAT WORRIED ABOUT ME?!
USA...
WE'LL GET OUT OF THIS PLACE ALIVE, I'M SURE OF IT...
BECAUSE... I'VE GOT THIS...

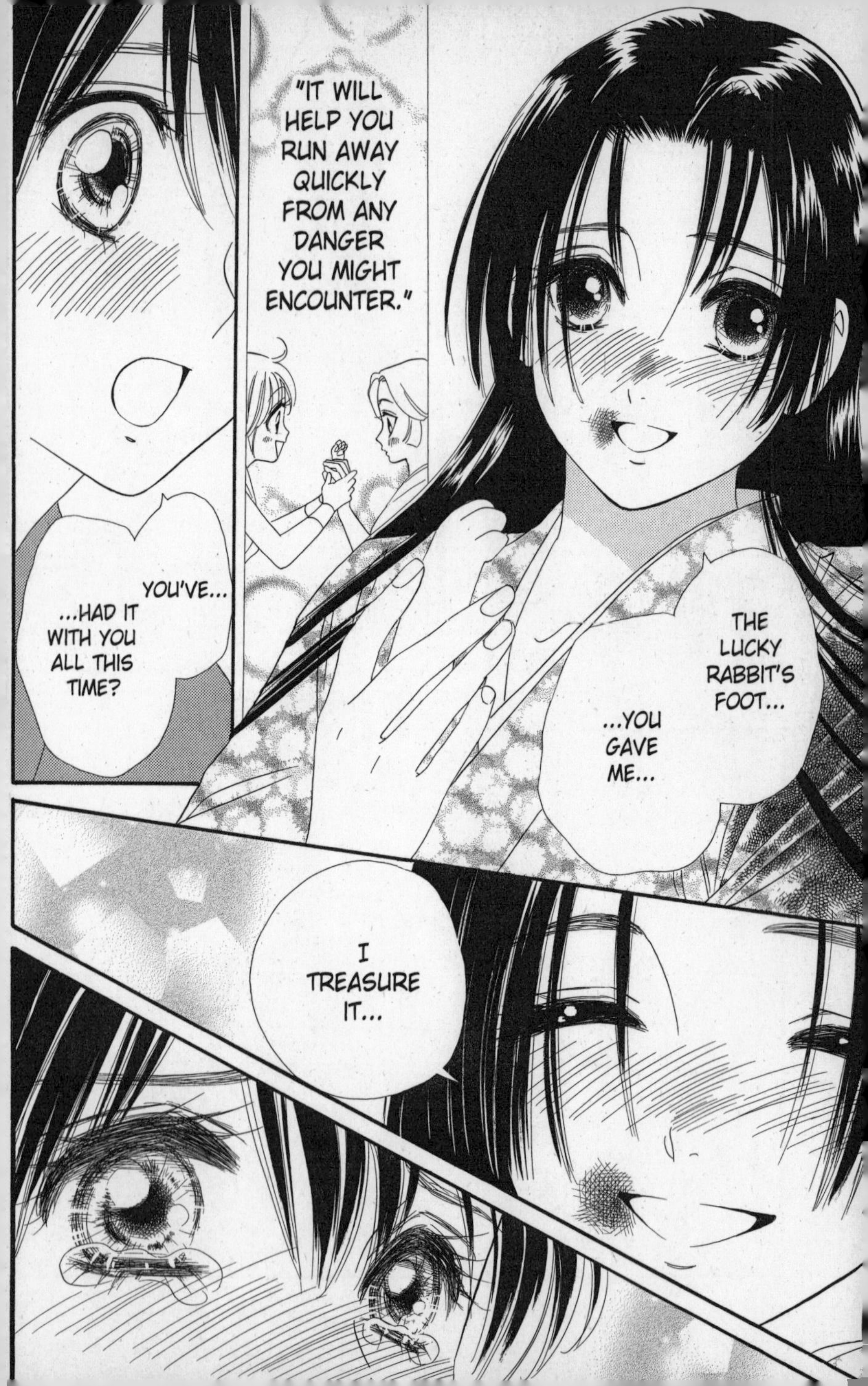
THE LUCKY RABBIT'S FOOT...
...YOU GAVE ME...
"IT WILL HELP YOU RUN AWAY QUICKLY FROM ANY DANGER YOU MIGHT ENCOUNTER."
YOU'VE...
...HAD IT WITH YOU ALL THIS TIME?
I TREASURE IT...

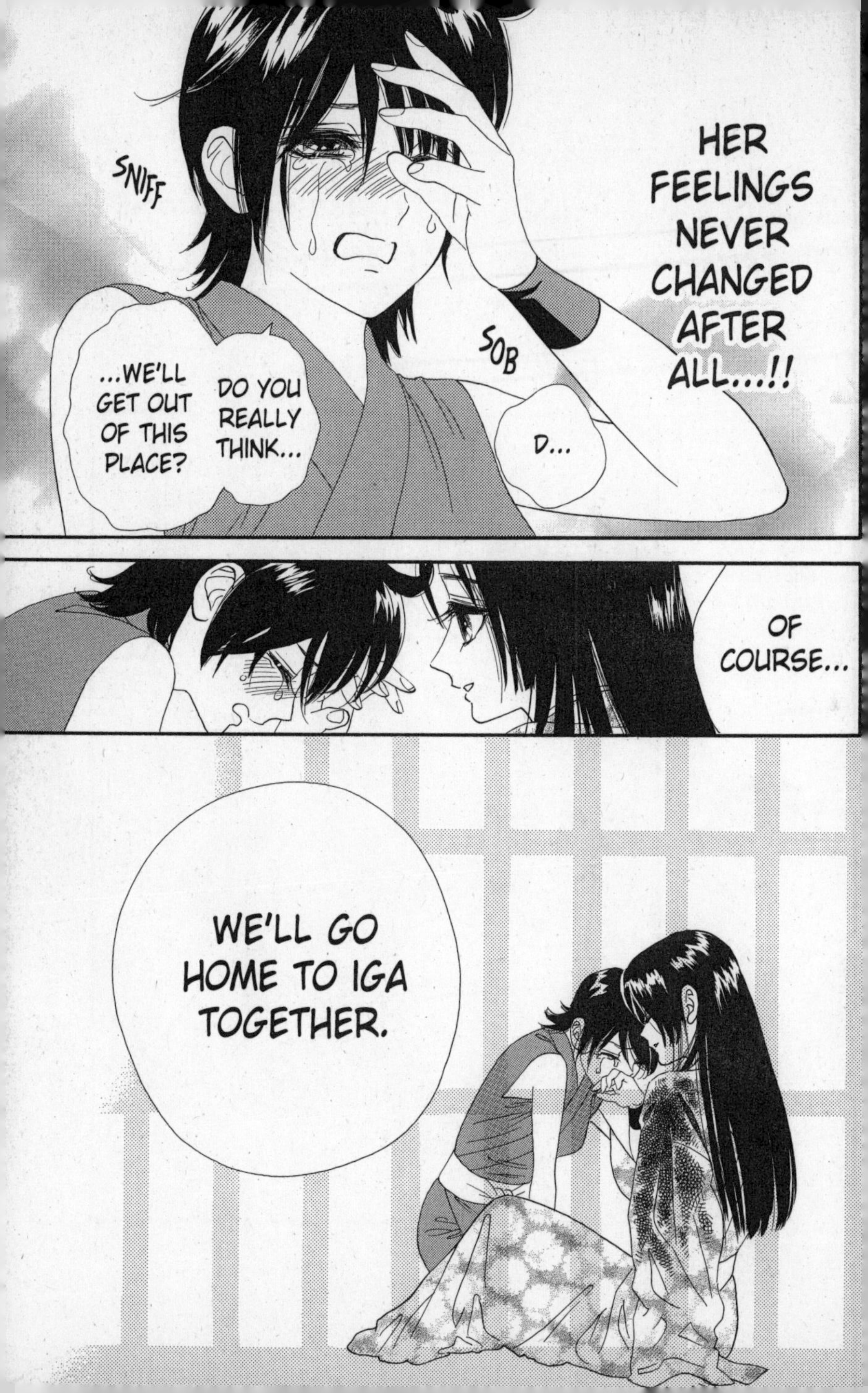
HER FEELINGS NEVER CHANGED AFTER ALL...!!
D...
SOB
DO YOU REALLY THINK...
...WE'LL GET OUT OF THIS PLACE?
SNIFF
OF COURSE...
WE'LL GO HOME TO IGA TOGETHER.

TAIL OF THE MOON EXTRA: TODAY'S MISSION

"I WANT TO SEE HANZO AS A SUPERHERO!"

-NAOKO NOGAMI, YAMAGUCHI PREFECTURE

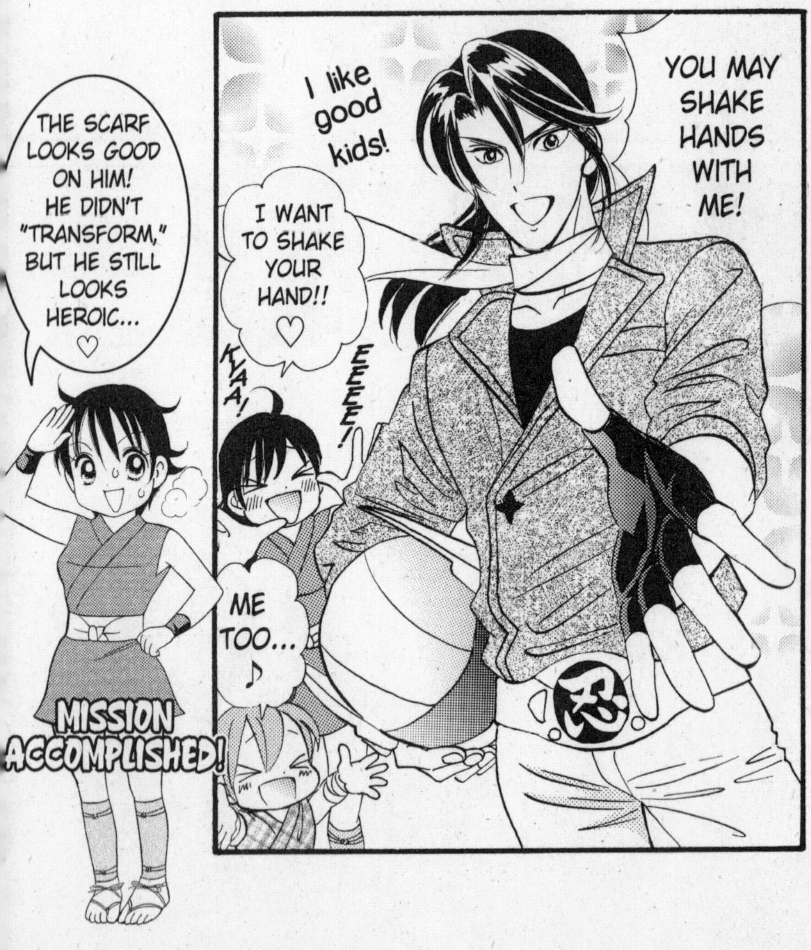
YOU MAY SHAKE HANDS WITH ME!
I like good kids!
I WANT TO SHAKE YOUR HAND!! ♡
EEEEE!
KYAA!
THE SCARF LOOKS GOOD ON HIM! HE DIDN'T "TRANSFORM," BUT HE STILL LOOKS HEROIC... ♡
ME TOO... ♪
MISSION ACCOMPLISHED!

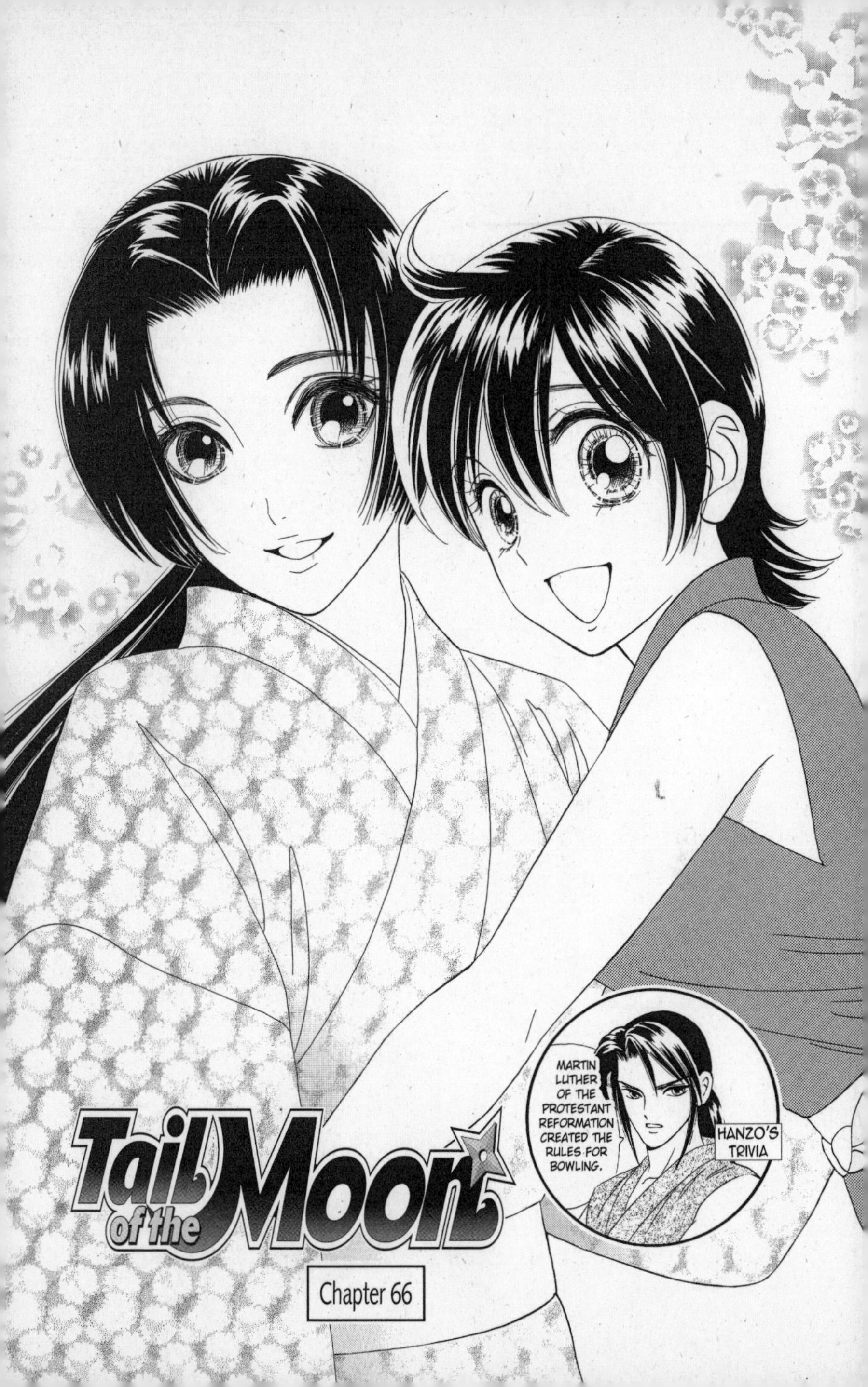

Tail of the Moon
MARTIN LUTHER OF THE PROTESTANT REFORMATION CREATED THE RULES FOR BOWLING.
HANZO'S TRIVIA
Chapter 66

WE'LL GO HOME TO IGA TOGETHER.
BY THE WAY, USA...
...WHAT DID YOU DO AFTER RANMARU TOOK YOU AWAY?

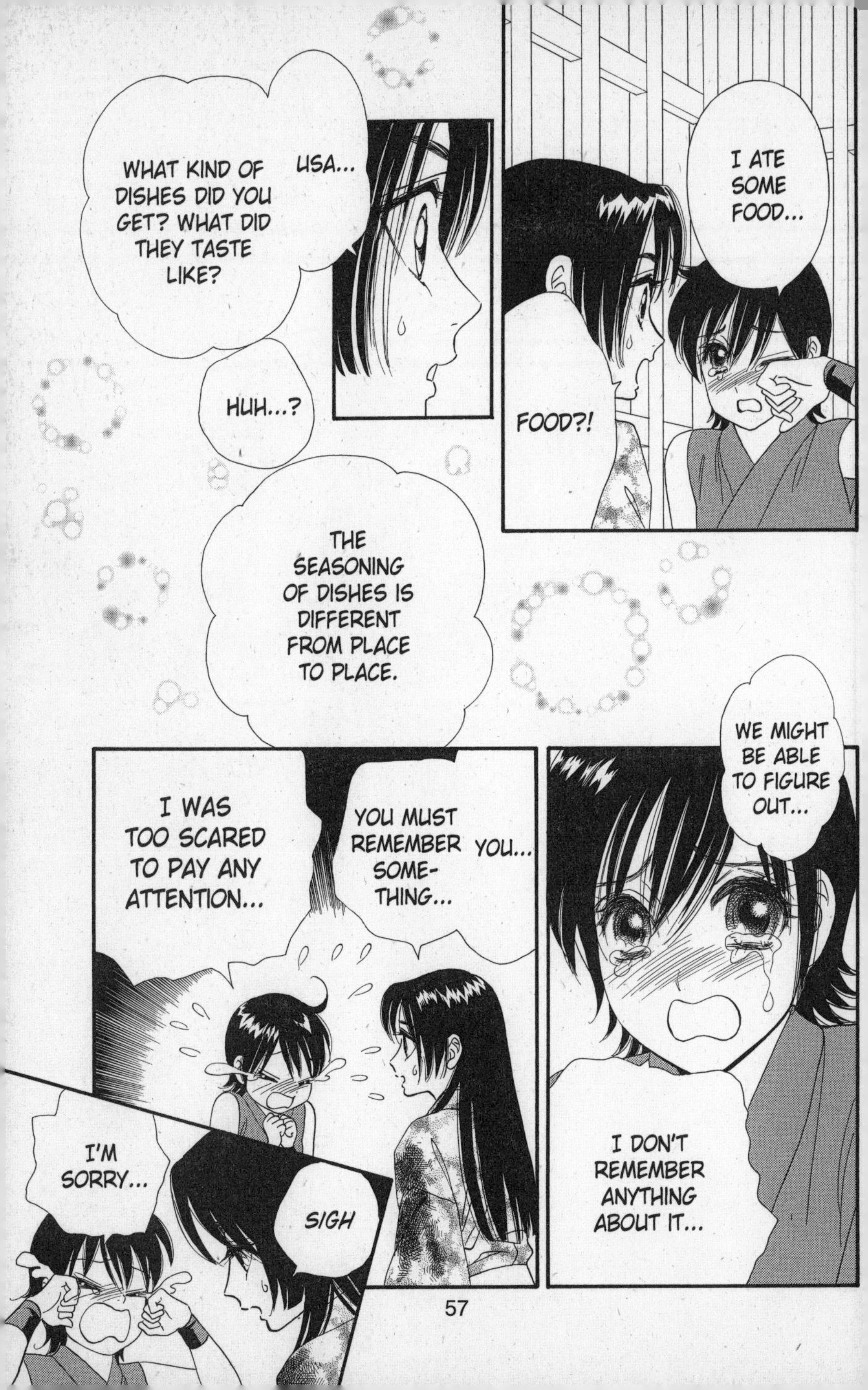

I ATE SOME FOOD...
FOOD?!
USA...
WHAT KIND OF DISHES DID YOU GET? WHAT DID THEY TASTE LIKE?
HUH...?
THE SEASONING OF DISHES IS DIFFERENT FROM PLACE TO PLACE.
WE MIGHT BE ABLE TO FIGURE OUT...
I DON'T REMEMBER ANYTHING ABOUT IT...
YOU...
YOU MUST REMEMBER SOME-THING...
I WAS TOO SCARED TO PAY ANY ATTENTION...
I'M SORRY...
SIGH

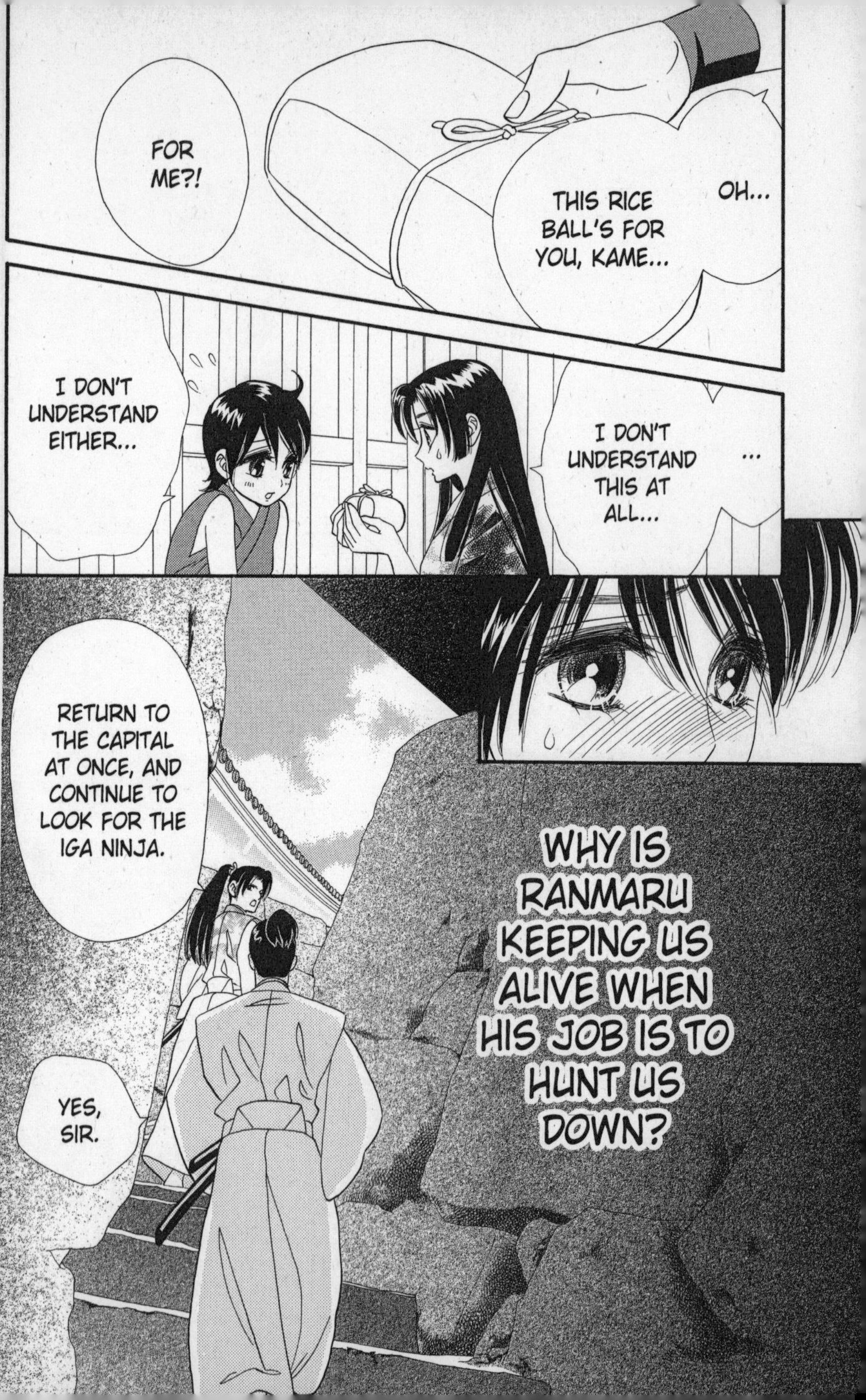
OH...
THIS RICE BALL'S FOR YOU, KAME...
FOR ME?!
...
I DON'T UNDERSTAND THIS AT ALL...
I DON'T UNDERSTAND EITHER...
RETURN TO THE CAPITAL AT ONCE, AND CONTINUE TO LOOK FOR THE IGA NINJA.
YES, SIR.
WHY IS RANMARU KEEPING US ALIVE WHEN HIS JOB IS TO HUNT US DOWN?

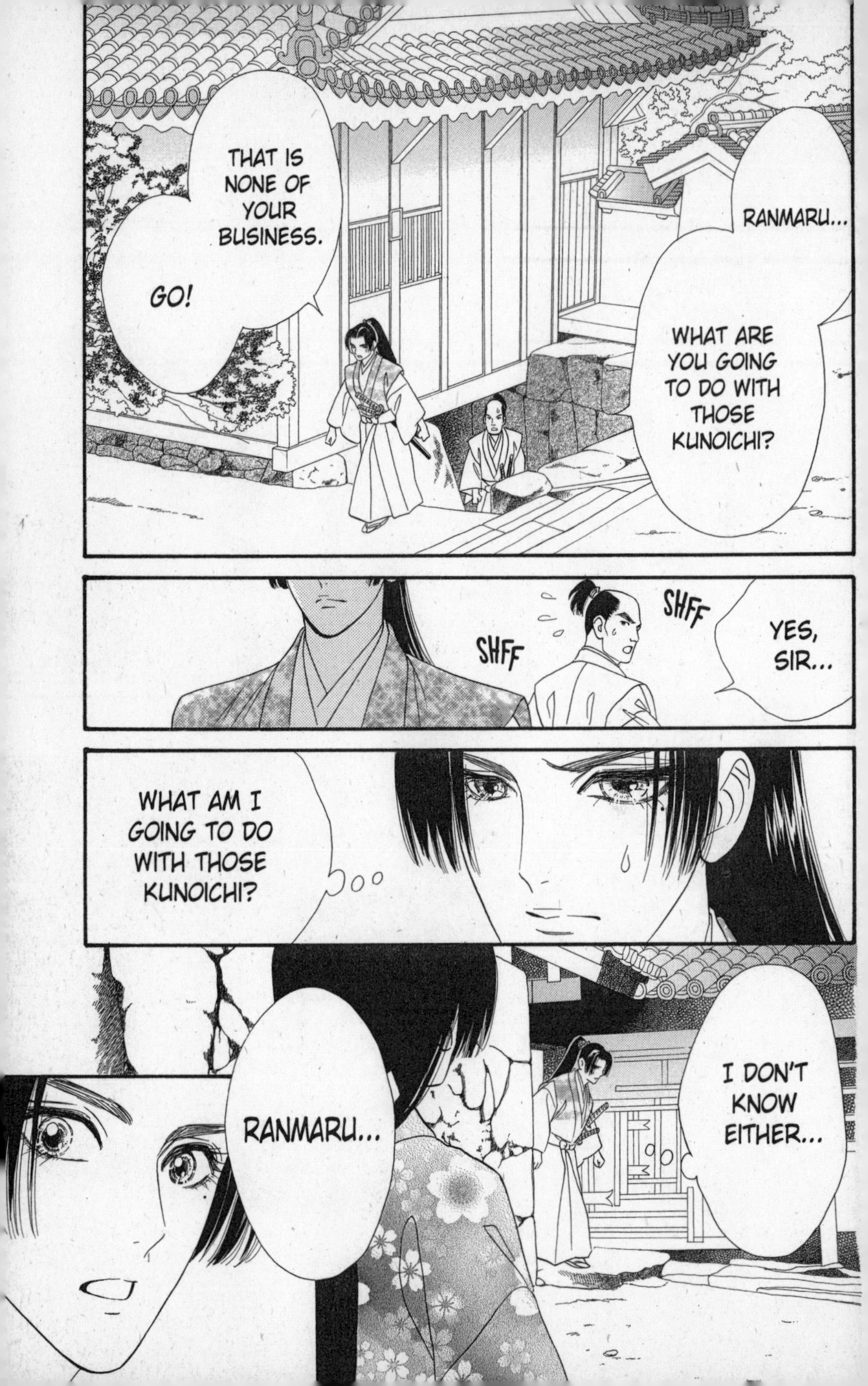
RANMARU...
WHAT ARE YOU GOING TO DO WITH THOSE KUNOICHI?
THAT IS NONE OF YOUR BUSINESS.
GO!
YES, SIR...
SHFF
SHFF
WHAT AM I GOING TO DO WITH THOSE KUNOICHI?
I DON'T KNOW EITHER...
RANMARU...

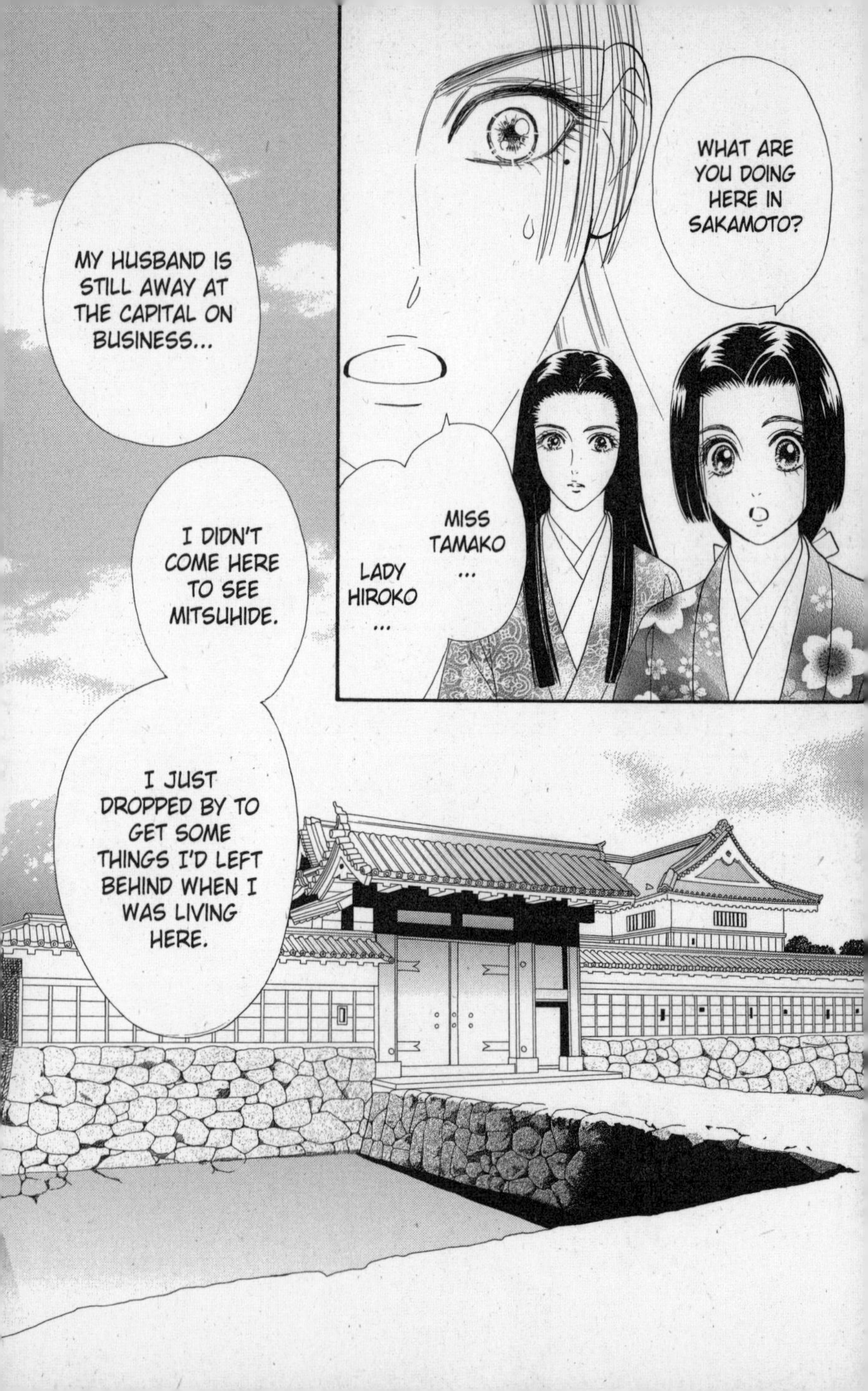
WHAT ARE YOU DOING HERE IN SAKAMOTO?
MISS TAMAKO ...
LADY HIROKO ...
MY HUSBAND IS STILL AWAY AT THE CAPITAL ON BUSINESS...
I DIDN'T COME HERE TO SEE MITSUHIDE.
I JUST DROPPED BY TO GET SOME THINGS I'D LEFT BEHIND WHEN I WAS LIVING HERE.

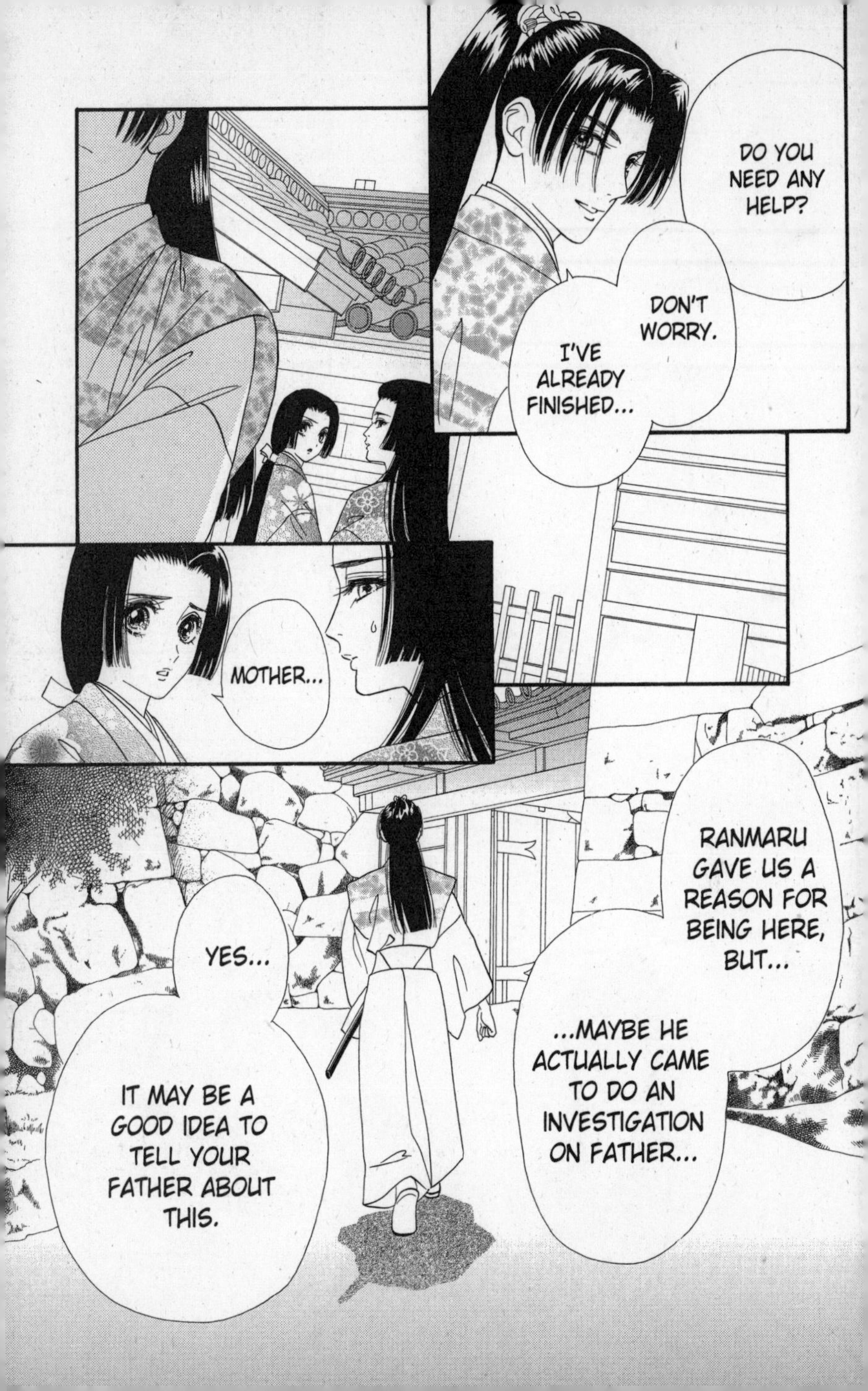
DO YOU NEED ANY HELP?
DON'T WORRY.
I'VE ALREADY FINISHED...
MOTHER...
RANMARU GAVE US A REASON FOR BEING HERE, BUT...
...MAYBE HE ACTUALLY CAME TO DO AN INVESTIGATION ON FATHER...
YES...
IT MAY BE A GOOD IDEA TO TELL YOUR FATHER ABOUT THIS.

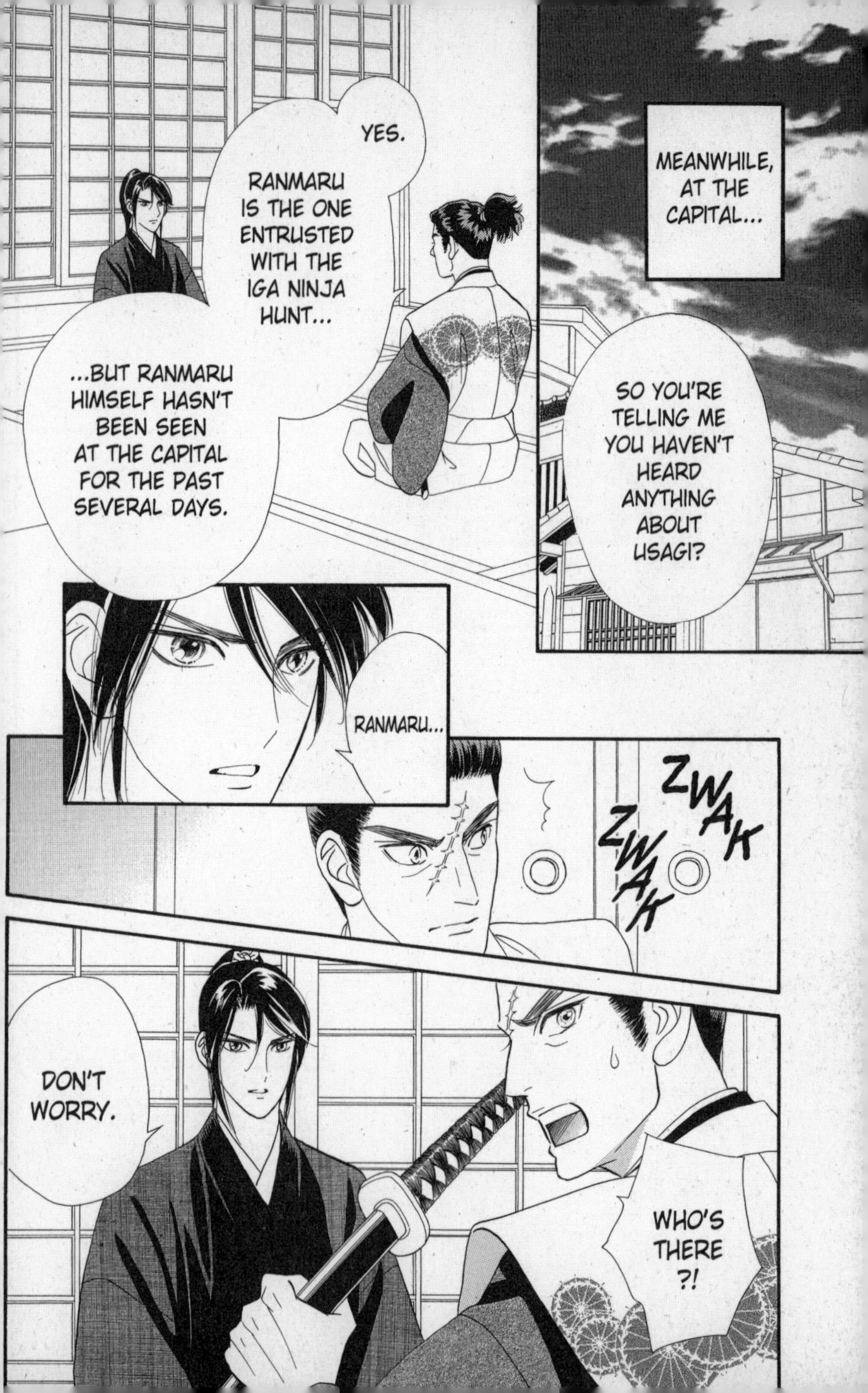
MEANWHILE, AT THE CAPITAL...
SO YOU'RE TELLING ME YOU HAVEN'T HEARD ANYTHING ABOUT USAGI?
YES.
RANMARU IS THE ONE ENTRUSTED WITH THE IGA NINJA HUNT...
...BUT RANMARU HIMSELF HASN'T BEEN SEEN AT THE CAPITAL FOR THE PAST SEVERAL DAYS.
RANMARU...
ZWAK
ZWAK
WHO'S THERE ?!
DON'T WORRY.

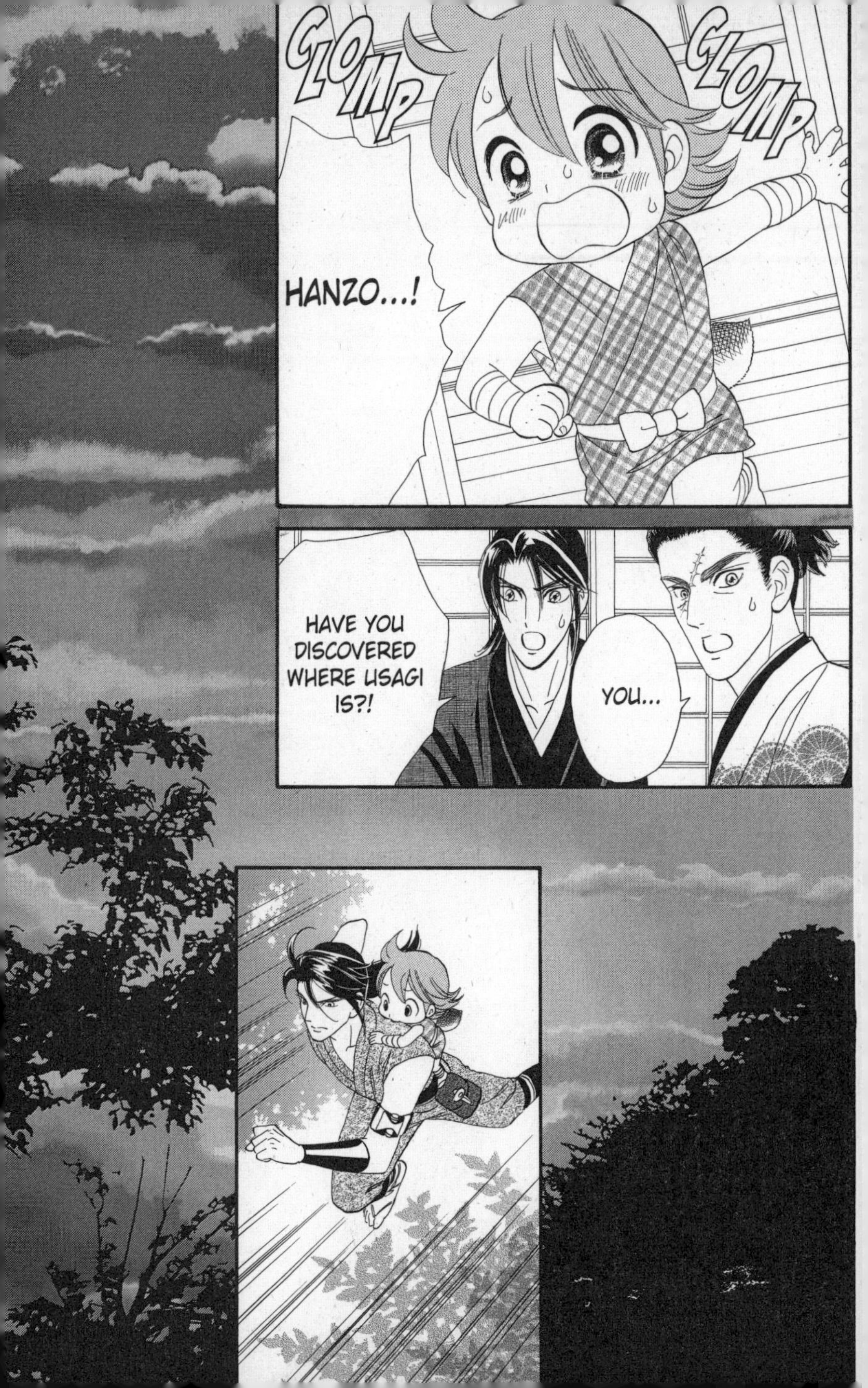
GLOMP
GLOMP
HANZO...!
YOU...
HAVE YOU DISCOVERED WHERE USAGI IS?!

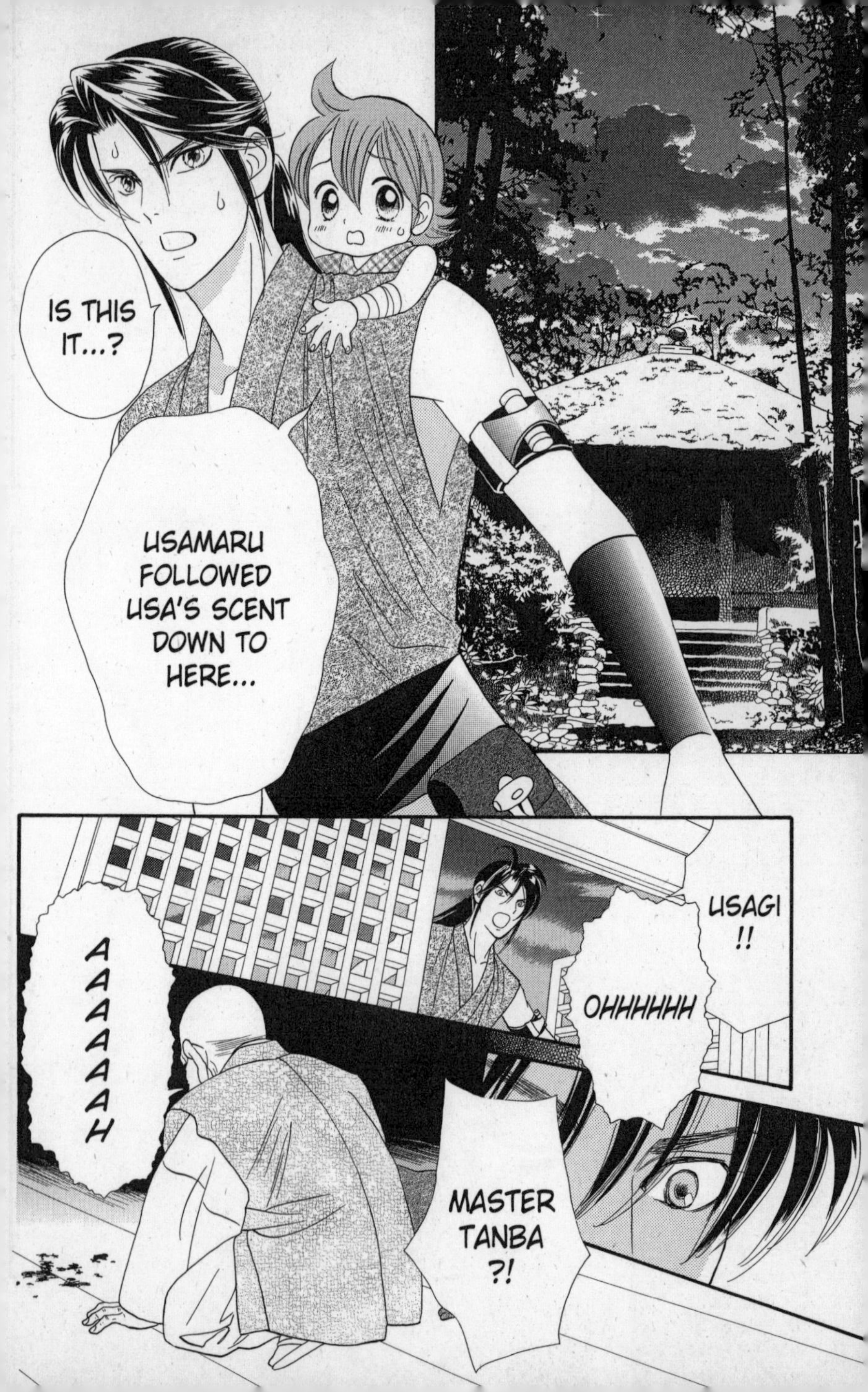
IS THIS IT...?
USAMARU FOLLOWED USA'S SCENT DOWN TO HERE...
USAGI !!
OHHHHHH
MASTER TANBA ?!
AAAAAAAH

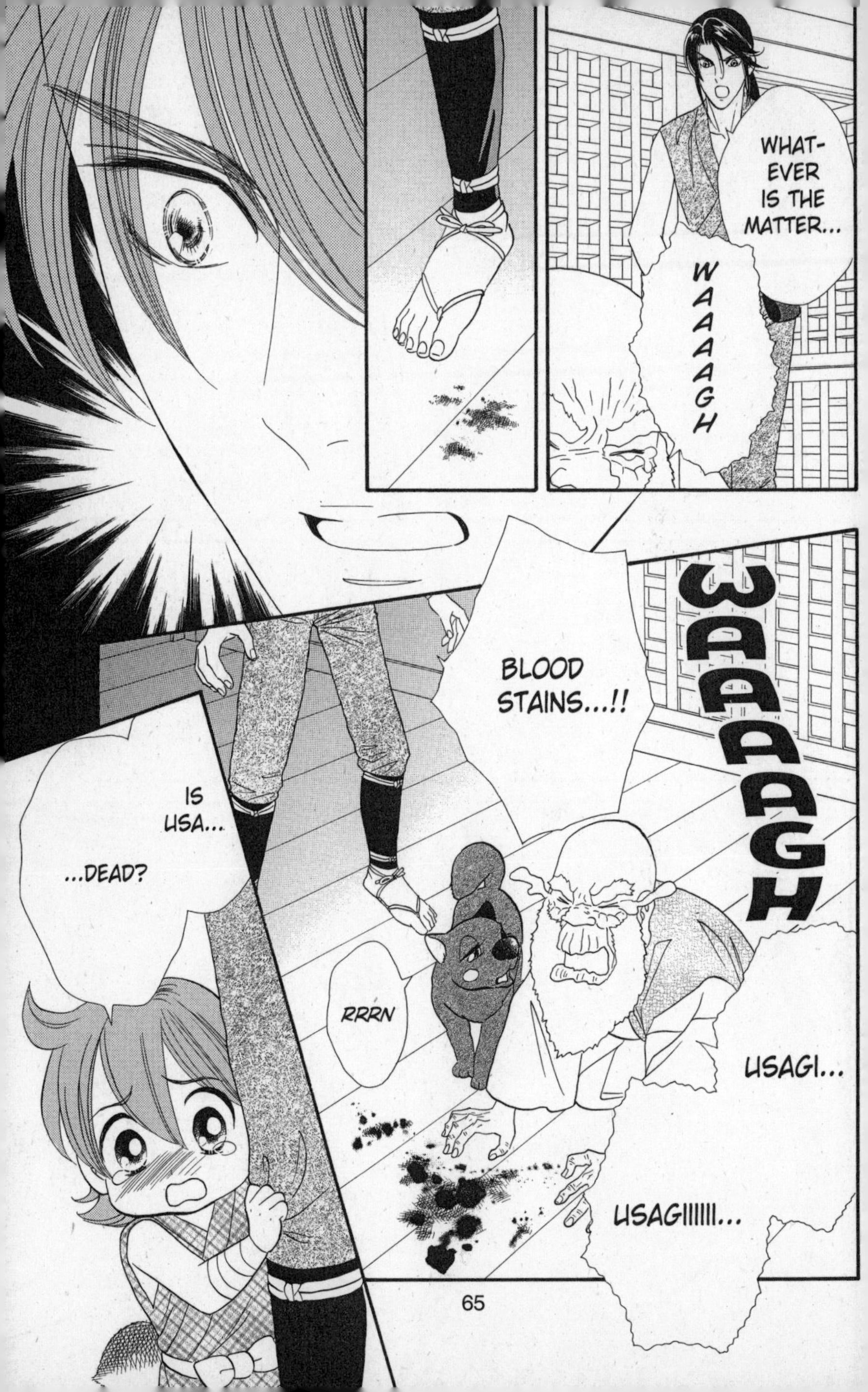
WHAT-EVER IS THE MATTER...
WAAAAGH
WAAAAGH
BLOOD STAINS...!!
RRRN
USAGI...
USAGIIIIII...
IS USA...
...DEAD?

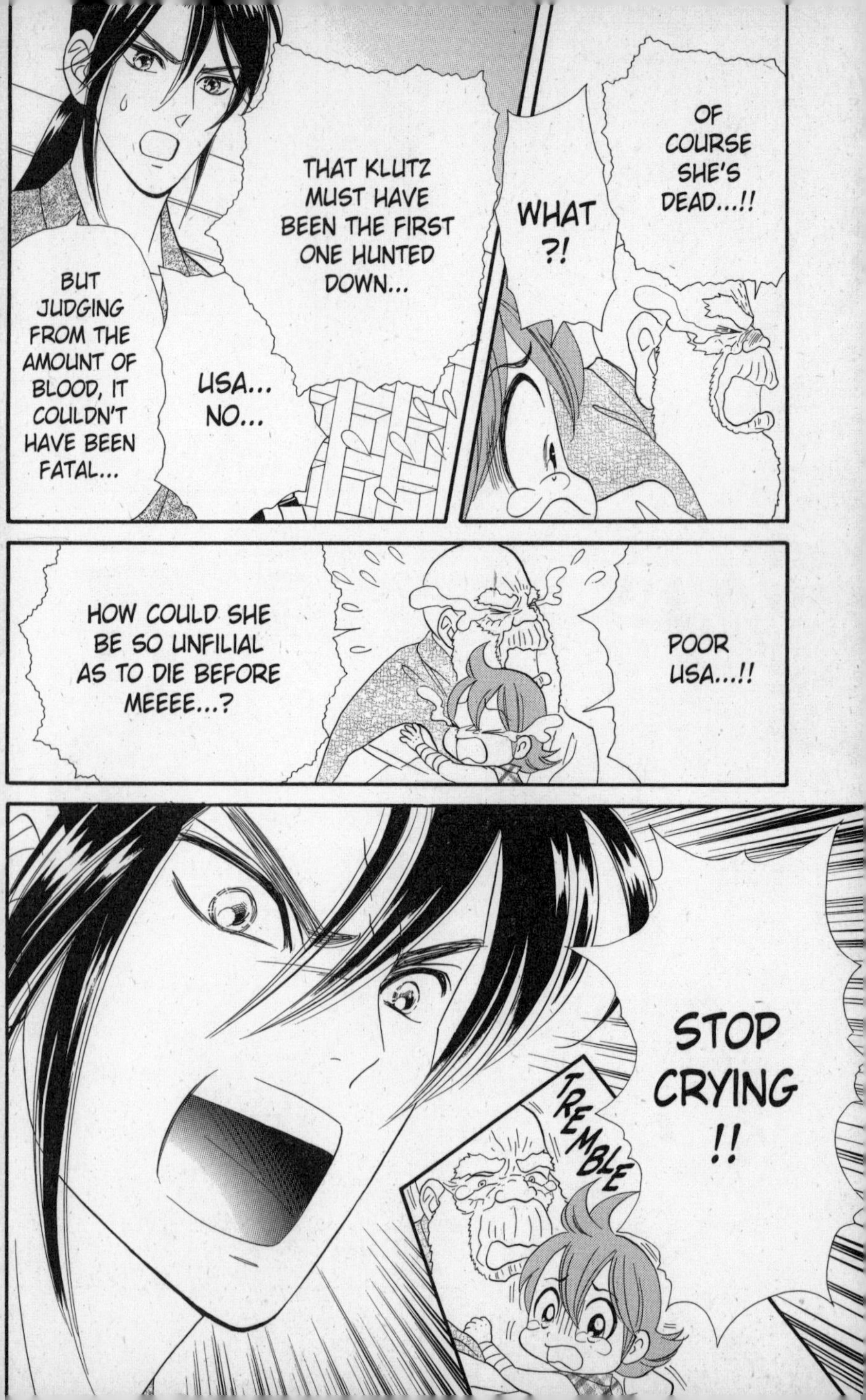
OF COURSE SHE'S DEAD...!!
WHAT ?!
THAT KLUTZ MUST HAVE BEEN THE FIRST ONE HUNTED DOWN...
USA... NO...
BUT JUDGING FROM THE AMOUNT OF BLOOD, IT COULDN'T HAVE BEEN FATAL...
POOR USA...!!
HOW COULD SHE BE SO UNFILIAL AS TO DIE BEFORE MEEEE...?
STOP CRYING !!
TREMBLE

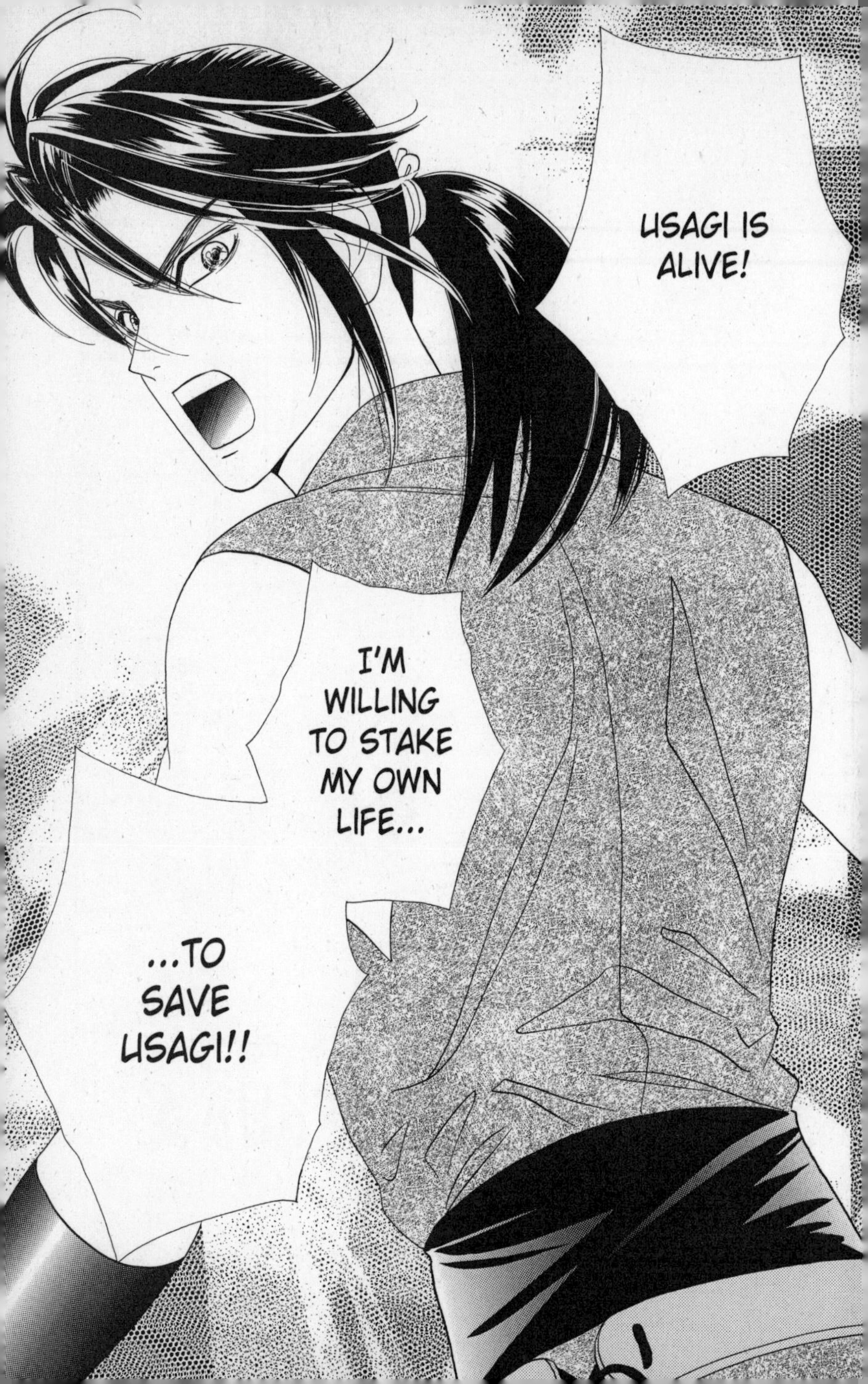
USAGI IS ALIVE!
I'M WILLING TO STAKE MY OWN LIFE...
...TO SAVE USAGI!!

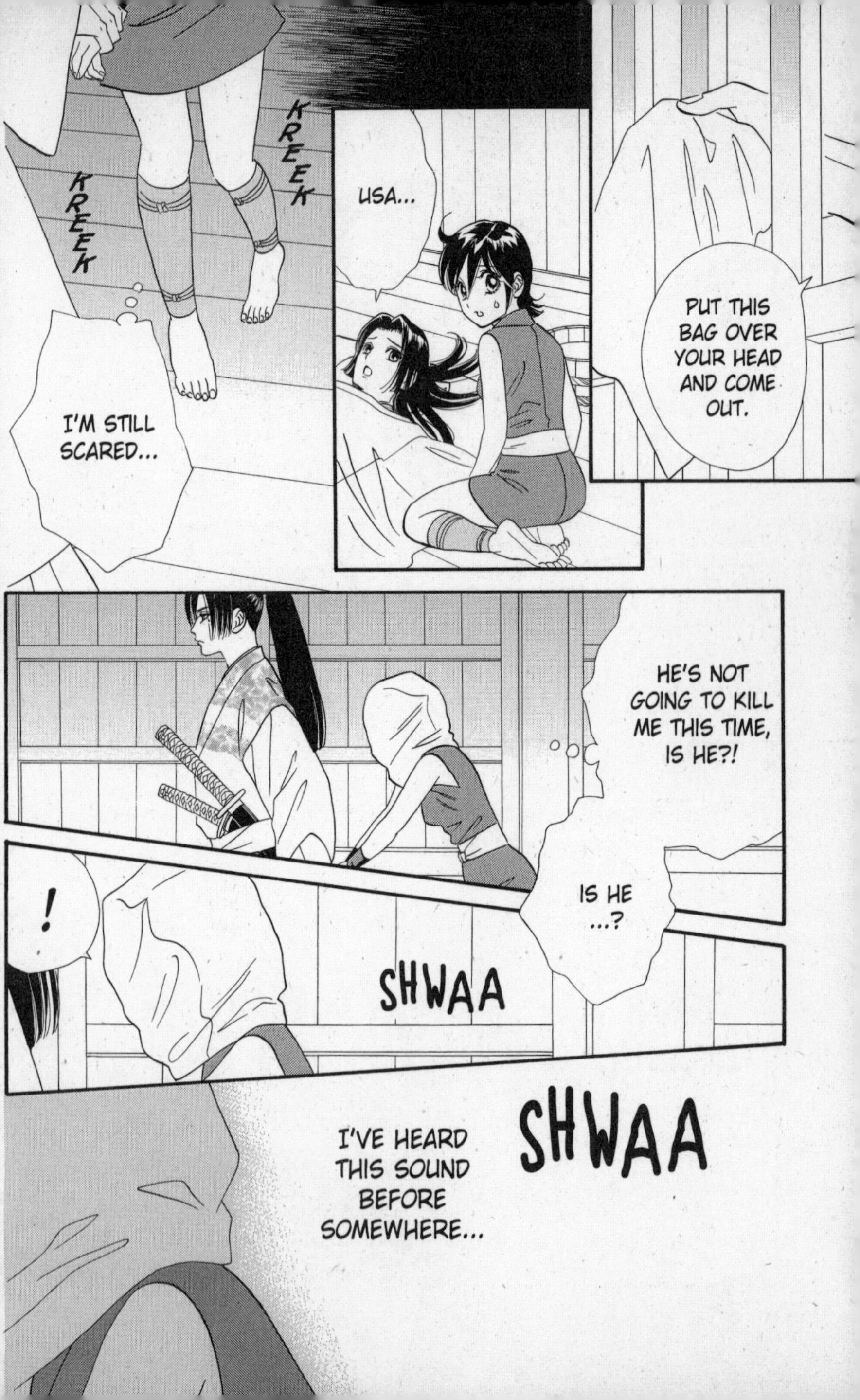
PUT THIS BAG OVER YOUR HEAD AND COME OUT.
USA...
KREEK
KREEK
I'M STILL SCARED...
HE'S NOT GOING TO KILL ME THIS TIME, IS HE?!
IS HE ...?
!
SHWAA
SHWAA
I'VE HEARD THIS SOUND BEFORE SOMEWHERE...

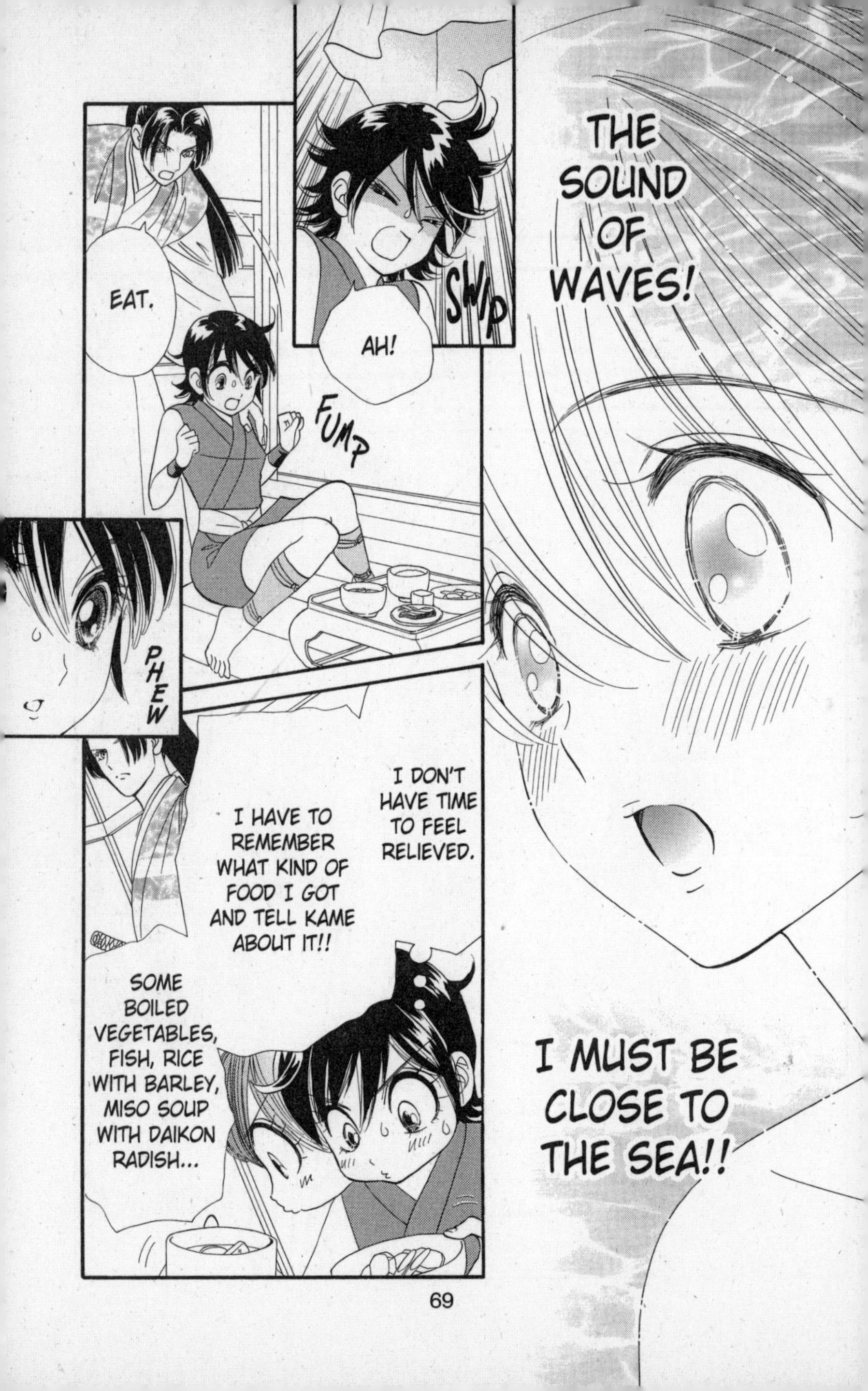
THE SOUND OF WAVES!
I MUST BE CLOSE TO THE SEA!!
SWIP
AH!
EAT.
FUMP
PHEW
I DON'T HAVE TIME TO FEEL RELIEVED.
I HAVE TO REMEMBER WHAT KIND OF FOOD I GOT AND TELL KAME ABOUT IT!!
SOME BOILED VEGETABLES, FISH, RICE WITH BARLEY, MISO SOUP WITH DAIKON RADISH...

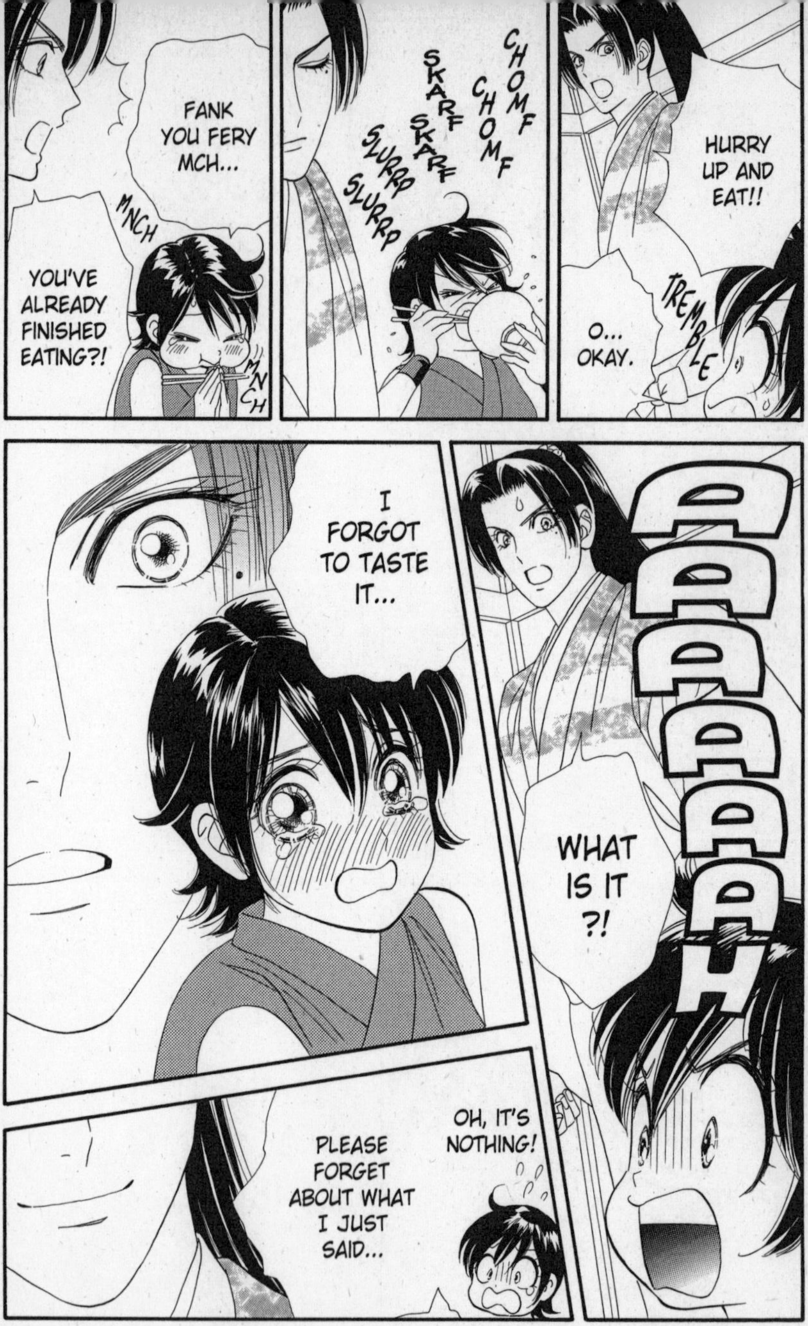
HURRY UP AND EAT!!
TREMBLE
O... OKAY.
CHOMF CHOMF
SKARF SKARF
SLURRP SLURRP
FANK YOU FERY MCH...
MNCH
YOU'VE ALREADY FINISHED EATING?!
MNCH
AAAAAAH
WHAT IS IT ?!
I FORGOT TO TASTE IT...
OH, IT'S NOTHING!
PLEASE FORGET ABOUT WHAT I JUST SAID...

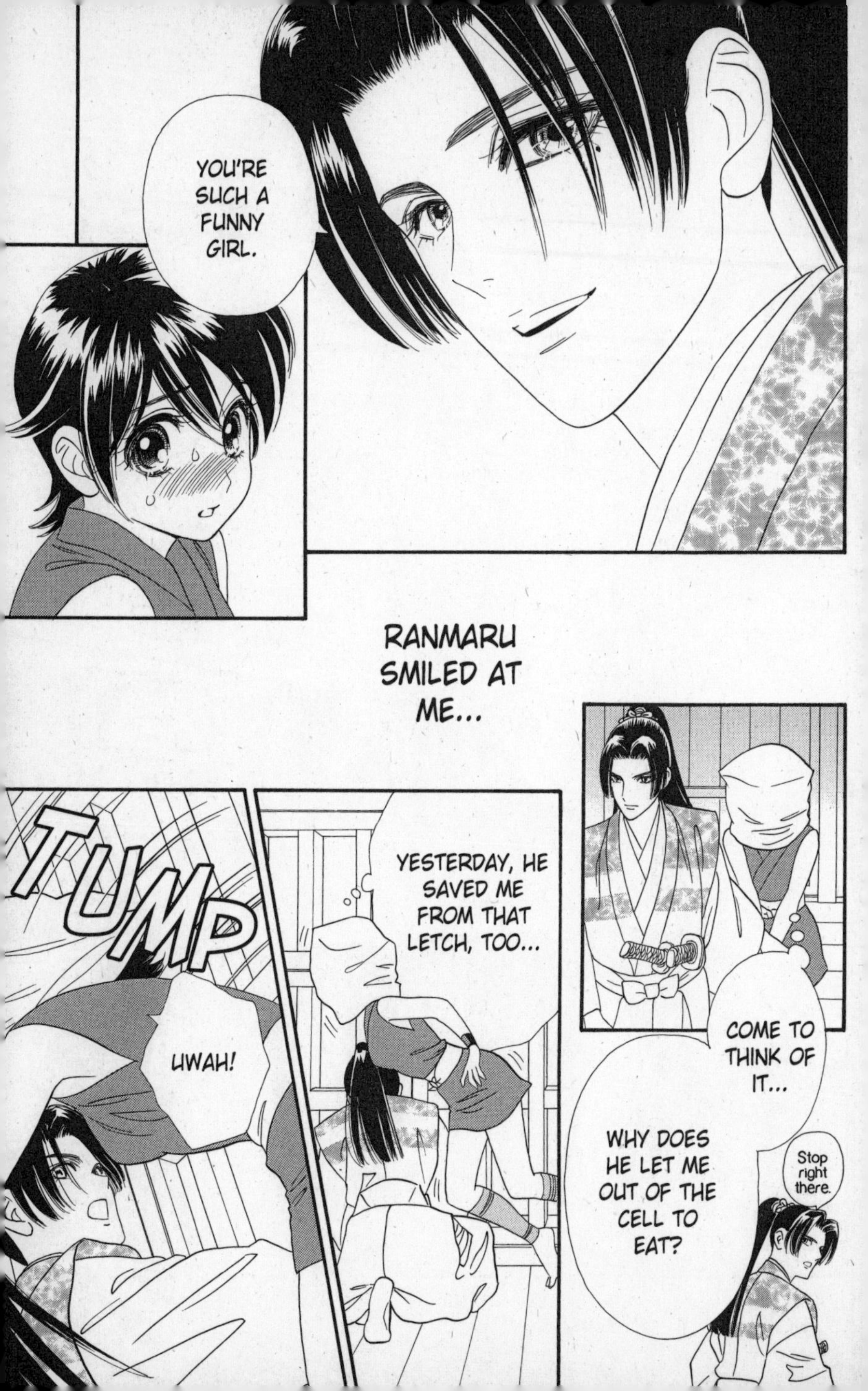
YOU'RE SUCH A FUNNY GIRL.
RANMARU SMILED AT ME...
COME TO THINK OF IT...
WHY DOES HE LET ME OUT OF THE CELL TO EAT?
Stop right there.
YESTERDAY, HE SAVED ME FROM THAT LETCH, TOO...
TUMP
UWAH!

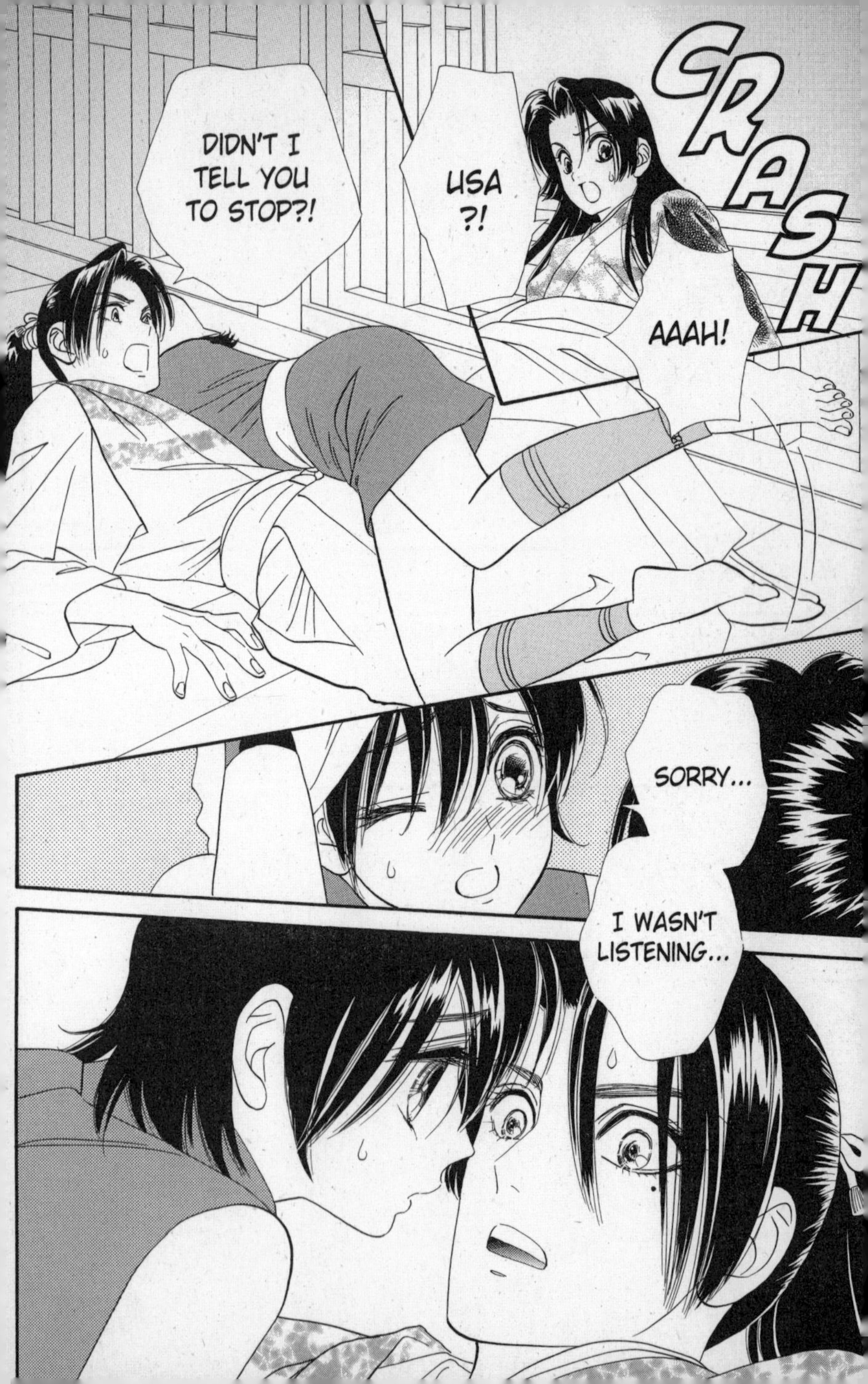
CRASH
AAAH!
USA ?!
DIDN'T I TELL YOU TO STOP?!
SORRY...
I WASN'T LISTENING...

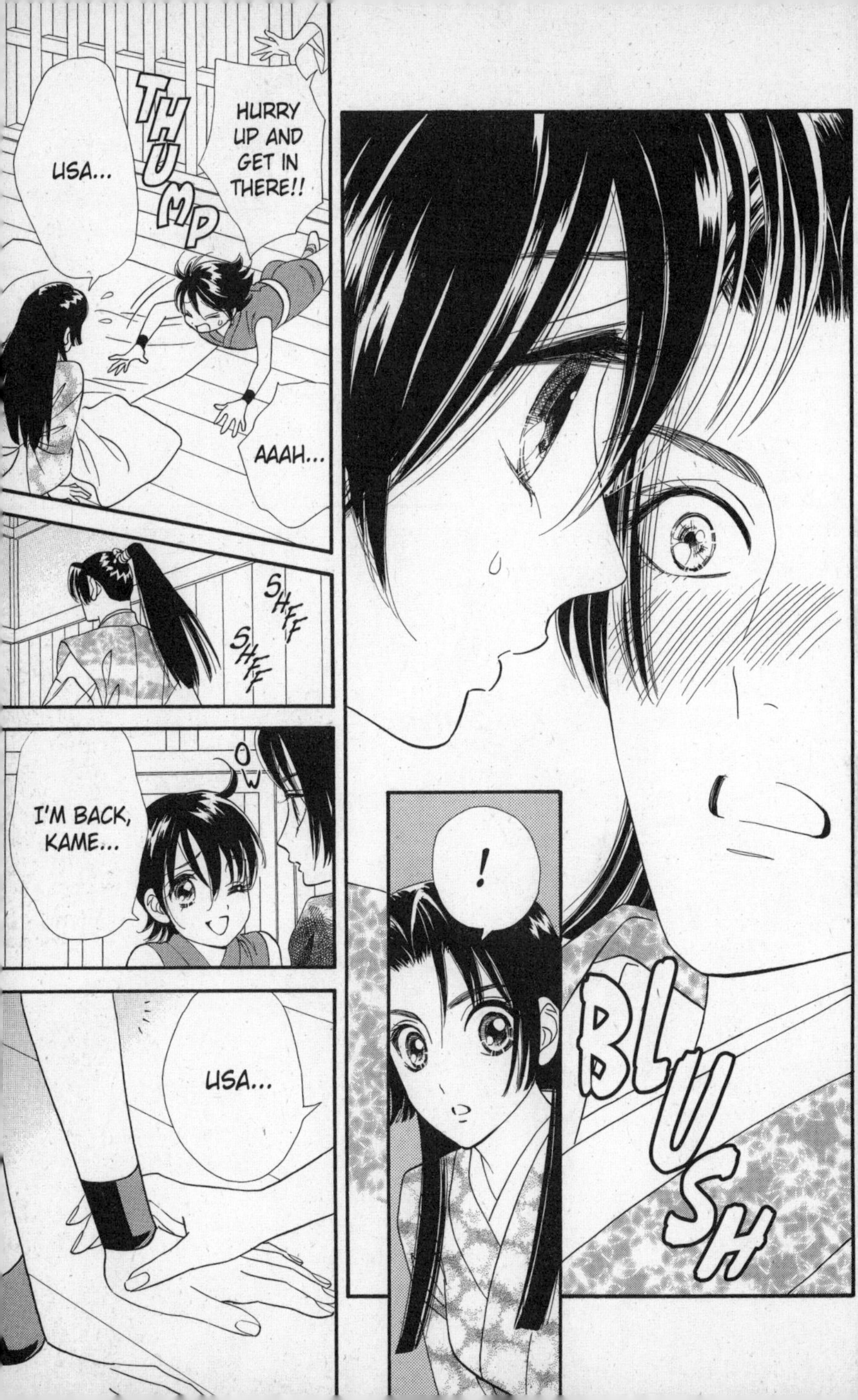
!
BLUSH
HURRY UP AND GET IN THERE!!
THUMP
USA...
AAAH...
SHFF
SHFF
OW
I'M BACK, KAME...
USA...

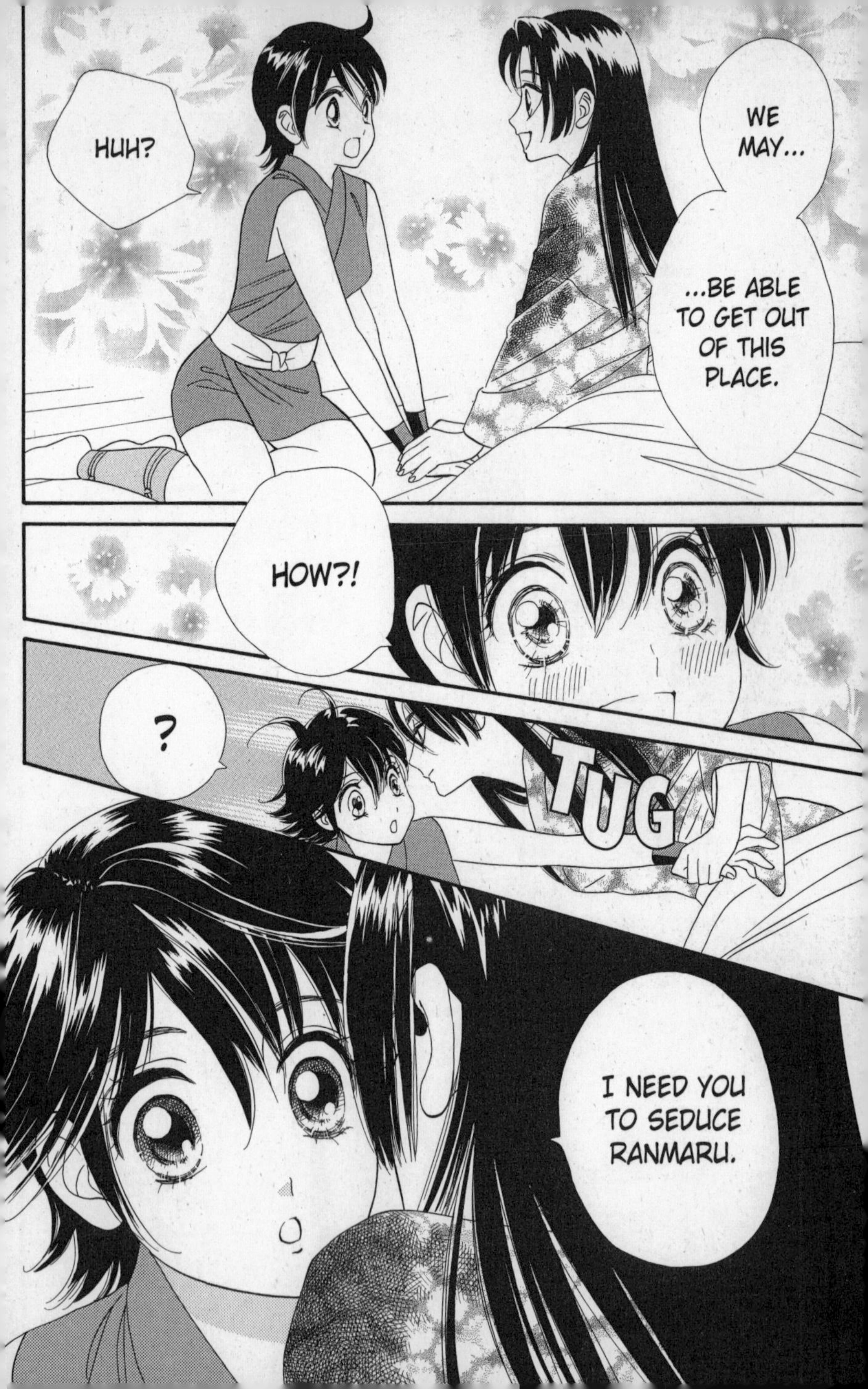
WE MAY...
...BE ABLE TO GET OUT OF THIS PLACE.
HUH?
HOW?!
TUG
?
I NEED YOU TO SEDUCE RANMARU.

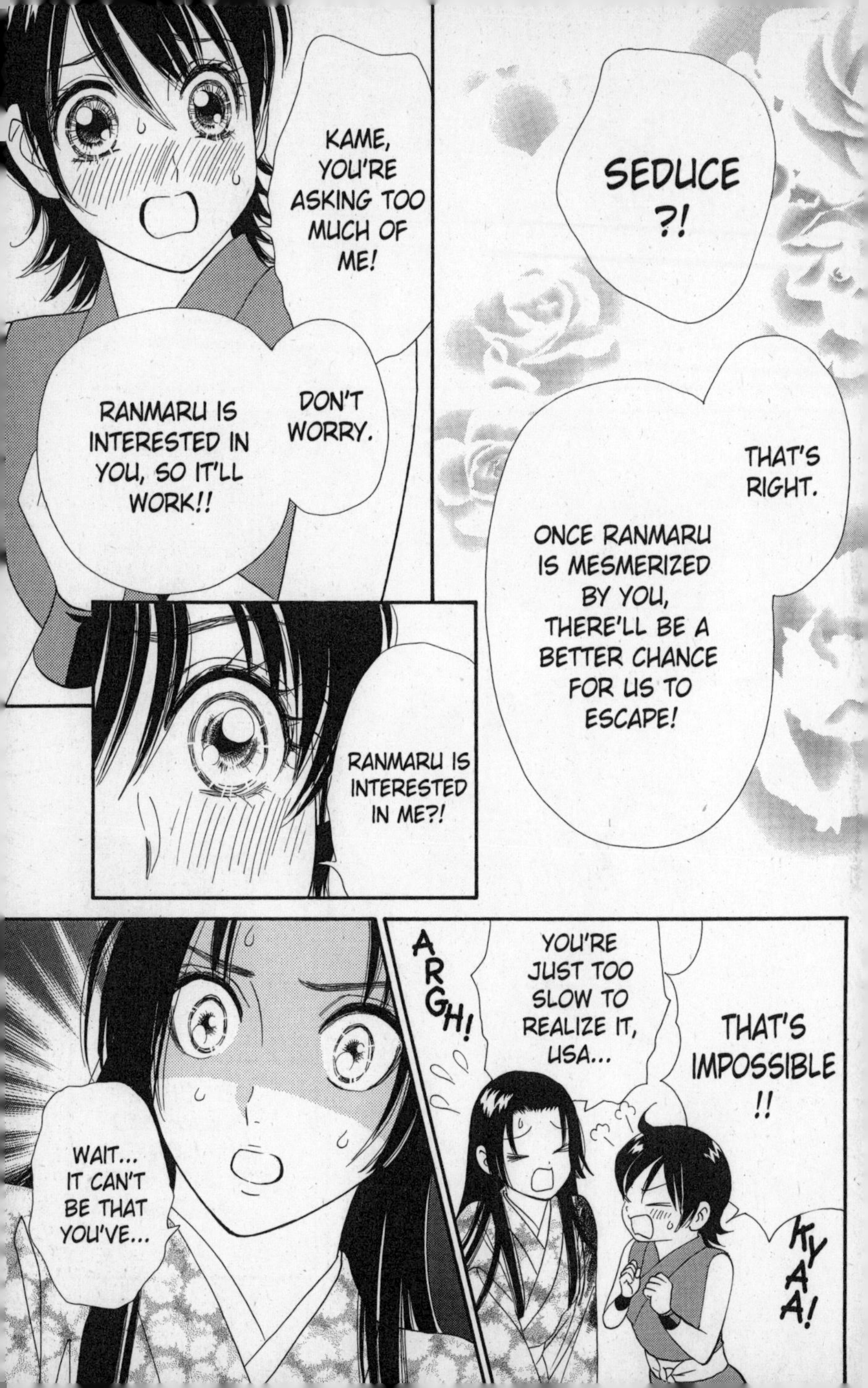
SEDUCE ?!
THAT'S RIGHT.
ONCE RANMARU IS MESMERIZED BY YOU, THERE'LL BE A BETTER CHANCE FOR US TO ESCAPE!
KAME, YOU'RE ASKING TOO MUCH OF ME!
DON'T WORRY.
RANMARU IS INTERESTED IN YOU, SO IT'LL WORK!!
RANMARU IS INTERESTED IN ME?!
THAT'S IMPOSSIBLE!!
KYAAA!
YOU'RE JUST TOO SLOW TO REALIZE IT, USA...
ARGH!
WAIT... IT CAN'T BE THAT YOU'VE...

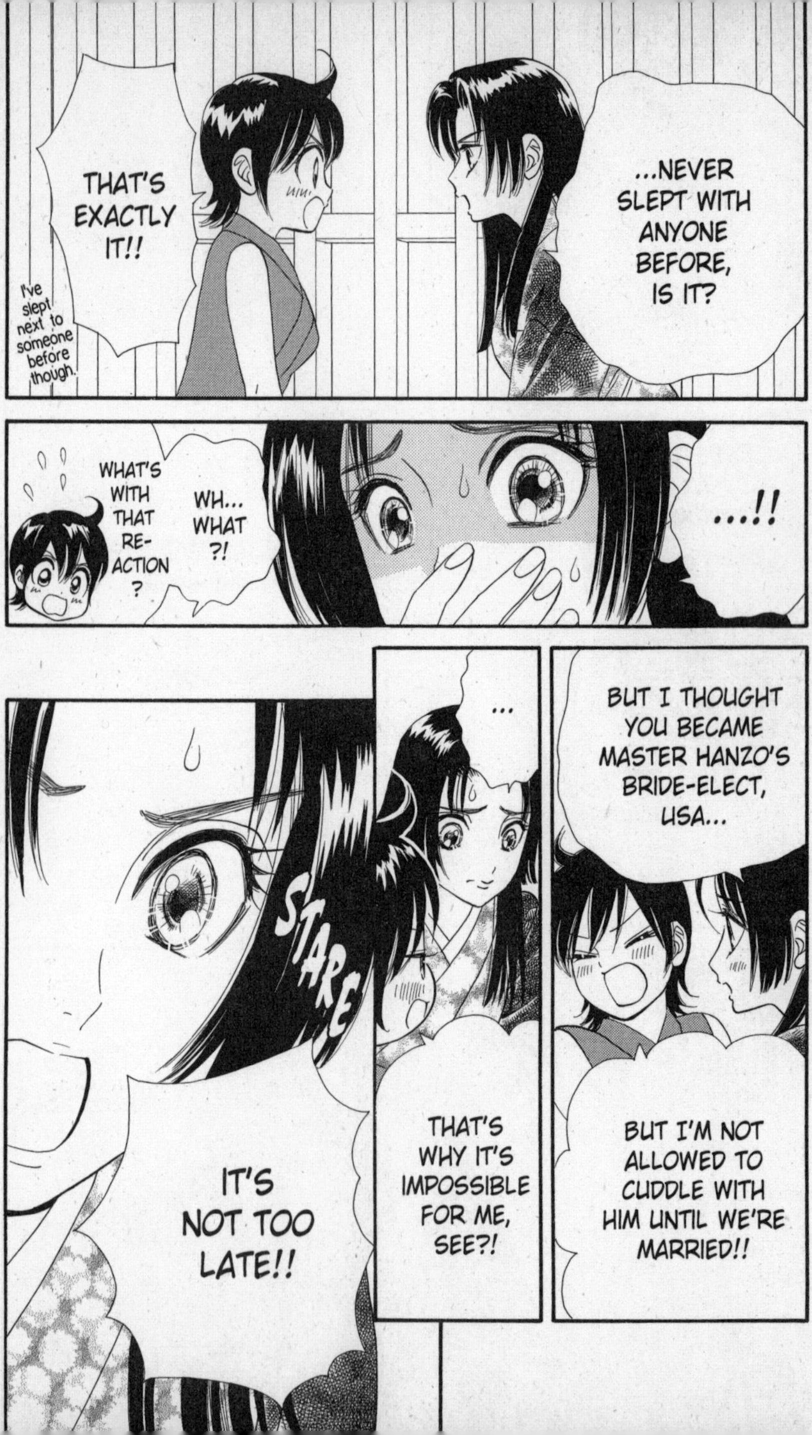
...NEVER SLEPT WITH ANYONE BEFORE, IS IT?
THAT'S EXACTLY IT!!
I've slept next to someone before though.
...!!
WH... WHAT?!
WHAT'S WITH THAT RE-ACTION?
BUT I THOUGHT YOU BECAME MASTER HANZO'S BRIDE-ELECT, USA...
BUT I'M NOT ALLOWED TO CUDDLE WITH HIM UNTIL WE'RE MARRIED!!
...
THAT'S WHY IT'S IMPOSSIBLE FOR ME, SEE?!
STARE
IT'S NOT TOO LATE!!

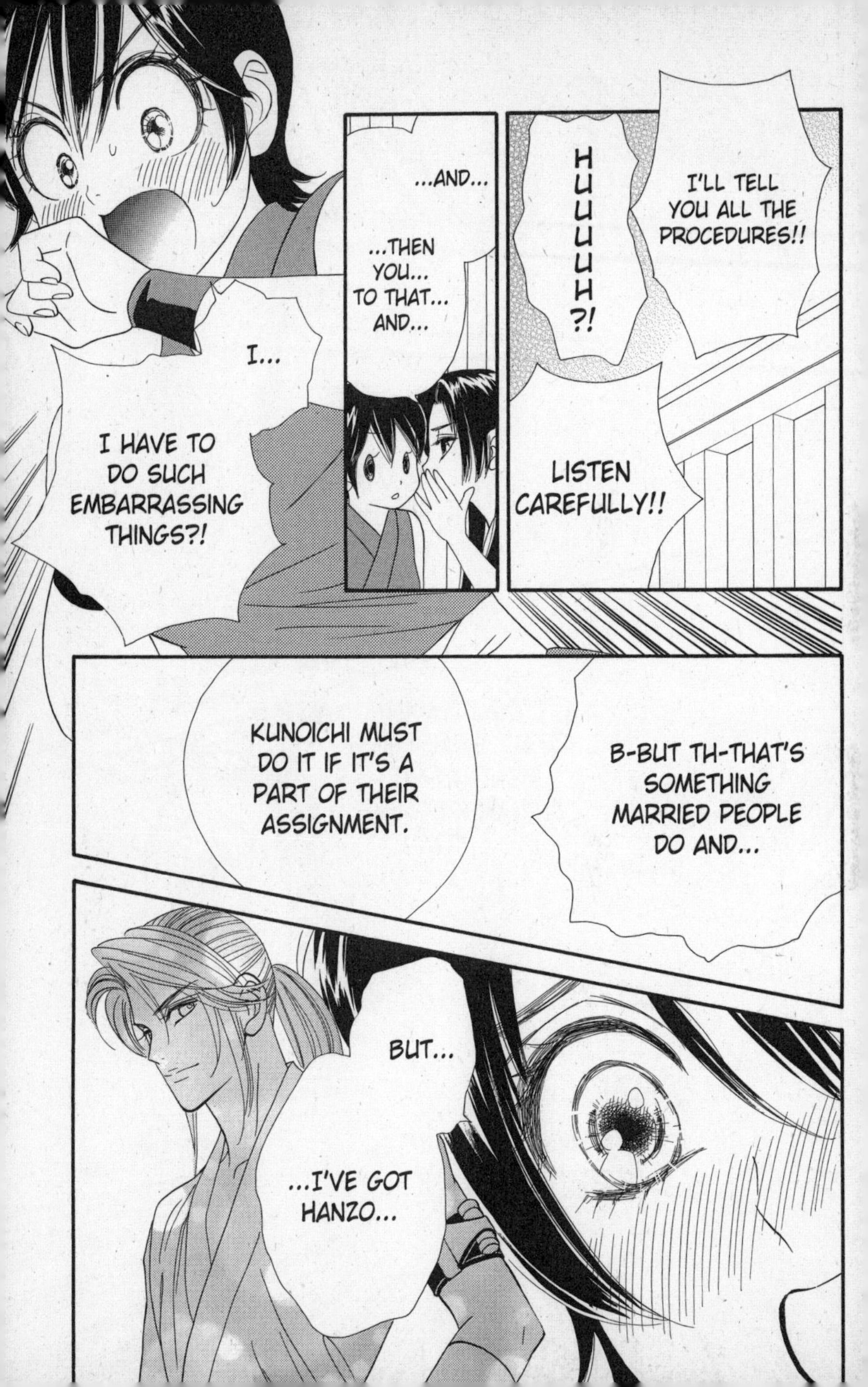
I'LL TELL YOU ALL THE PROCEDURES!!
HUUUUUH?!
LISTEN CAREFULLY!!
...AND...
...THEN YOU... TO THAT... AND...
I...
I HAVE TO DO SUCH EMBARRASSING THINGS?!
B-BUT TH-THAT'S SOMETHING MARRIED PEOPLE DO AND...
KUNOICHI MUST DO IT IF IT'S A PART OF THEIR ASSIGNMENT.
BUT...
...I'VE GOT HANZO...

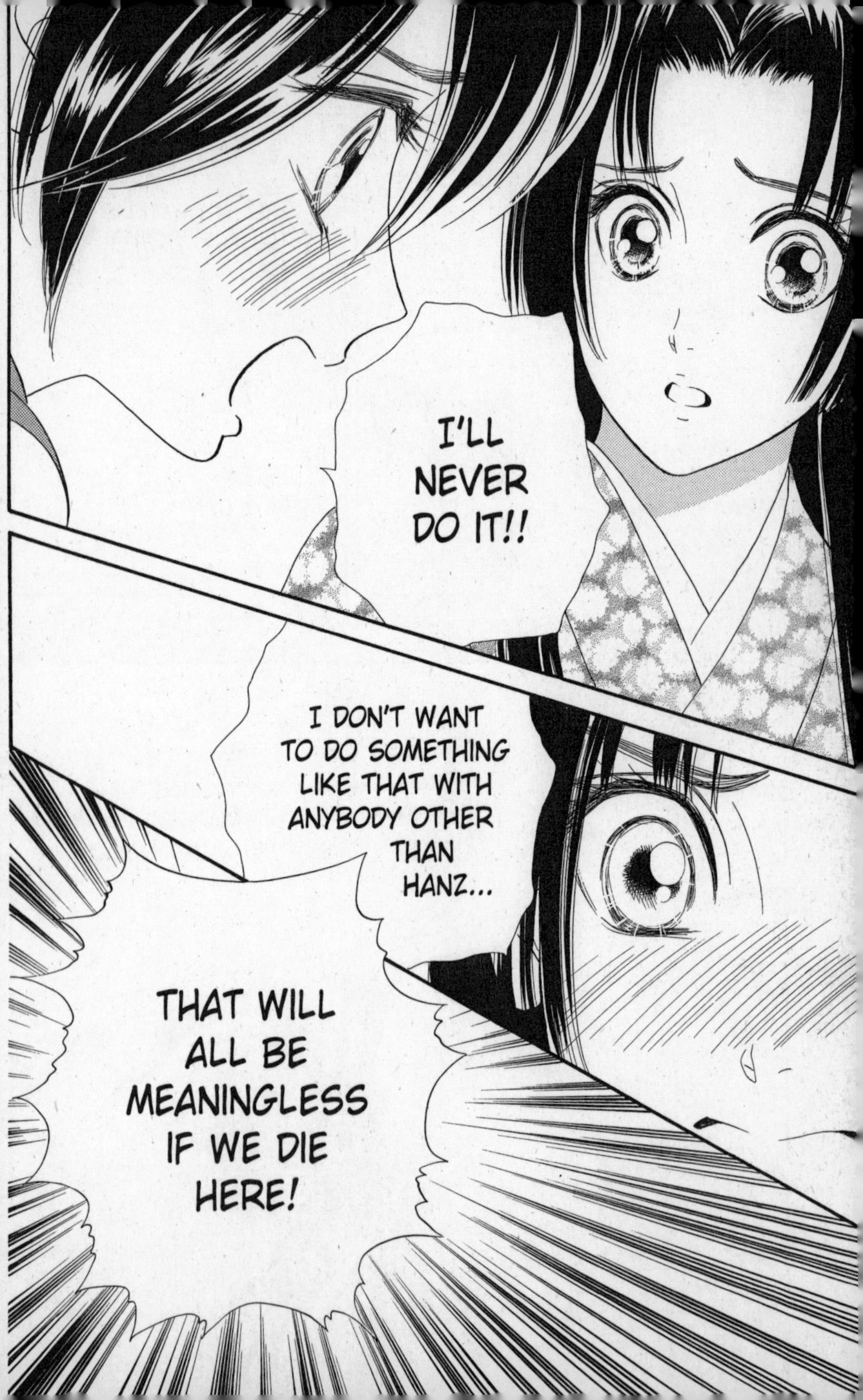
I'LL NEVER DO IT!!
I DON'T WANT TO DO SOMETHING LIKE THAT WITH ANYBODY OTHER THAN HANZ...
THAT WILL ALL BE MEANINGLESS IF WE DIE HERE!

KAME...
YOU MAY NEVER BE ABLE TO MEET YOUR LOVED ONE AGAIN, USA! DO YOU WANT THAT?!

TAIL OF THE MOON EXTRA: TODAY'S MISSION

"I WANT TO SEE HANZO EATING A PARFAIT!"

-RIKO, NARA PREFECTURE

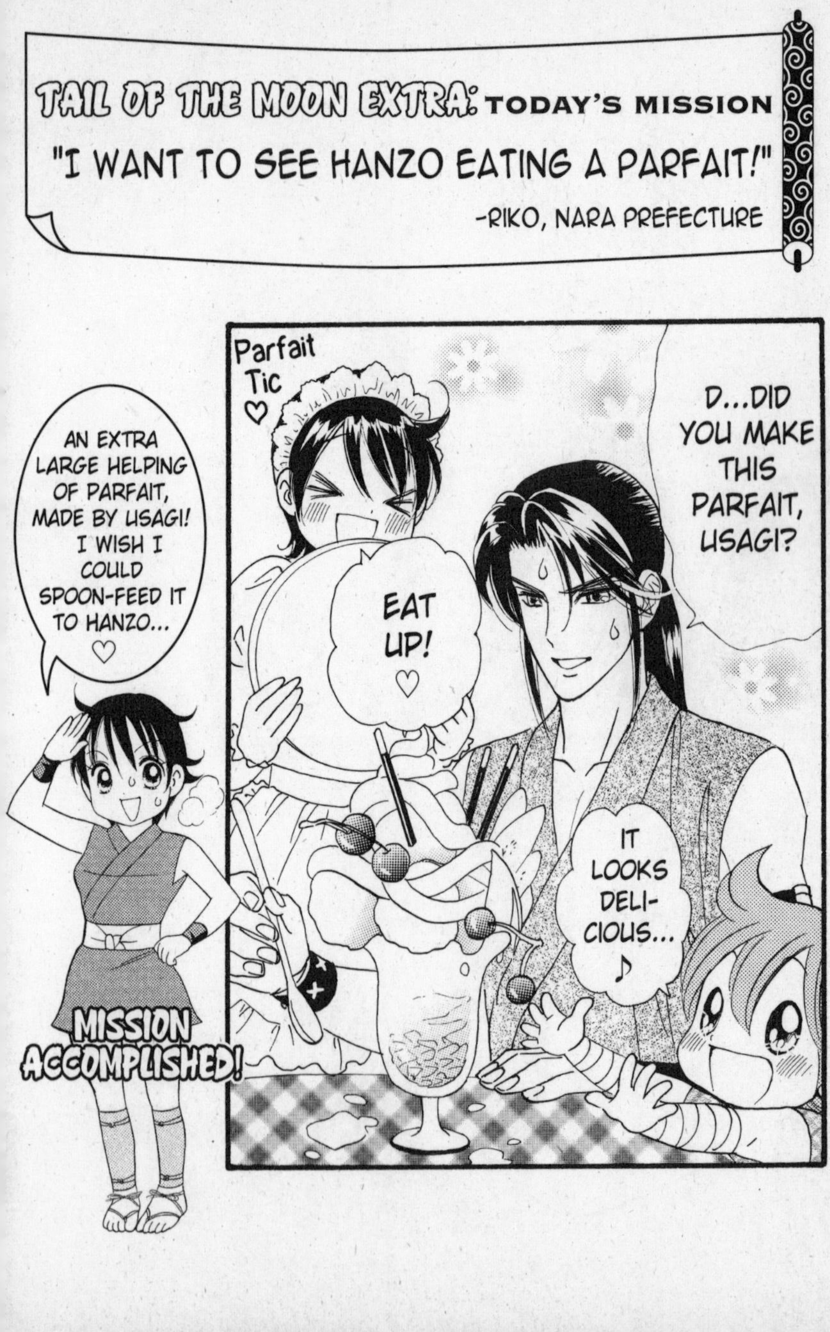
D...DID YOU MAKE THIS PARFAIT, USAGI?
Parfait Tic ♡
EAT UP! ♡
IT LOOKS DELICIOUS... ♪
AN EXTRA LARGE HELPING OF PARFAIT, MADE BY USAGI! I WISH I COULD SPOON-FEED IT TO HANZO... ♡
MISSION ACCOMPLISHED!

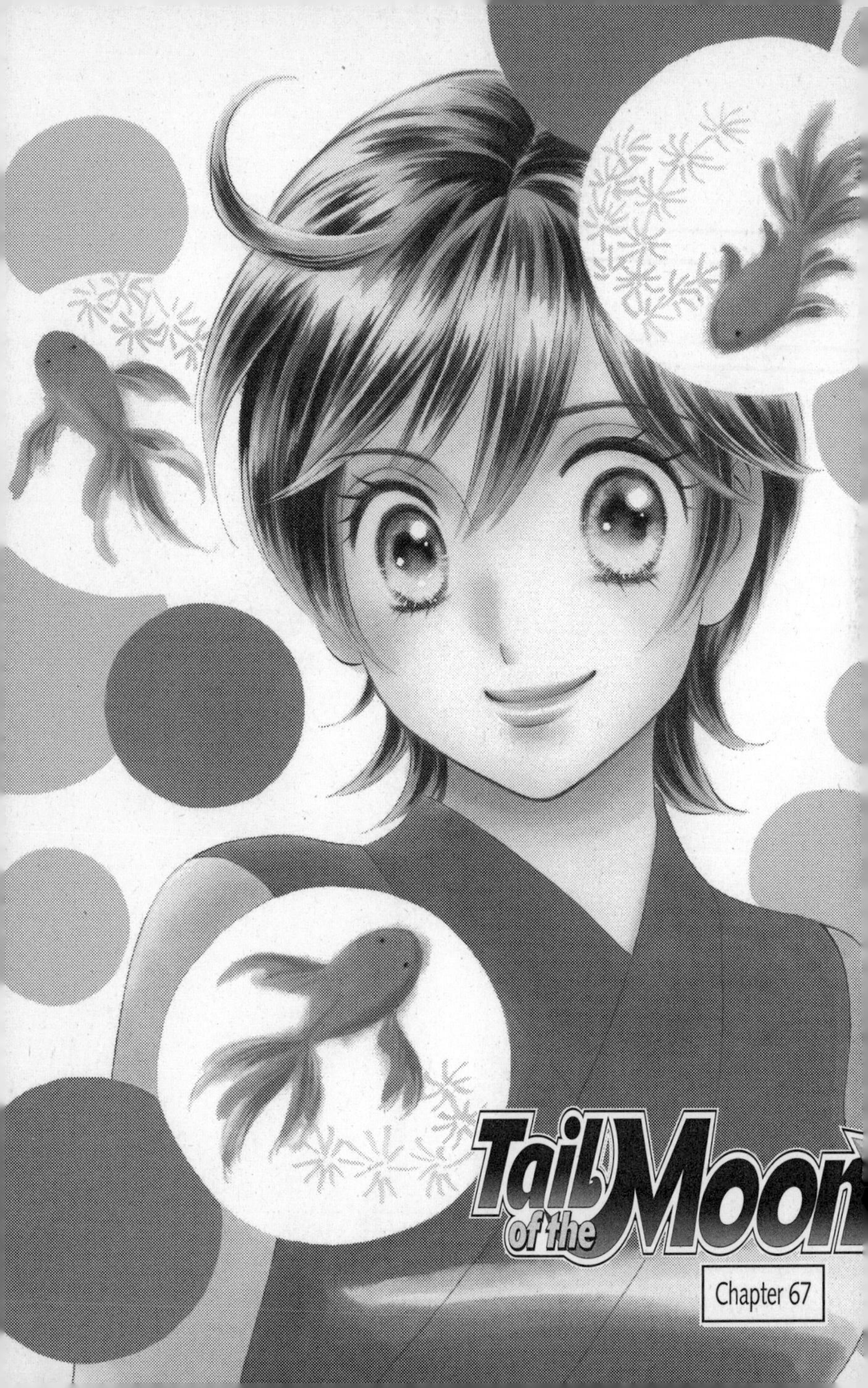

Tail of the Moon
Chapter 67

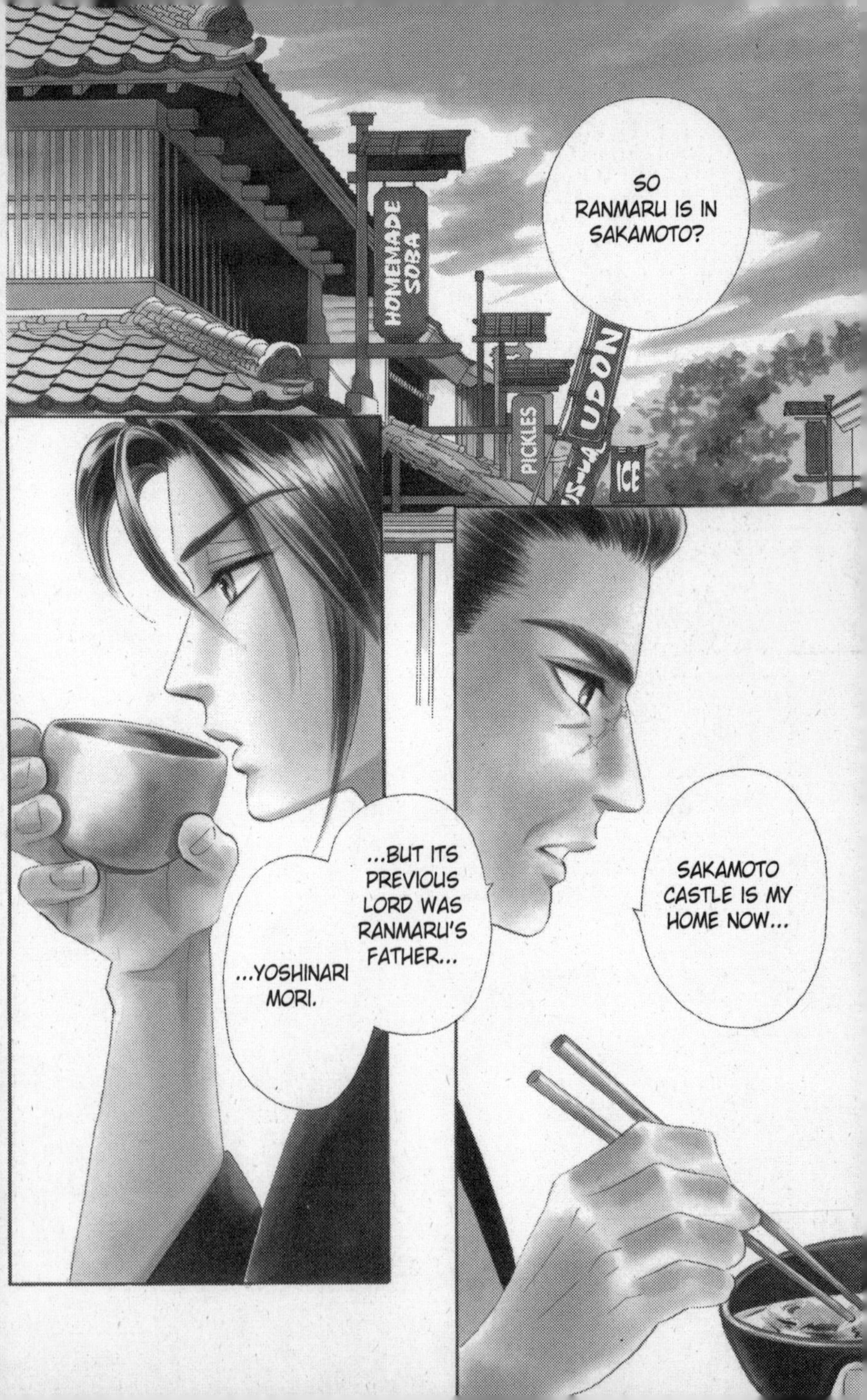
SO RANMARU IS IN SAKAMOTO?
HOMEMADE SOBA
UDON
PICKLES
ICE
SAKAMOTO CASTLE IS MY HOME NOW...
...BUT ITS PREVIOUS LORD WAS RANMARU'S FATHER...
...YOSHINARI MORI.

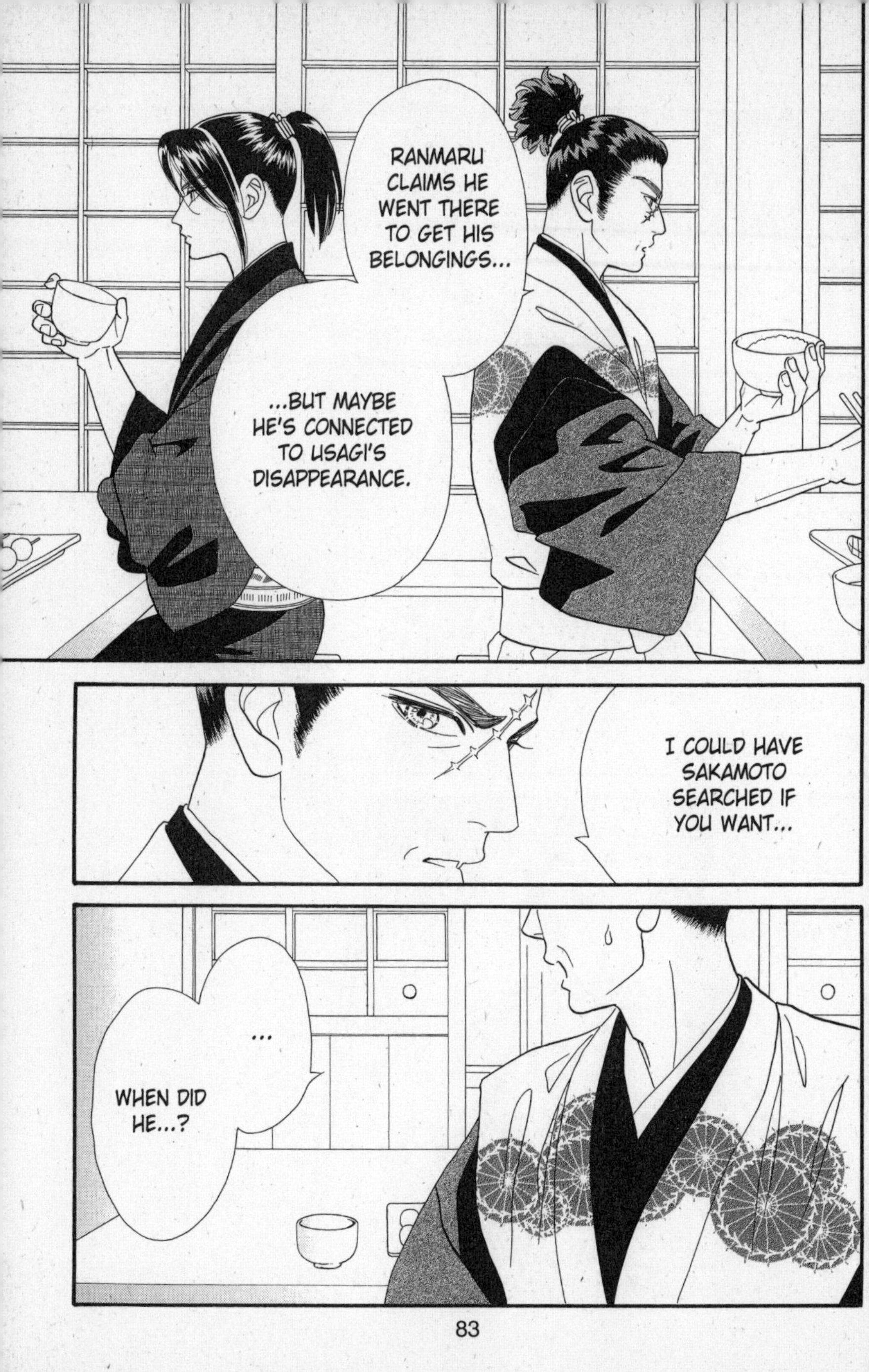
RANMARU CLAIMS HE WENT THERE TO GET HIS BELONGINGS...
...BUT MAYBE HE'S CONNECTED TO USAGI'S DISAPPEARANCE.
I COULD HAVE SAKAMOTO SEARCHED IF YOU WANT...
...
WHEN DID HE...?

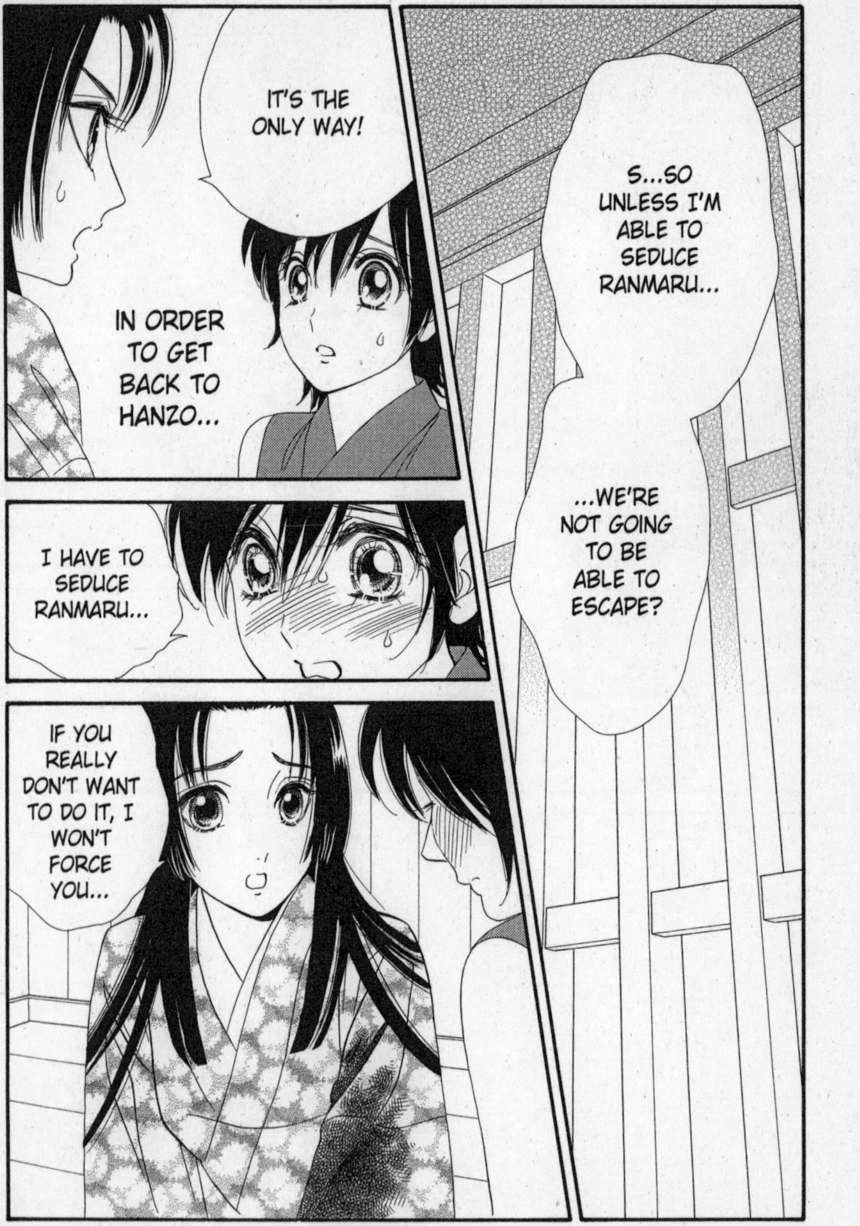
S...SO UNLESS I'M ABLE TO SEDUCE RANMARU...
...WE'RE NOT GOING TO BE ABLE TO ESCAPE?
IT'S THE ONLY WAY!
IN ORDER TO GET BACK TO HANZO...
I HAVE TO SEDUCE RANMARU...
IF YOU REALLY DON'T WANT TO DO IT, I WON'T FORCE YOU...

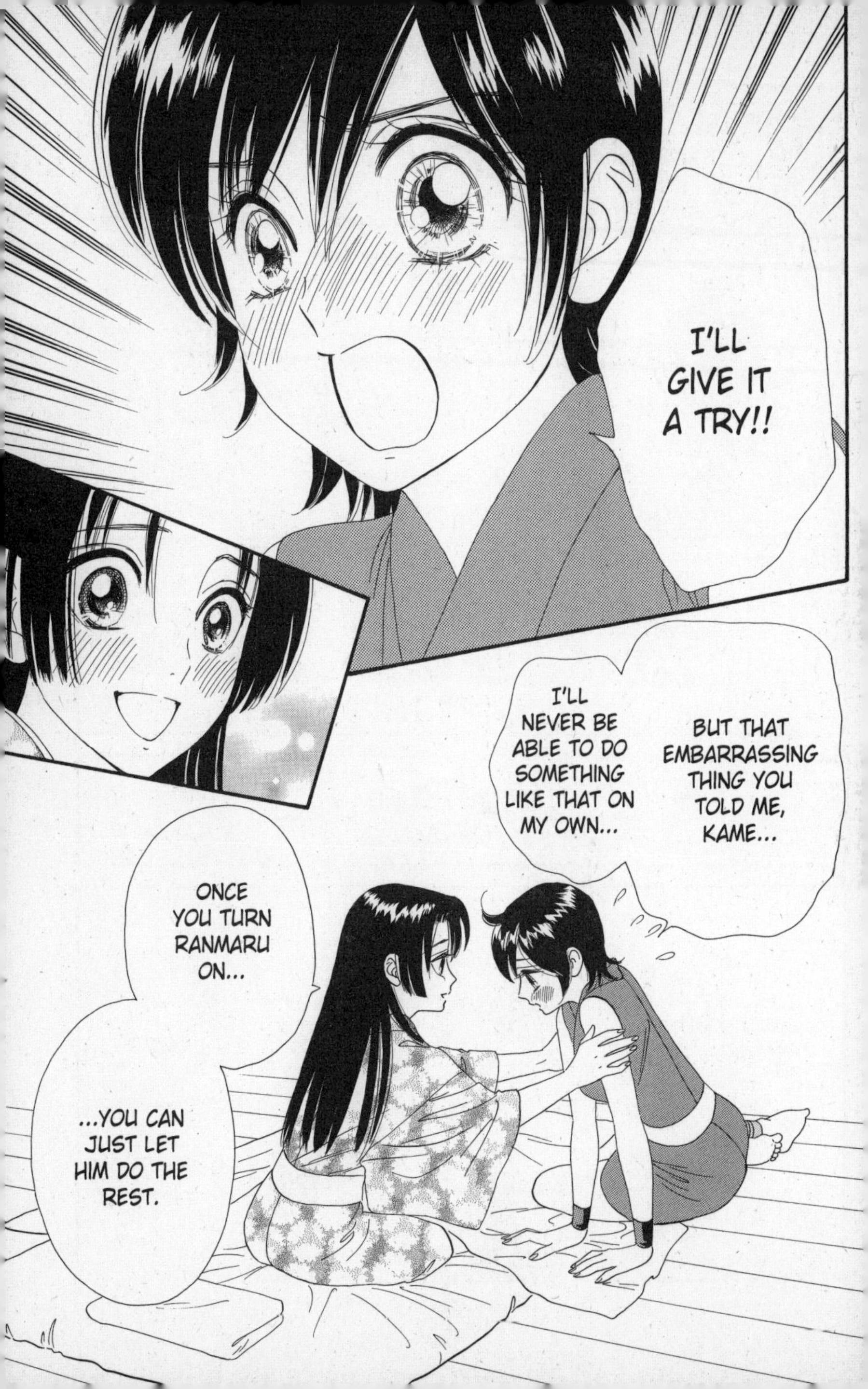
I'LL GIVE IT A TRY!!
BUT THAT EMBARRASSING THING YOU TOLD ME, KAME...
I'LL NEVER BE ABLE TO DO SOMETHING LIKE THAT ON MY OWN...
ONCE YOU TURN RANMARU ON...
...YOU CAN JUST LET HIM DO THE REST.

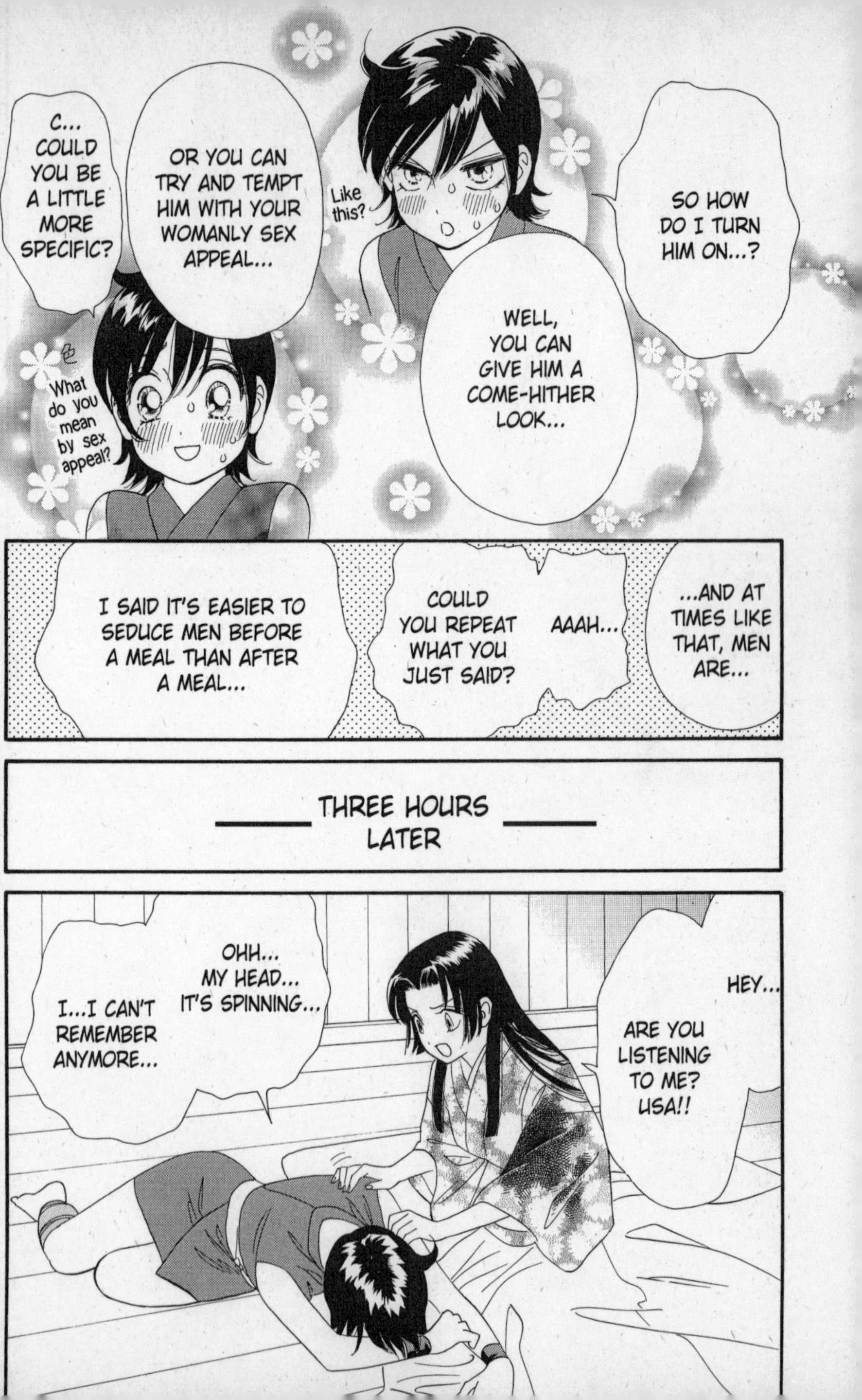
SO HOW DO I TURN HIM ON...?
WELL, YOU CAN GIVE HIM A COME-HITHER LOOK...
Like this?
OR YOU CAN TRY AND TEMPT HIM WITH YOUR WOMANLY SEX APPEAL...
C... COULD YOU BE A LITTLE MORE SPECIFIC?
What do you mean by sex appeal?
...AND AT TIMES LIKE THAT, MEN ARE...
AAAH...
COULD YOU REPEAT WHAT YOU JUST SAID?
I SAID IT'S EASIER TO SEDUCE MEN BEFORE A MEAL THAN AFTER A MEAL...
THREE HOURS LATER
HEY...
ARE YOU LISTENING TO ME? USA!!
OHH... MY HEAD... IT'S SPINNING...
I...I CAN'T REMEMBER ANYMORE...

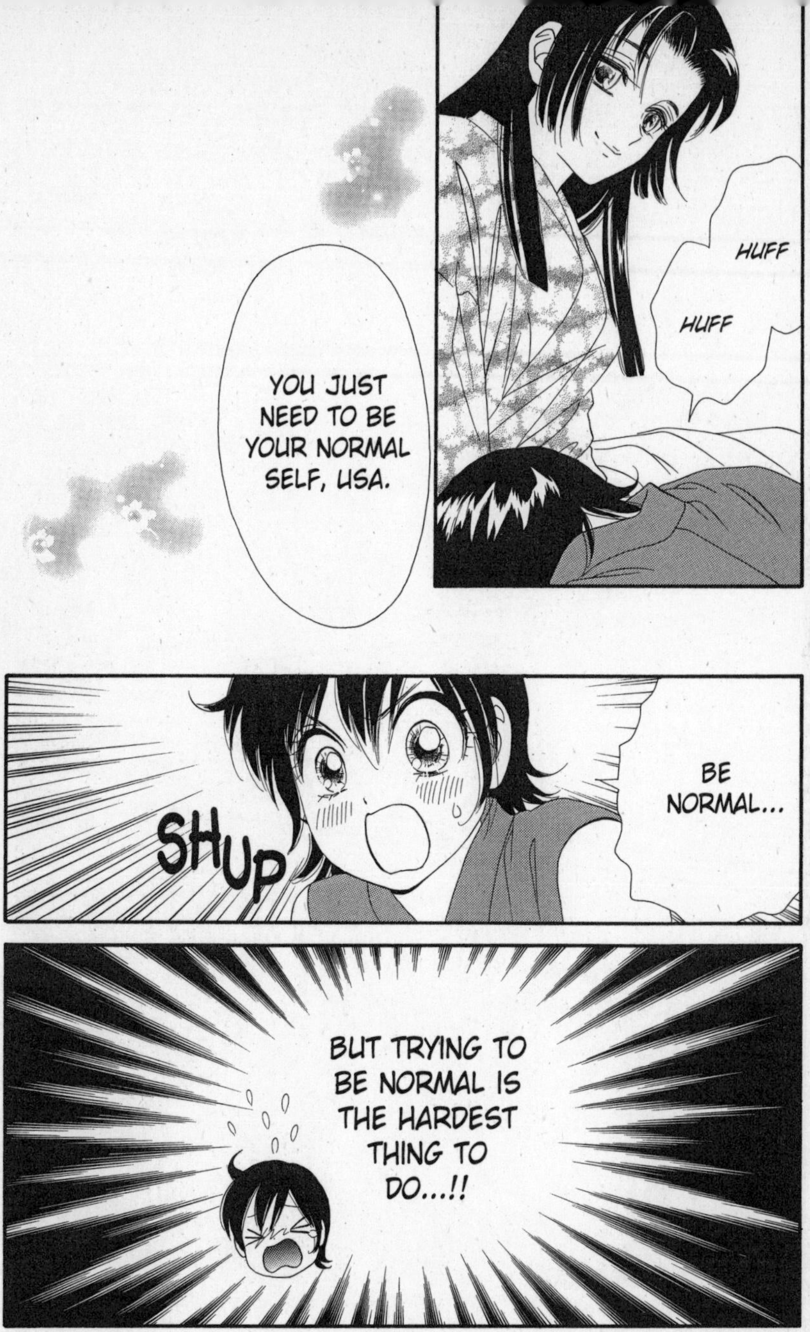
HUFF
HUFF
YOU JUST NEED TO BE YOUR NORMAL SELF, USA.
BE NORMAL...
SHUP
BUT TRYING TO BE NORMAL IS THE HARDEST THING TO DO...!!

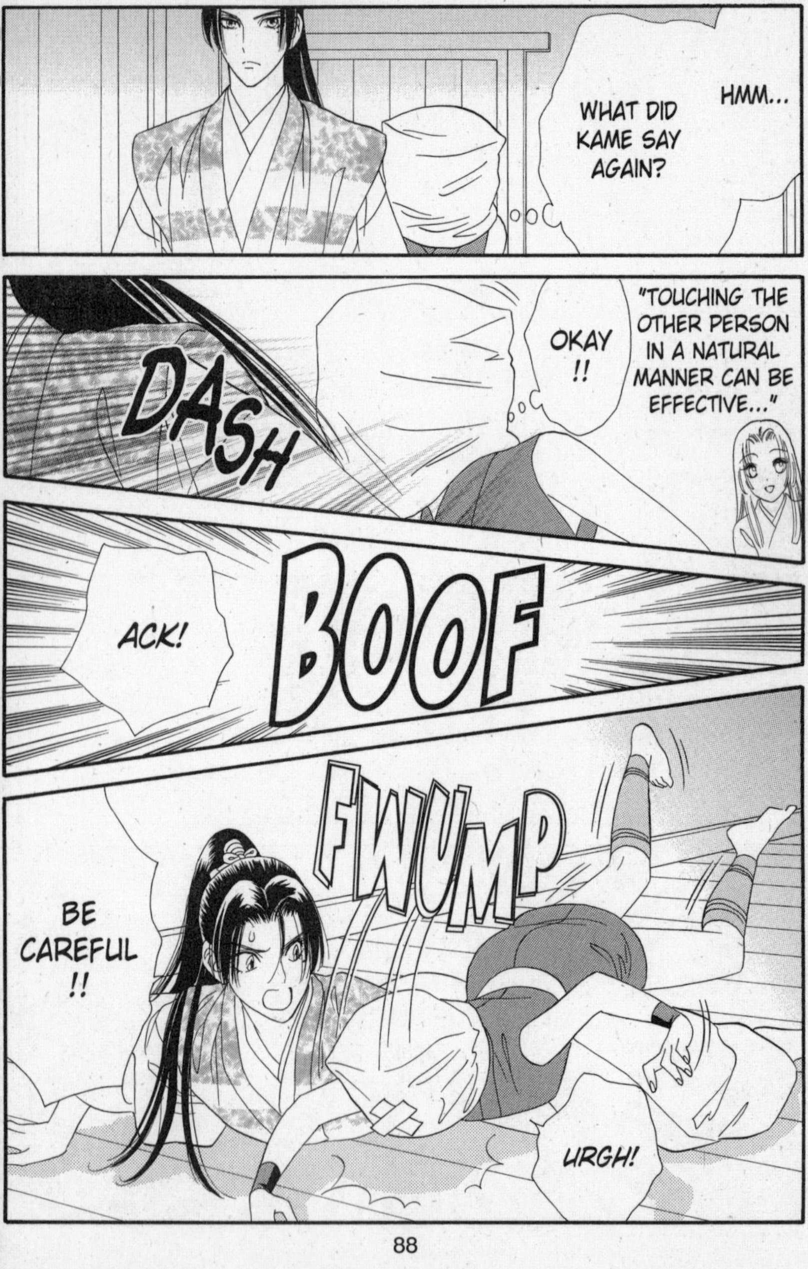
HMM...
WHAT DID KAME SAY AGAIN?
"TOUCHING THE OTHER PERSON IN A NATURAL MANNER CAN BE EFFECTIVE..."
OKAY !!
DASH
BOOF
ACK!
FWUMP
BE CAREFUL !!
URGH!

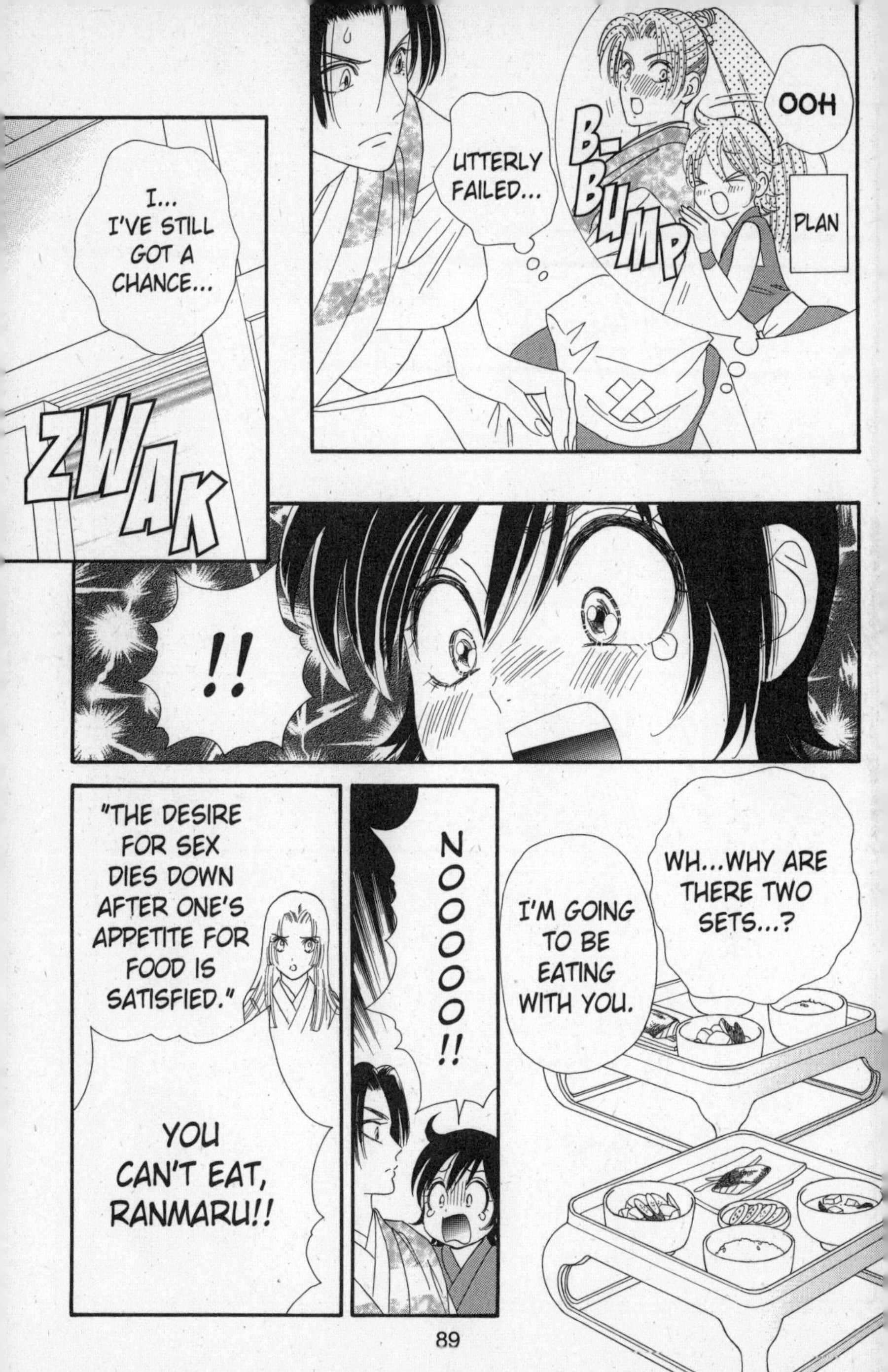
OOH
PLAN
B-BUMP
UTTERLY FAILED...
I... I'VE STILL GOT A CHANCE...
ZWAK
!!
WH...WHY ARE THERE TWO SETS...?
I'M GOING TO BE EATING WITH YOU.
NOOOOOO!!
"THE DESIRE FOR SEX DIES DOWN AFTER ONE'S APPETITE FOR FOOD IS SATISFIED."
YOU CAN'T EAT, RANMARU!!

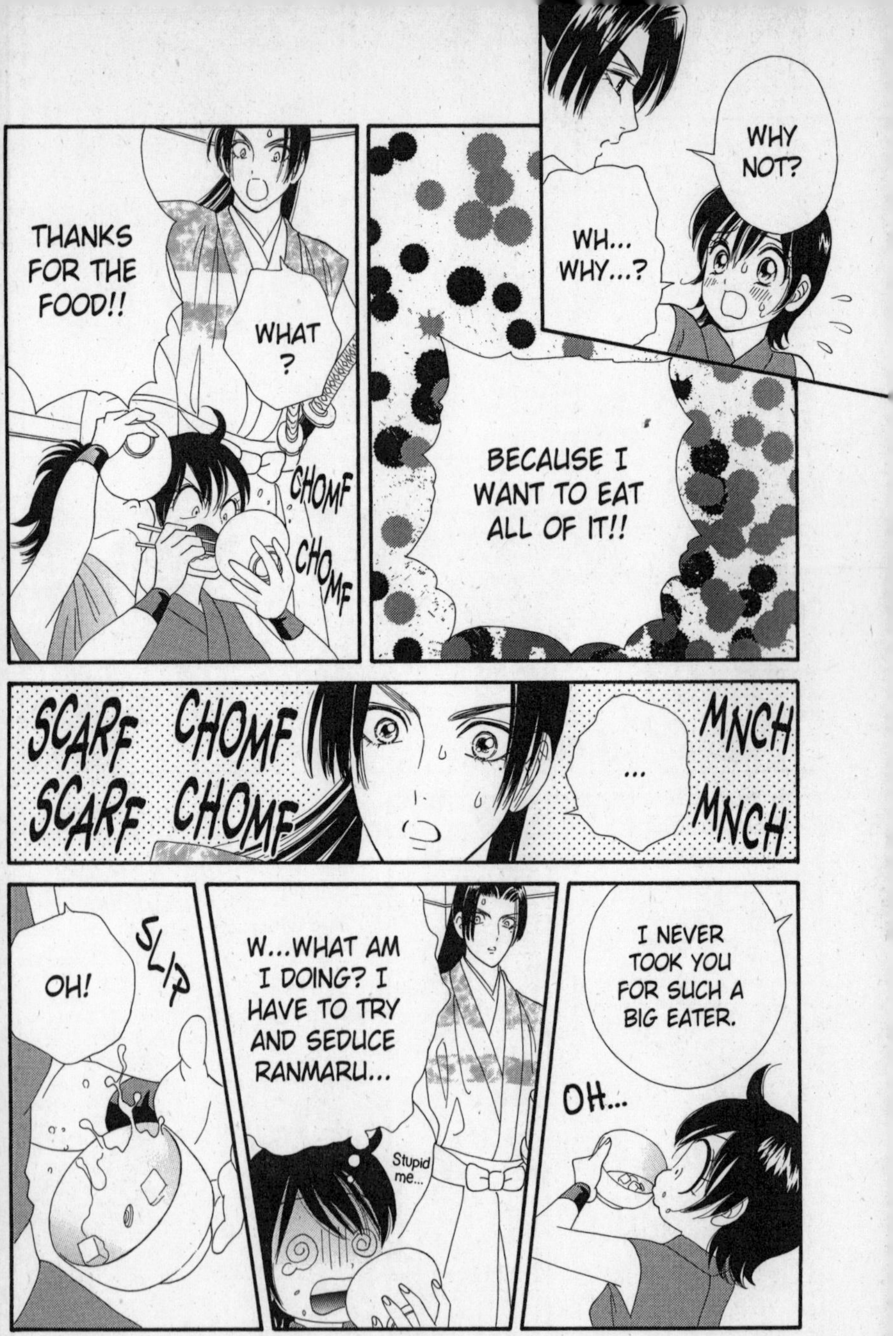
WHY NOT?
WH... WHY...?
BECAUSE I WANT TO EAT ALL OF IT!!
THANKS FOR THE FOOD!!
WHAT ?
CHOMF
CHOMF
MNCH MNCH
...
SCARF CHOMF SCARF CHOMF
I NEVER TOOK YOU FOR SUCH A BIG EATER.
OH...
W...WHAT AM I DOING? I HAVE TO TRY AND SEDUCE RANMARU...
Stupid me...
SLIP
OH!

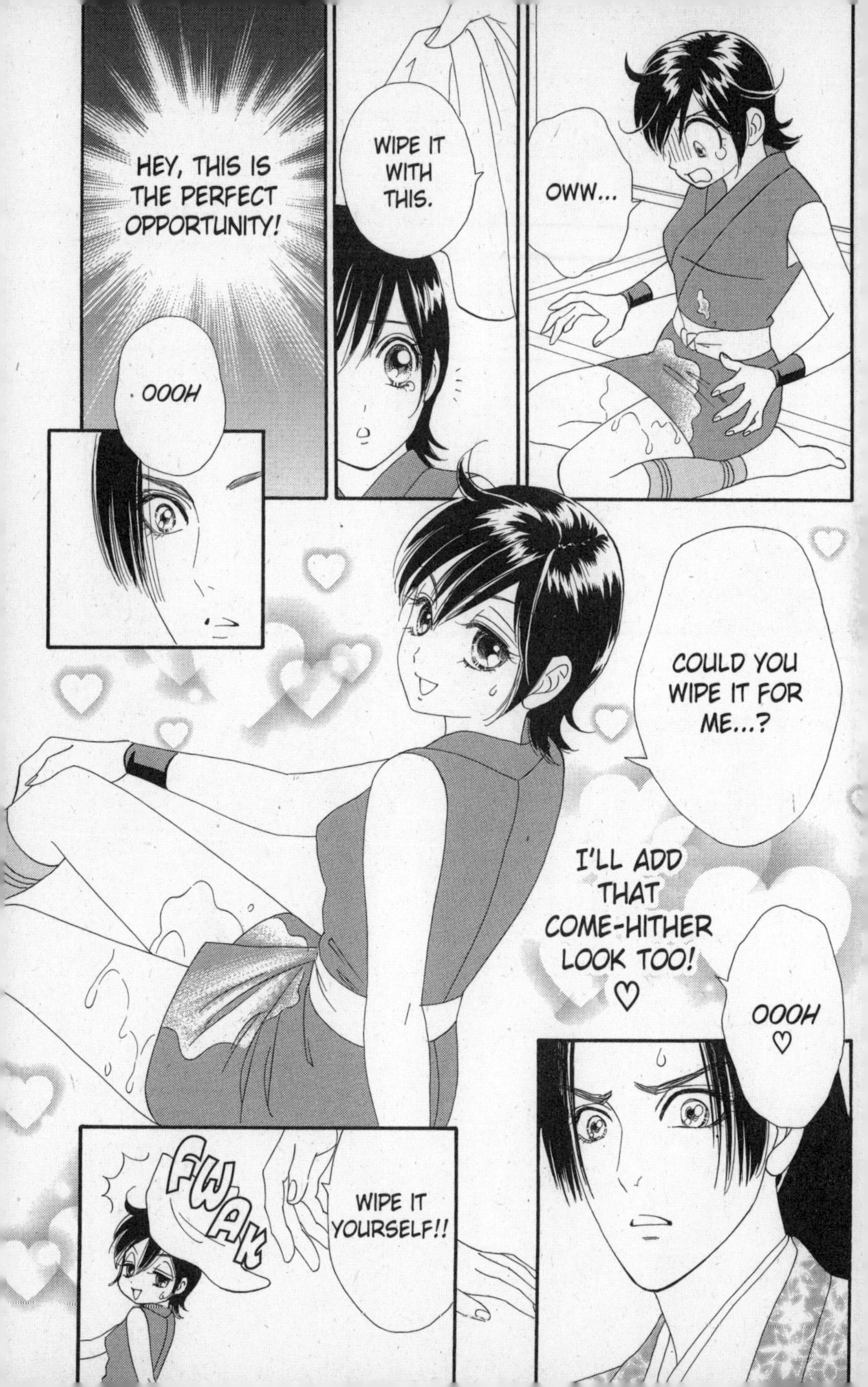
OWW...
WIPE IT WITH THIS.
HEY, THIS IS THE PERFECT OPPORTUNITY!
OOOH
COULD YOU WIPE IT FOR ME...?
I'LL ADD THAT COME-HITHER LOOK TOO! ♡
OOOH ♡
WIPE IT YOURSELF!!
FWAK

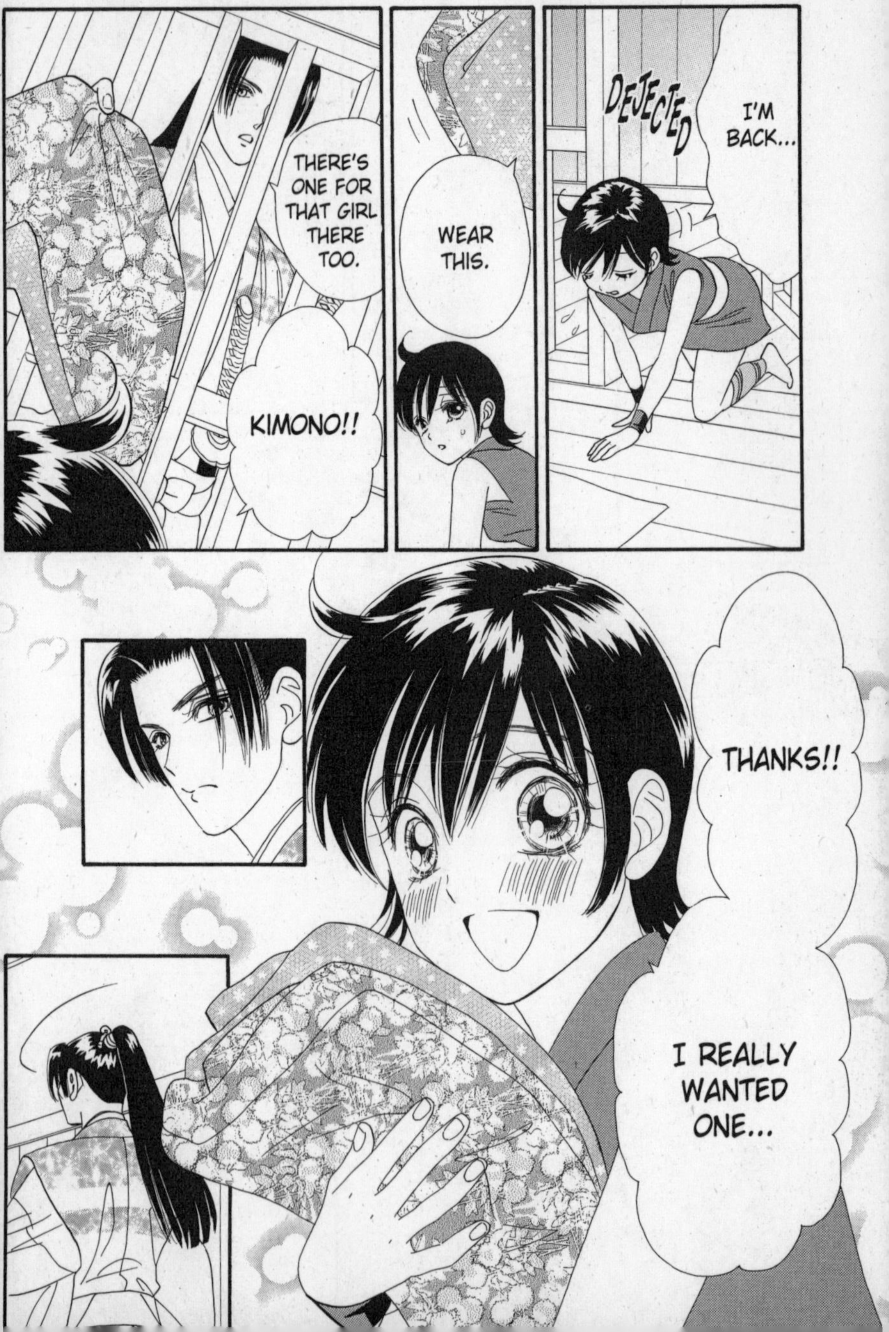

DEJECTED
I'M BACK...
WEAR THIS.
THERE'S ONE FOR THAT GIRL THERE TOO.
KIMONO!!
THANKS!!
I REALLY WANTED ONE...

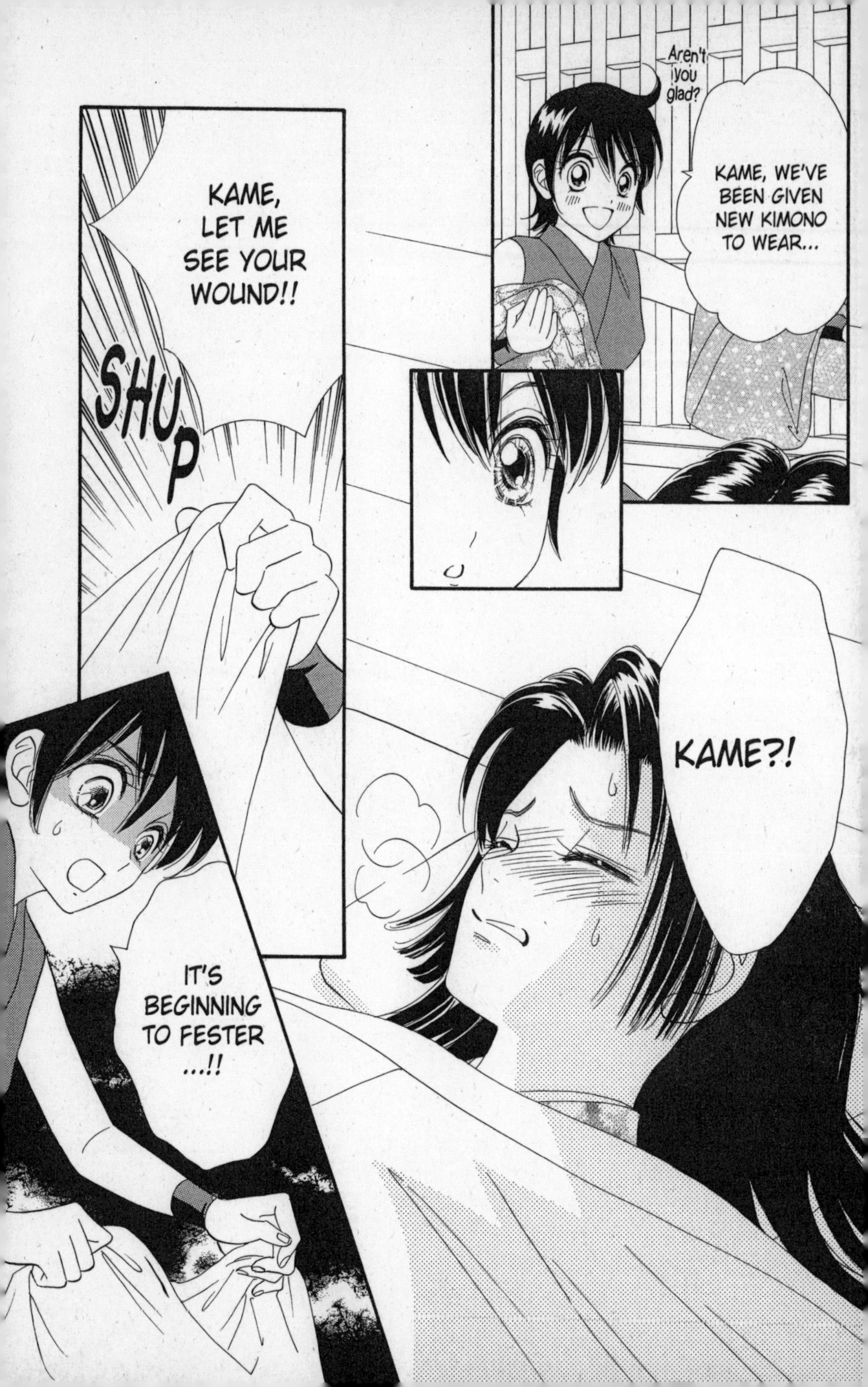

KAME, WE'VE BEEN GIVEN NEW KIMONO TO WEAR...
Aren't you glad?
KAME, LET ME SEE YOUR WOUND!!
SHUP
KAME?!
IT'S BEGINNING TO FESTER ...!!

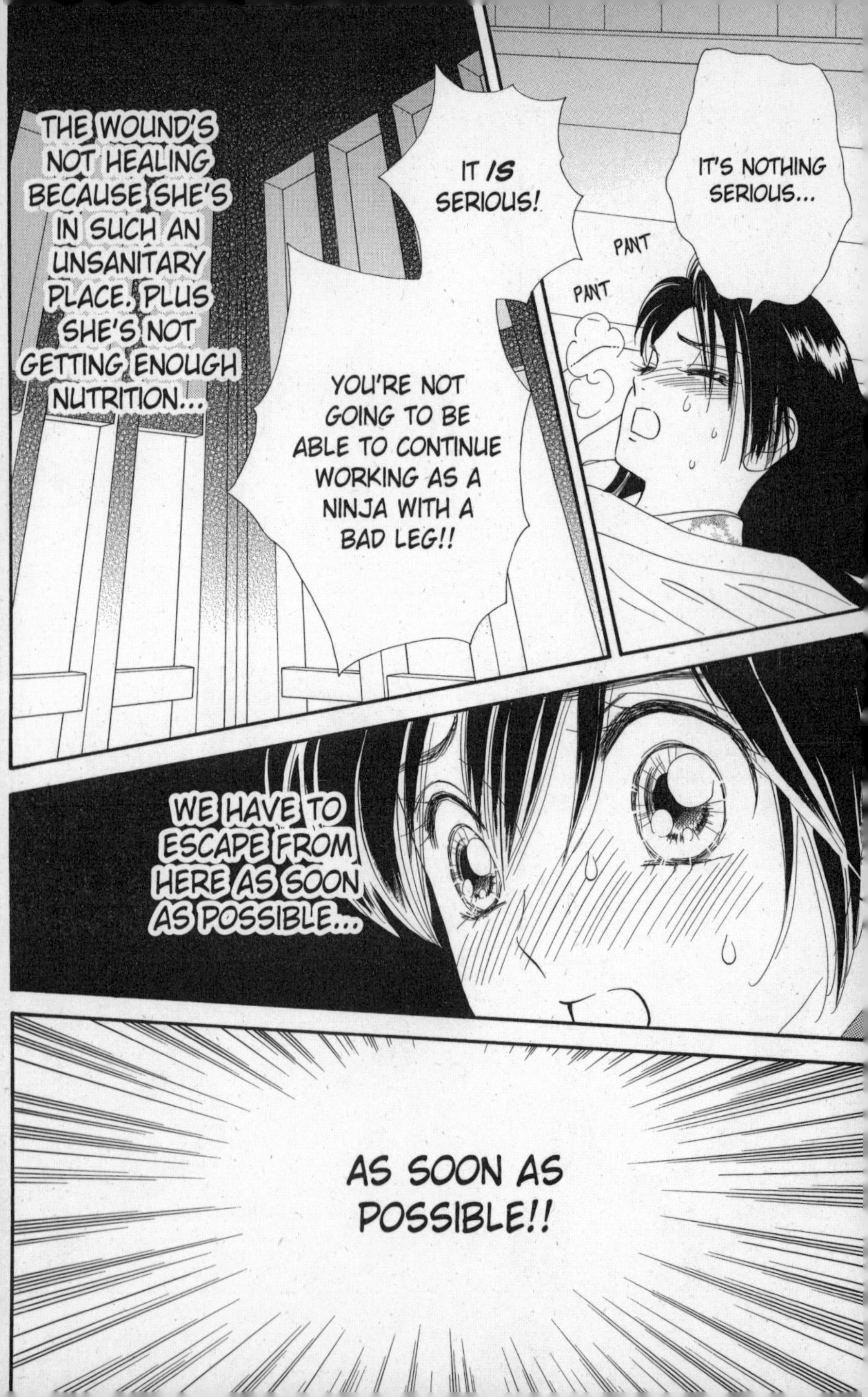
IT'S NOTHING SERIOUS...
PANT
PANT
IT IS SERIOUS!
THE WOUND'S NOT HEALING BECAUSE SHE'S IN SUCH AN UNSANITARY PLACE. PLUS SHE'S NOT GETTING ENOUGH NUTRITION...
YOU'RE NOT GOING TO BE ABLE TO CONTINUE WORKING AS A NINJA WITH A BAD LEG!!
WE HAVE TO ESCAPE FROM HERE AS SOON AS POSSIBLE...
AS SOON AS POSSIBLE!!

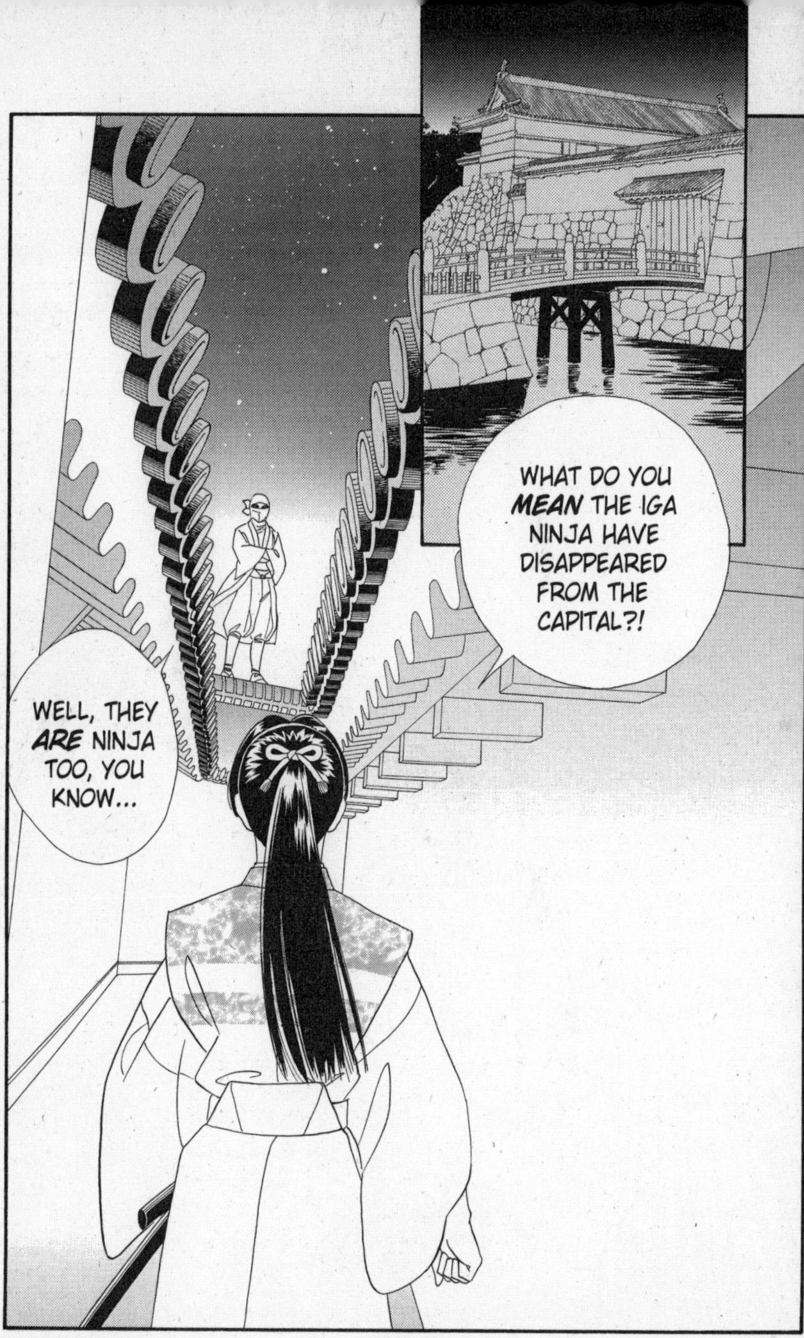
WHAT DO YOU *MEAN* THE IGA NINJA HAVE DISAPPEARED FROM THE CAPITAL?!
WELL, THEY *ARE* NINJA TOO, YOU KNOW...

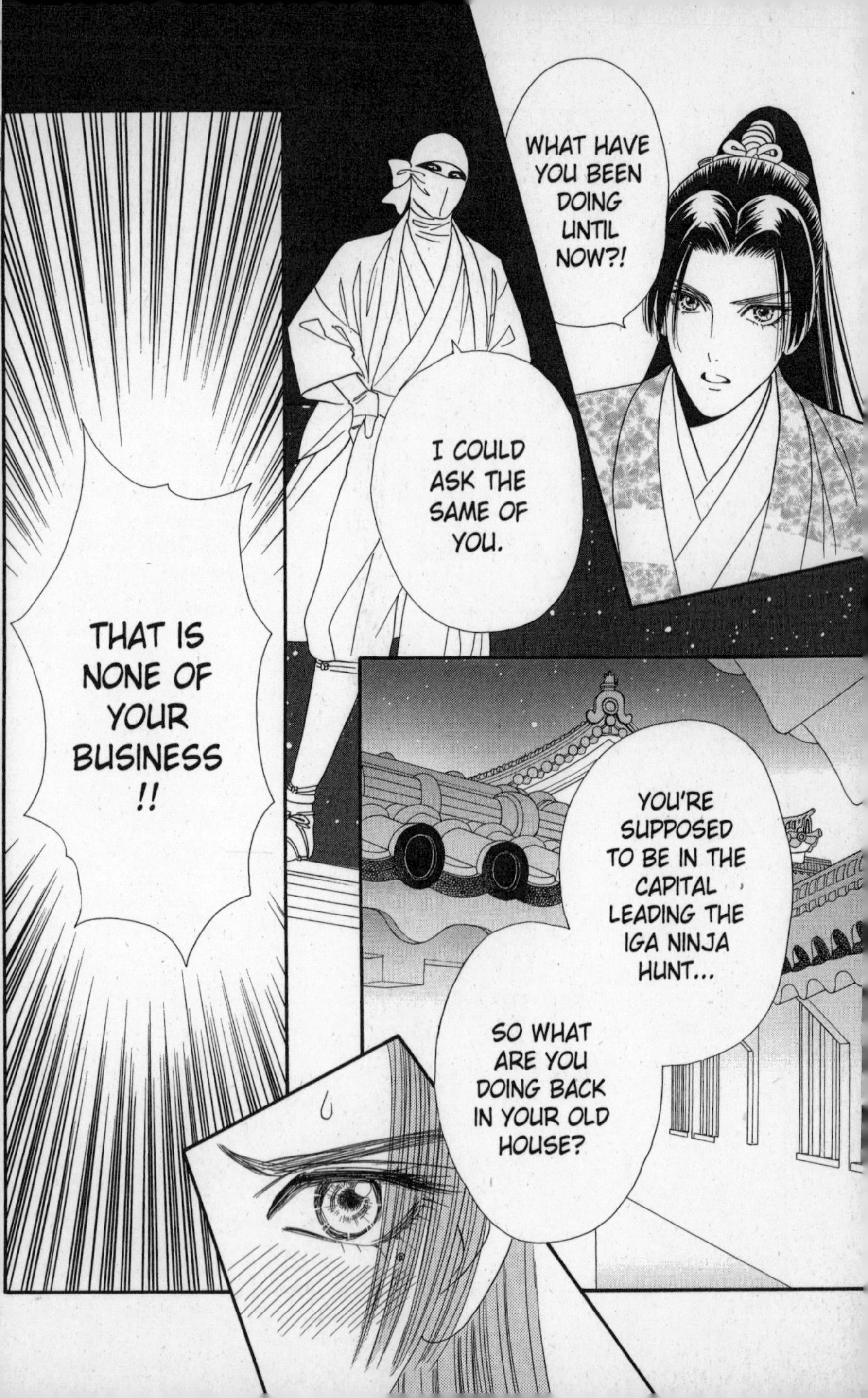
WHAT HAVE YOU BEEN DOING UNTIL NOW?!
I COULD ASK THE SAME OF YOU.
YOU'RE SUPPOSED TO BE IN THE CAPITAL LEADING THE IGA NINJA HUNT...
SO WHAT ARE YOU DOING BACK IN YOUR OLD HOUSE?
THAT IS NONE OF YOUR BUSINESS!!

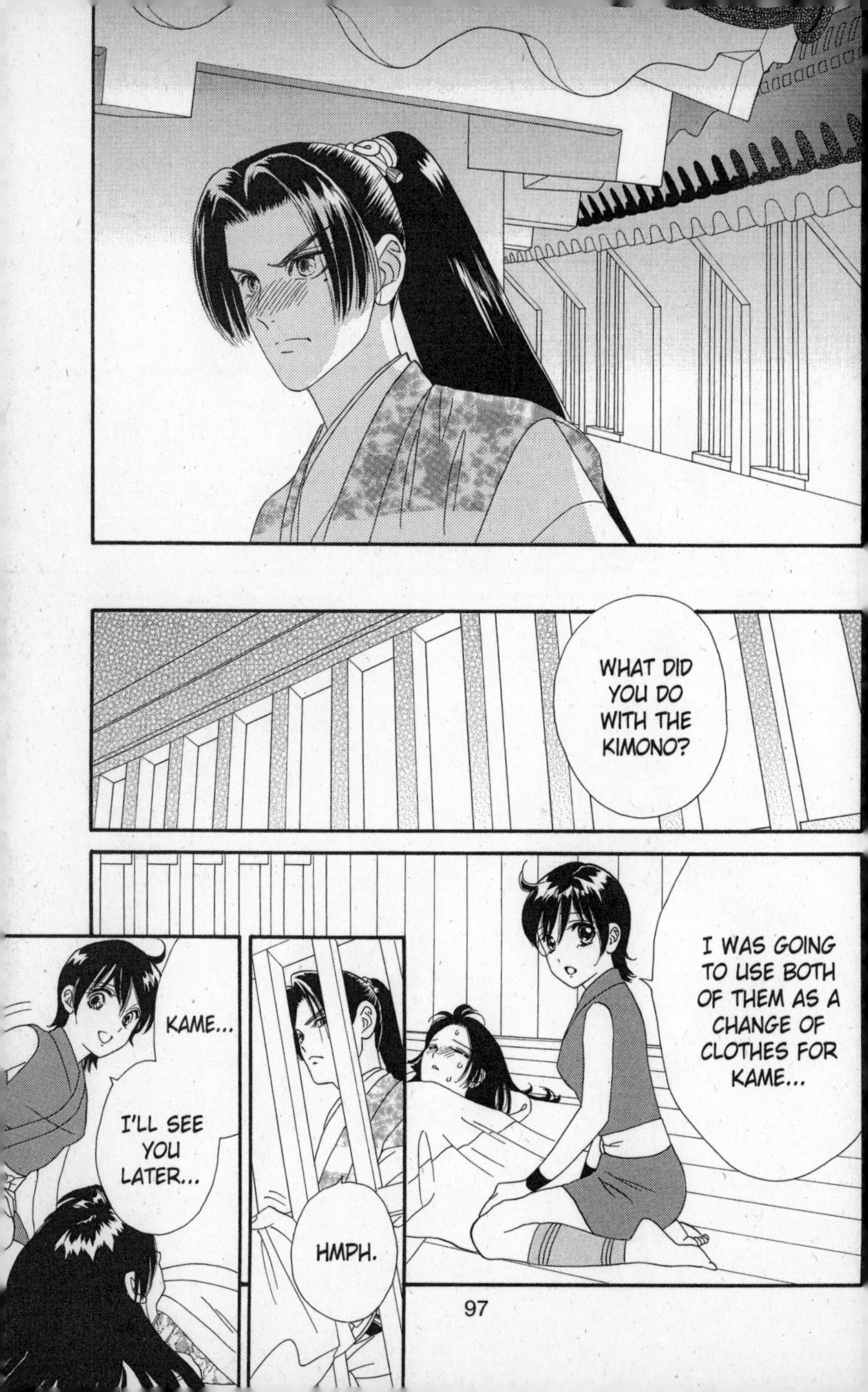
WHAT DID YOU DO WITH THE KIMONO?
I WAS GOING TO USE BOTH OF THEM AS A CHANGE OF CLOTHES FOR KAME...
HMPH.
KAME...
I'LL SEE YOU LATER...

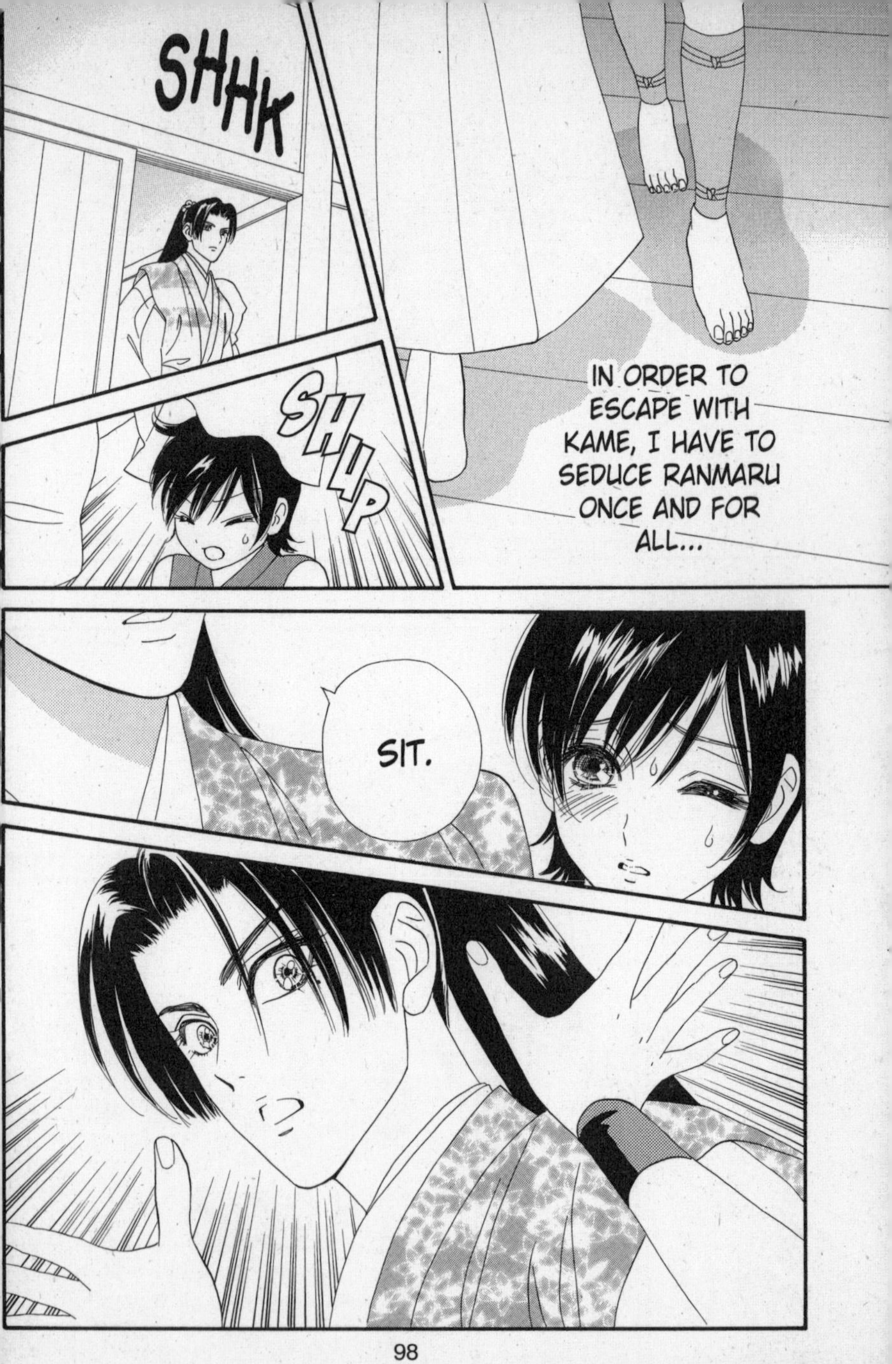
IN ORDER TO ESCAPE WITH KAME, I HAVE TO SEDUCE RANMARU ONCE AND FOR ALL...
SHHK
SHUP
SIT.

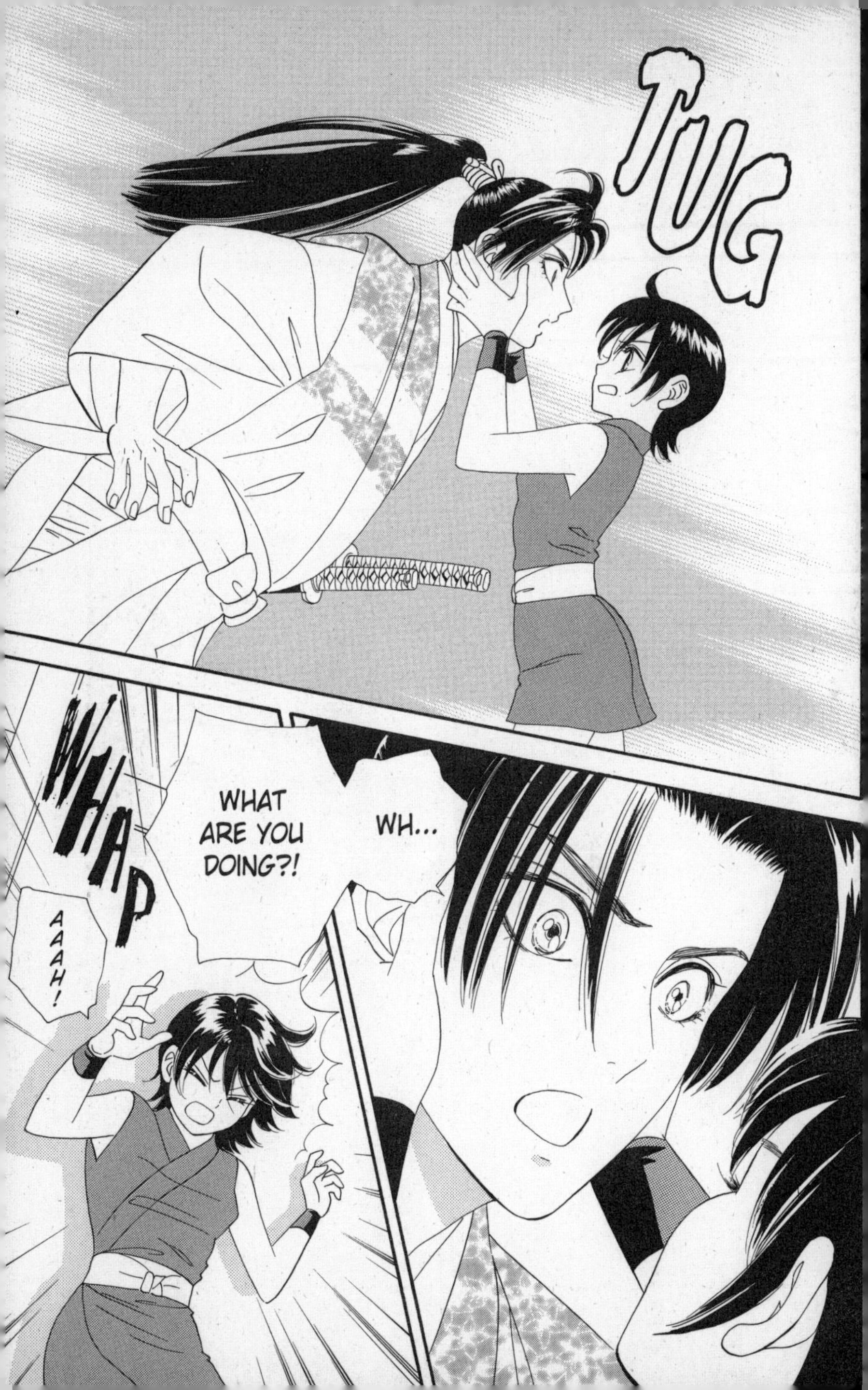
TUG
WH...
WHAT ARE YOU DOING?!
WHAP
AAAH!

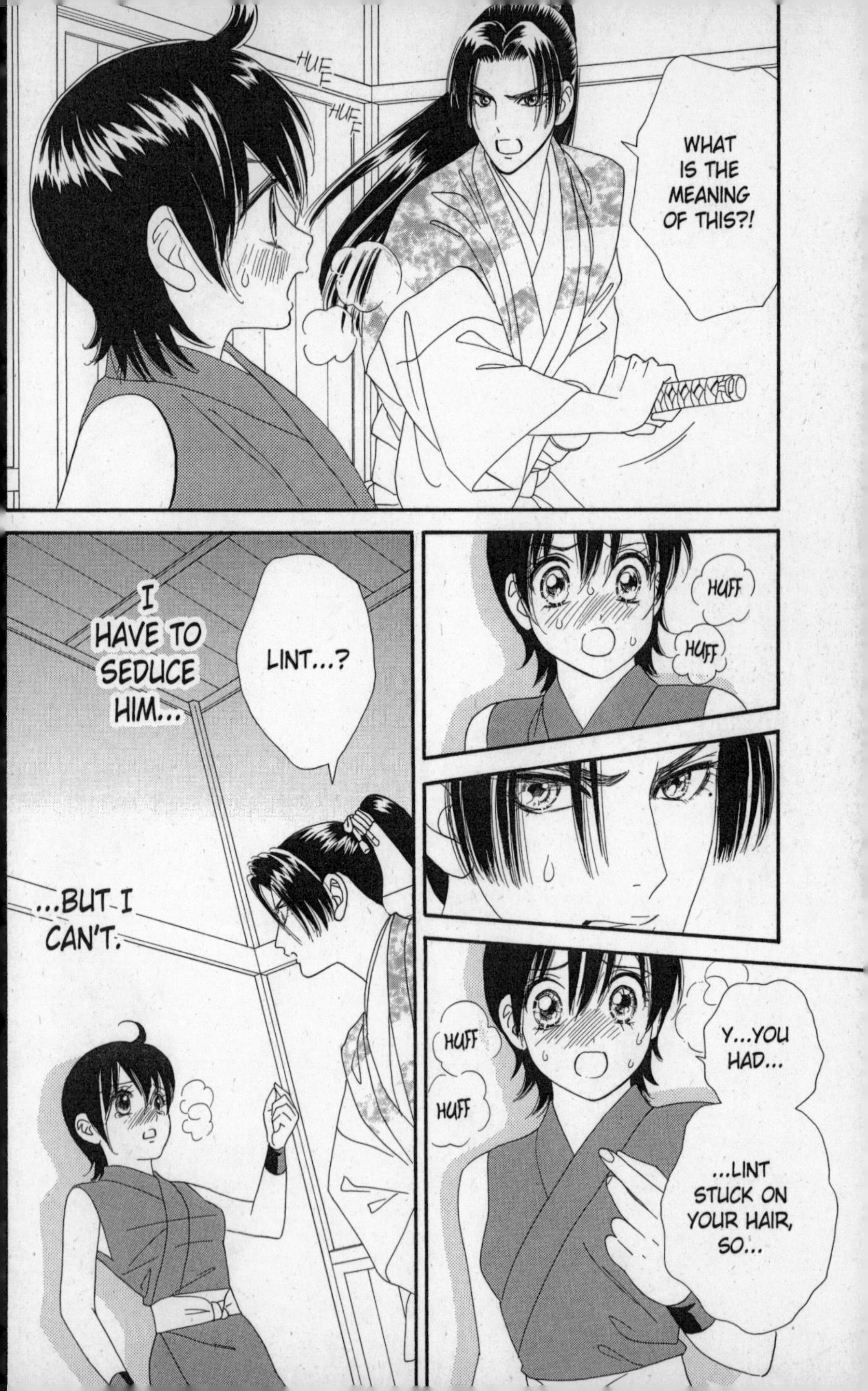
WHAT IS THE MEANING OF THIS?!
HUFF
HUFF
HUFF
HUFF
Y...YOU HAD...
...LINT STUCK ON YOUR HAIR, SO...
HUFF
HUFF
LINT...?
I HAVE TO SEDUCE HIM...
...BUT I CAN'T.

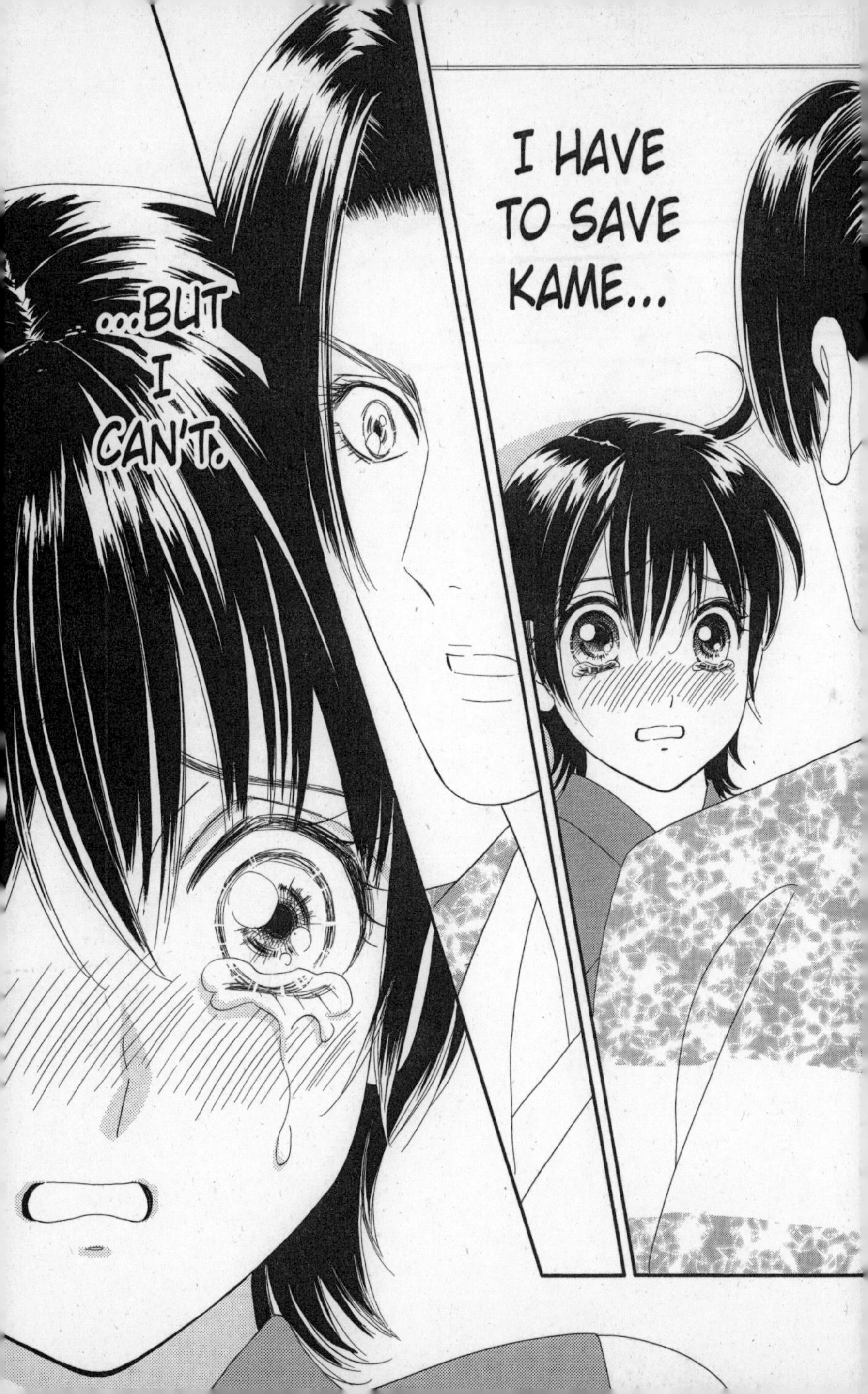
I HAVE TO SAVE KAME...
...BUT I CAN'T.

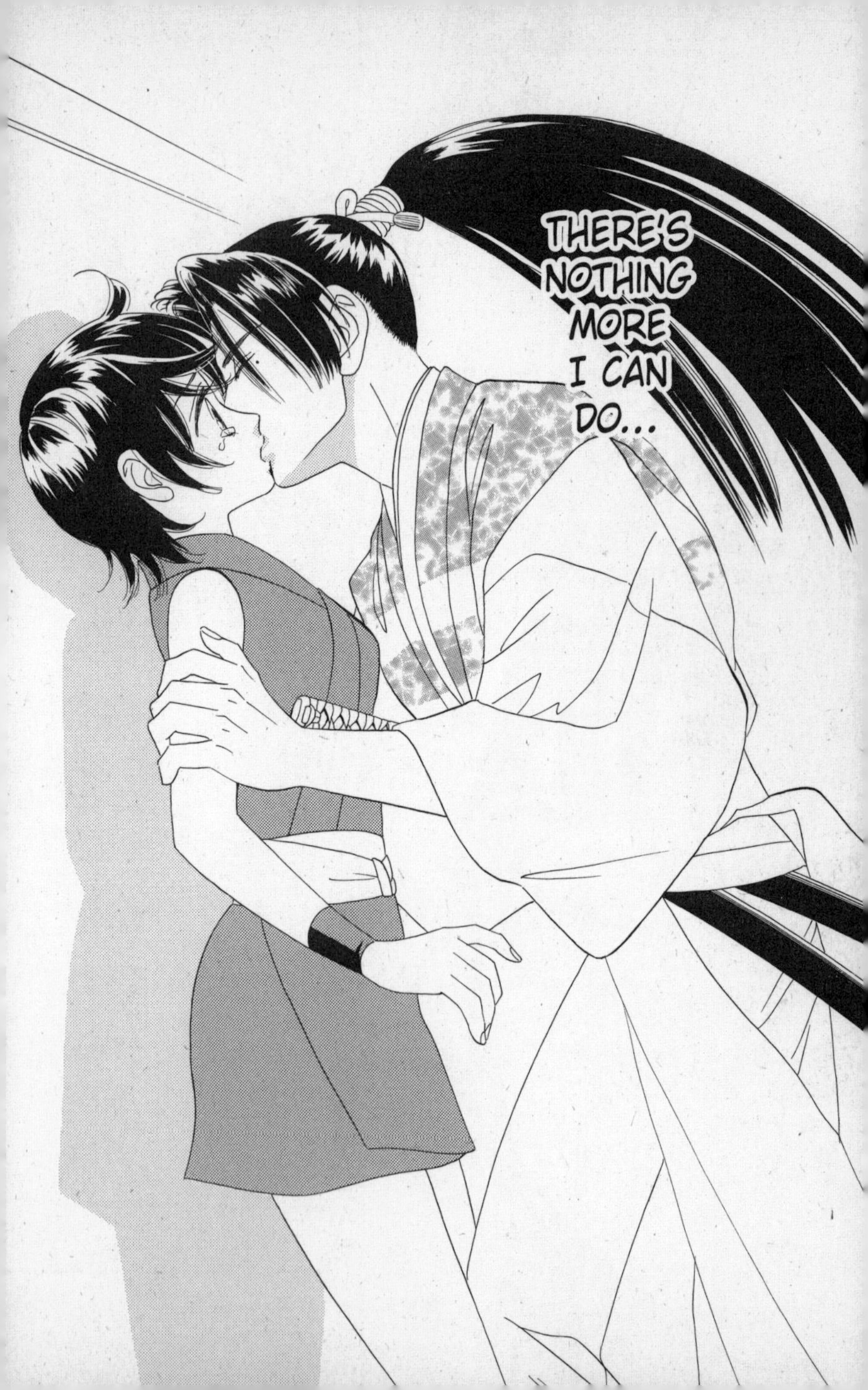
THERE'S NOTHING MORE I CAN DO...

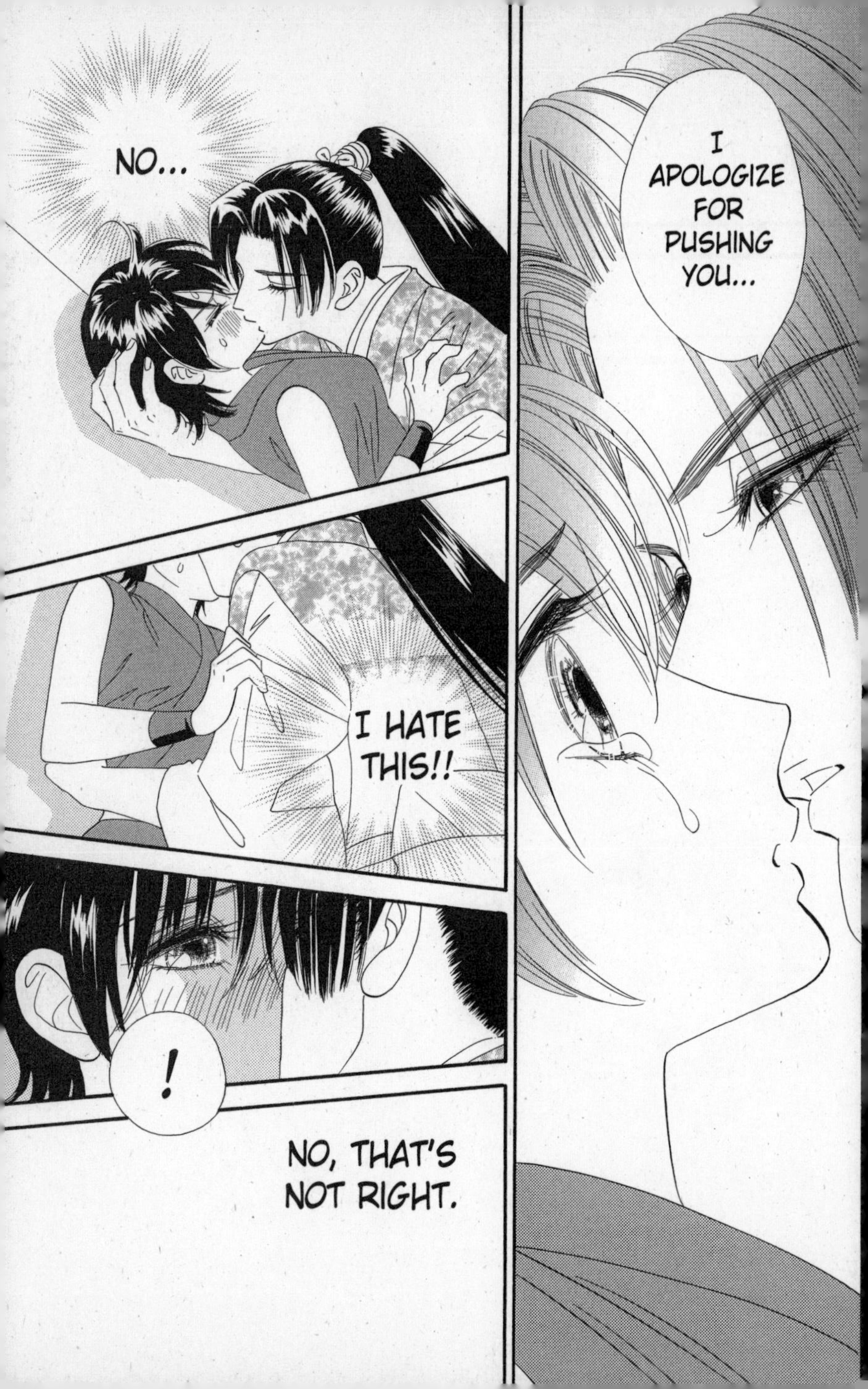
I APOLOGIZE FOR PUSHING YOU...
NO...
I HATE THIS!!
!
NO, THAT'S NOT RIGHT.

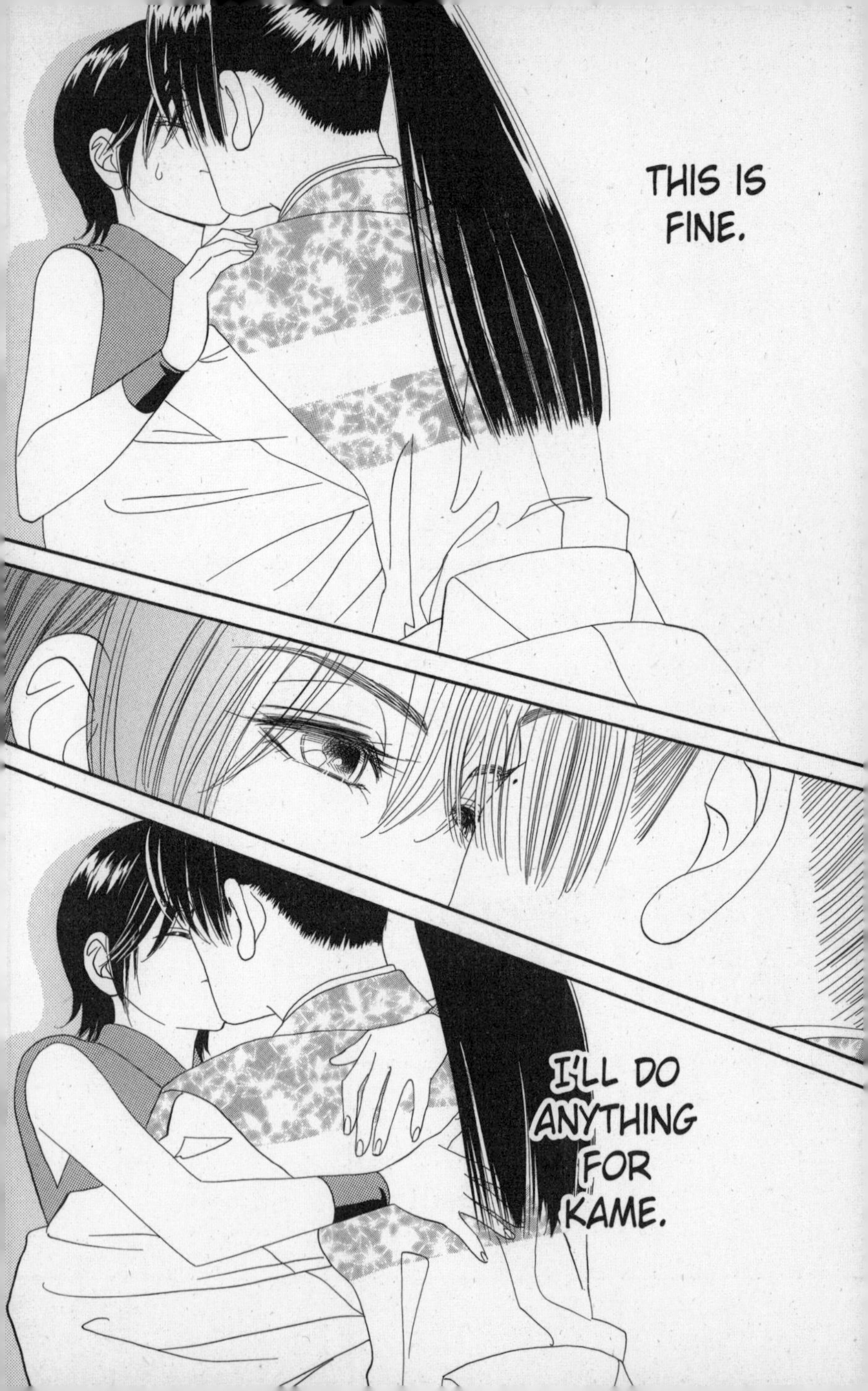
THIS IS FINE.
I'LL DO ANYTHING FOR KAME.

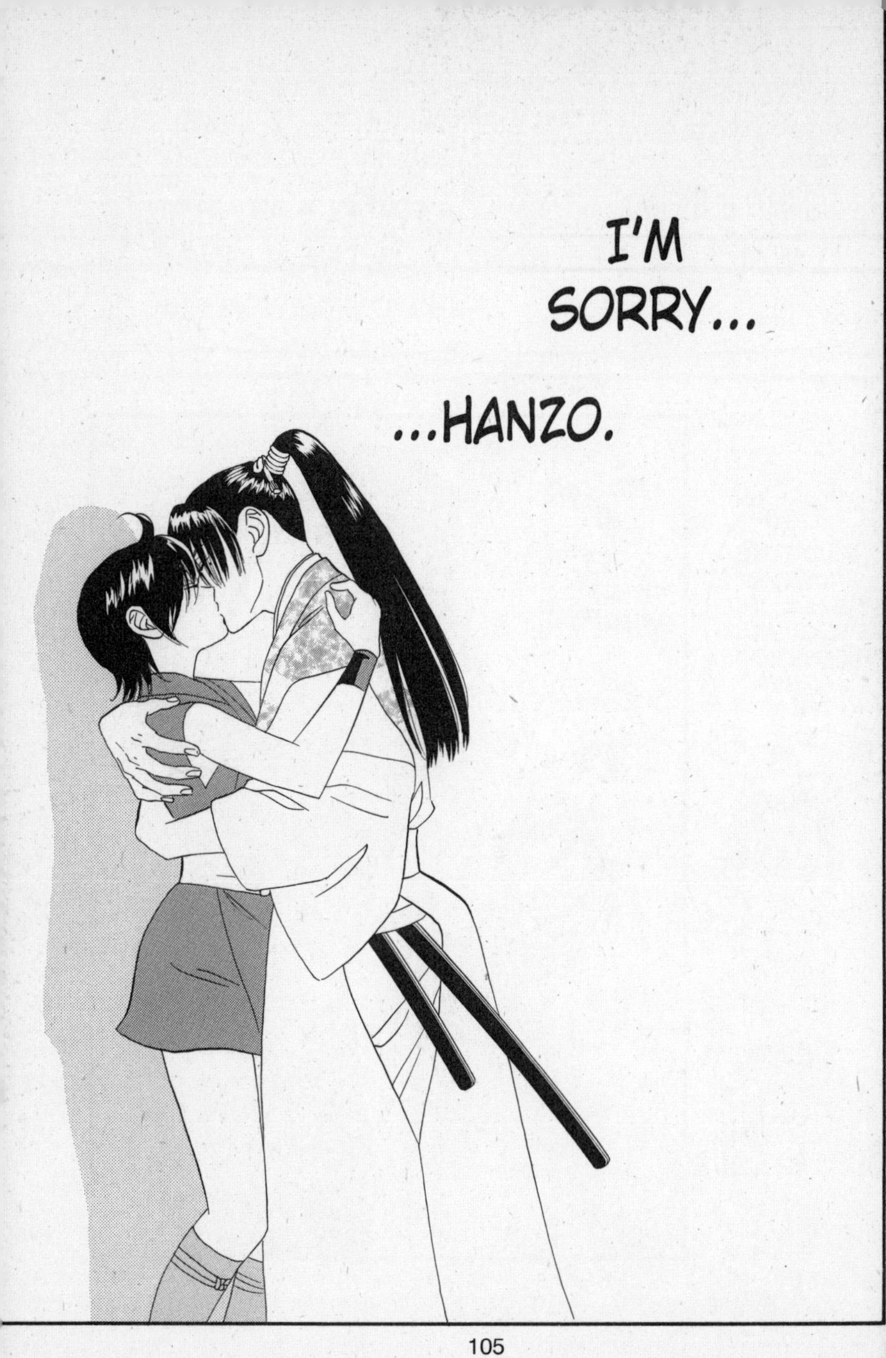
I'M SORRY...
...HANZO.

TAIL OF THE MOON EXTRA: TODAY'S MISSION

"I WANT TO SEE HANZO DIET-WALKING!"

-KAYO, EHIME PREFECTURE

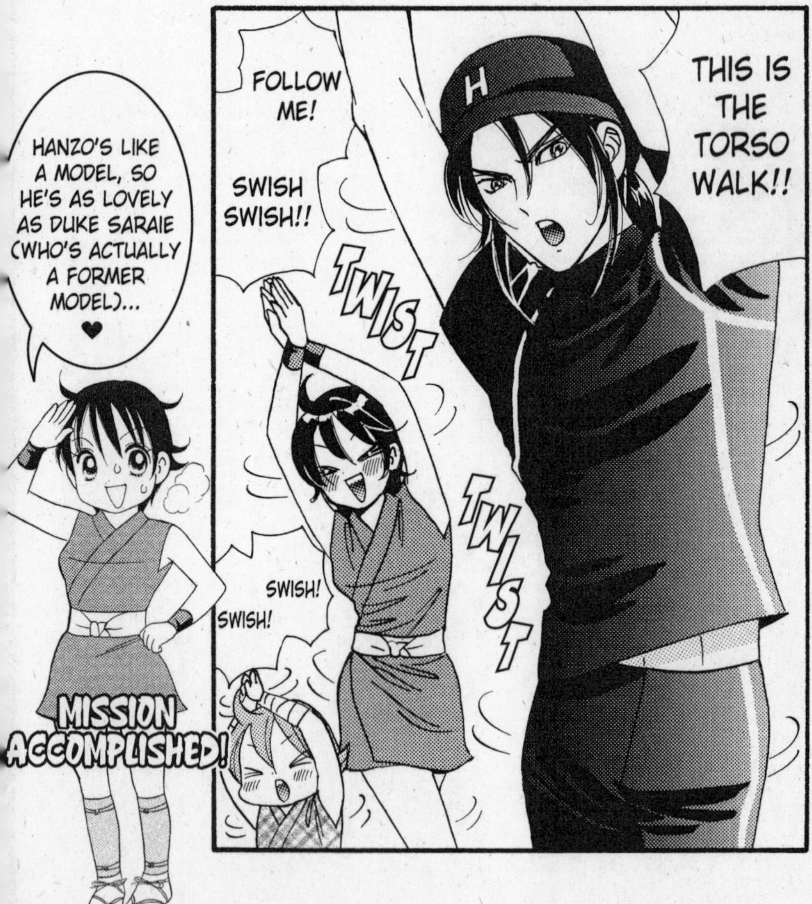
THIS IS THE TORSO WALK!!
FOLLOW ME!
SWISH SWISH!!
TWIST
TWIST
SWISH!
SWISH!
HANZO'S LIKE A MODEL, SO HE'S AS LOVELY AS DUKE SARAIE (WHO'S ACTUALLY A FORMER MODEL)... ♥
MISSION ACCOMPLISHED!

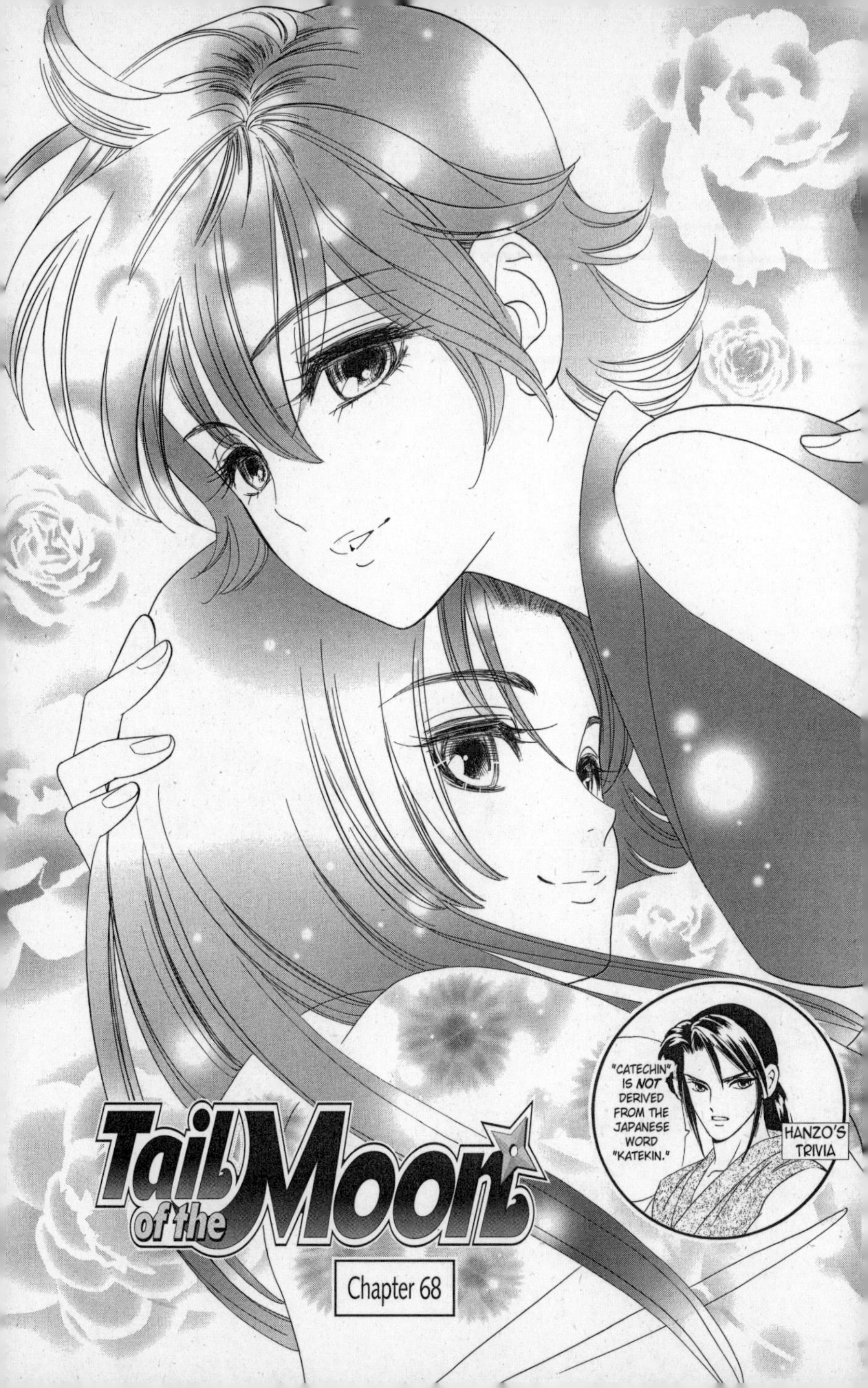
Tail of the Moon
Chapter 68
"CATECHIN" IS NOT DERIVED FROM THE JAPANESE WORD "KATEKIN."
HANZO'S TRIVIA

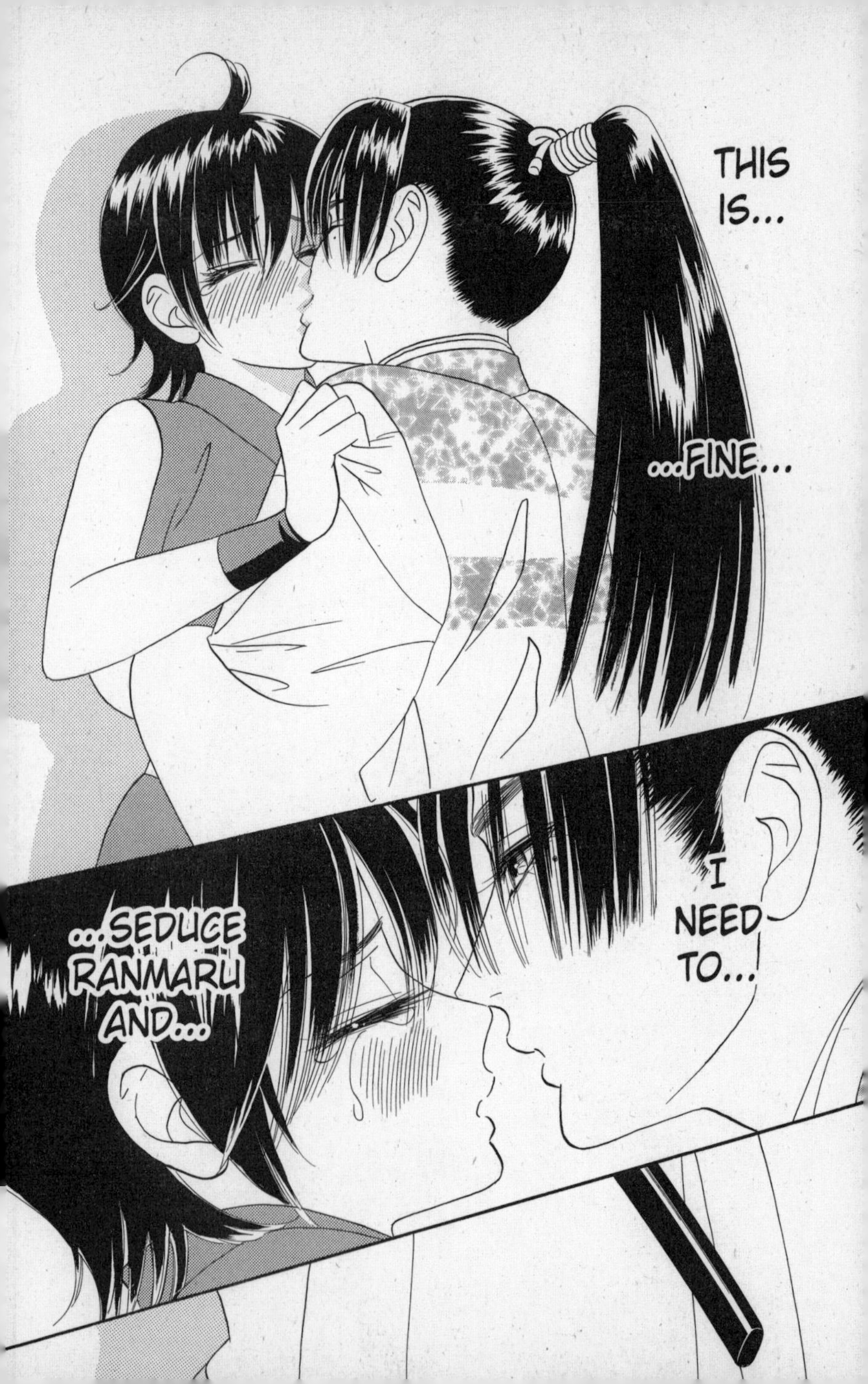
THIS IS...
...FINE...
I NEED TO...
...SEDUCE RANMARU AND...

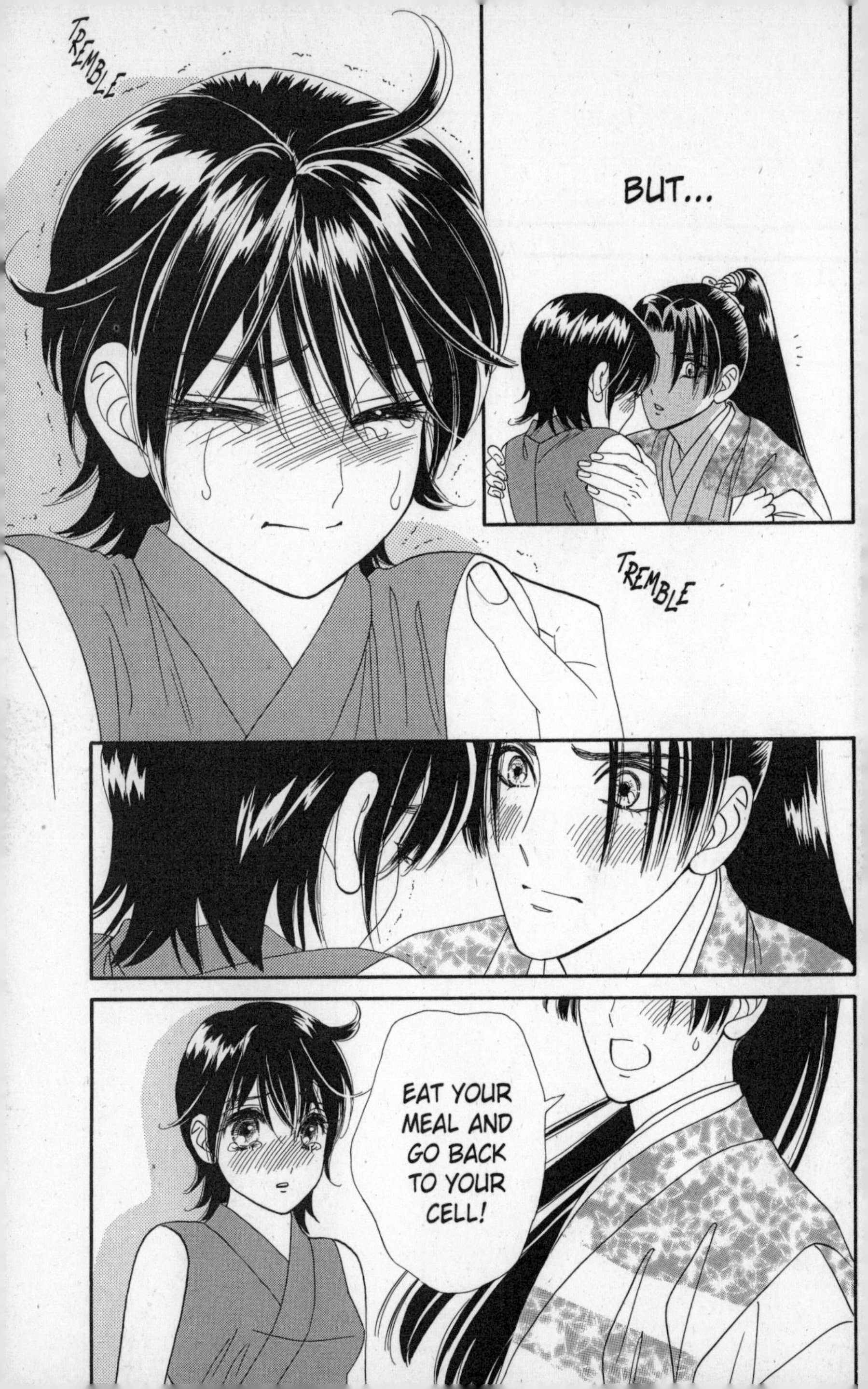
BUT...
TREMBLE
TREMBLE
EAT YOUR MEAL AND GO BACK TO YOUR CELL!

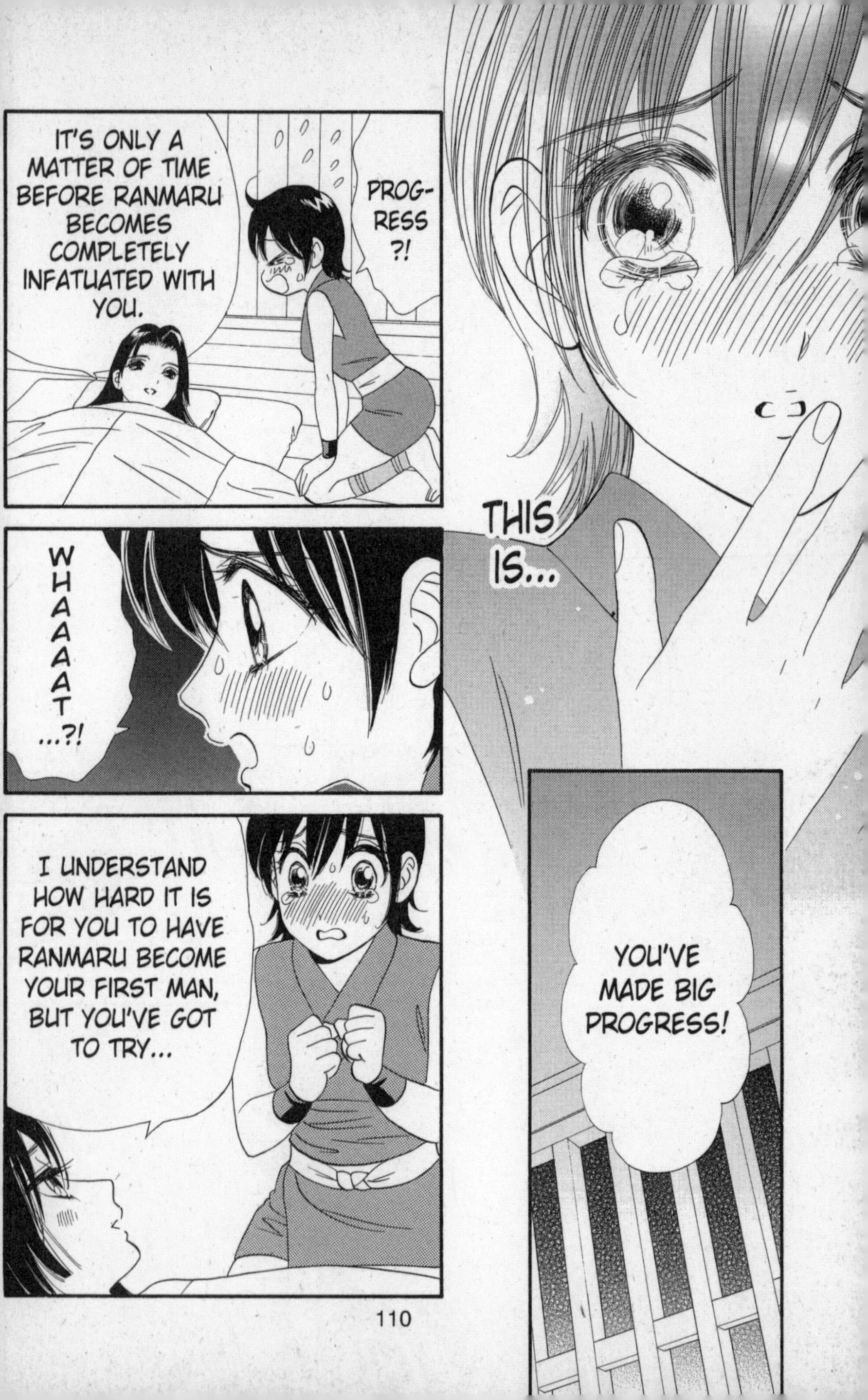
THIS IS...
YOU'VE MADE BIG PROGRESS!
PROG-RESS?!
IT'S ONLY A MATTER OF TIME BEFORE RANMARU BECOMES COMPLETELY INFATUATED WITH YOU.
WHAAAAAT...?!
I UNDERSTAND HOW HARD IT IS FOR YOU TO HAVE RANMARU BECOME YOUR FIRST MAN, BUT YOU'VE GOT TO TRY...

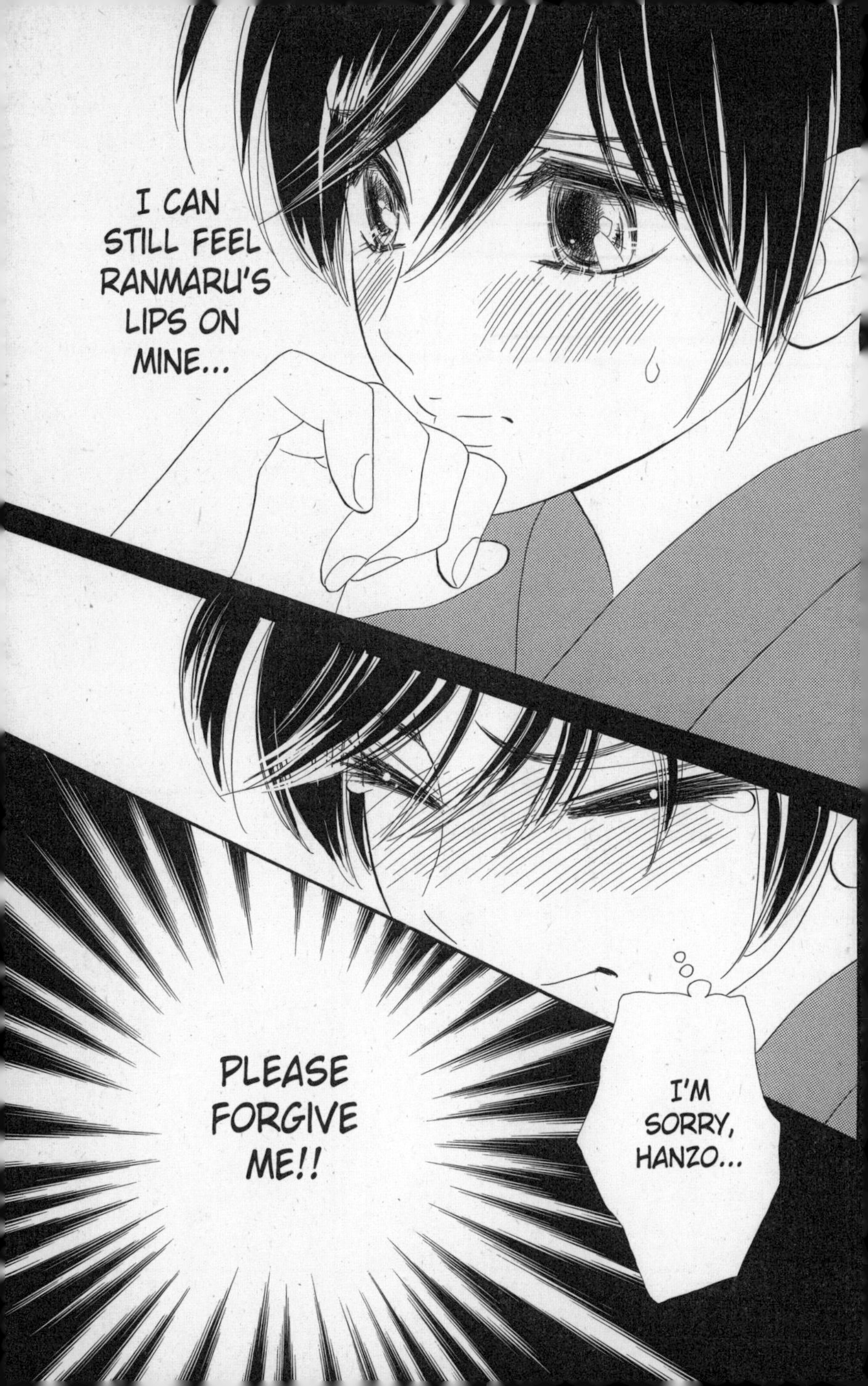
I CAN STILL FEEL RANMARU'S LIPS ON MINE...
I'M SORRY, HANZO...
PLEASE FORGIVE ME!!

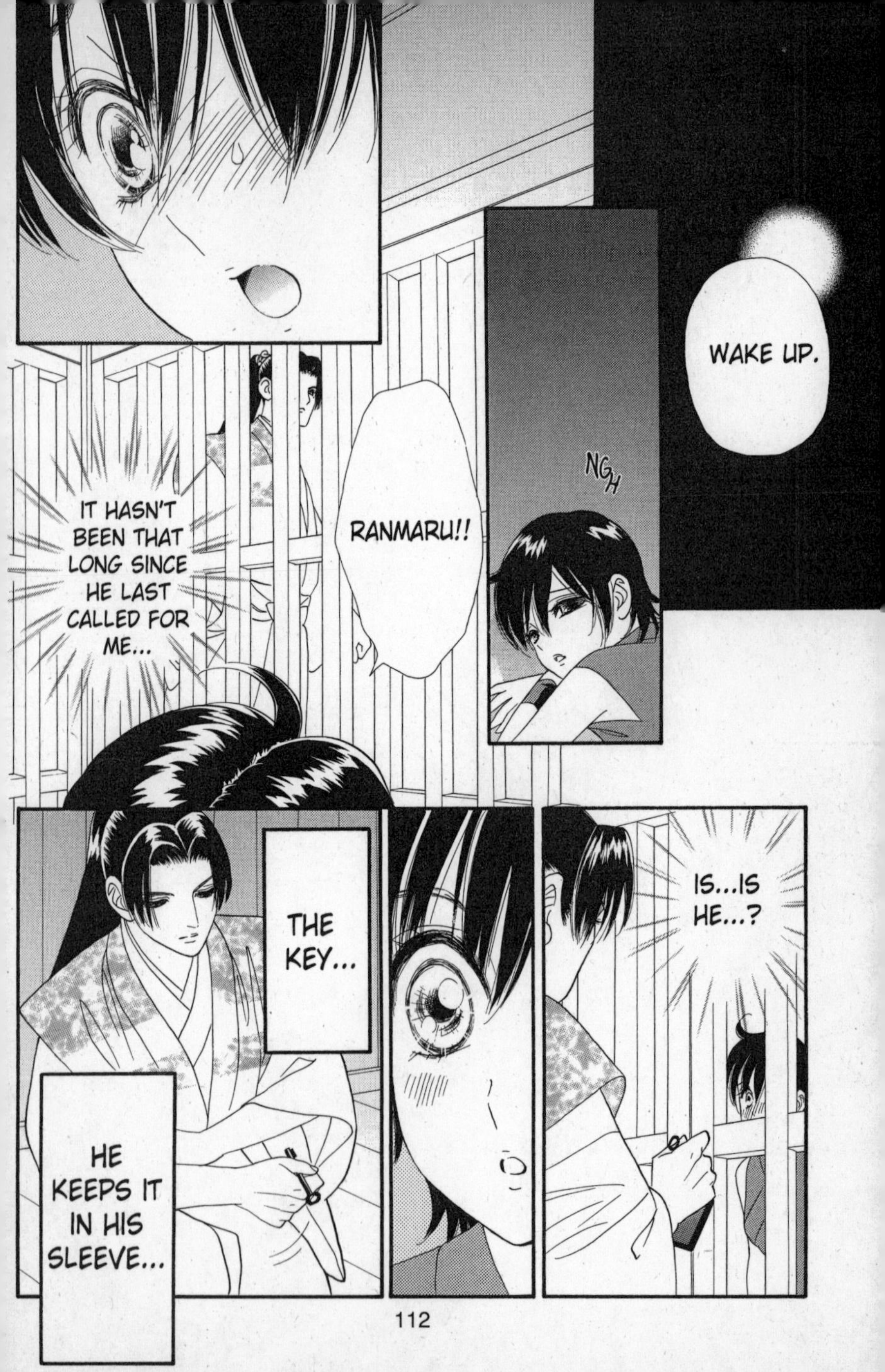

WAKE UP.
NGH
RANMARU!!
IT HASN'T BEEN THAT LONG SINCE HE LAST CALLED FOR ME...
IS...IS HE...?
THE KEY...
HE KEEPS IT IN HIS SLEEVE...

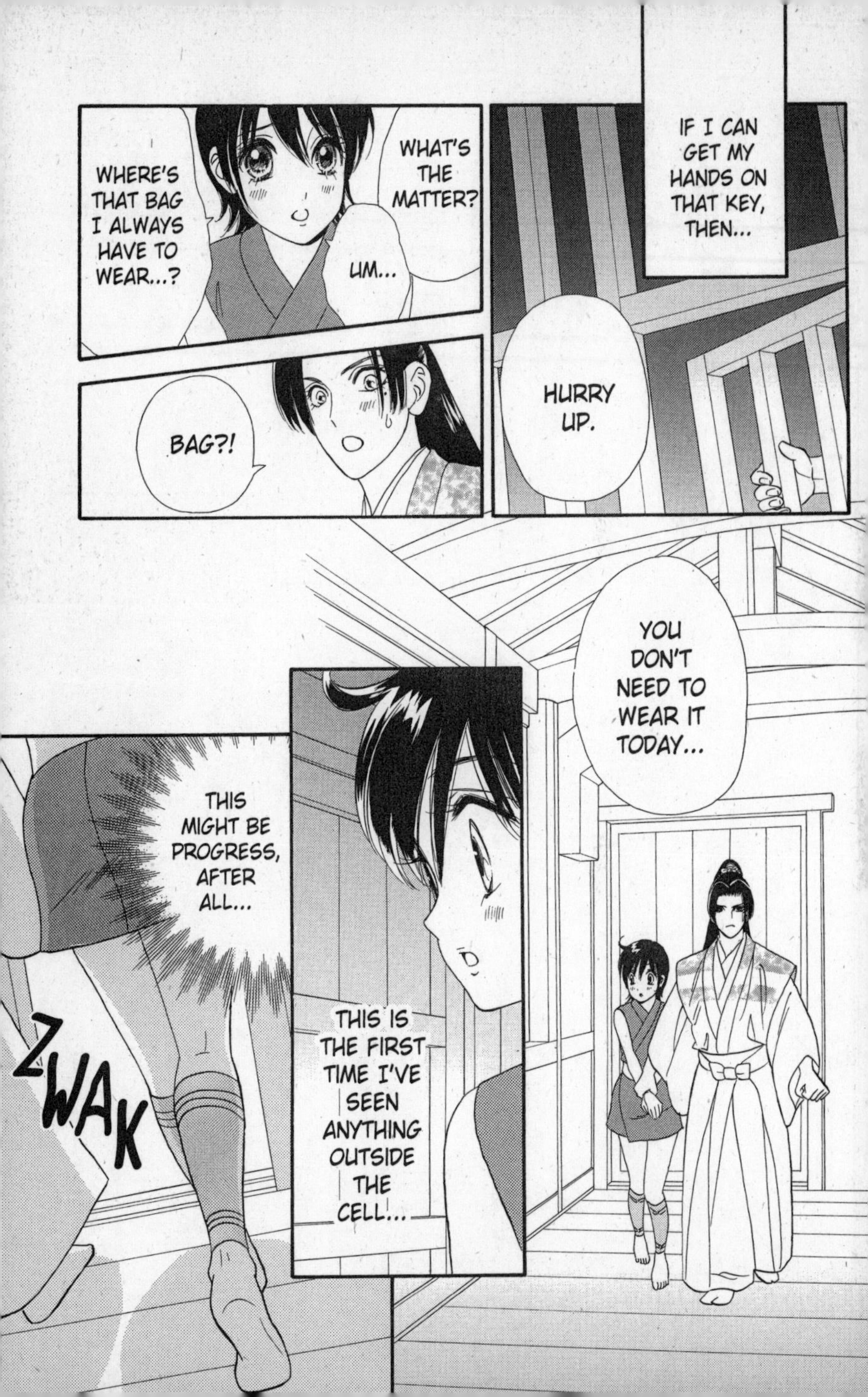
IF I CAN GET MY HANDS ON THAT KEY, THEN...
HURRY UP.
WHAT'S THE MATTER?
UM...
WHERE'S THAT BAG I ALWAYS HAVE TO WEAR...?
BAG?!
YOU DON'T NEED TO WEAR IT TODAY...
THIS IS THE FIRST TIME I'VE SEEN ANYTHING OUTSIDE THE CELL...
THIS MIGHT BE PROGRESS, AFTER ALL...
ZWAK

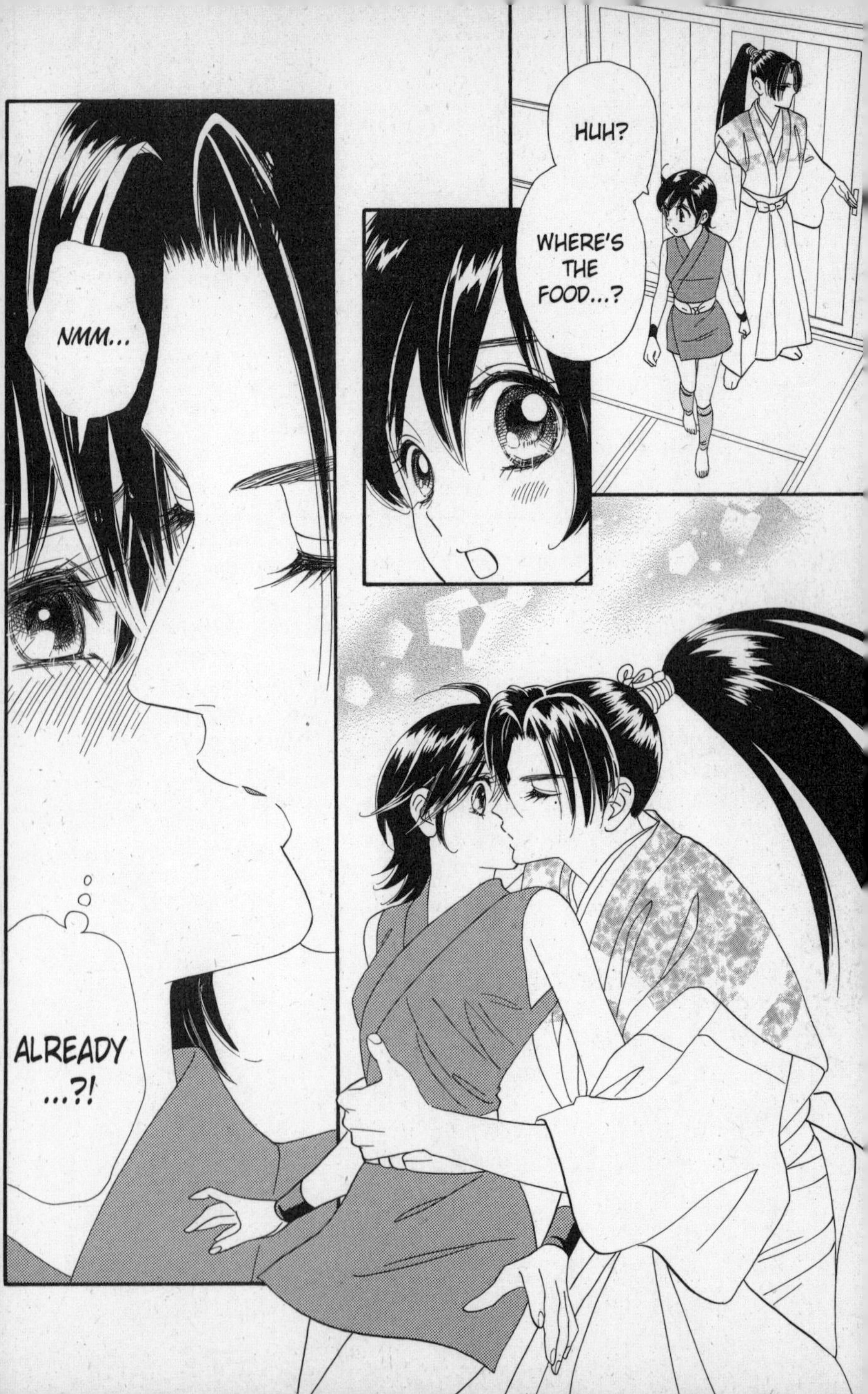
HUH?
WHERE'S THE FOOD...?
NMM...
ALREADY ...?!

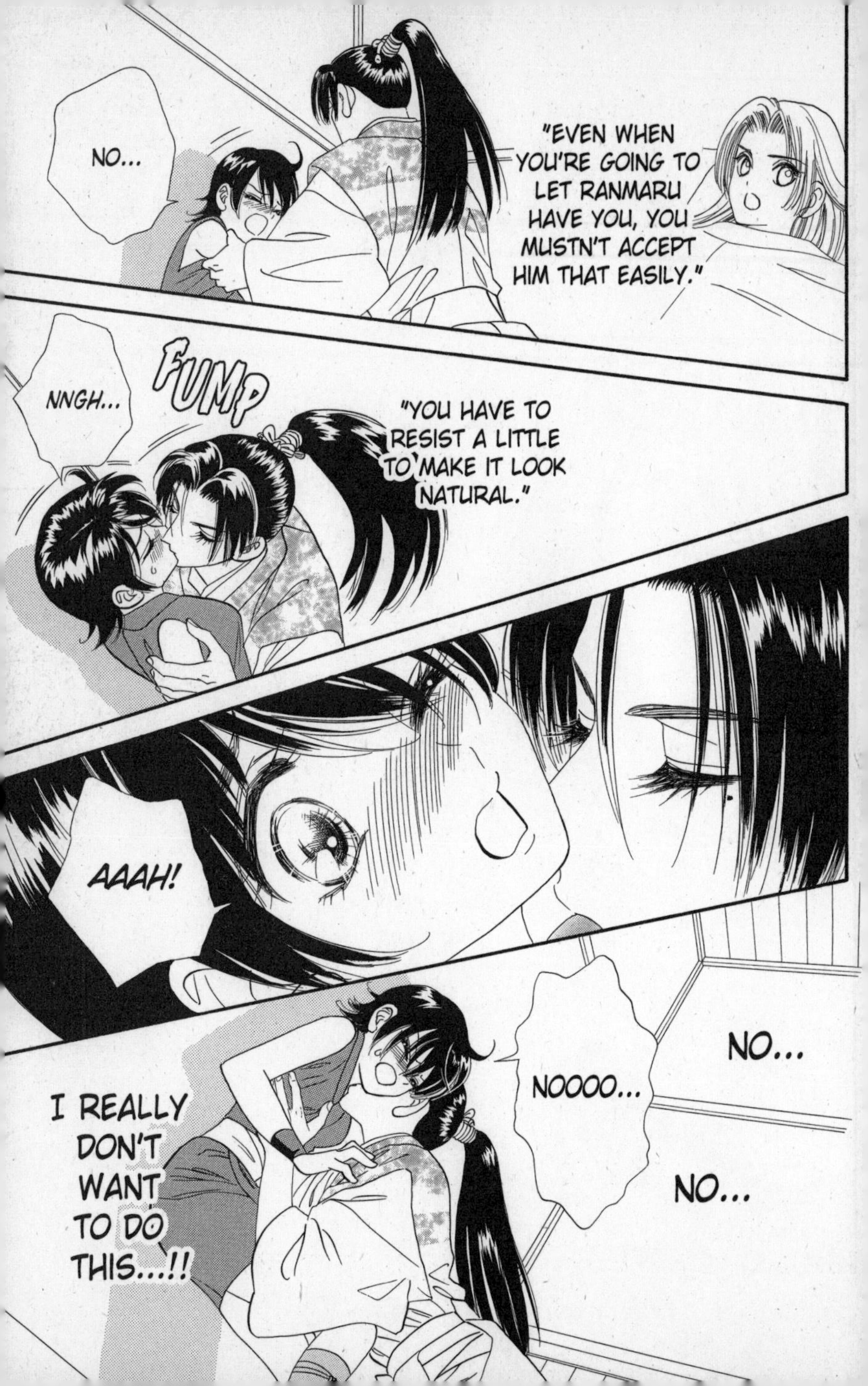
"EVEN WHEN YOU'RE GOING TO LET RANMARU HAVE YOU, YOU MUSTN'T ACCEPT HIM THAT EASILY."
NO...
"YOU HAVE TO RESIST A LITTLE TO MAKE IT LOOK NATURAL."
FUMP
NNGH...
AAAH!
NO...
NO...
NOOOO...
I REALLY DON'T WANT TO DO THIS...!!

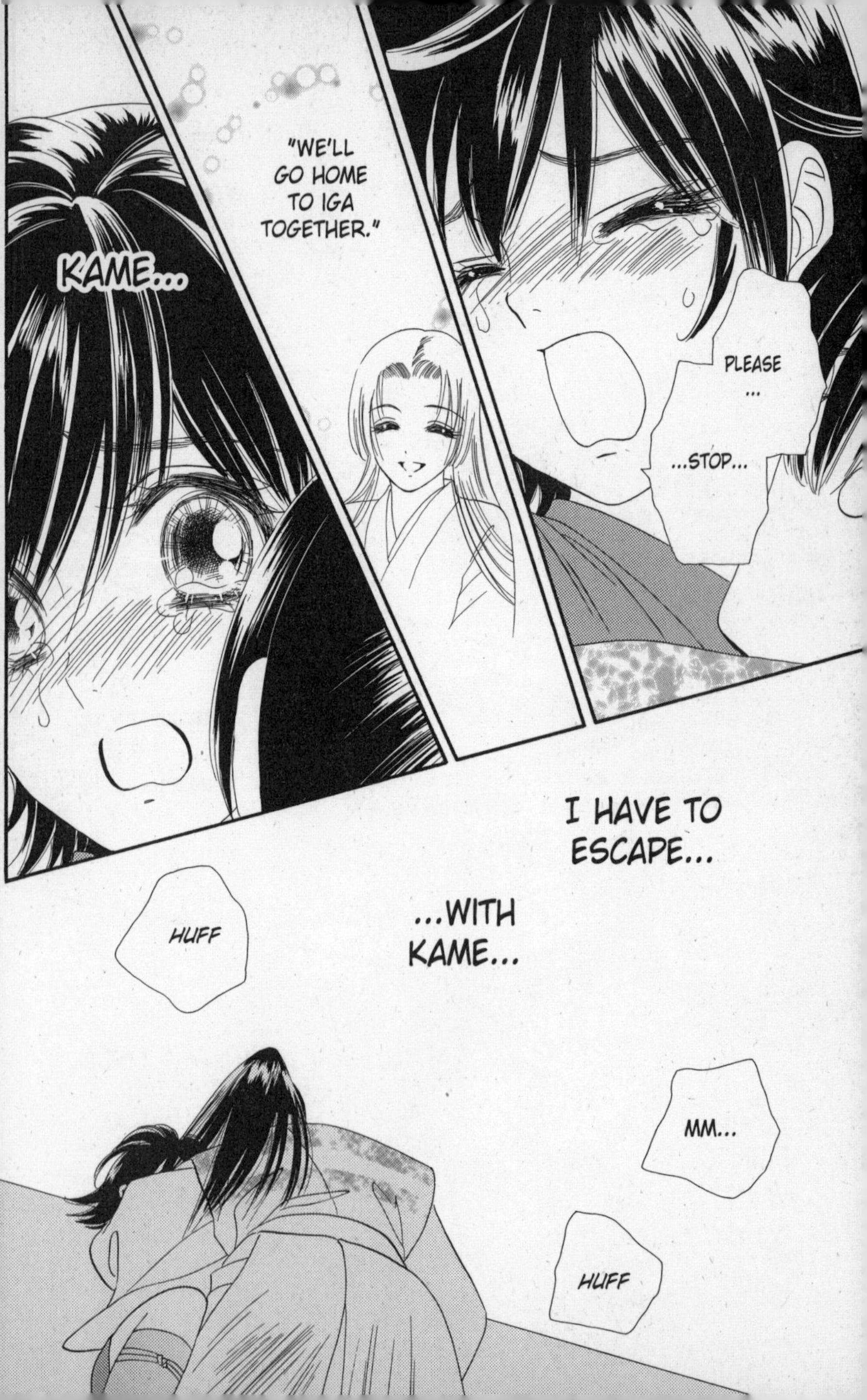
PLEASE ...
...STOP...
"WE'LL GO HOME TO IGA TOGETHER."
KAME...
I HAVE TO ESCAPE...
...WITH KAME...
HUFF
MM...
HUFF

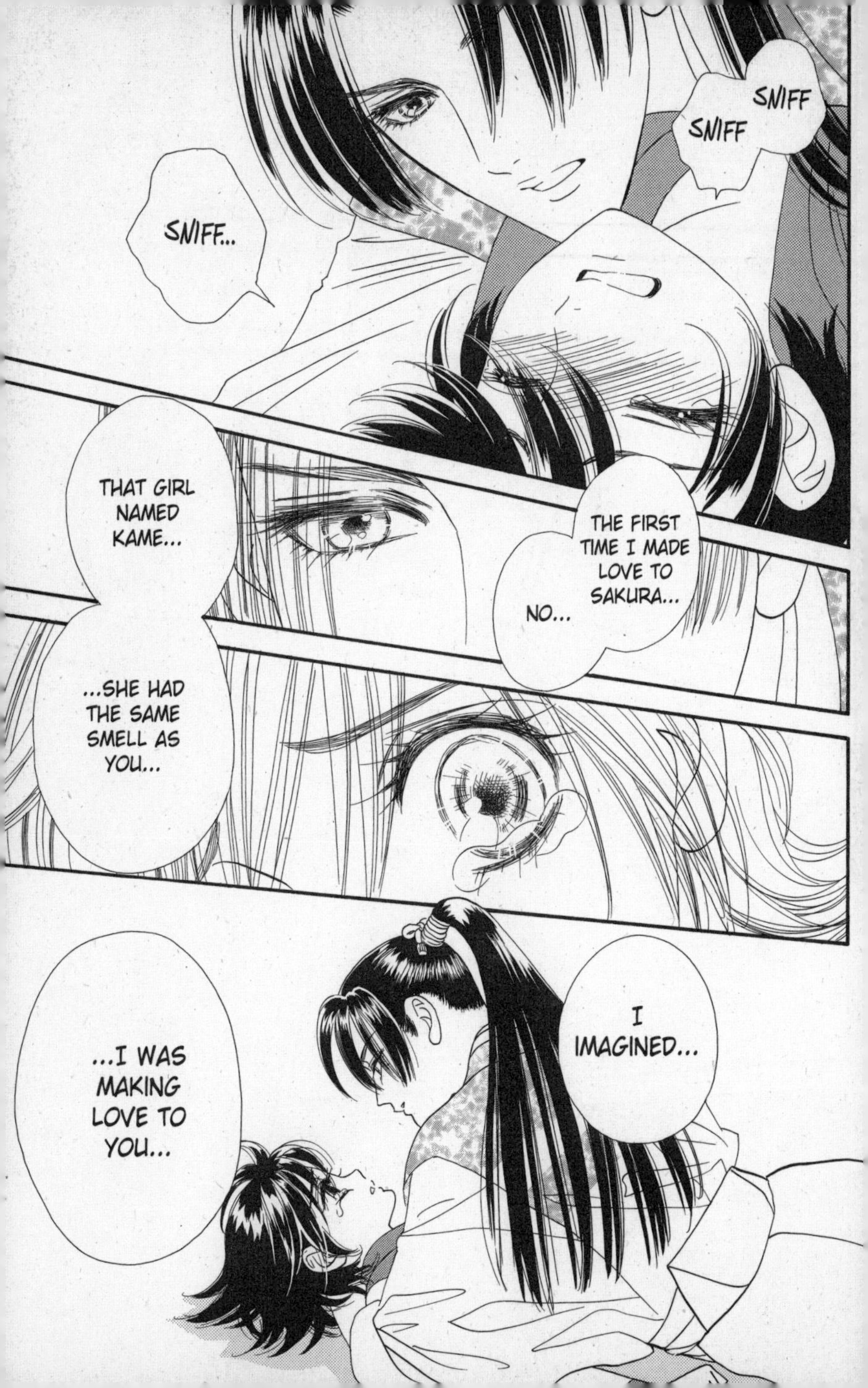
SNIFF
SNIFF
SNIFF...
THAT GIRL NAMED KAME...
...SHE HAD THE SAME SMELL AS YOU...
NO...
THE FIRST TIME I MADE LOVE TO SAKURA...
I IMAGINED...
...I WAS MAKING LOVE TO YOU...

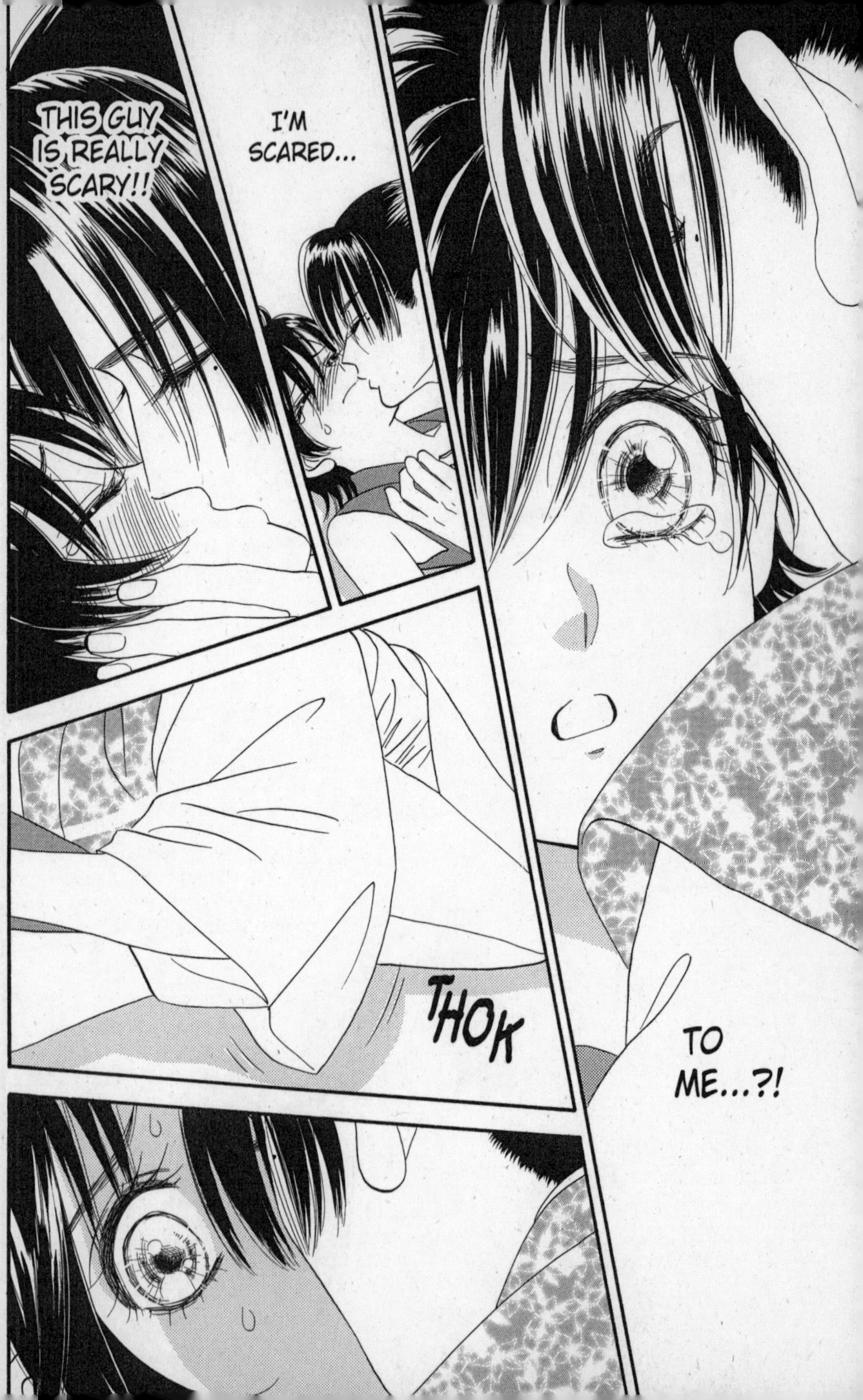
TO ME...?!
I'M SCARED...
THIS GUY IS REALLY SCARY!!
THOK

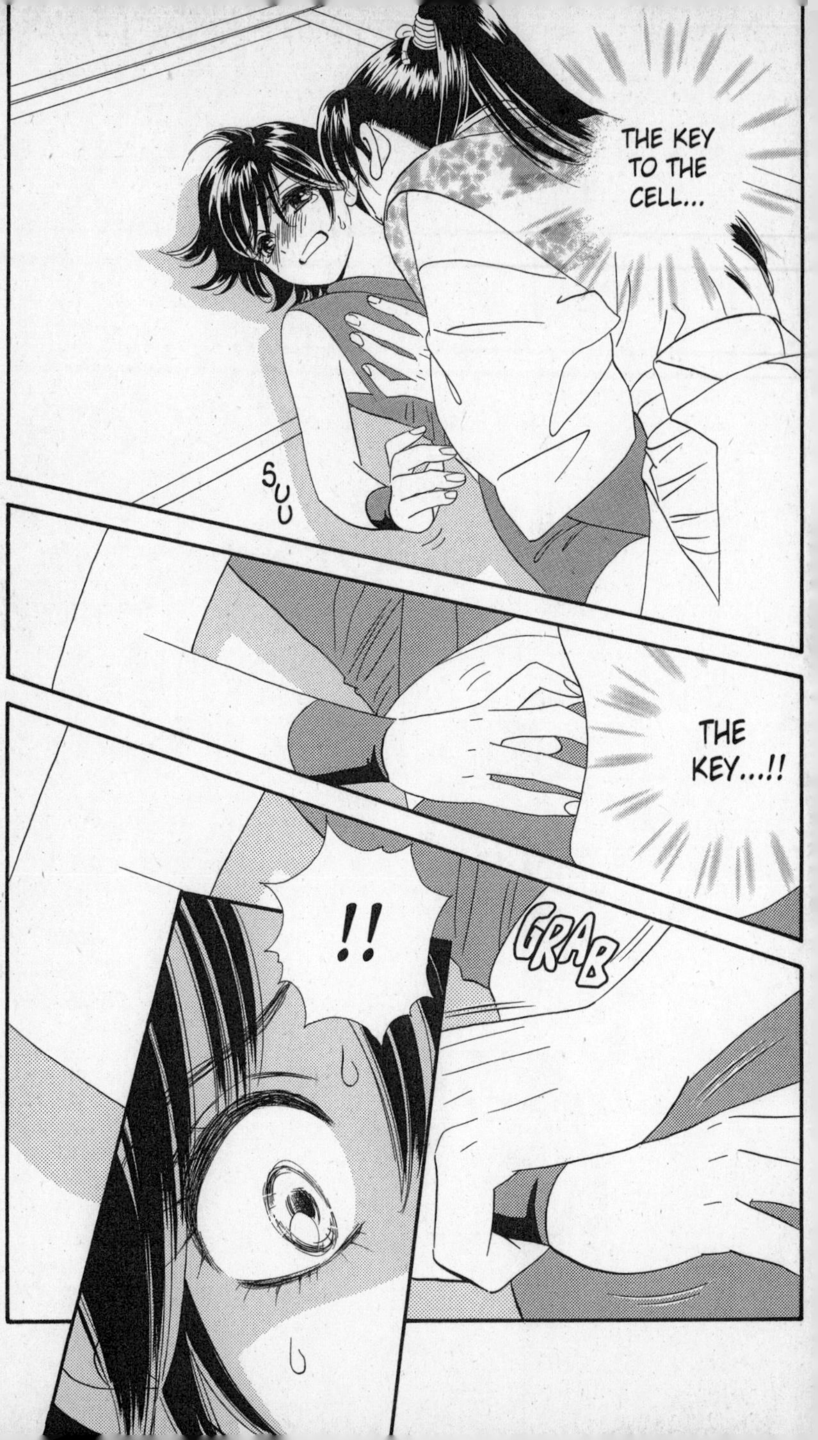
THE KEY TO THE CELL...
SUU
THE KEY...!!
GRAB
!!

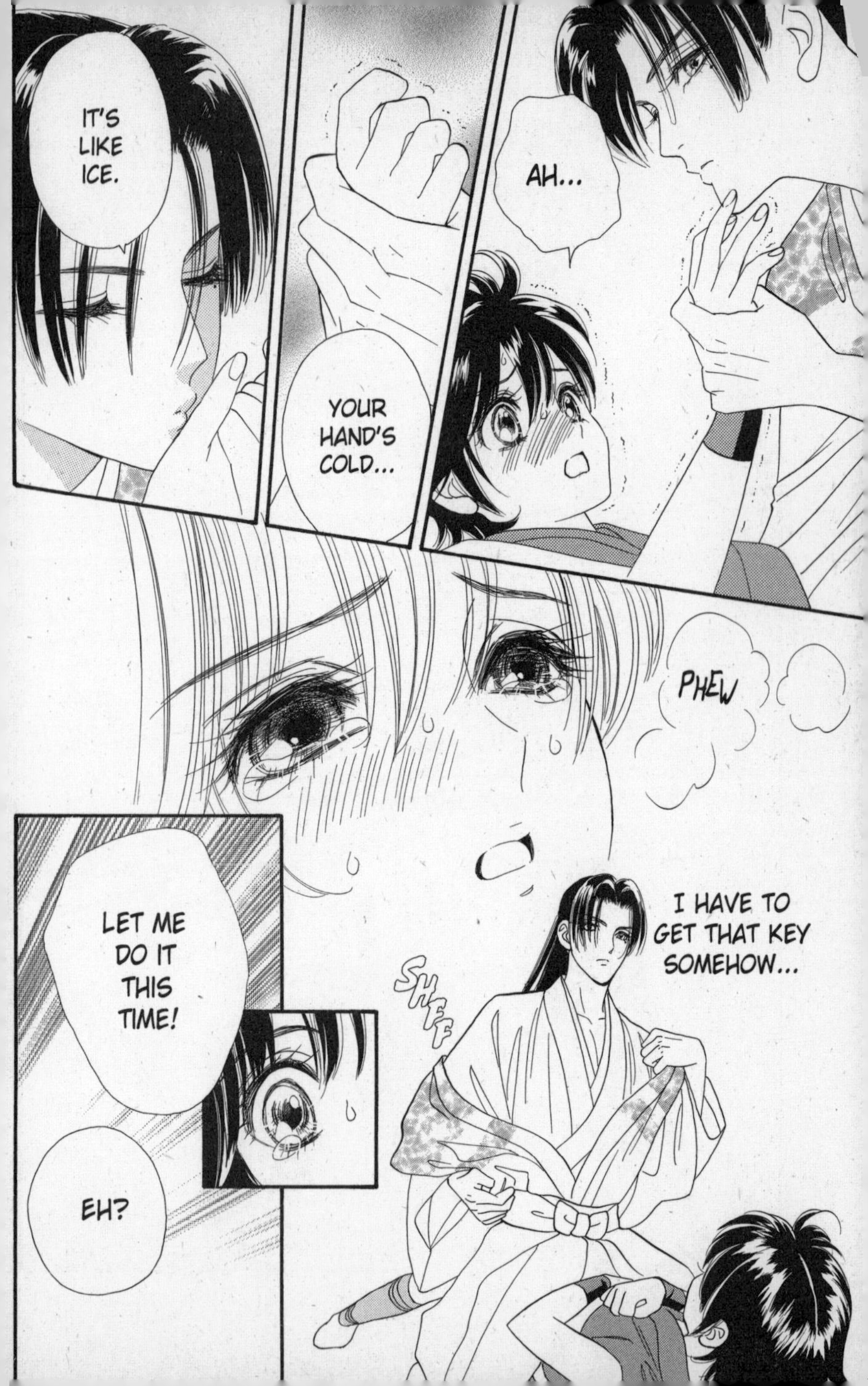
AH...
YOUR HAND'S COLD...
IT'S LIKE ICE.
PHEW
I HAVE TO GET THAT KEY SOMEHOW...
SHFF
LET ME DO IT THIS TIME!
EH?

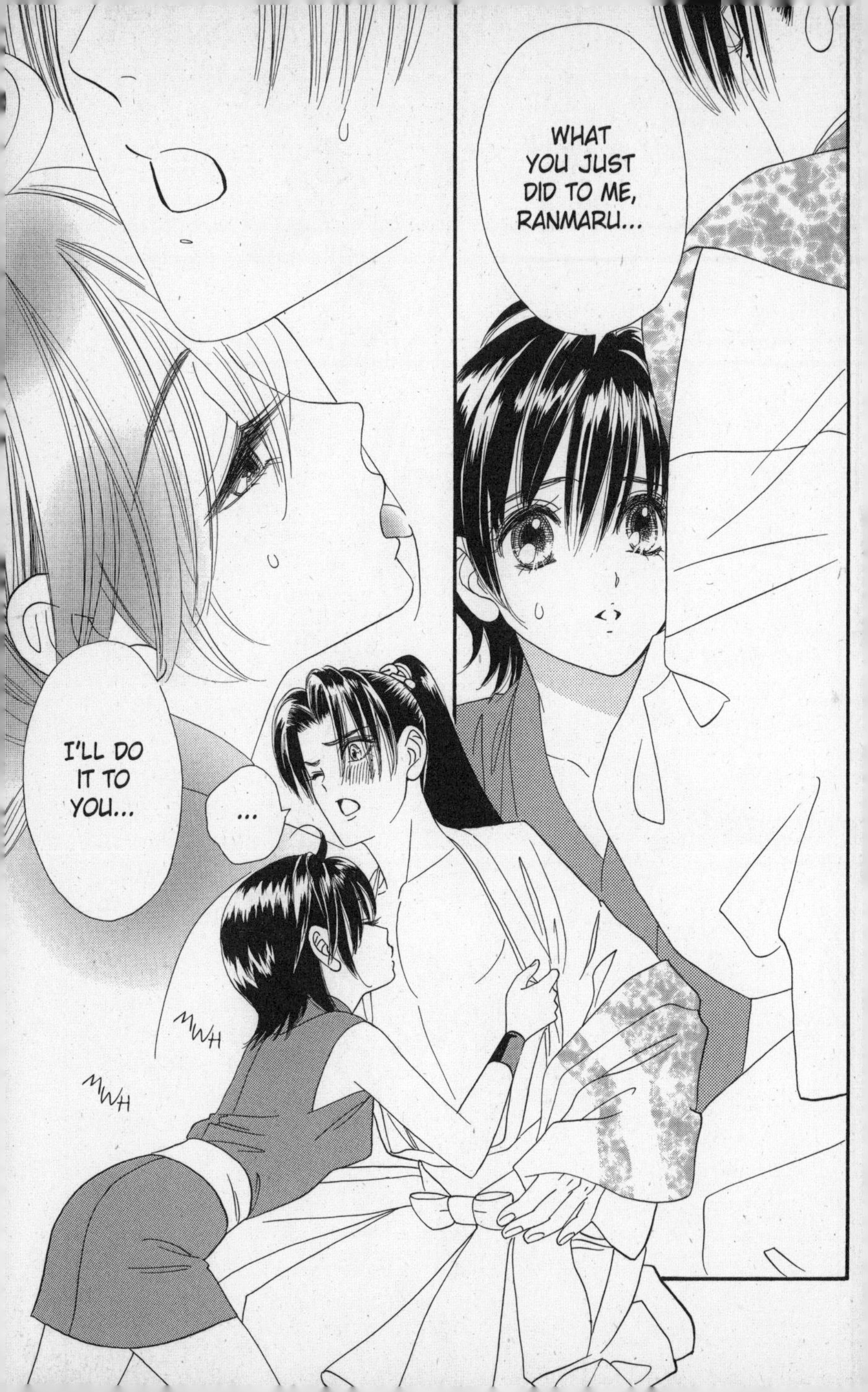
WHAT YOU JUST DID TO ME, RANMARU...
I'LL DO IT TO YOU...
...
MWH
MWH

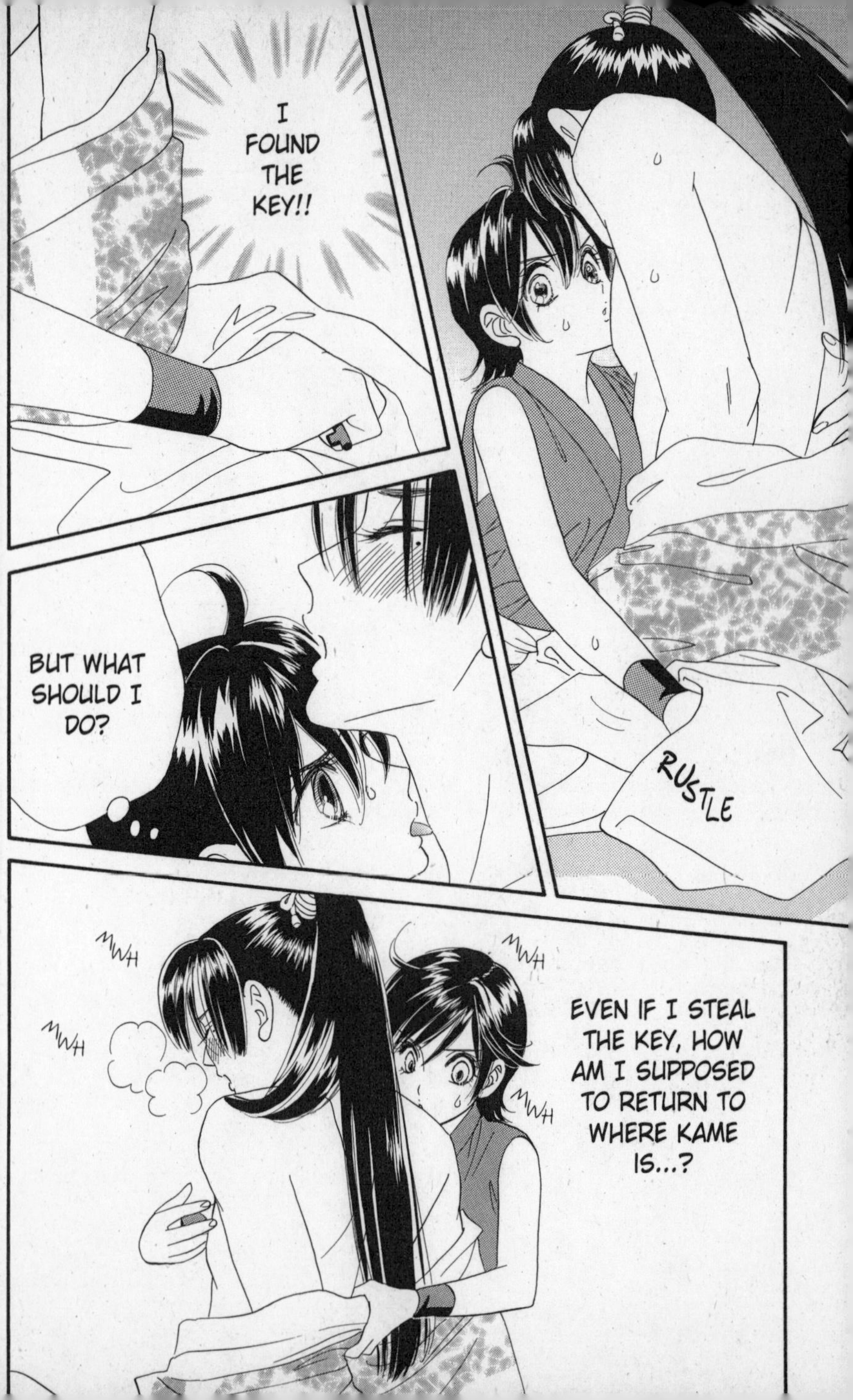
RUSTLE
I FOUND THE KEY!!
BUT WHAT SHOULD I DO?
MWH
EVEN IF I STEAL THE KEY, HOW AM I SUPPOSED TO RETURN TO WHERE KAME IS...?
MWH
MWH
MWH

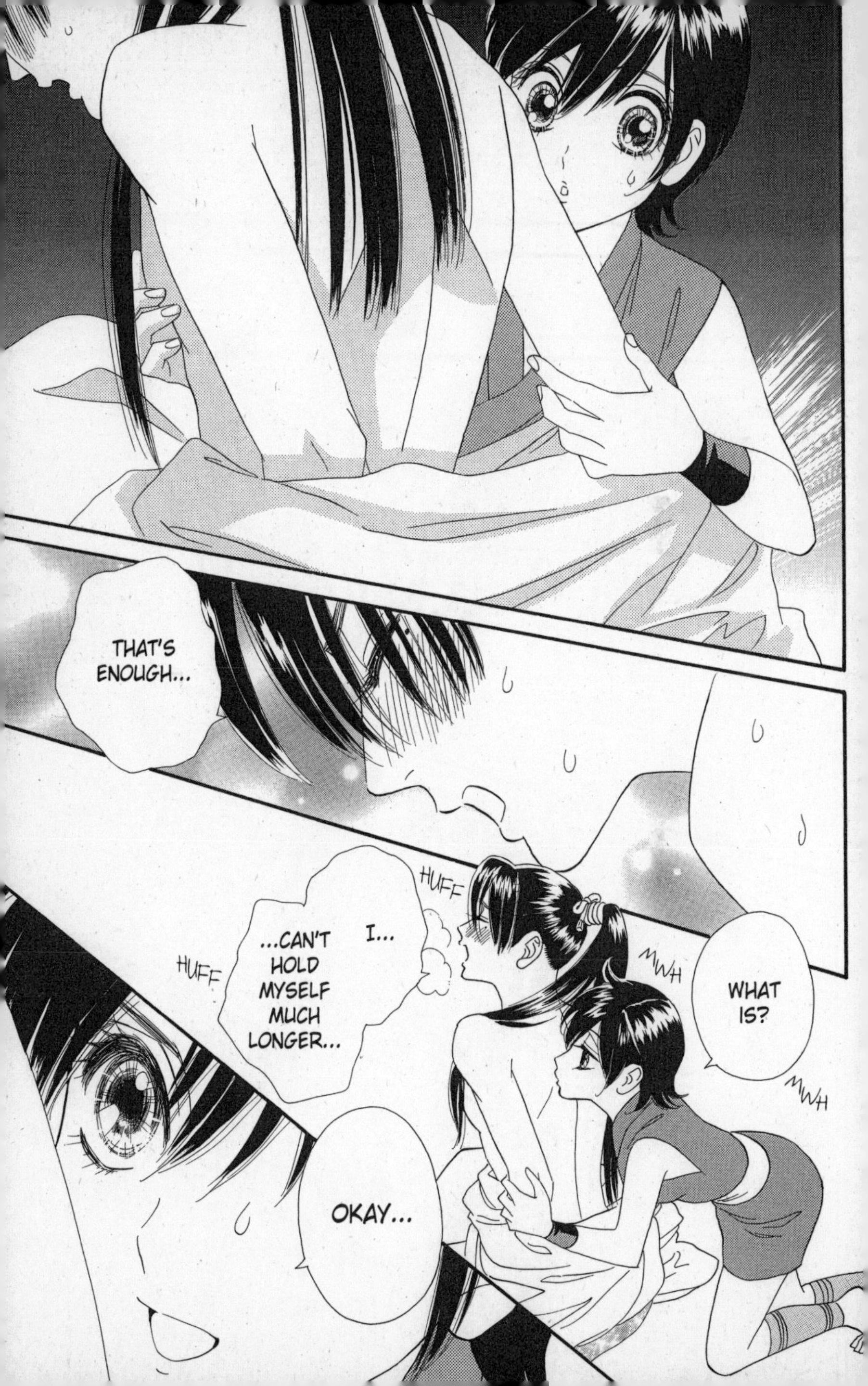
THAT'S ENOUGH...
MWH
WHAT IS?
MWH
HUFF
I...
...CAN'T HOLD MYSELF MUCH LONGER...
HUFF
OKAY...

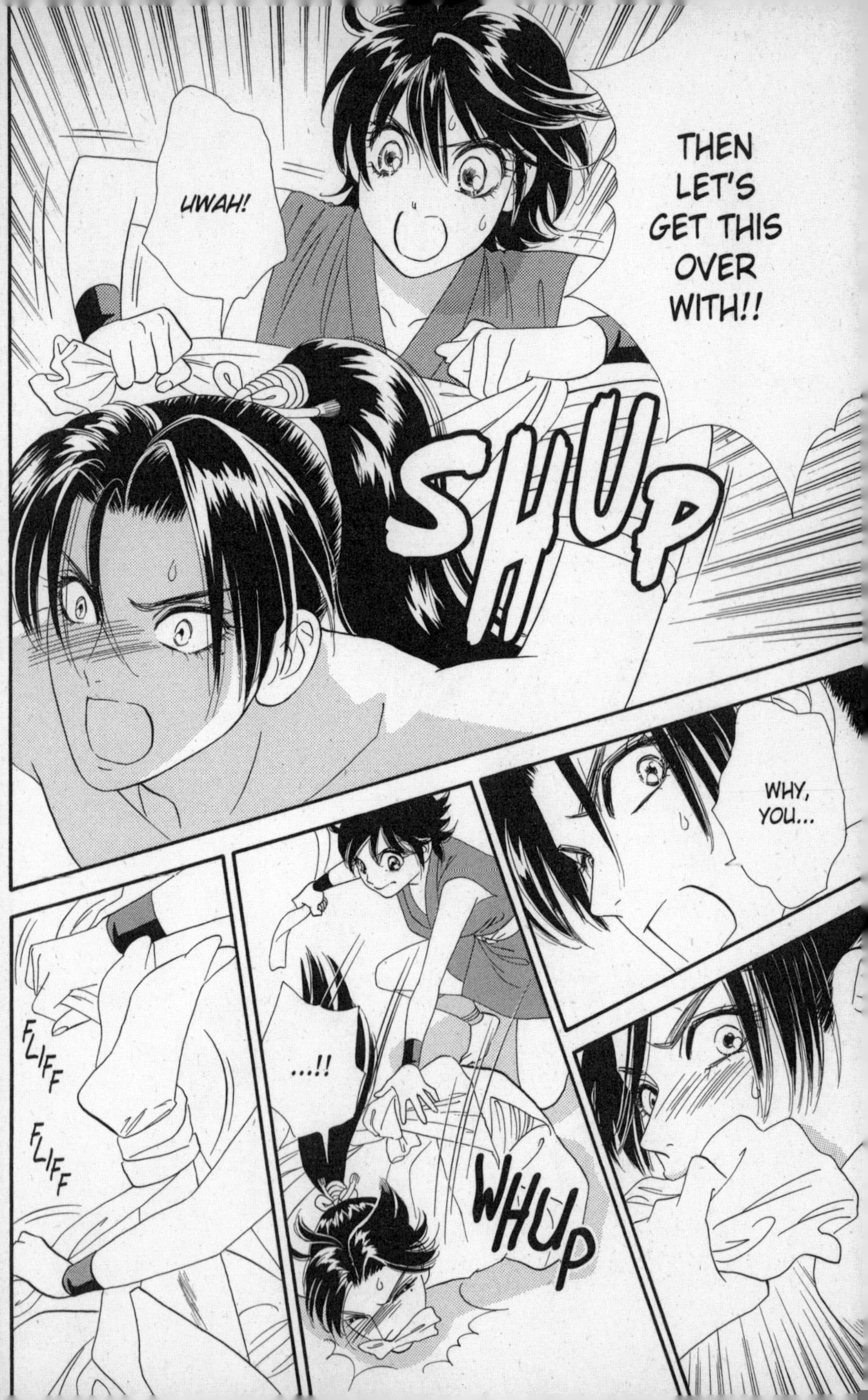
THEN LET'S GET THIS OVER WITH!!
SHUP
UWAH!
WHY, YOU...
...!!
WHUP
FLIFF
FLIFF

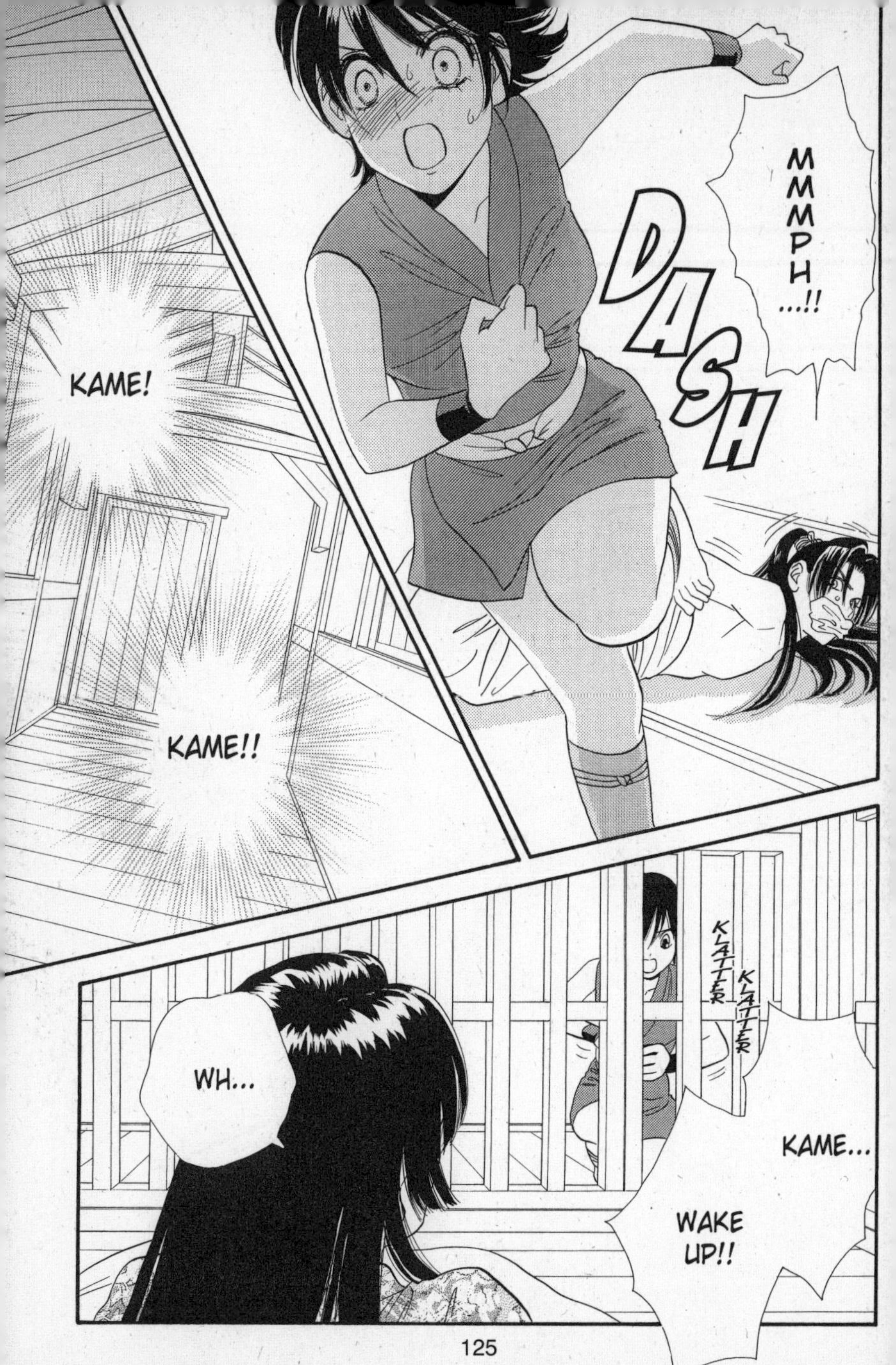
MMMPH...!!
DASH
KAME!
KAME!!
KLATTER KLATTER
KAME...
WAKE UP!!
WH...

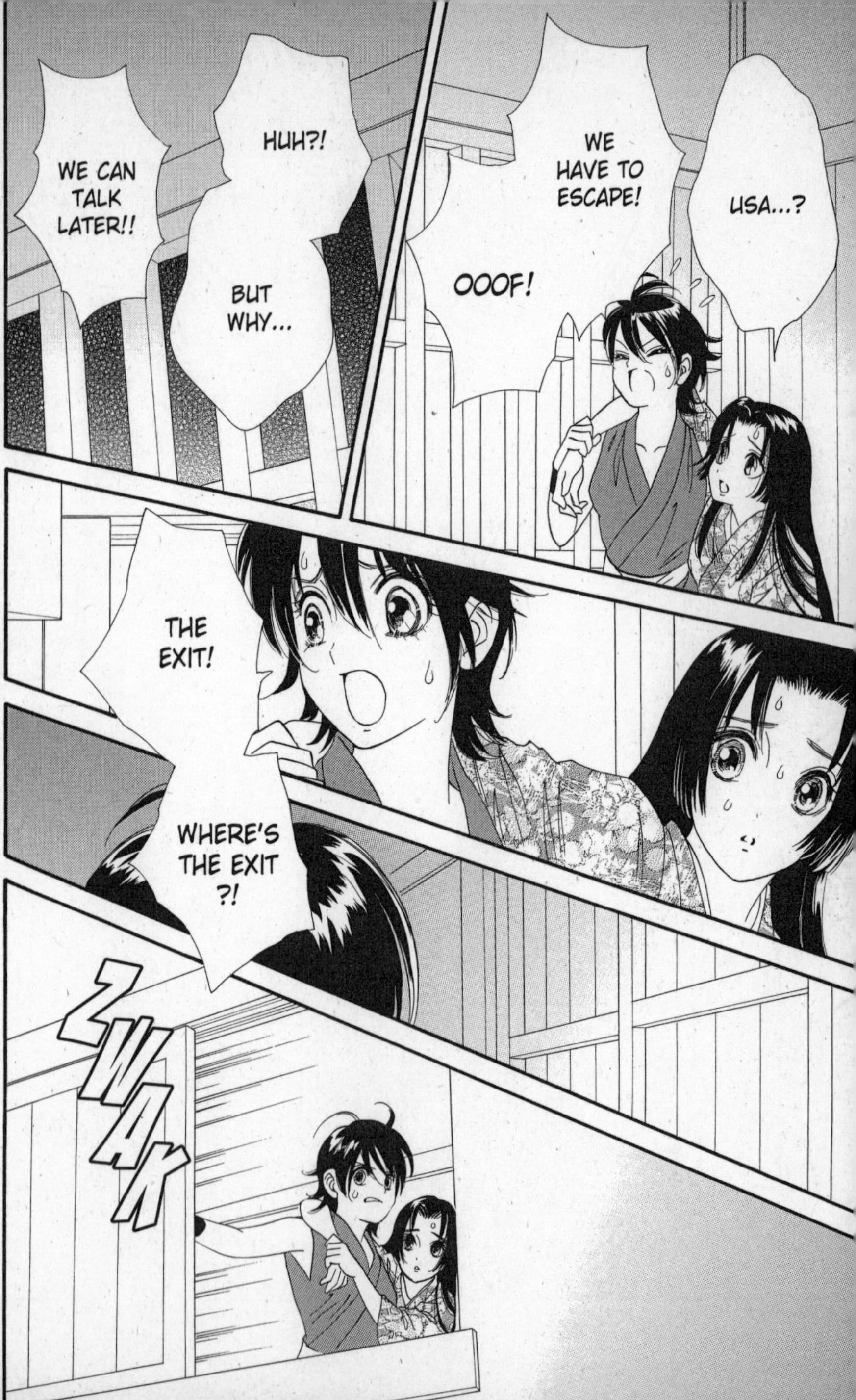
USA...?
WE HAVE TO ESCAPE!
OOOF!
HUH?!
BUT WHY...
WE CAN TALK LATER!!
THE EXIT!
WHERE'S THE EXIT ?!
ZWAK

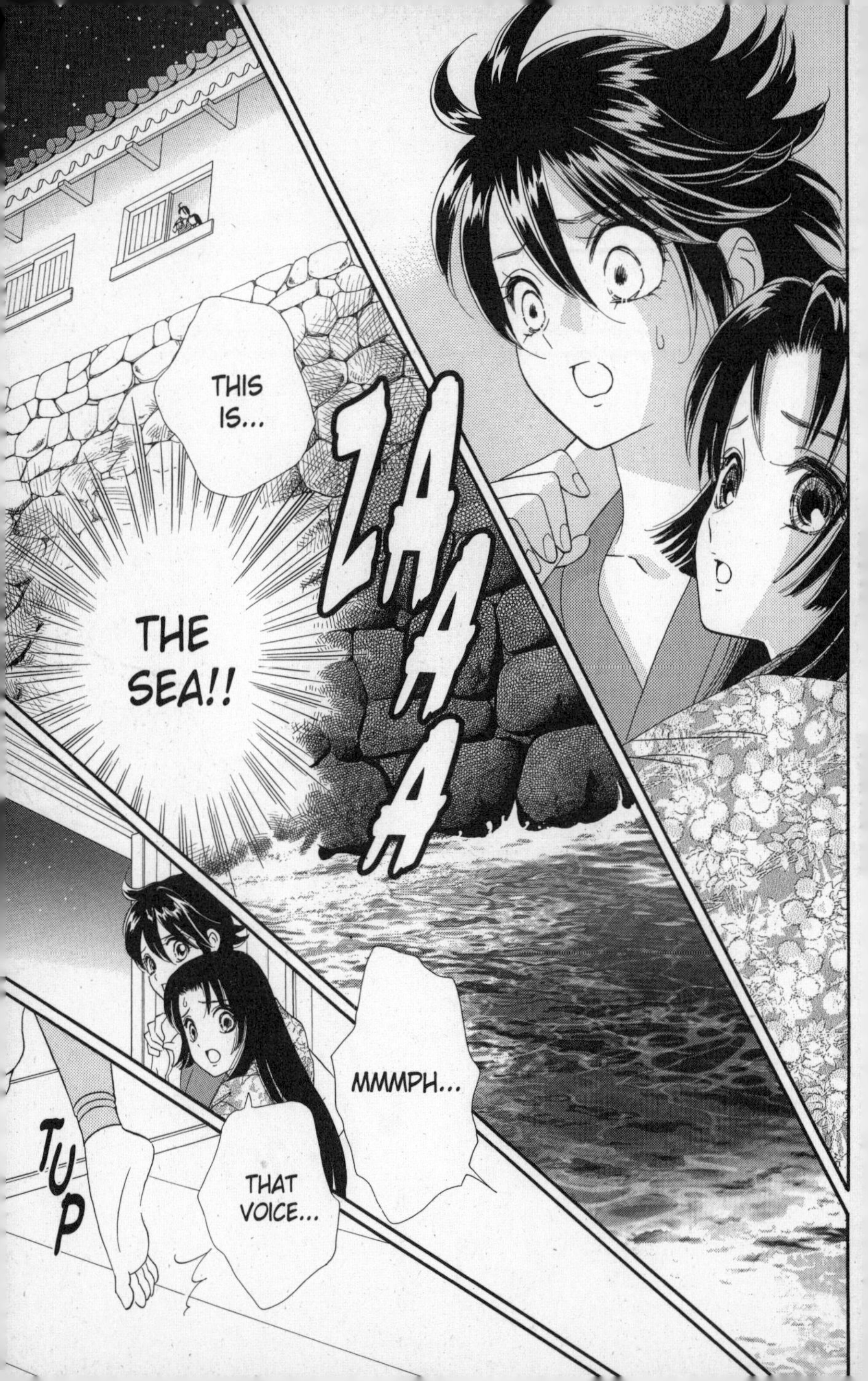
THIS IS...
ZAAA
THE SEA!!
MMMPH...
THAT VOICE...
TUP

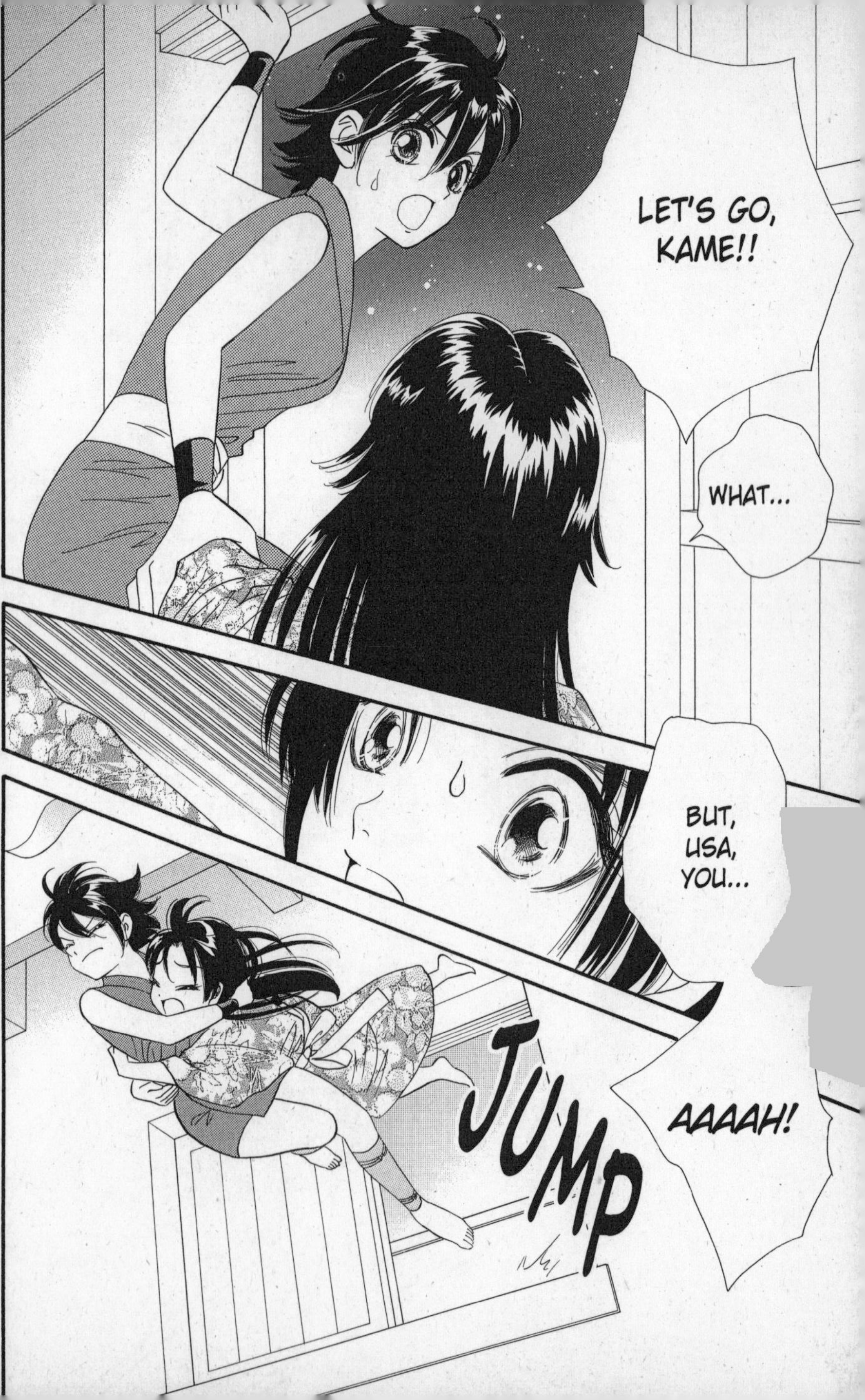
LET'S GO, KAME!!
WHAT...
BUT, USA, YOU...
AAAAH!
JUMP

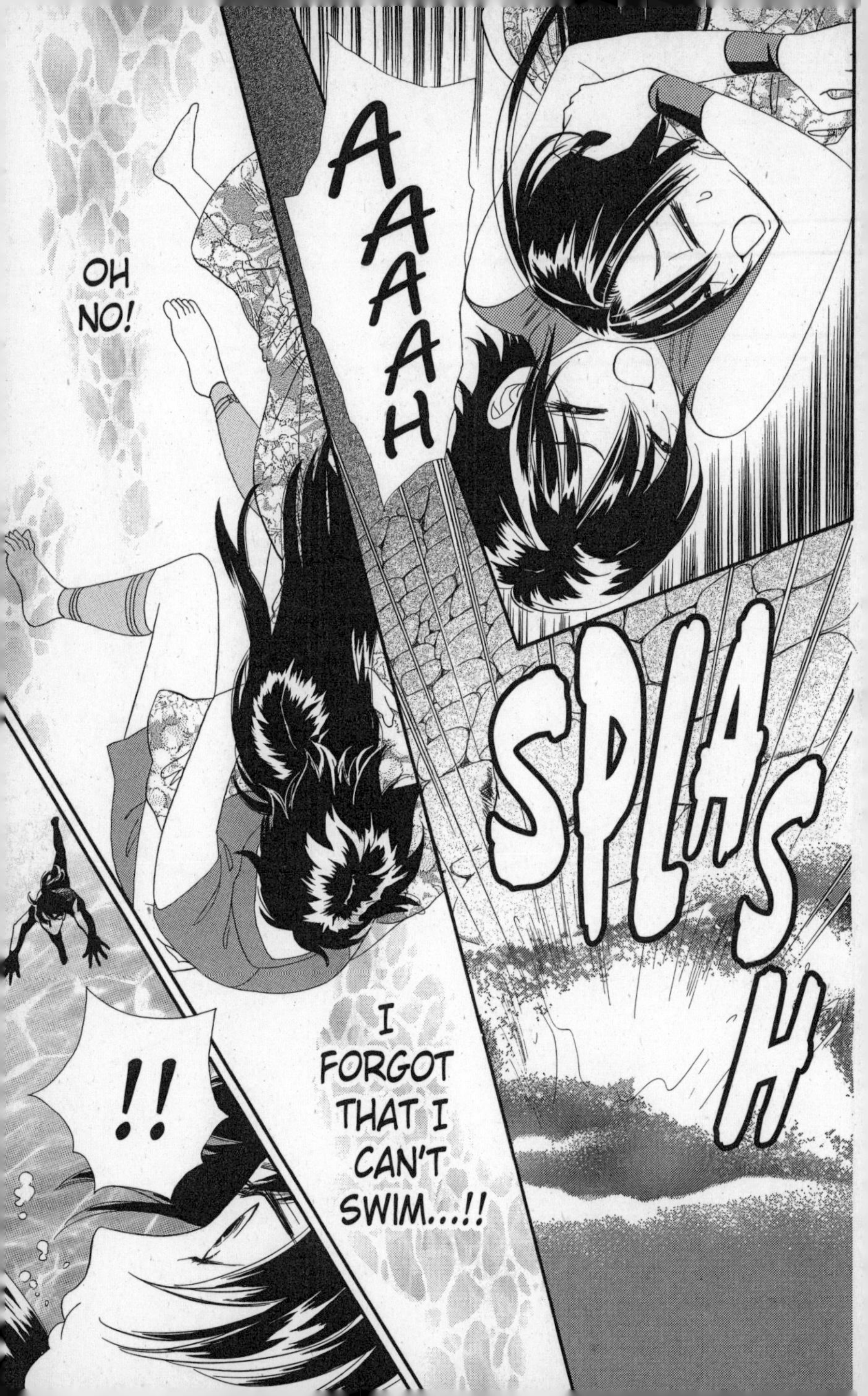
AAAAAH
SPLASH
OH NO!
I FORGOT THAT I CAN'T SWIM...!!
!!

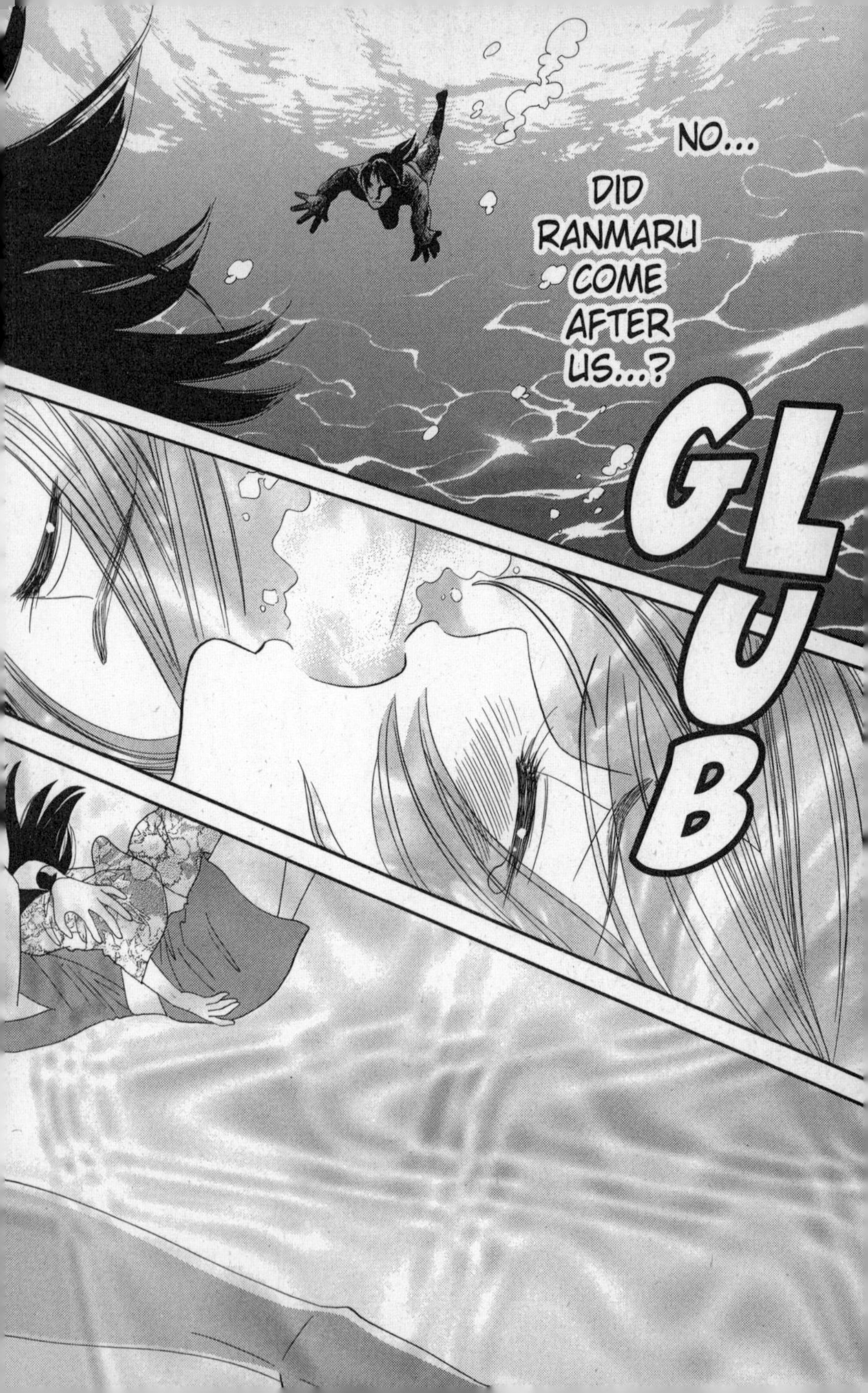
NO...
DID RANMARU COME AFTER US...?
GLUB

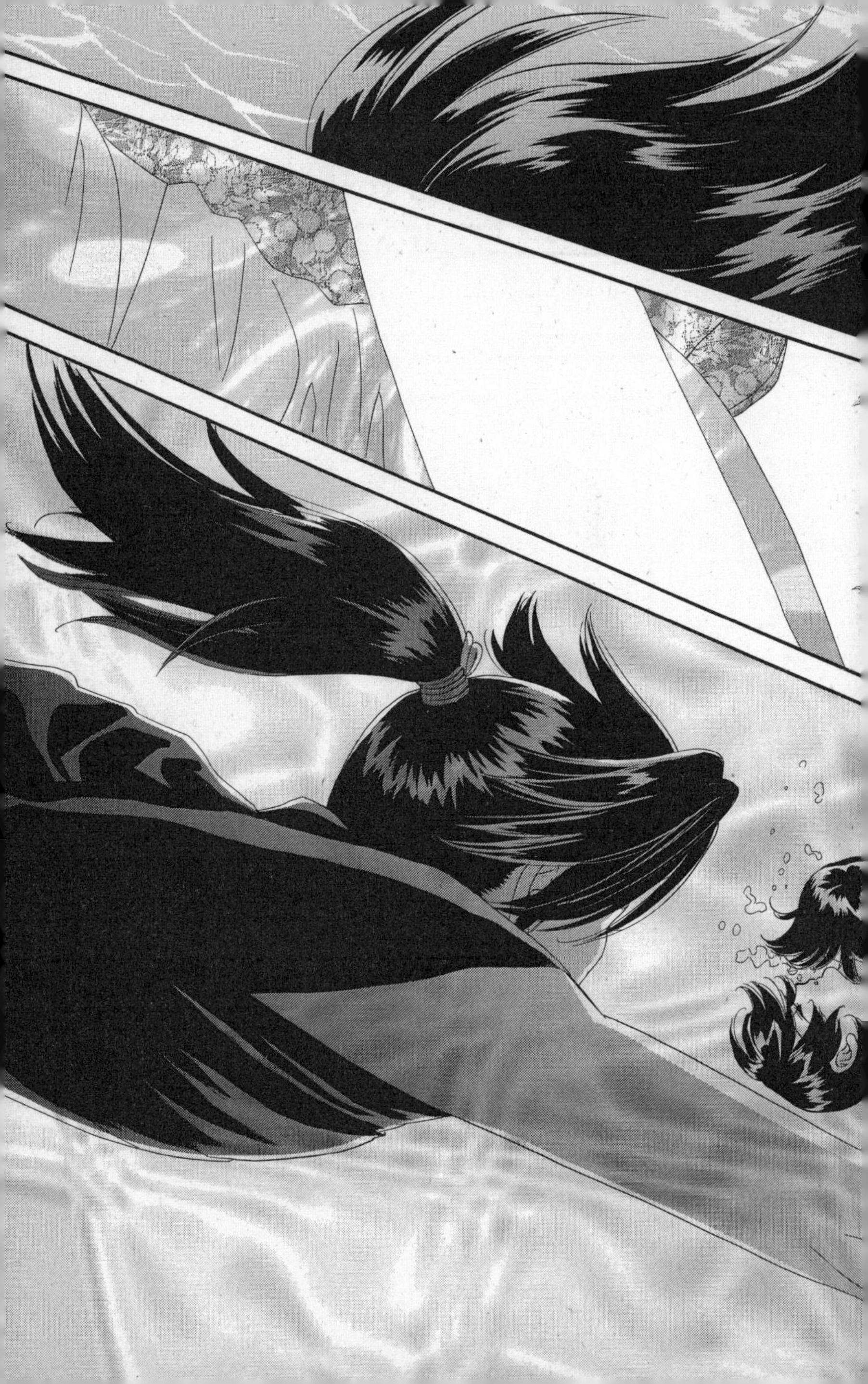

TAIL OF THE MOON EXTRA: TODAY'S MISSION
"I WANT TO SEE USAGI AS A BOY!"
-AI, ISHIKAWA PREFECTURE

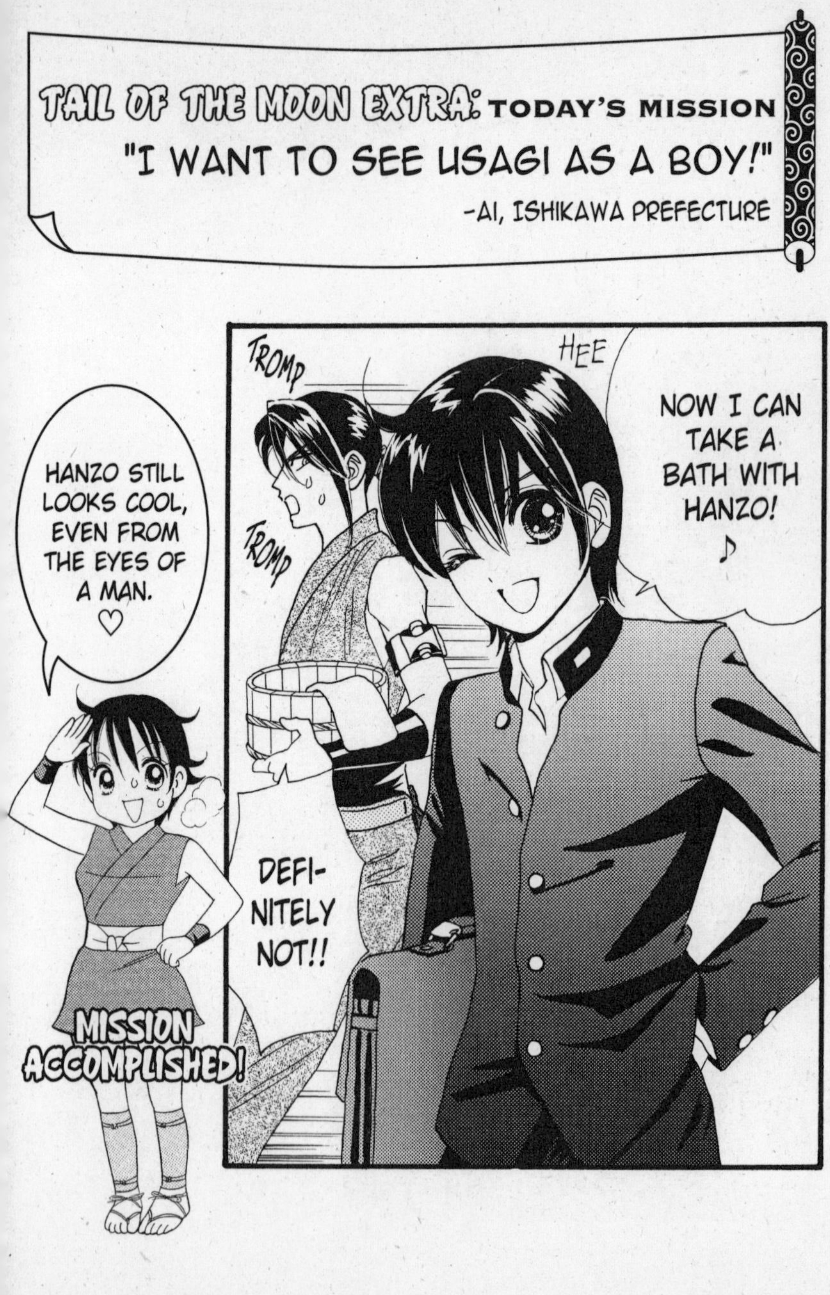
HEE
NOW I CAN TAKE A BATH WITH HANZO! ♪
TROMP
TROMP
DEFI-NITELY NOT!!
HANZO STILL LOOKS COOL, EVEN FROM THE EYES OF A MAN. ♡
MISSION ACCOMPLISHED!

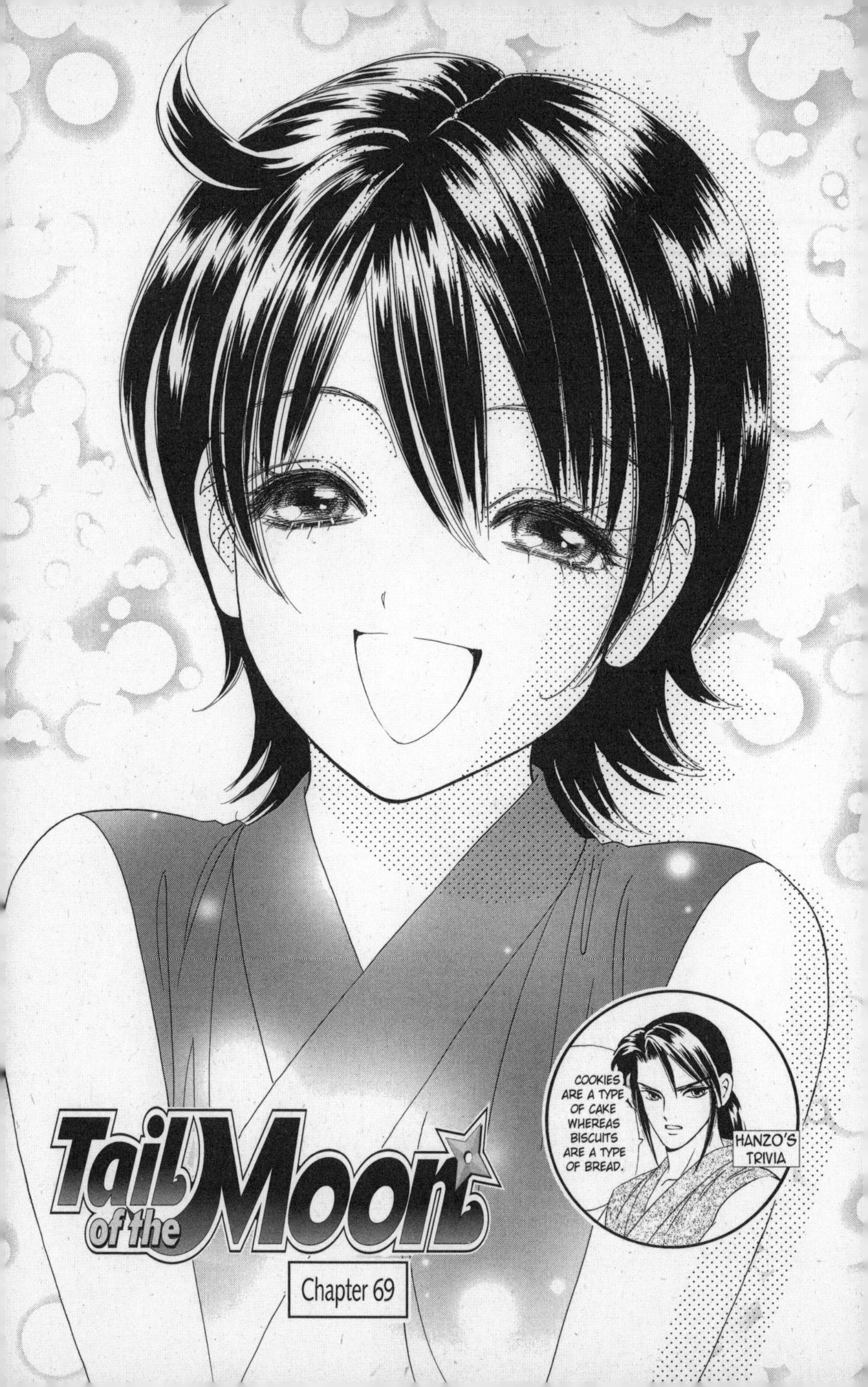
Tail of the Moon
Chapter 69
COOKIES ARE A TYPE OF CAKE WHEREAS BISCUITS ARE A TYPE OF BREAD.
HANZO'S TRIVIA

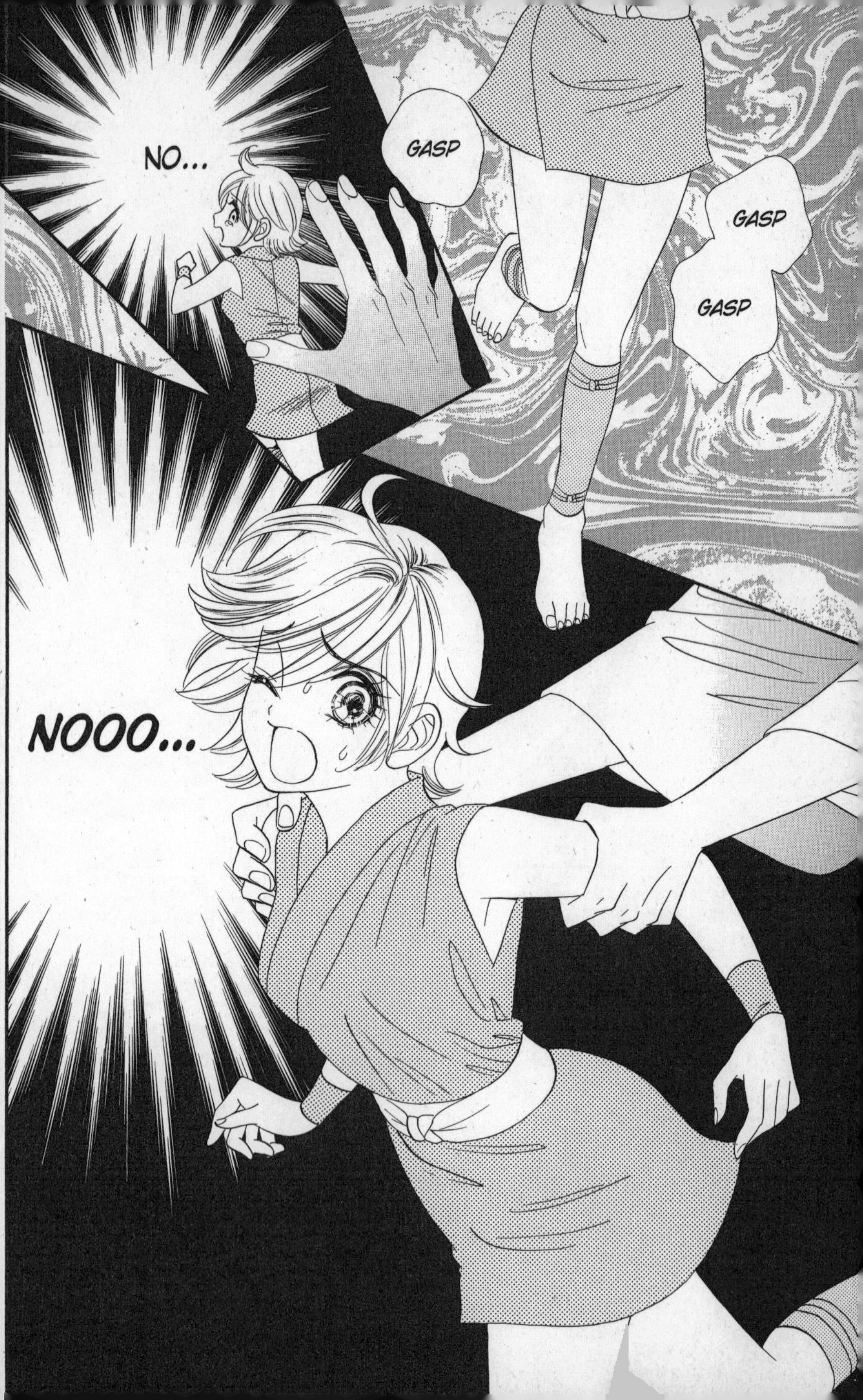

GASP
GASP
GASP
NO...
NOOO...

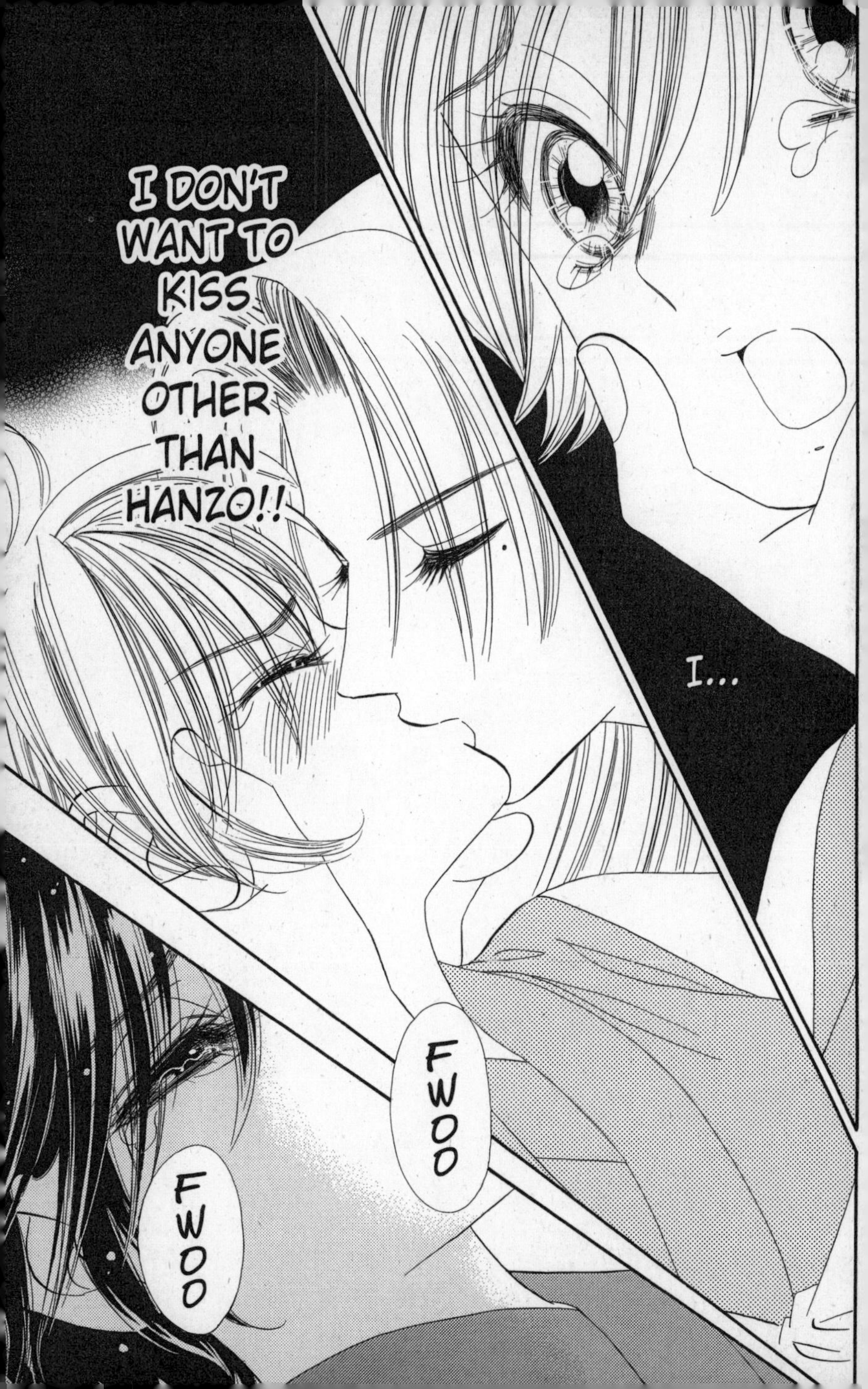
I...
I DON'T WANT TO KISS ANYONE OTHER THAN HANZO!!
FWOO
FWOO

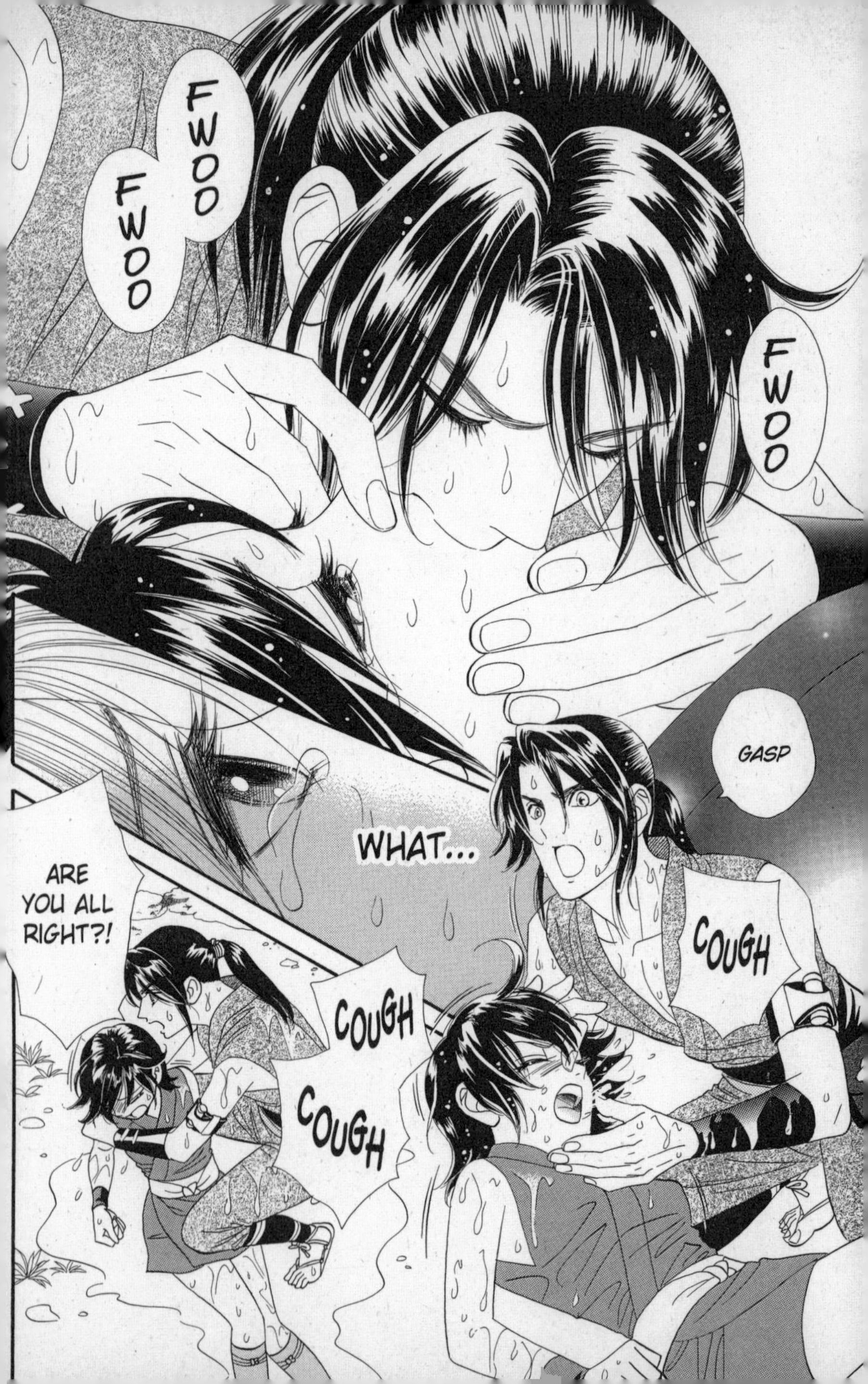
FWOO
FWOO
FWOO
GASP
WHAT...
COUGH
COUGH
COUGH
ARE YOU ALL RIGHT?!

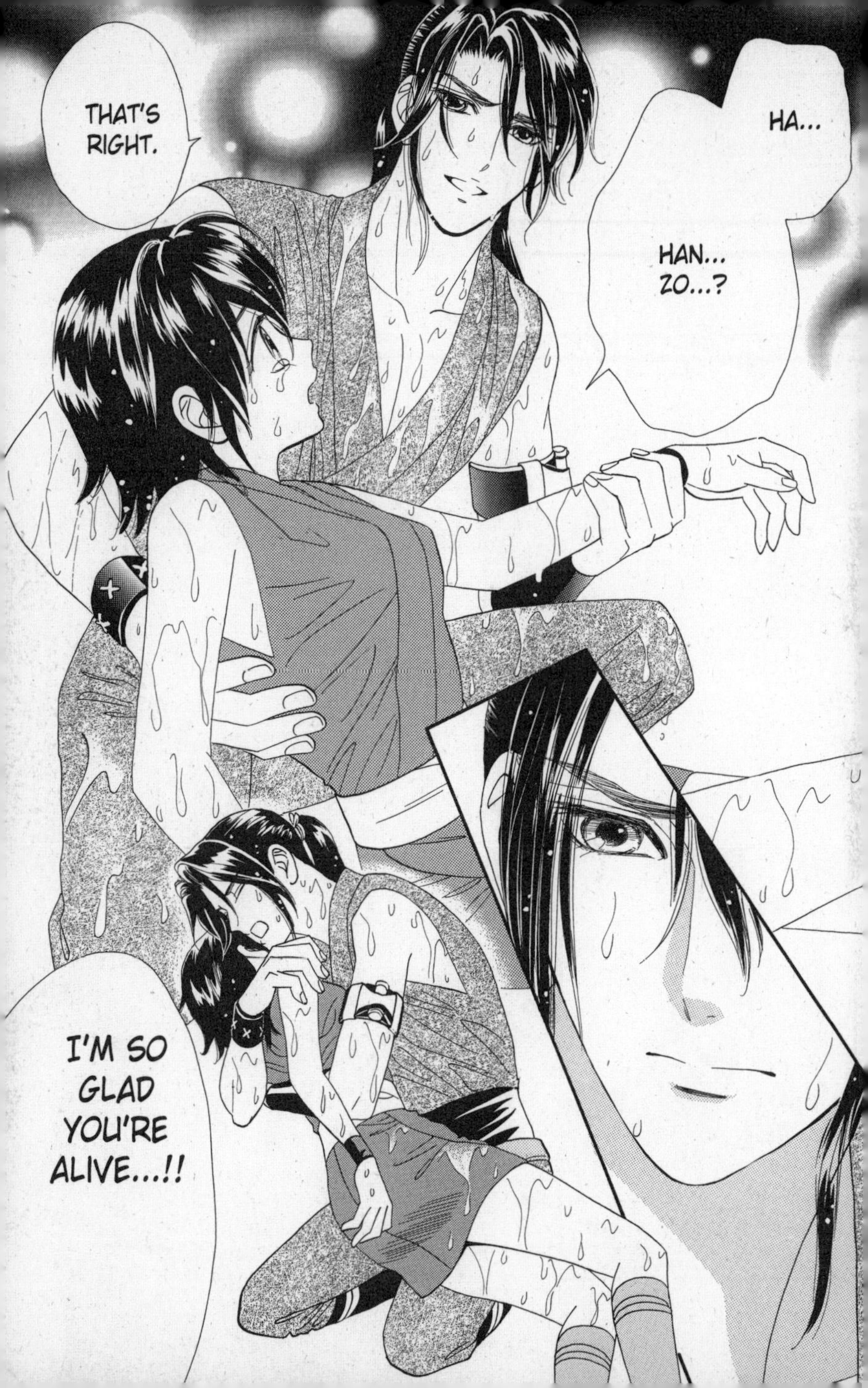
HA...
HAN... ZO...?
THAT'S RIGHT.
I'M SO GLAD YOU'RE ALIVE...!!

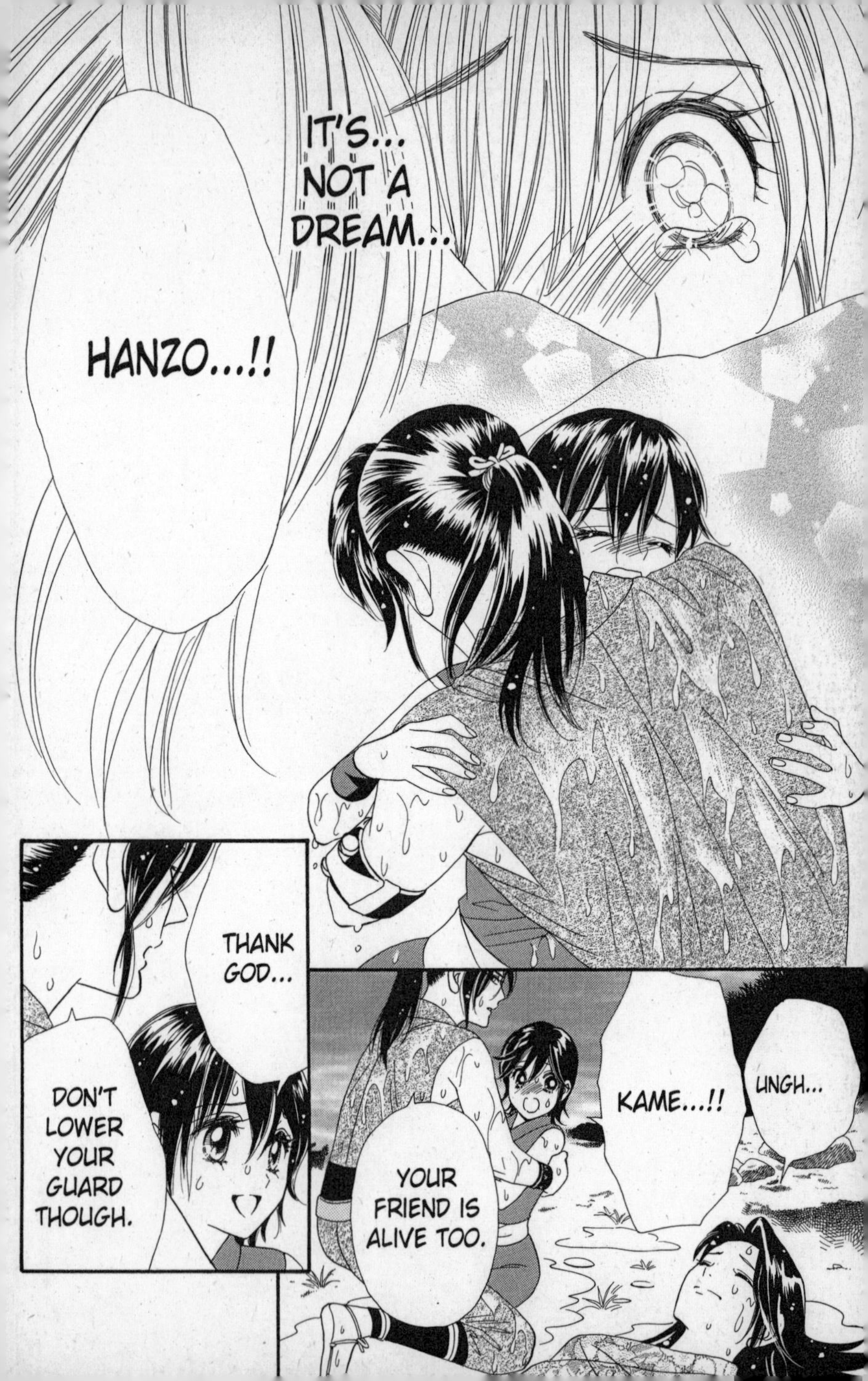
IT'S... NOT A DREAM...
HANZO...!!
THANK GOD...
DON'T LOWER YOUR GUARD THOUGH.
UNGH...
KAME...!!
YOUR FRIEND IS ALIVE TOO.

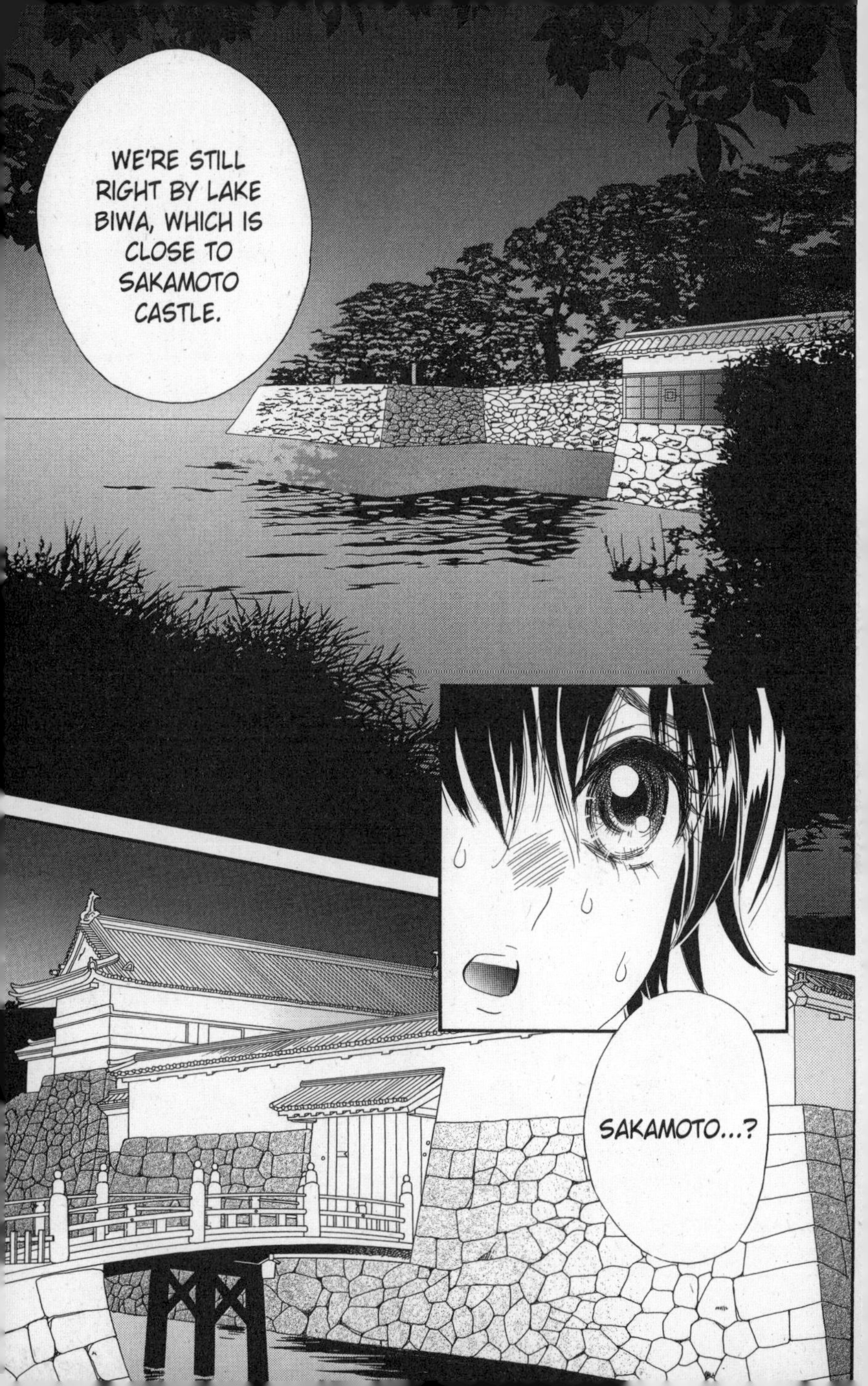
WE'RE STILL RIGHT BY LAKE BIWA, WHICH IS CLOSE TO SAKAMOTO CASTLE.
SAKAMOTO...?

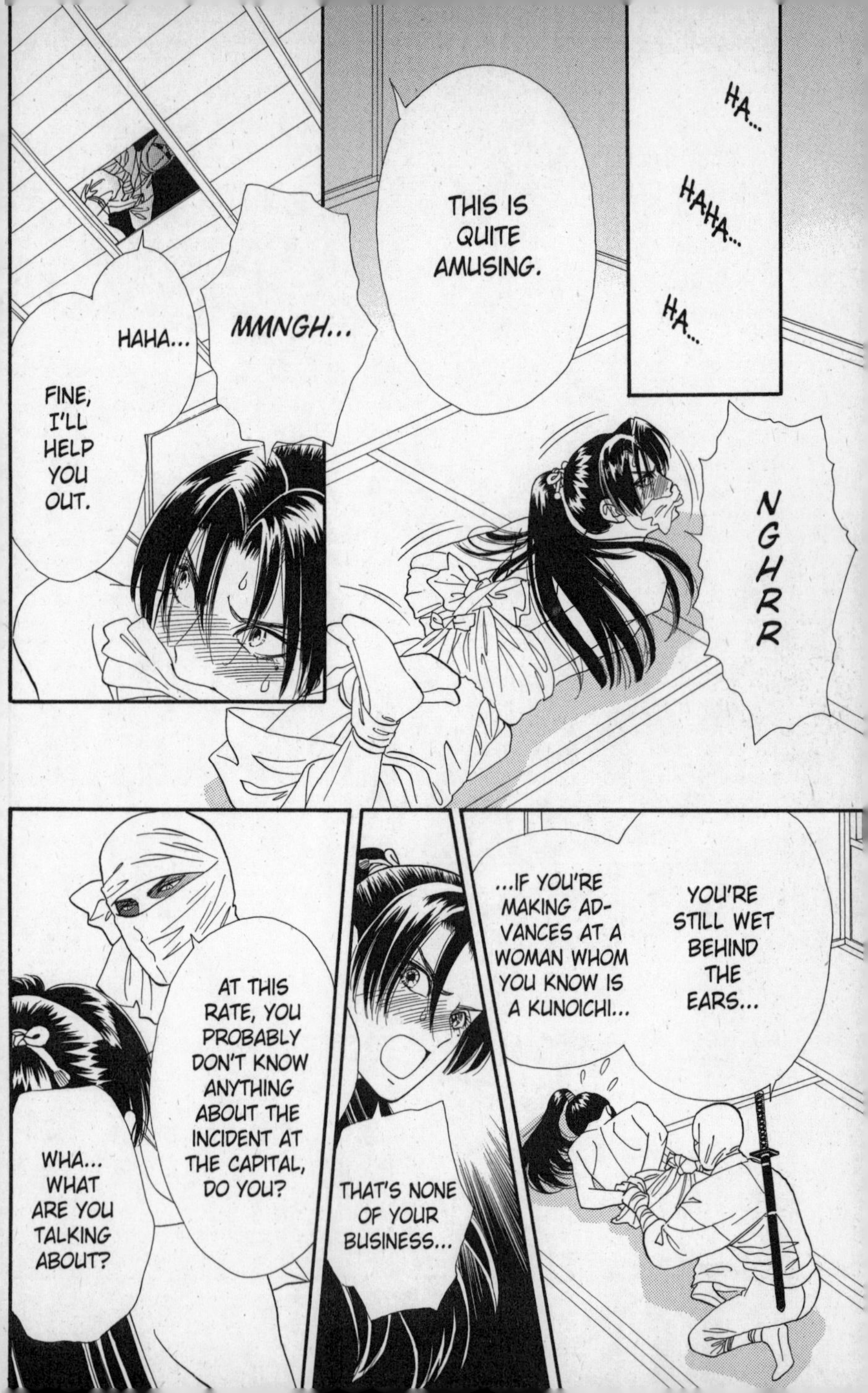
HA...
HAHA...
HA...
THIS IS QUITE AMUSING.
NGHRR
MMNGH...
HAHA...
FINE, I'LL HELP YOU OUT.
YOU'RE STILL WET BEHIND THE EARS...
...IF YOU'RE MAKING AD-VANCES AT A WOMAN WHOM YOU KNOW IS A KUNOICHI...
THAT'S NONE OF YOUR BUSINESS...
AT THIS RATE, YOU PROBABLY DON'T KNOW ANYTHING ABOUT THE INCIDENT AT THE CAPITAL, DO YOU?
WHA... WHAT ARE YOU TALKING ABOUT?

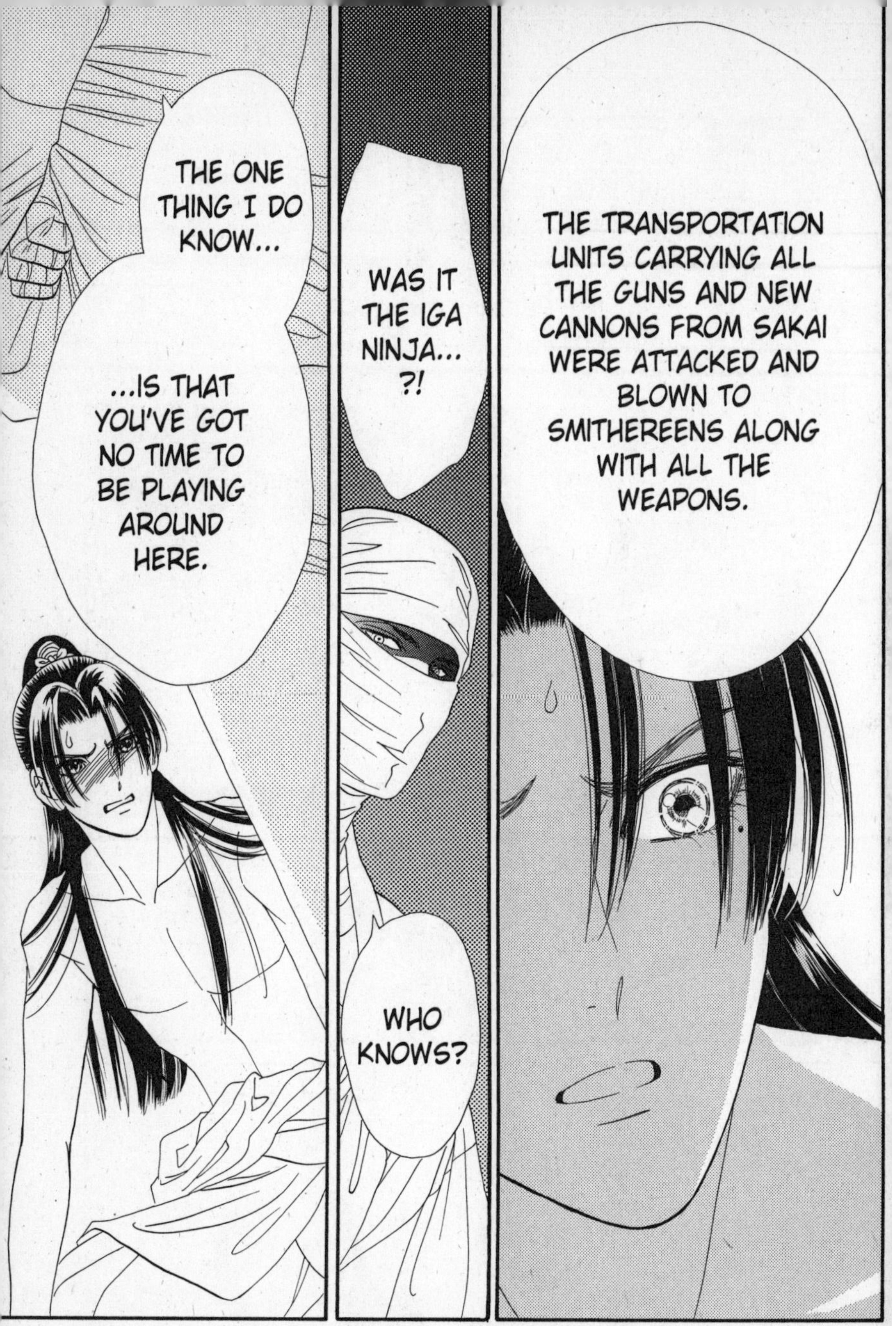
THE TRANSPORTATION UNITS CARRYING ALL THE GUNS AND NEW CANNONS FROM SAKAI WERE ATTACKED AND BLOWN TO SMITHEREENS ALONG WITH ALL THE WEAPONS.
WAS IT THE IGA NINJA...?!
WHO KNOWS?
THE ONE THING I DO KNOW...
...IS THAT YOU'VE GOT NO TIME TO BE PLAYING AROUND HERE.

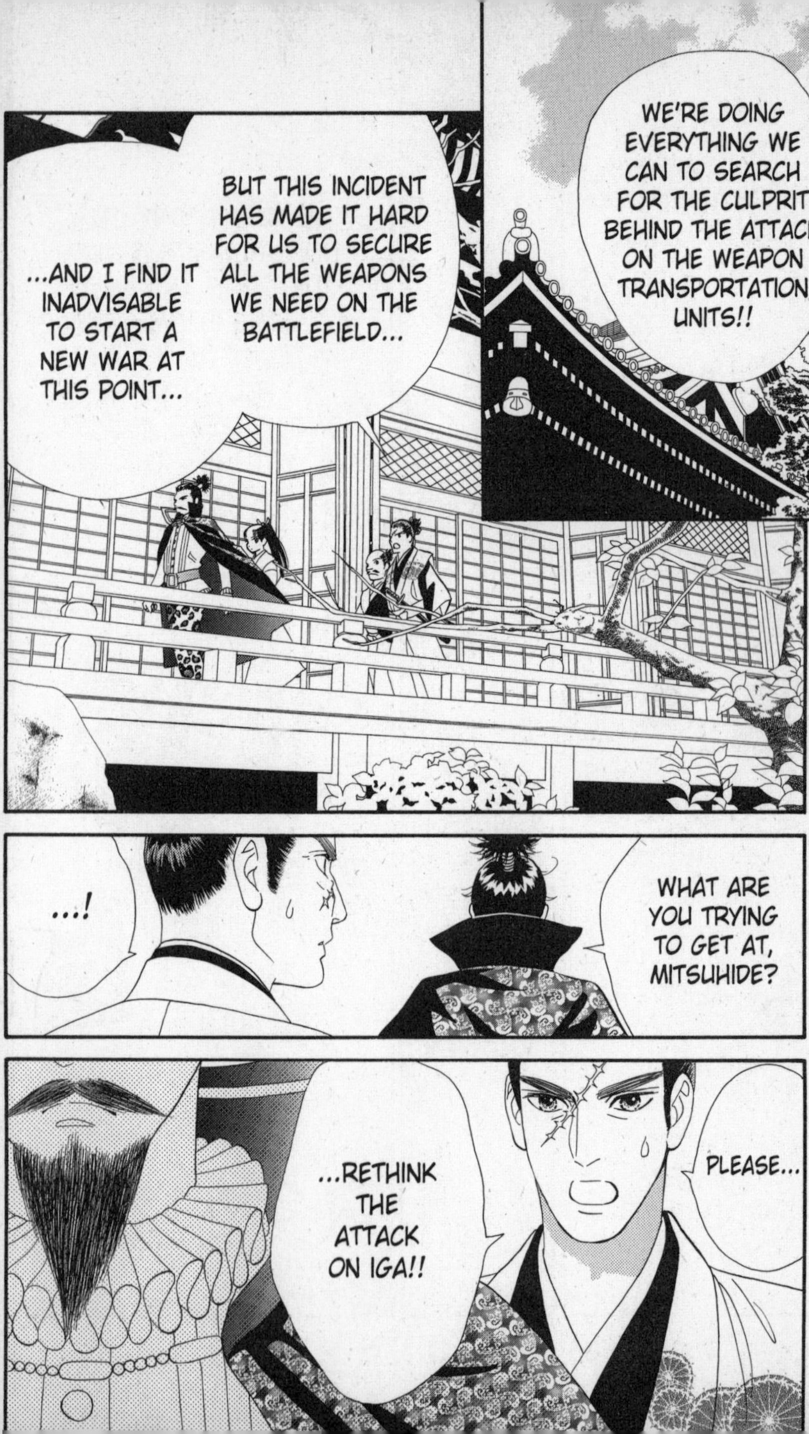
WE'RE DOING EVERYTHING WE CAN TO SEARCH FOR THE CULPRIT BEHIND THE ATTACK ON THE WEAPON TRANSPORTATION UNITS!!
BUT THIS INCIDENT HAS MADE IT HARD FOR US TO SECURE ALL THE WEAPONS WE NEED ON THE BATTLEFIELD...
...AND I FIND IT INADVISABLE TO START A NEW WAR AT THIS POINT...
WHAT ARE YOU TRYING TO GET AT, MITSUHIDE?
...!
PLEASE...
...RETHINK THE ATTACK ON IGA!!

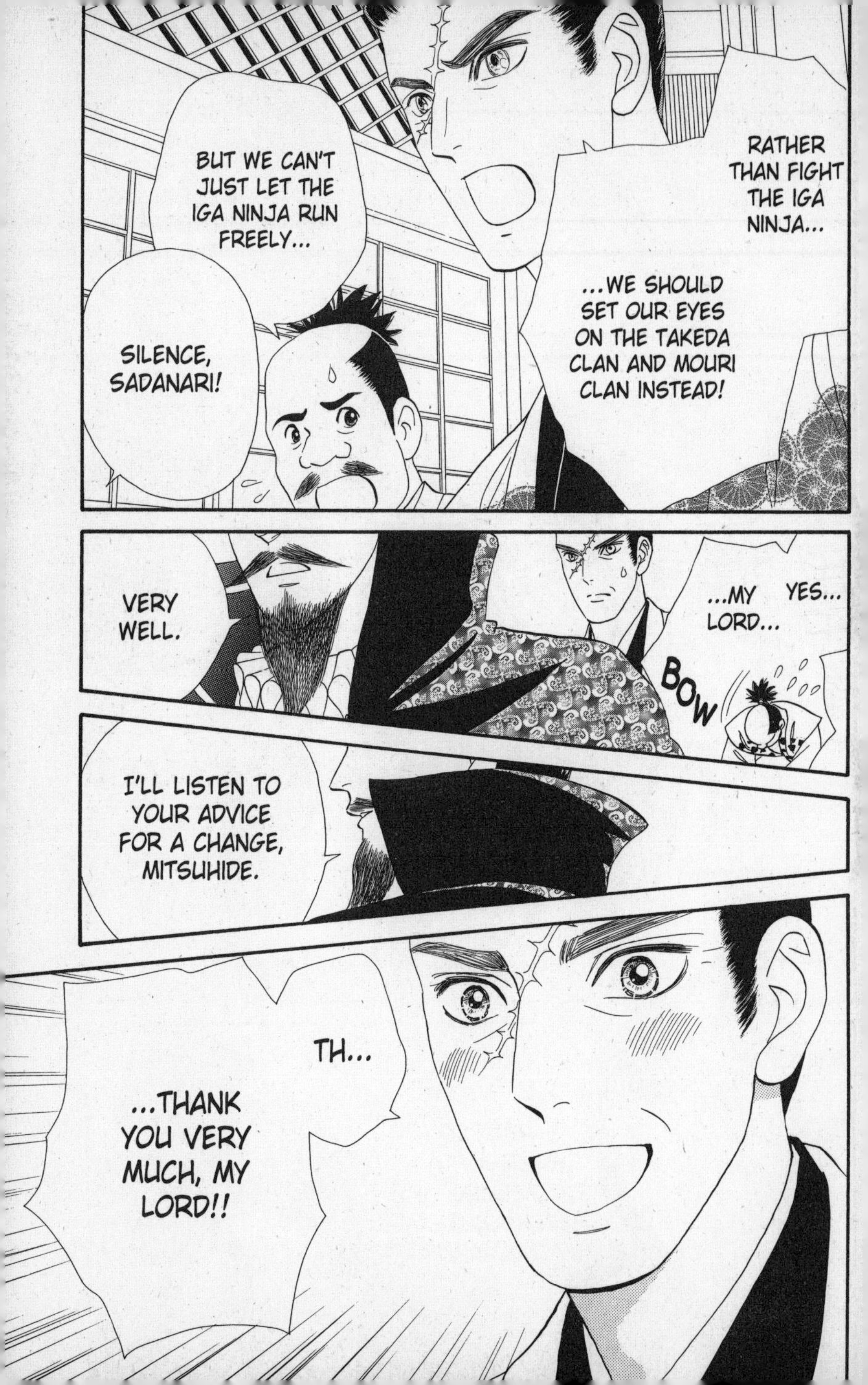
RATHER THAN FIGHT THE IGA NINJA...
...WE SHOULD SET OUR EYES ON THE TAKEDA CLAN AND MOURI CLAN INSTEAD!
BUT WE CAN'T JUST LET THE IGA NINJA RUN FREELY...
SILENCE, SADANARI!
YES...
...MY LORD...
BOW
VERY WELL.
I'LL LISTEN TO YOUR ADVICE FOR A CHANGE, MITSUHIDE.
TH...
...THANK YOU VERY MUCH, MY LORD!!

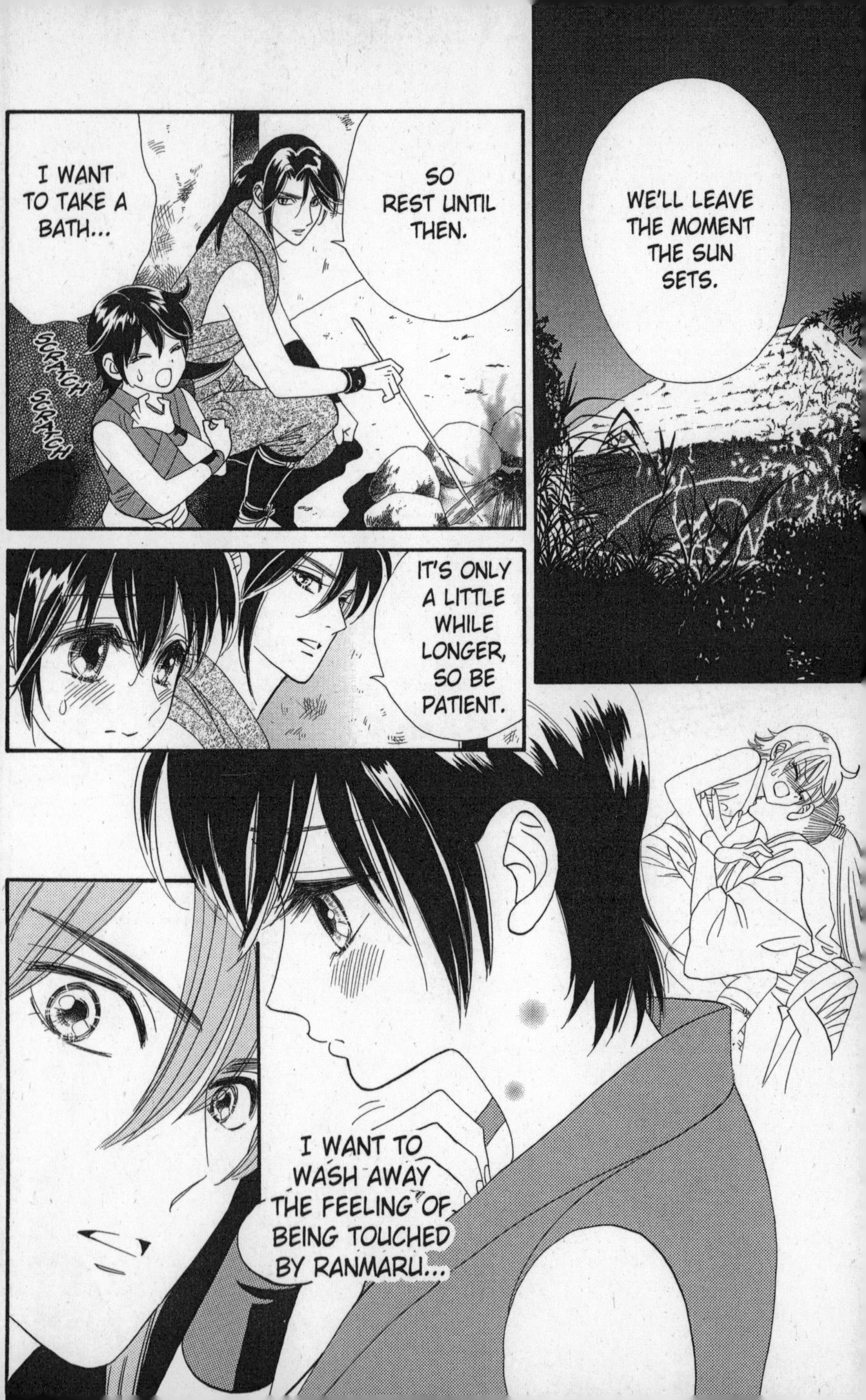
WE'LL LEAVE THE MOMENT THE SUN SETS.
SO REST UNTIL THEN.
I WANT TO TAKE A BATH...
SCRATCH SCRATCH
IT'S ONLY A LITTLE WHILE LONGER, SO BE PATIENT.
I WANT TO WASH AWAY THE FEELING OF BEING TOUCHED BY RANMARU...

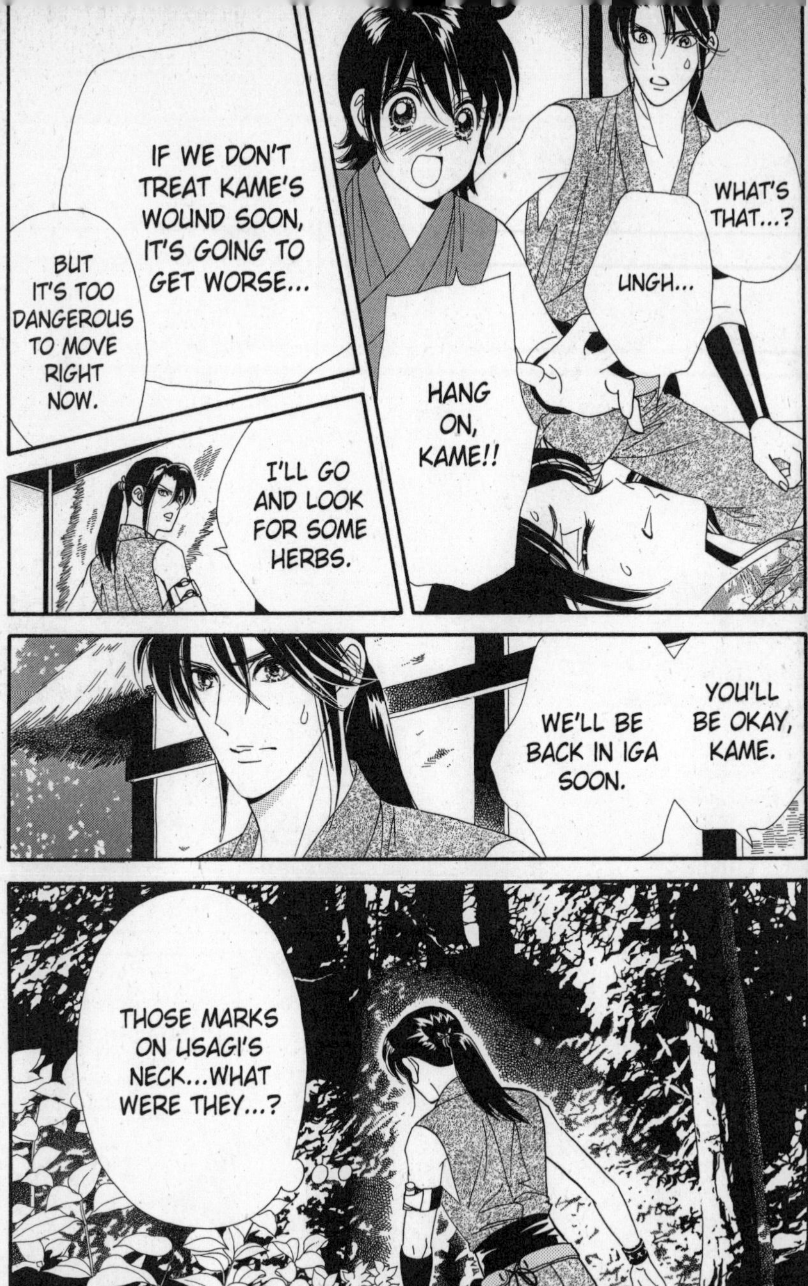
WHAT'S THAT...?
UNGH...
HANG ON, KAME!!
IF WE DON'T TREAT KAME'S WOUND SOON, IT'S GOING TO GET WORSE...
BUT IT'S TOO DANGEROUS TO MOVE RIGHT NOW.
I'LL GO AND LOOK FOR SOME HERBS.
YOU'LL BE OKAY, KAME.
WE'LL BE BACK IN IGA SOON.
THOSE MARKS ON USAGI'S NECK...WHAT WERE THEY...?

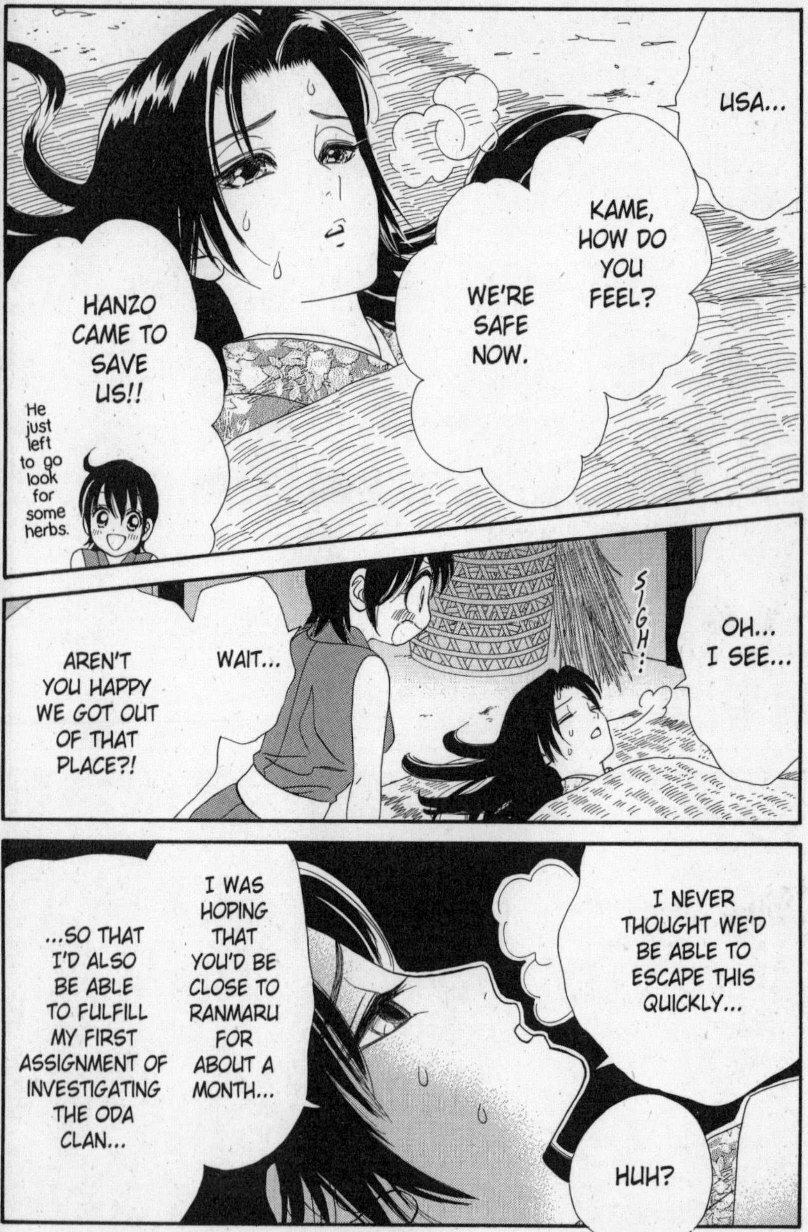
USA...
KAME, HOW DO YOU FEEL?
WE'RE SAFE NOW.
HANZO CAME TO SAVE US!!
He just left to go look for some herbs.
OH... I SEE...
SIGH...
WAIT...
AREN'T YOU HAPPY WE GOT OUT OF THAT PLACE?!
I NEVER THOUGHT WE'D BE ABLE TO ESCAPE THIS QUICKLY...
HUH?
I WAS HOPING THAT YOU'D BE CLOSE TO RANMARU FOR ABOUT A MONTH...
...SO THAT I'D ALSO BE ABLE TO FULFILL MY FIRST ASSIGNMENT OF INVESTIGATING THE ODA CLAN...

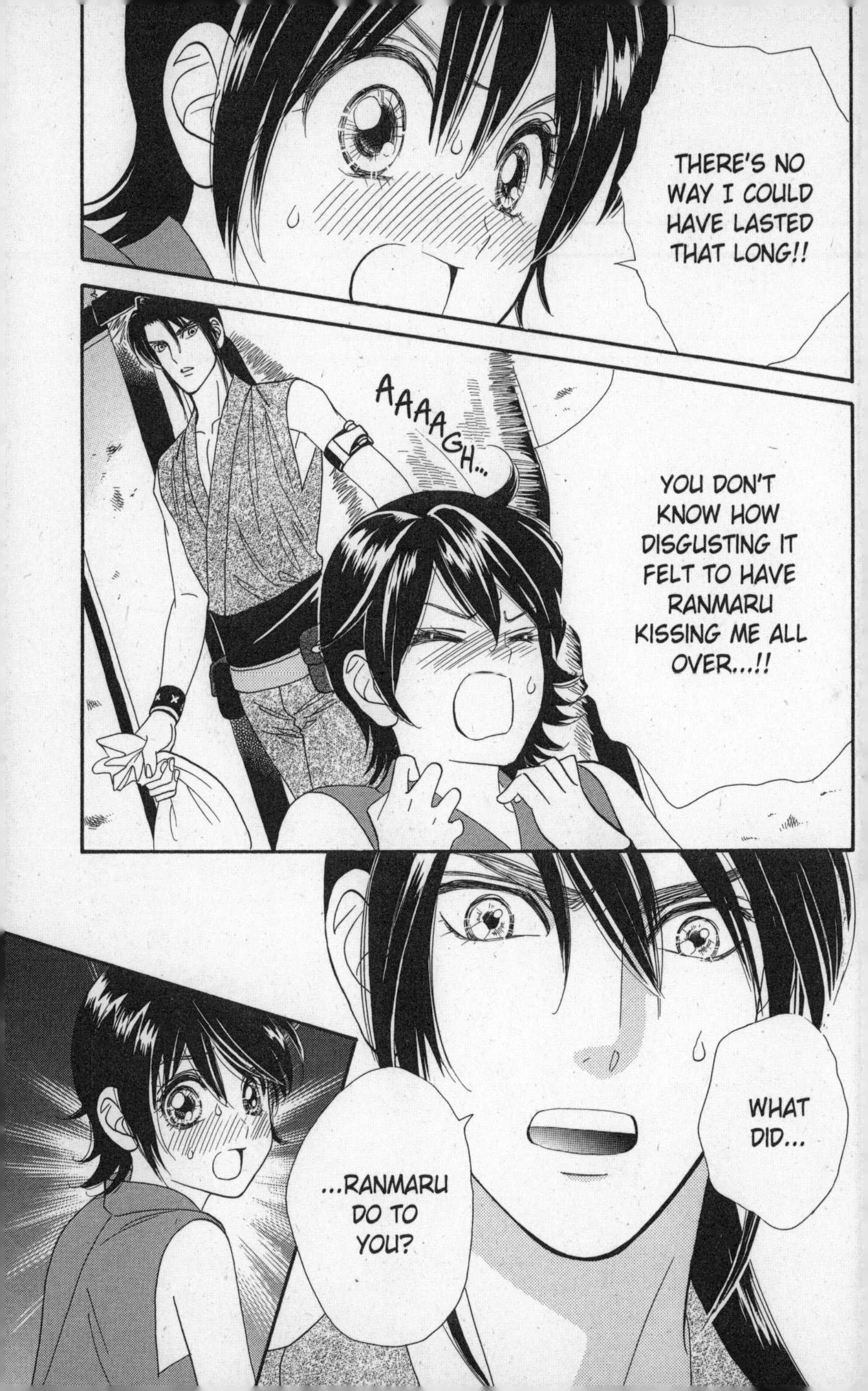
THERE'S NO WAY I COULD HAVE LASTED THAT LONG!!
YOU DON'T KNOW HOW DISGUSTING IT FELT TO HAVE RANMARU KISSING ME ALL OVER...!!
AAAAGH...
WHAT DID...
...RANMARU DO TO YOU?

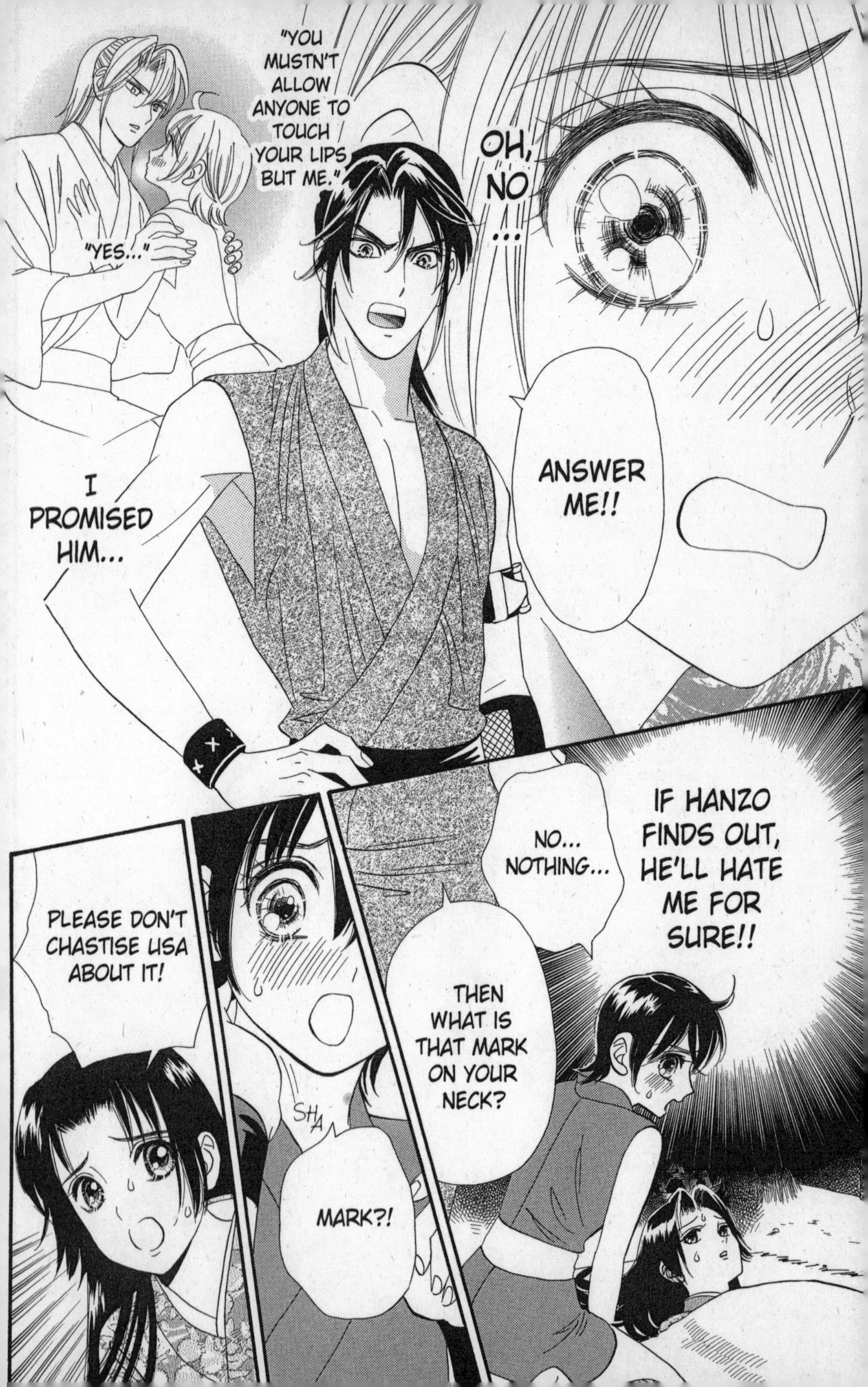
OH, NO ...
"YOU MUSTN'T ALLOW ANYONE TO TOUCH YOUR LIPS BUT ME."
"YES..."
ANSWER ME!!
I PROMISED HIM...
IF HANZO FINDS OUT, HE'LL HATE ME FOR SURE!!
NO... NOTHING...
THEN WHAT IS THAT MARK ON YOUR NECK?
SHA
MARK?!
PLEASE DON'T CHASTISE USA ABOUT IT!

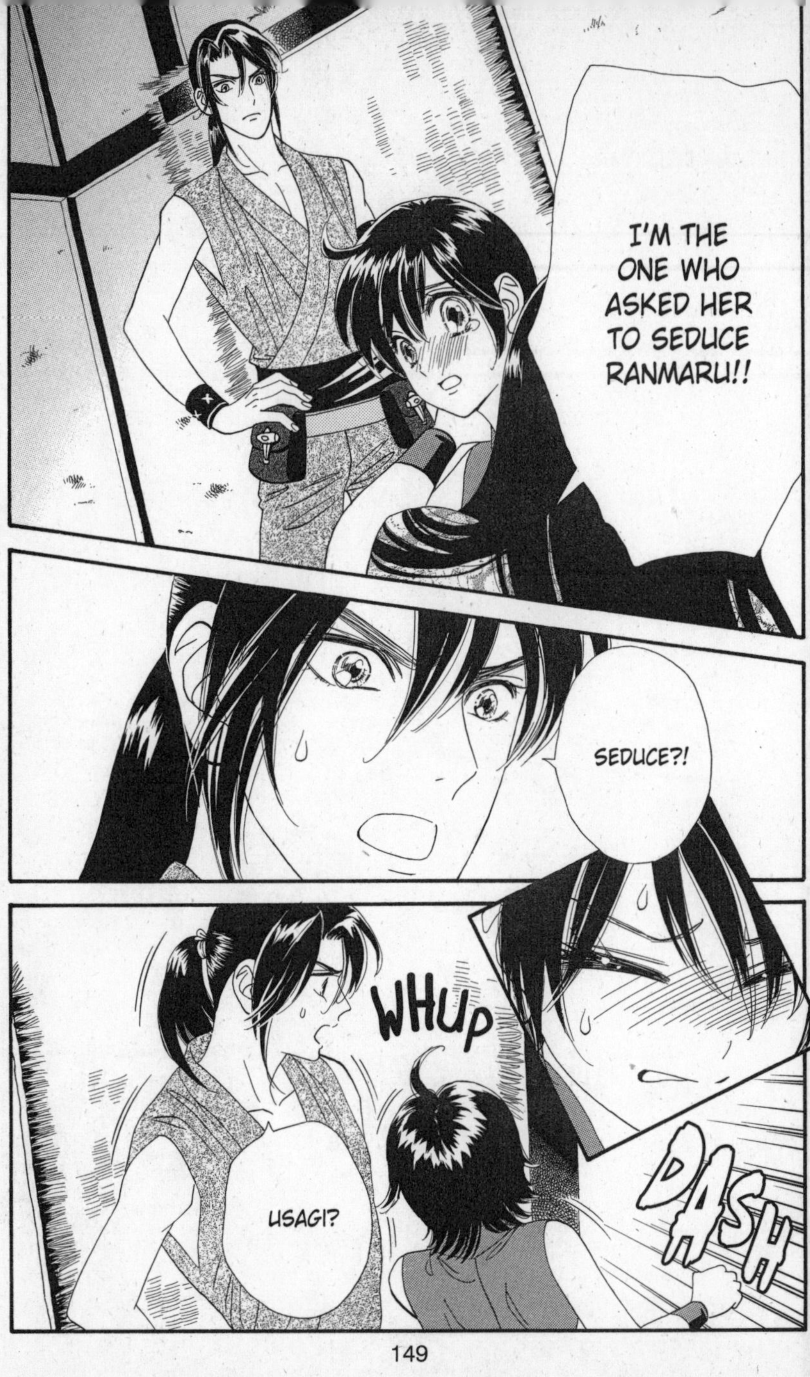
I'M THE ONE WHO ASKED HER TO SEDUCE RANMARU!!
SEDUCE?!
DASH
WHUP
USAGI?

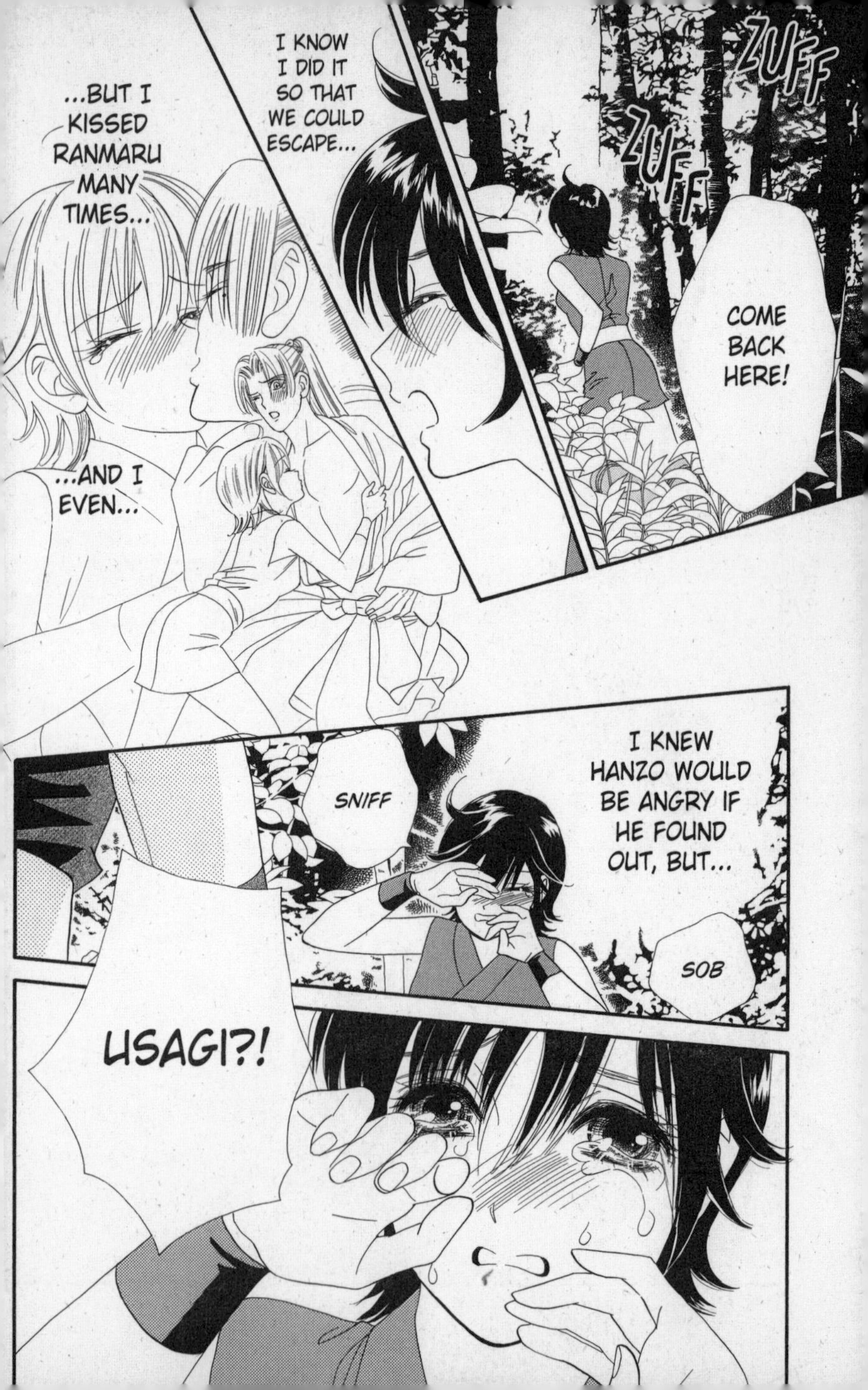
ZUFF
ZUFF
COME BACK HERE!
I KNOW I DID IT SO THAT WE COULD ESCAPE...
...BUT I KISSED RANMARU MANY TIMES...
...AND I EVEN...
I KNEW HANZO WOULD BE ANGRY IF HE FOUND OUT, BUT...
SNIFF
SOB
USAGI?!

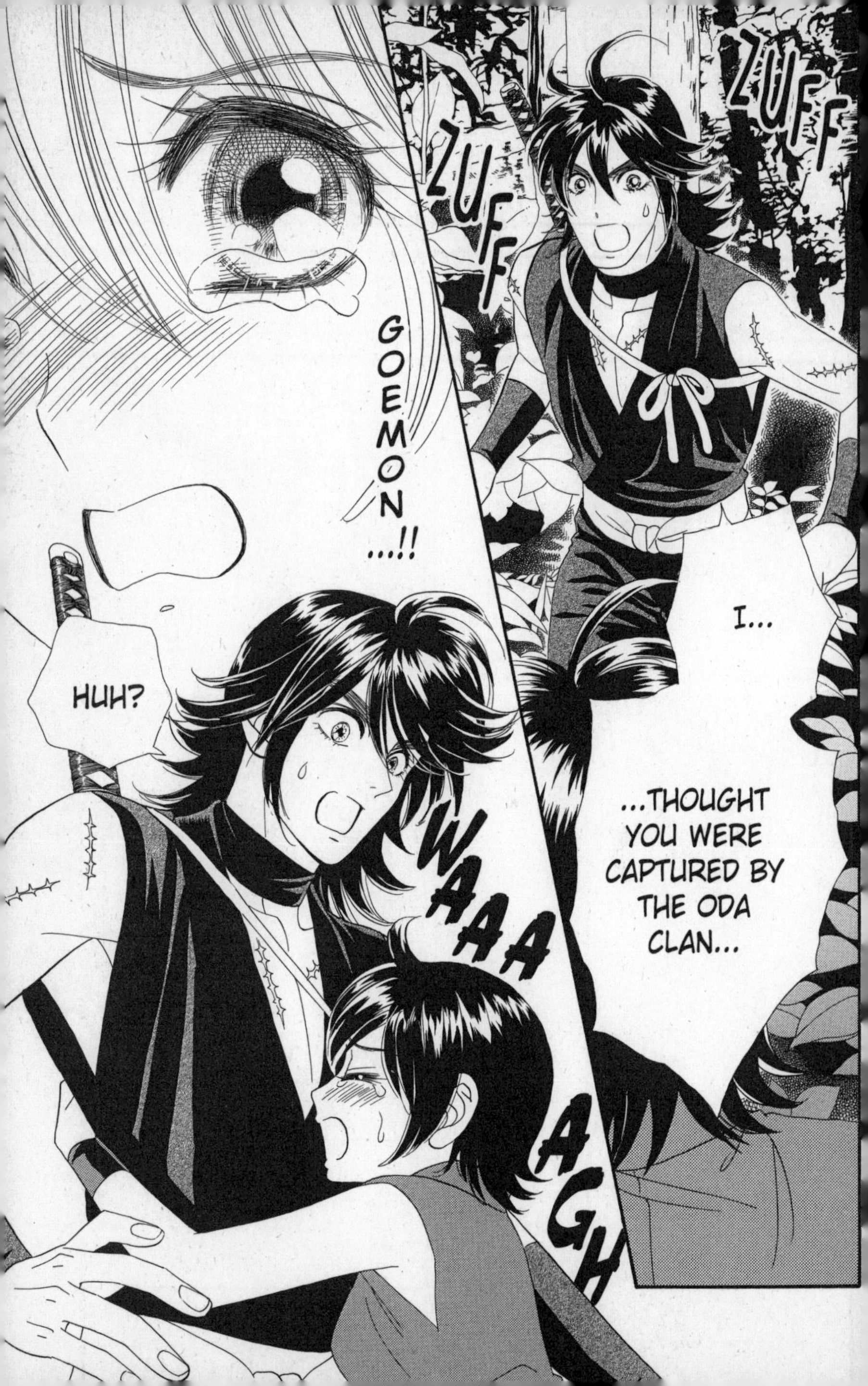
ZUFF
ZUFF
I...
...THOUGHT YOU WERE CAPTURED BY THE ODA CLAN...
GOEMON...!!
HUH?
WAAAAGH

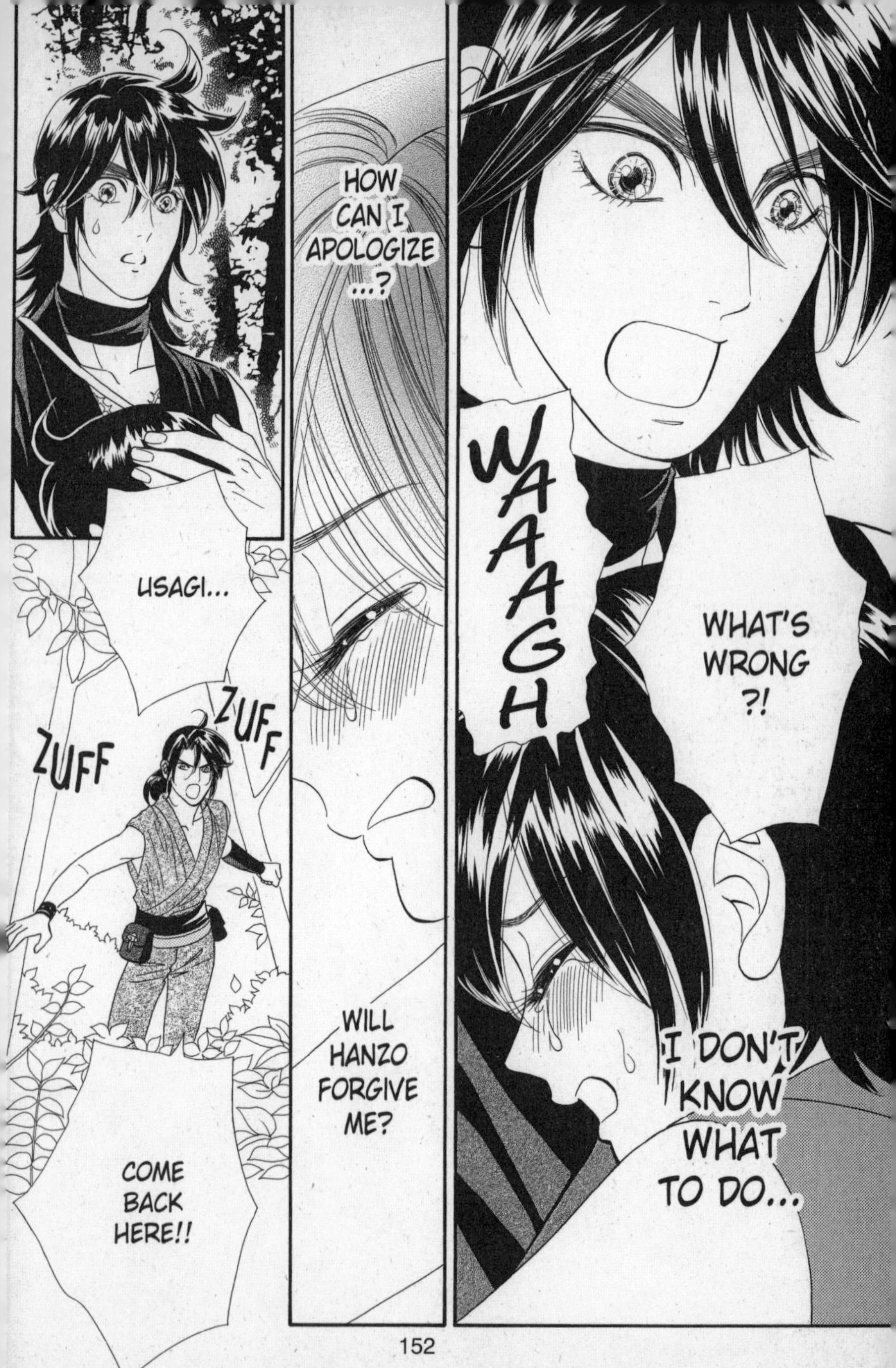
WAAAGH
WHAT'S WRONG ?!
I DON'T KNOW WHAT TO DO...
HOW CAN I APOLOGIZE ...?
WILL HANZO FORGIVE ME?
USAGI...
ZUFF
ZUFF
COME BACK HERE!!

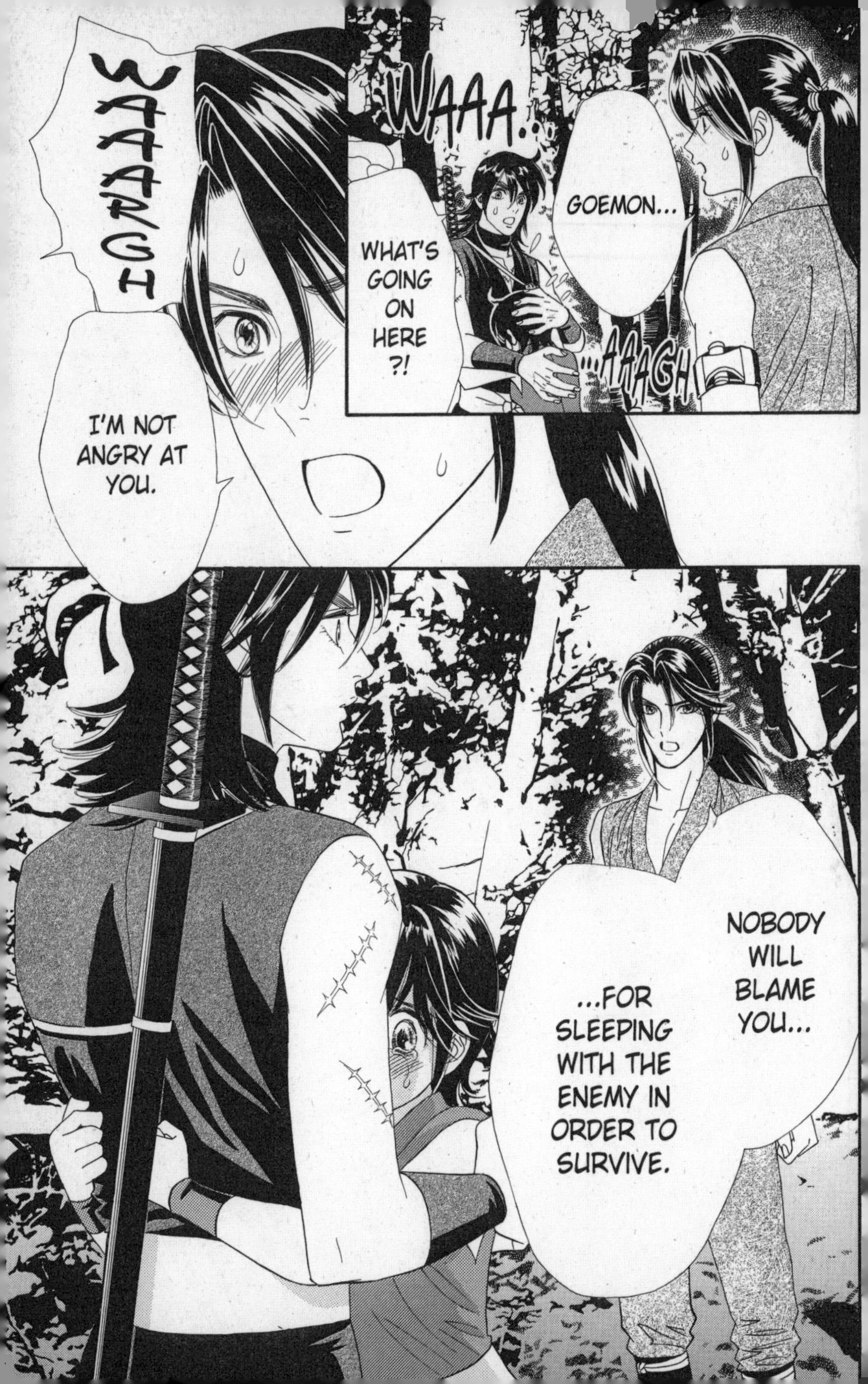
GOEMON...
WAAA...
WHAT'S GOING ON HERE?!
...AAAGH
WAAARGH
I'M NOT ANGRY AT YOU.
NOBODY WILL BLAME YOU...
...FOR SLEEPING WITH THE ENEMY IN ORDER TO SURVIVE.

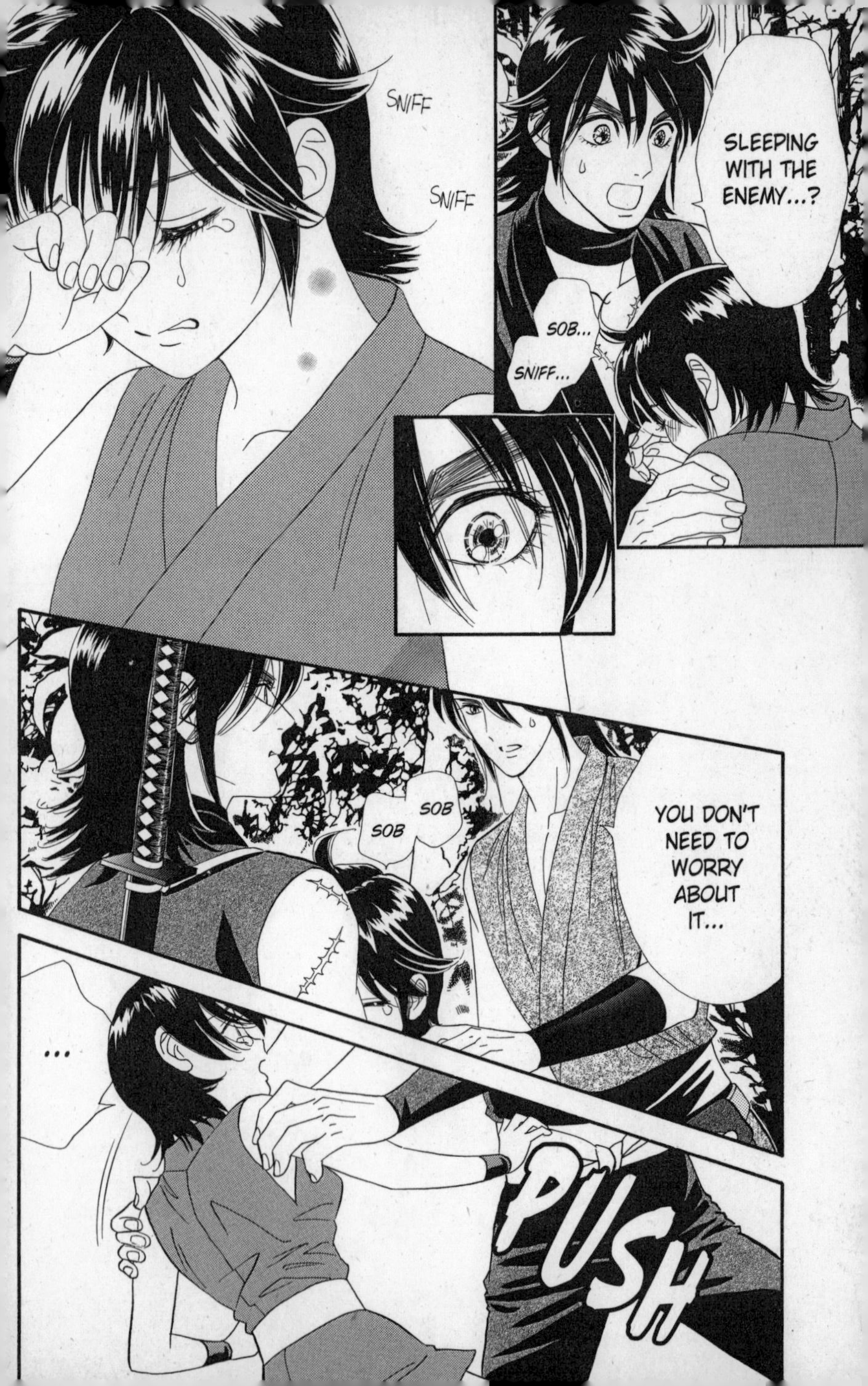
SLEEPING WITH THE ENEMY...?
SOB...
SNIFF...
SNIFF
SNIFF
YOU DON'T NEED TO WORRY ABOUT IT...
SOB
SOB
PUSH
...

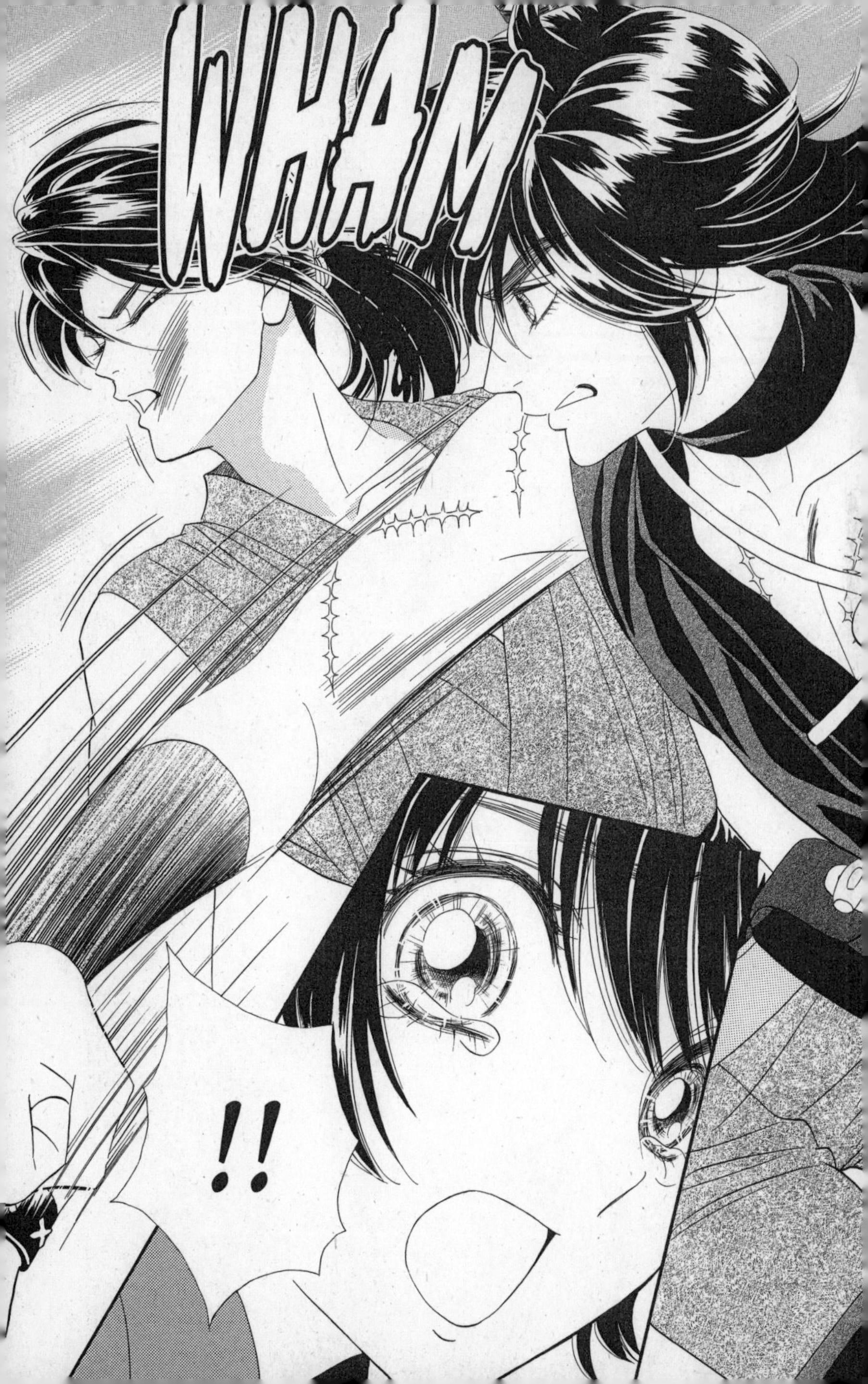
WHAM
!!

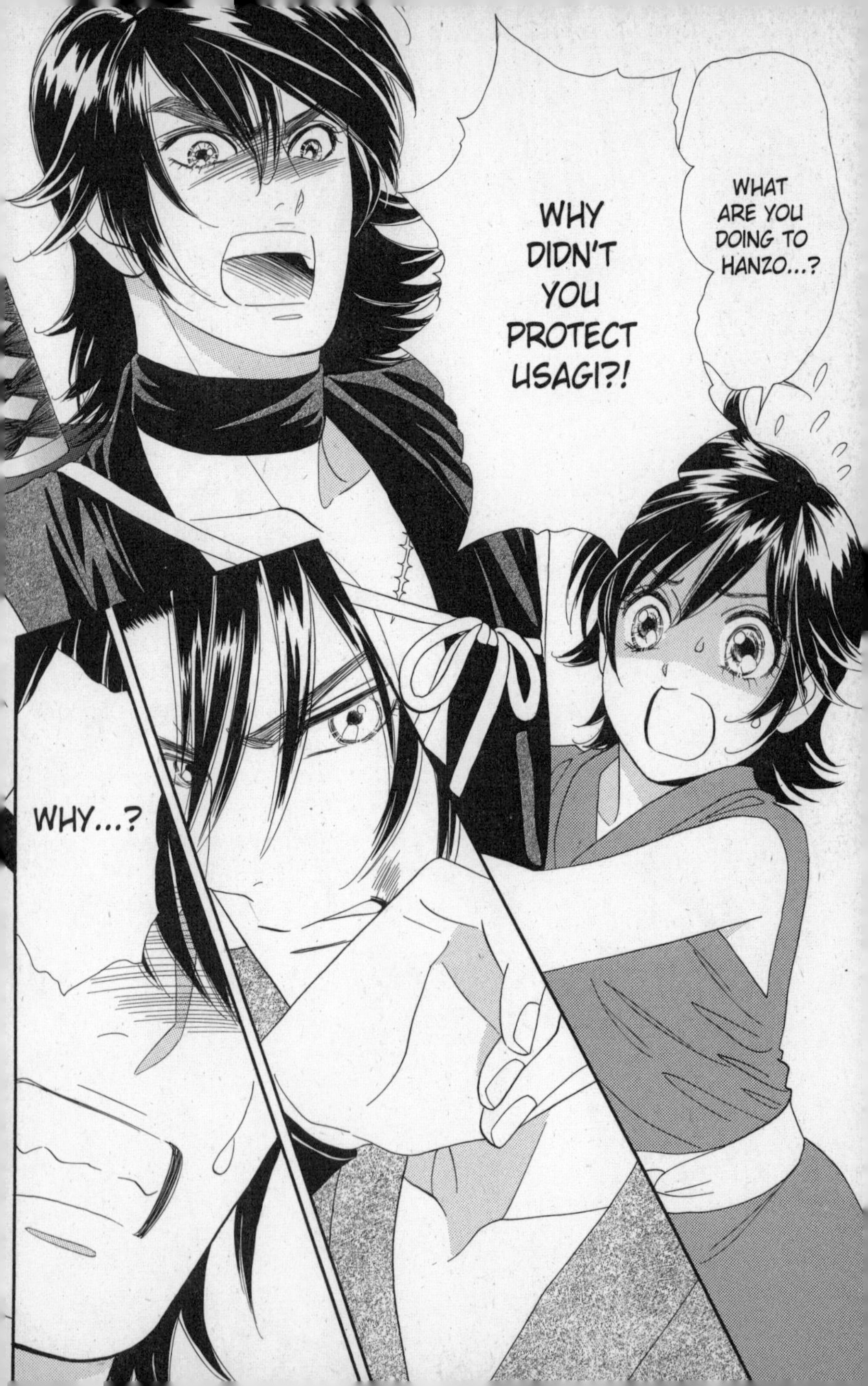
WHAT ARE YOU DOING TO HANZO...?
WHY DIDN'T YOU PROTECT USAGI?!
WHY...?

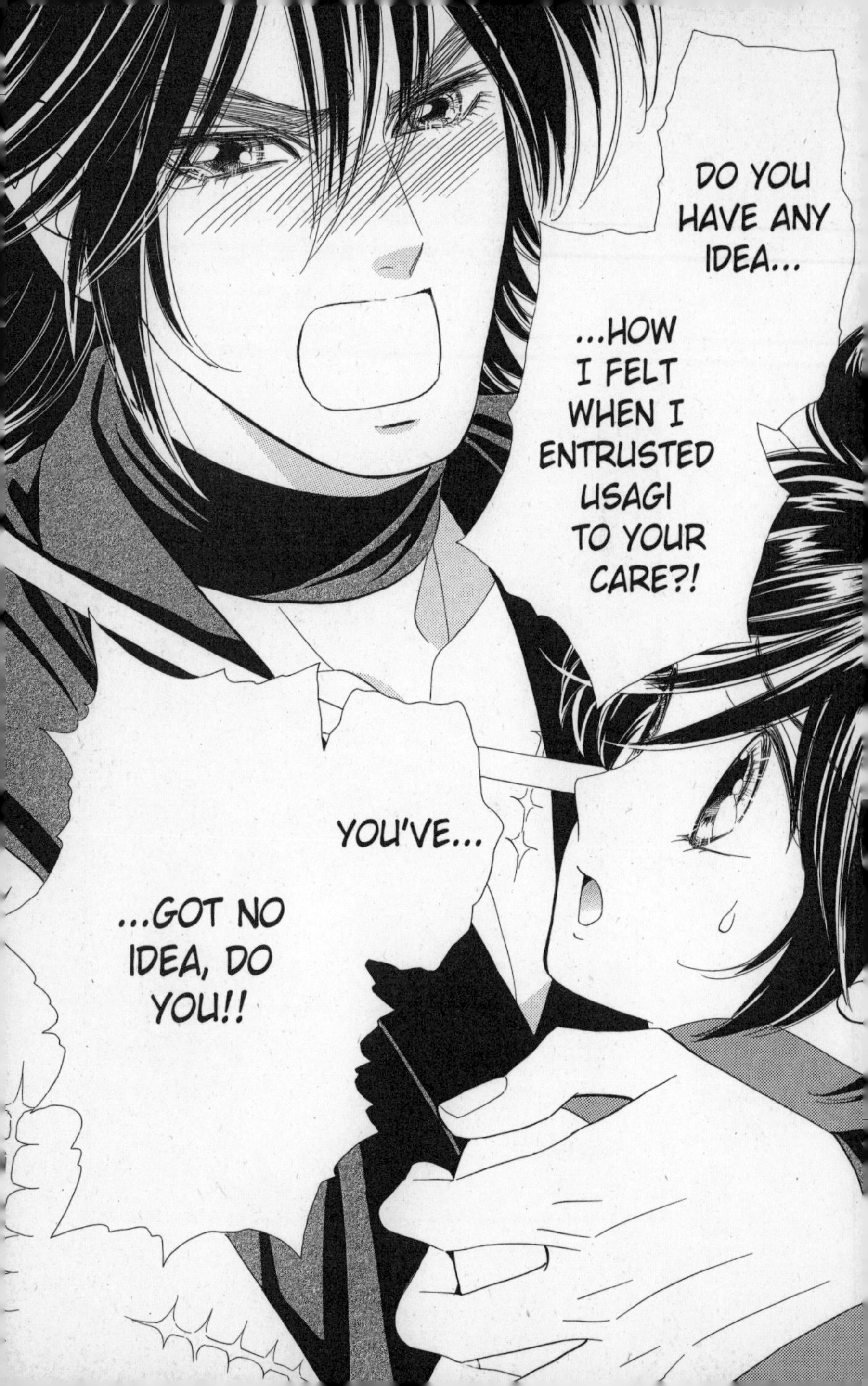
DO YOU HAVE ANY IDEA...
...HOW I FELT WHEN I ENTRUSTED USAGI TO YOUR CARE?!
YOU'VE...
...GOT NO IDEA, DO YOU!!

TAIL OF THE MOON EXTRA: TODAY'S MISSION

"I WANT TO SEE HANZO AS SANTA CLAUS!"

-YUKO, FUKUOKA PREFECTURE

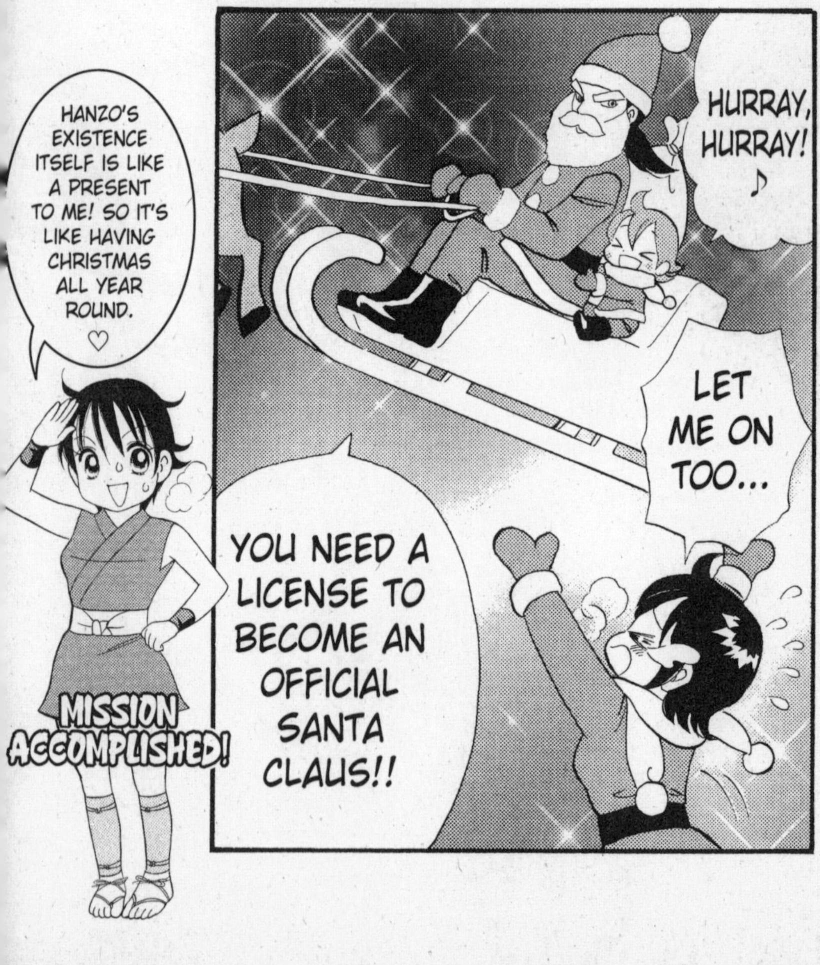
HURRAY, HURRAY! ♪
LET ME ON TOO...
YOU NEED A LICENSE TO BECOME AN OFFICIAL SANTA CLAUS!!
HANZO'S EXISTENCE ITSELF IS LIKE A PRESENT TO ME! SO IT'S LIKE HAVING CHRISTMAS ALL YEAR ROUND. ♡
MISSION ACCOMPLISHED!

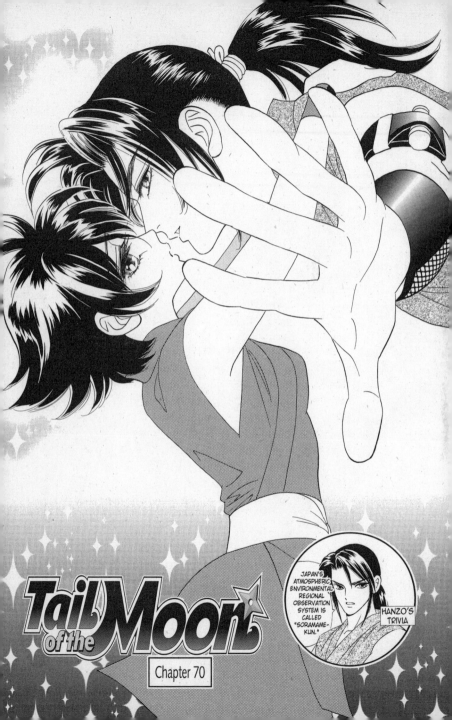

Tail *of the* Moon

Chapter 70

JAPAN'S
ATMOSPHERIC
ENVIRONMENTAL
REGIONAL
OBSERVATION
SYSTEM IS
CALLED
"SORAMAME-
KUN."

HANZO'S
TRIVIA

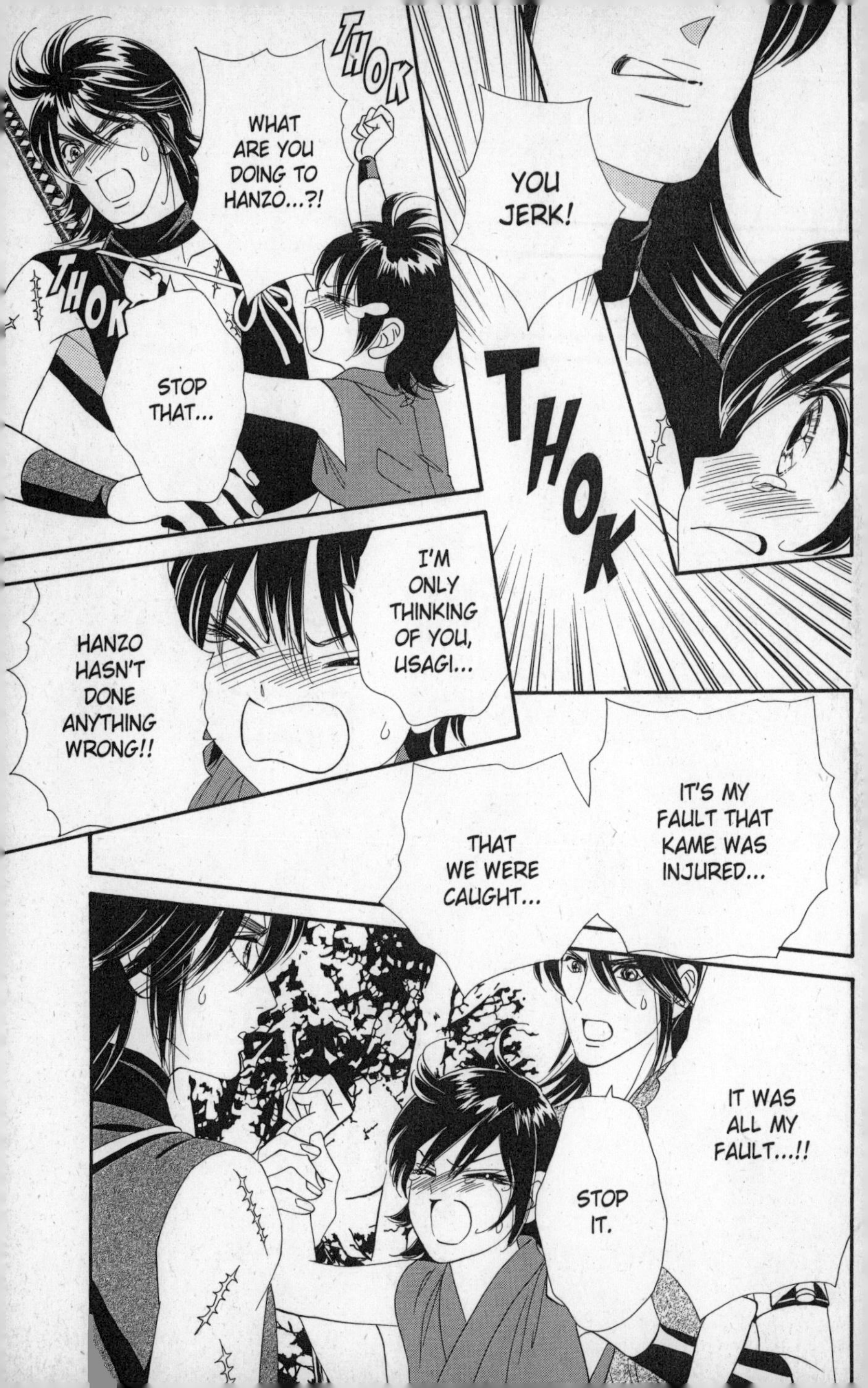
YOU JERK!
THOK
THOK
WHAT ARE YOU DOING TO HANZO...?!
THOK
STOP THAT...
I'M ONLY THINKING OF YOU, USAGI...
HANZO HASN'T DONE ANYTHING WRONG!!
IT'S MY FAULT THAT KAME WAS INJURED...
THAT WE WERE CAUGHT...
IT WAS ALL MY FAULT...!!
STOP IT.

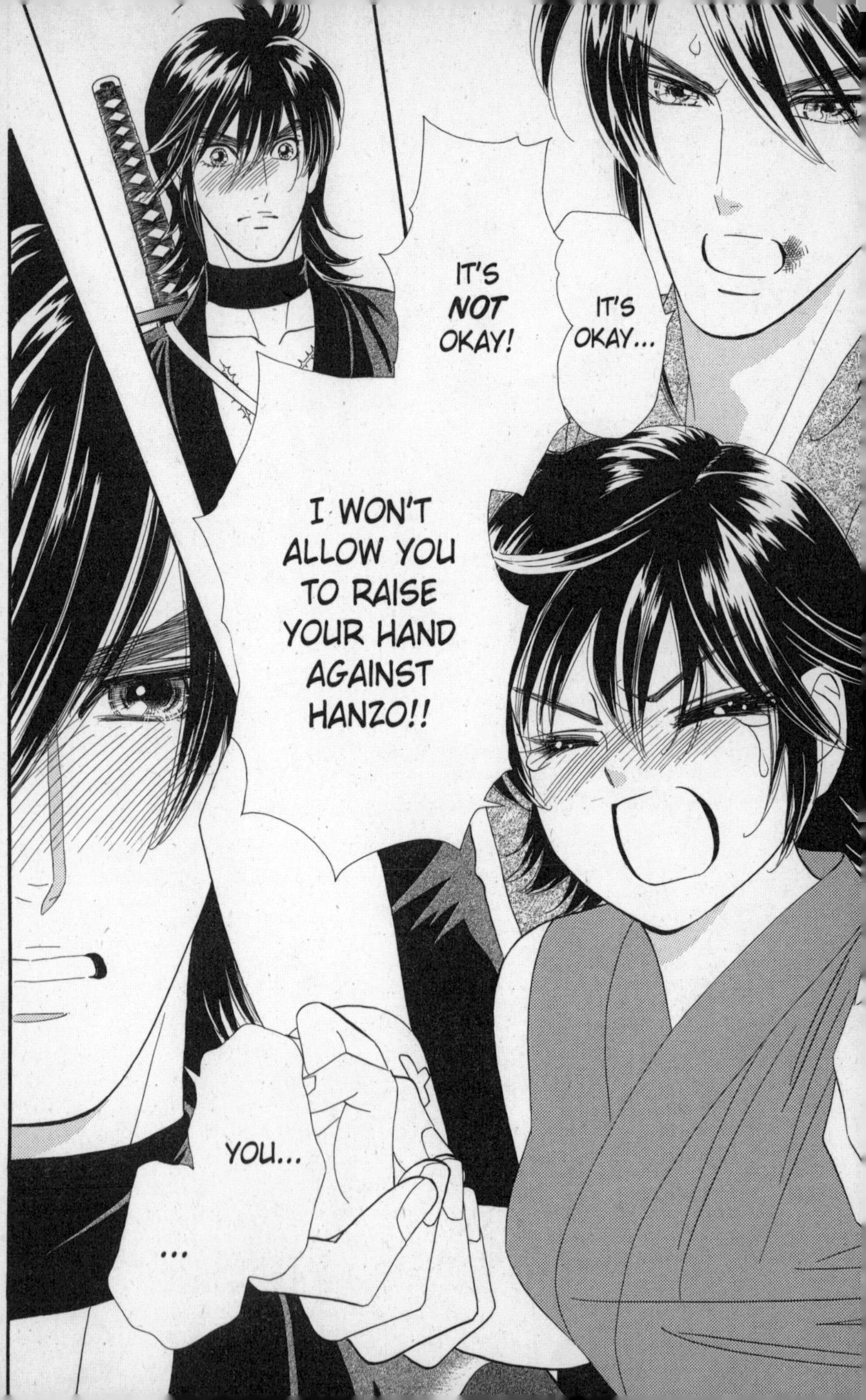
IT'S OKAY...
IT'S NOT OKAY!
I WON'T ALLOW YOU TO RAISE YOUR HAND AGAINST HANZO!!
YOU...
...

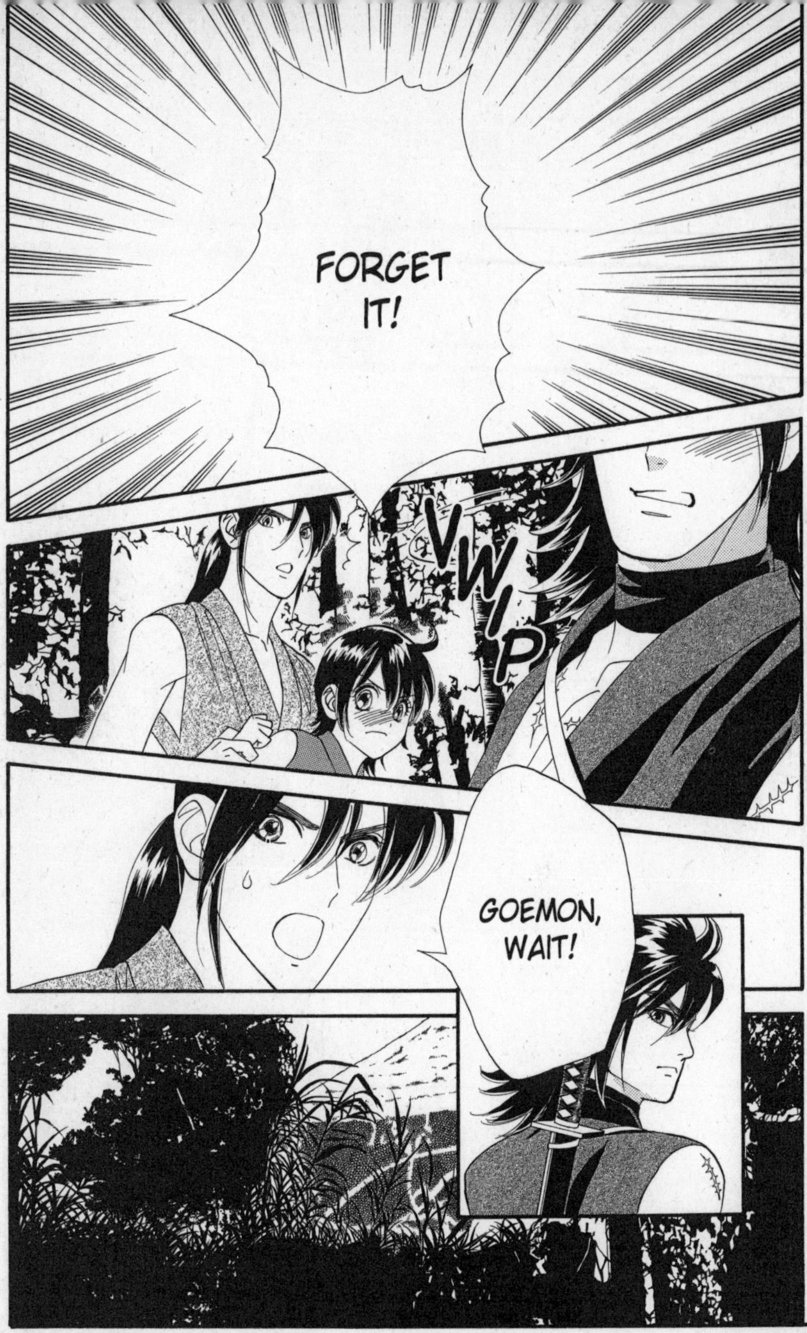
FORGET IT!
VWIP
GOEMON, WAIT!

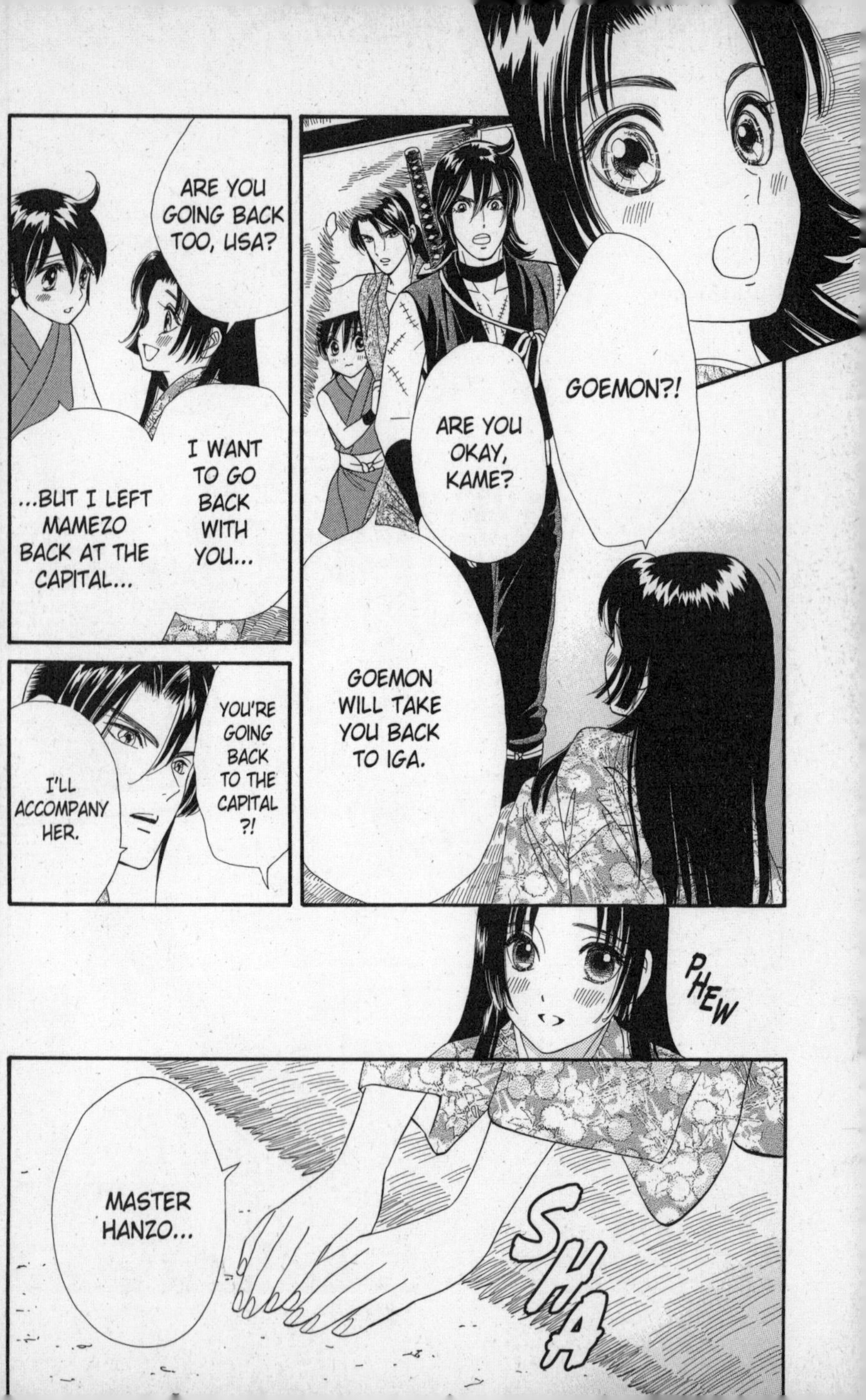
GOEMON?!
ARE YOU OKAY, KAME?
GOEMON WILL TAKE YOU BACK TO IGA.
ARE YOU GOING BACK TOO, USA?
I WANT TO GO BACK WITH YOU...
...BUT I LEFT MAMEZO BACK AT THE CAPITAL...
YOU'RE GOING BACK TO THE CAPITAL?!
I'LL ACCOMPANY HER.
PHEW
SHA
MASTER HANZO...

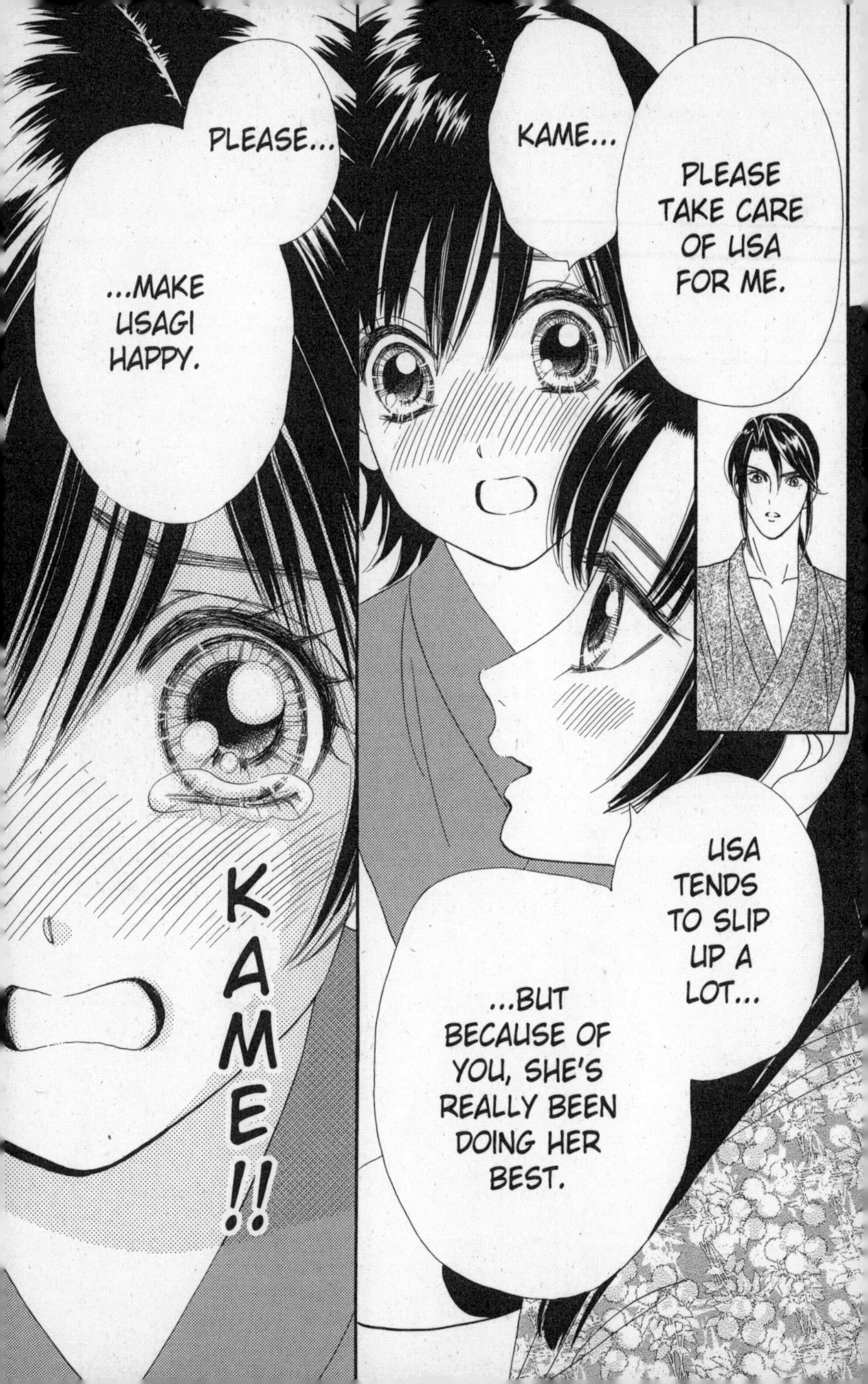
KAME...
PLEASE TAKE CARE OF USA FOR ME.
USA TENDS TO SLIP UP A LOT...
...BUT BECAUSE OF YOU, SHE'S REALLY BEEN DOING HER BEST.
PLEASE...
...MAKE USAGI HAPPY.
KAME!!

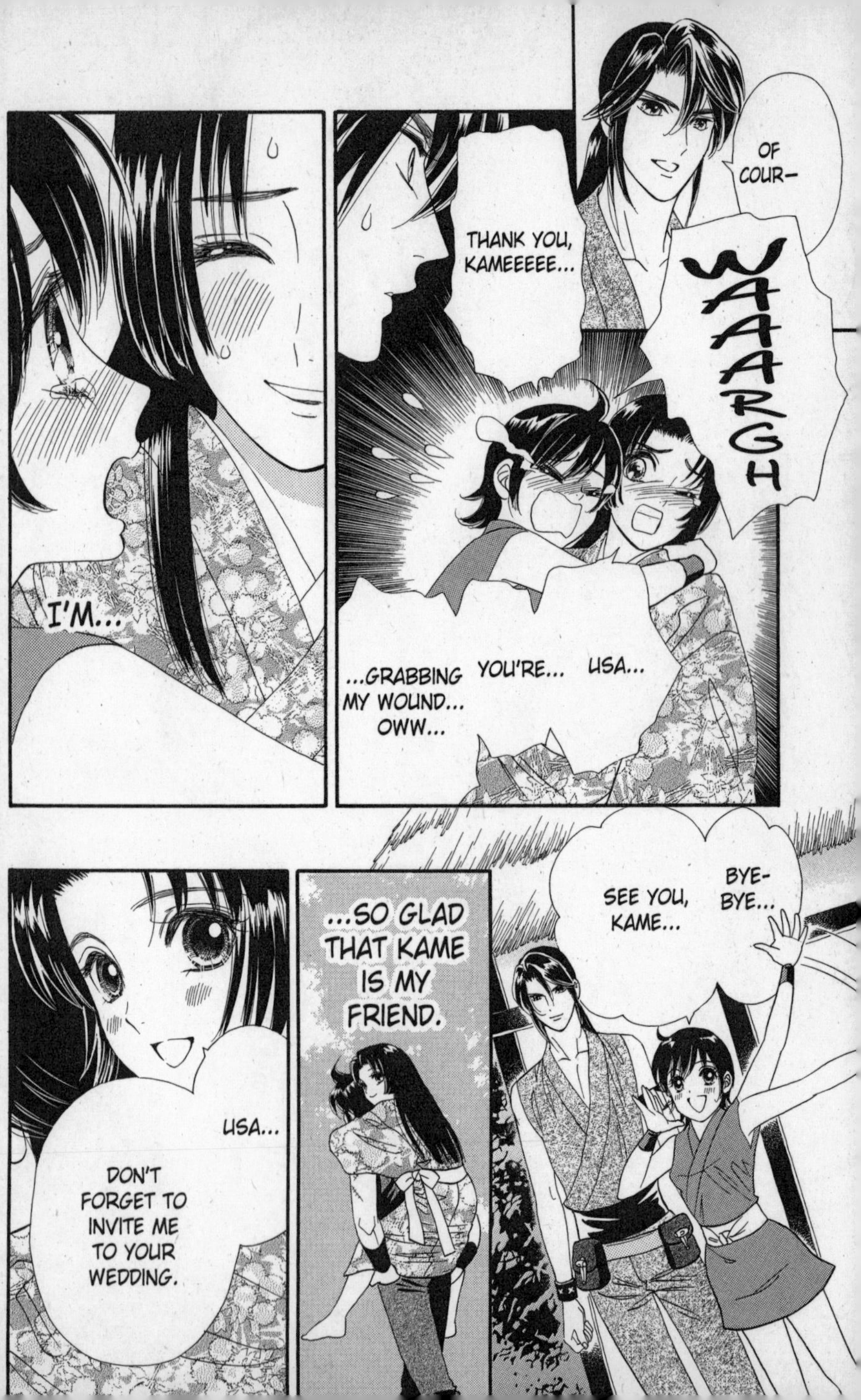
OF COUR–
WAAARGH
THANK YOU, KAMEEEEE...
USA...
YOU'RE...
...GRABBING MY WOUND... OWW...
I'M...
BYE-BYE...
SEE YOU, KAME...
...SO GLAD THAT KAME IS MY FRIEND.
USA...
DON'T FORGET TO INVITE ME TO YOUR WEDDING.

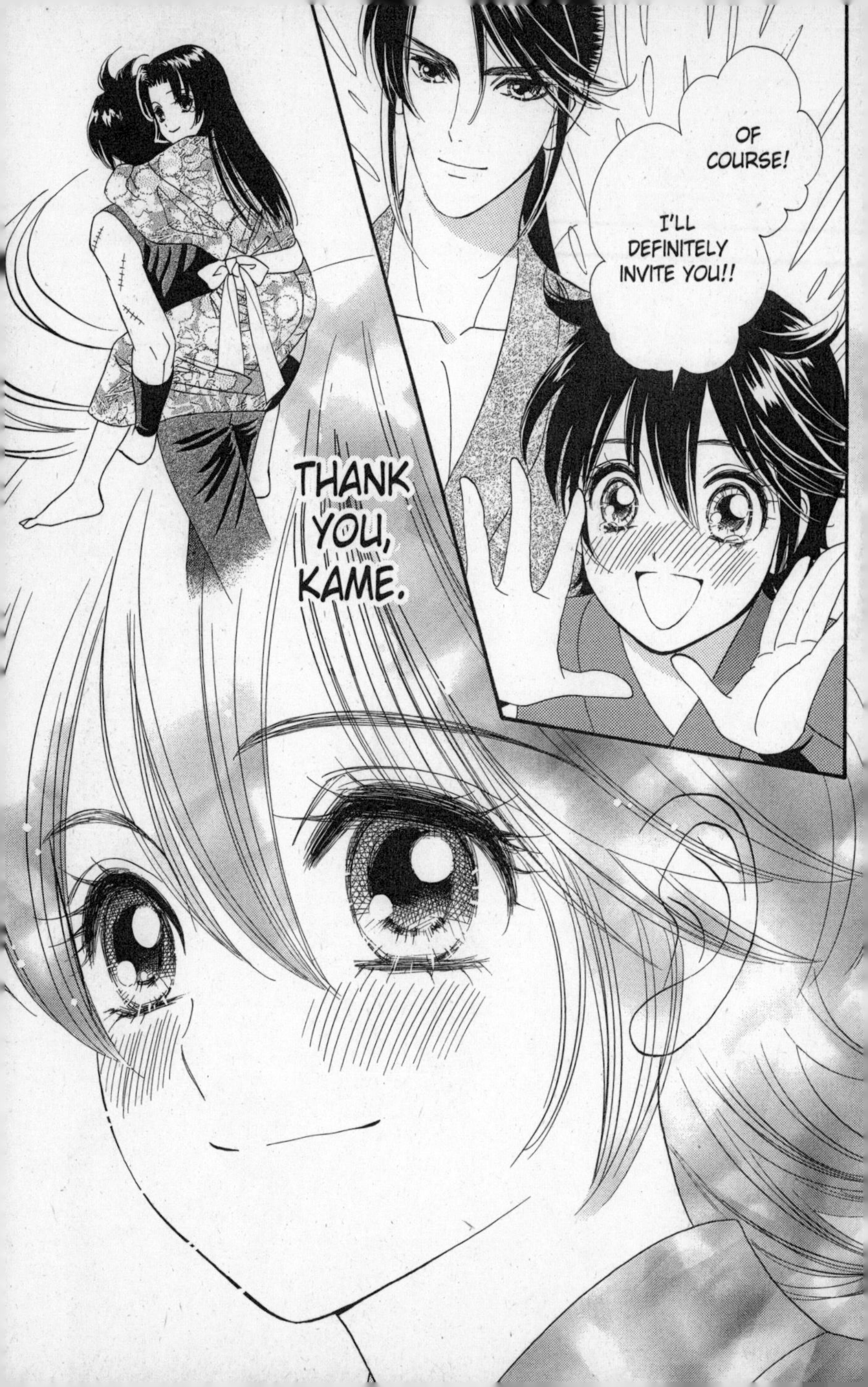
OF COURSE!
I'LL DEFINITELY INVITE YOU!!
THANK YOU, KAME.

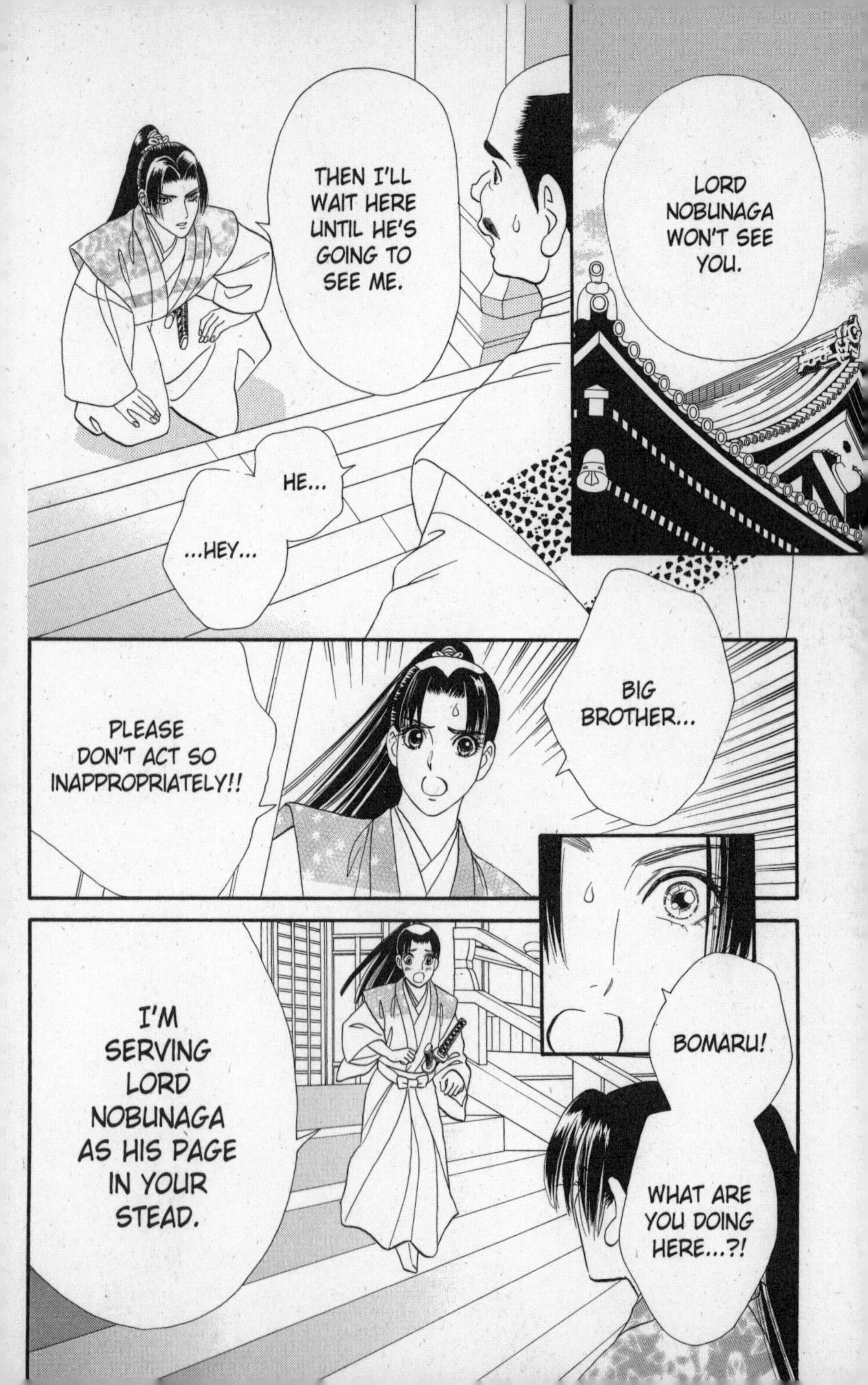
LORD NOBUNAGA WON'T SEE YOU.
THEN I'LL WAIT HERE UNTIL HE'S GOING TO SEE ME.
HE...
...HEY...
BIG BROTHER...
PLEASE DON'T ACT SO INAPPROPRIATELY!!
BOMARU!
WHAT ARE YOU DOING HERE...?!
I'M SERVING LORD NOBUNAGA AS HIS PAGE IN YOUR STEAD.

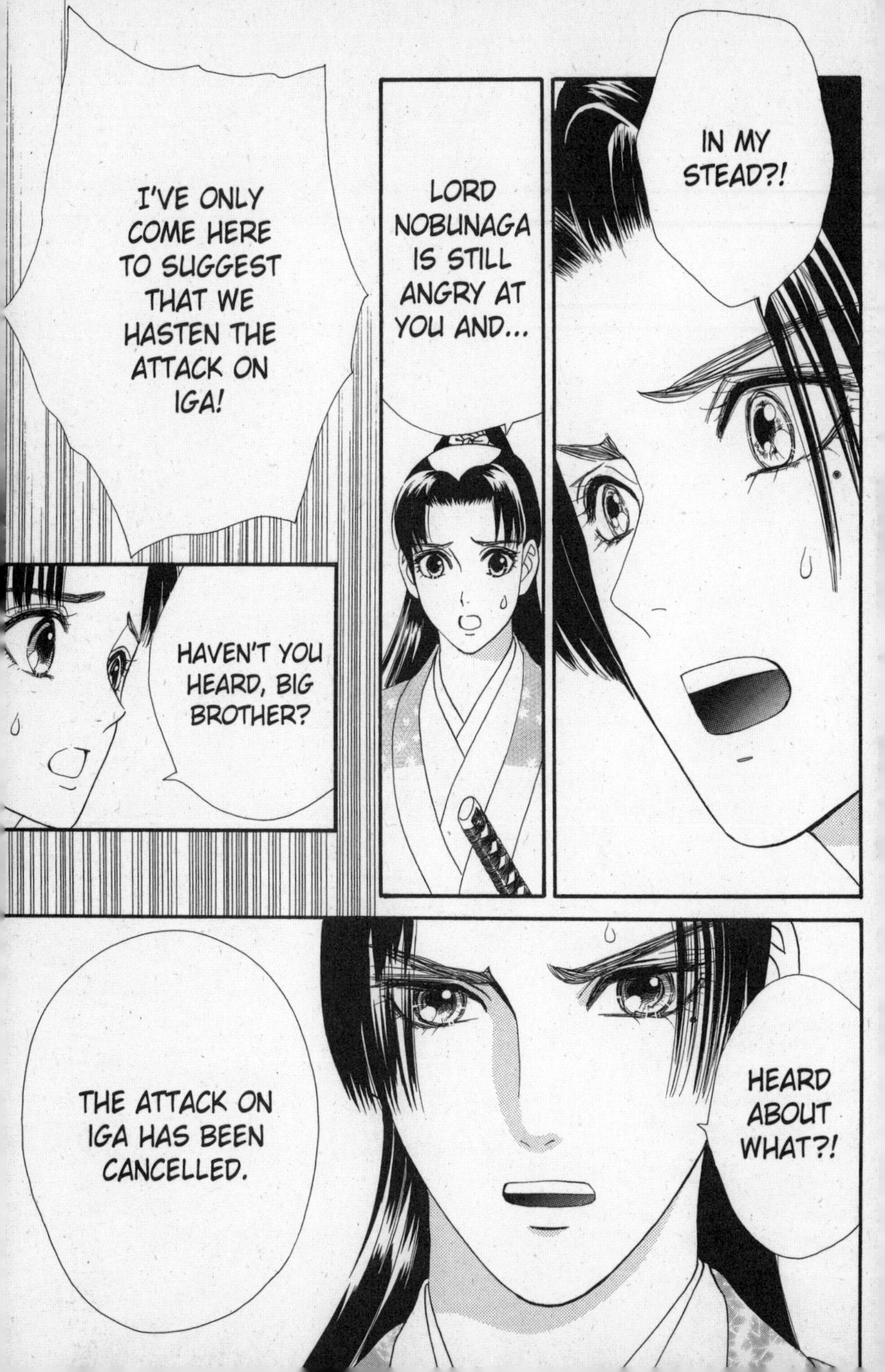
IN MY STEAD?!
LORD NOBUNAGA IS STILL ANGRY AT YOU AND...
I'VE ONLY COME HERE TO SUGGEST THAT WE HASTEN THE ATTACK ON IGA!
HAVEN'T YOU HEARD, BIG BROTHER?
HEARD ABOUT WHAT?!
THE ATTACK ON IGA HAS BEEN CANCELLED.

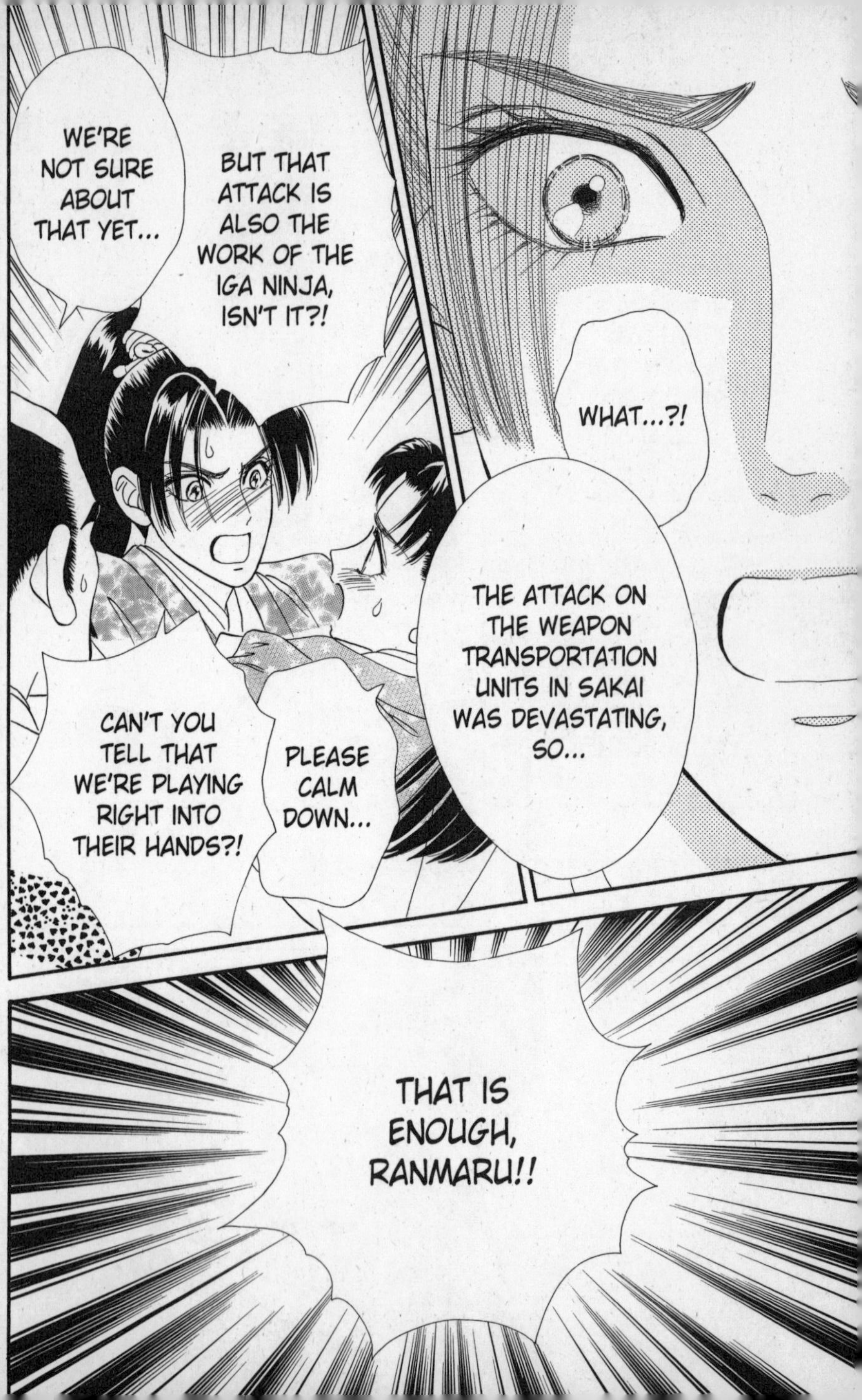
WHAT...?!
THE ATTACK ON THE WEAPON TRANSPORTATION UNITS IN SAKAI WAS DEVASTATING, SO...
BUT THAT ATTACK IS ALSO THE WORK OF THE IGA NINJA, ISN'T IT?!
WE'RE NOT SURE ABOUT THAT YET...
CAN'T YOU TELL THAT WE'RE PLAYING RIGHT INTO THEIR HANDS?!
PLEASE CALM DOWN...
THAT IS ENOUGH, RANMARU!!

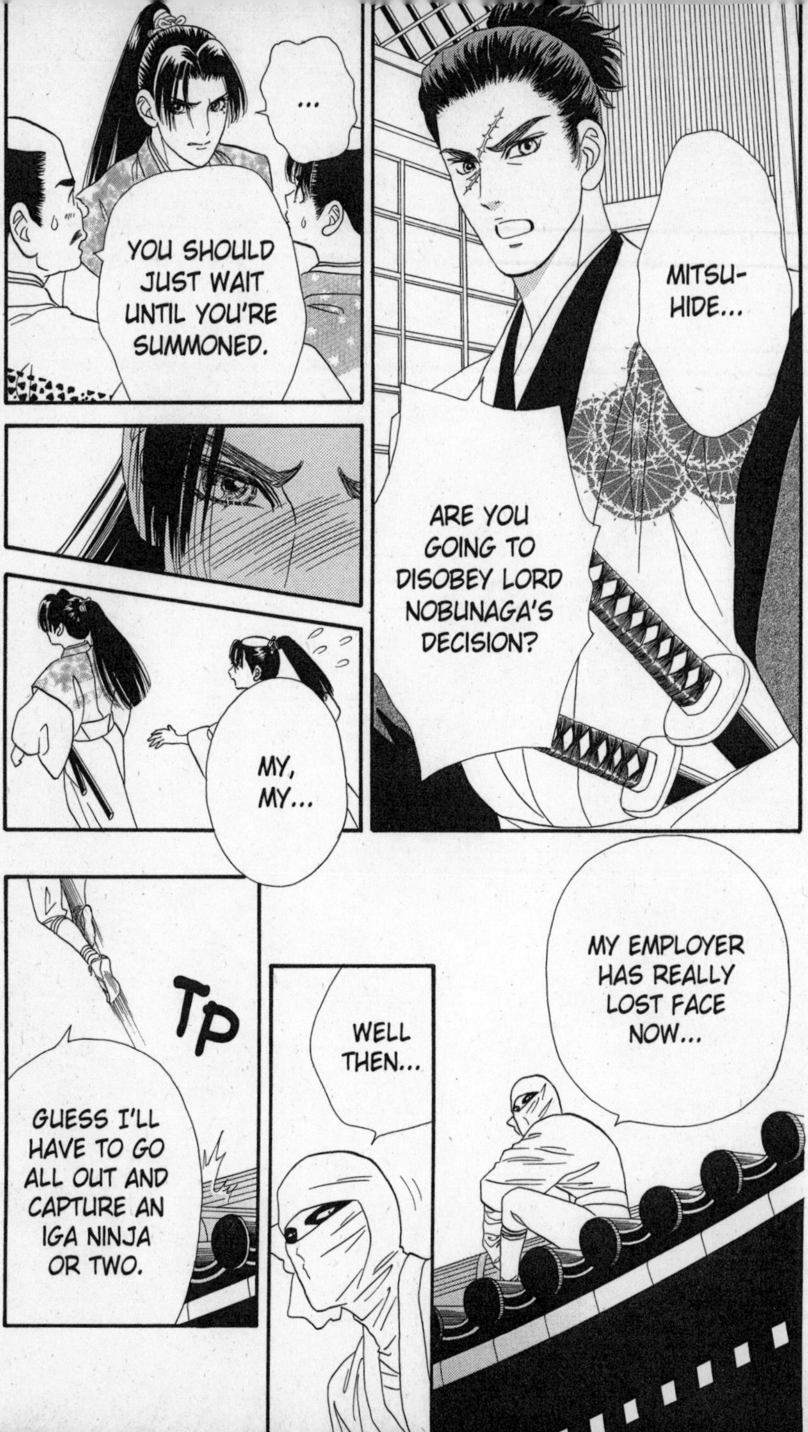
MITSU-HIDE...
ARE YOU GOING TO DISOBEY LORD NOBUNAGA'S DECISION?
...
YOU SHOULD JUST WAIT UNTIL YOU'RE SUMMONED.
MY, MY...
MY EMPLOYER HAS REALLY LOST FACE NOW...
WELL THEN...
TP
GUESS I'LL HAVE TO GO ALL OUT AND CAPTURE AN IGA NINJA OR TWO.

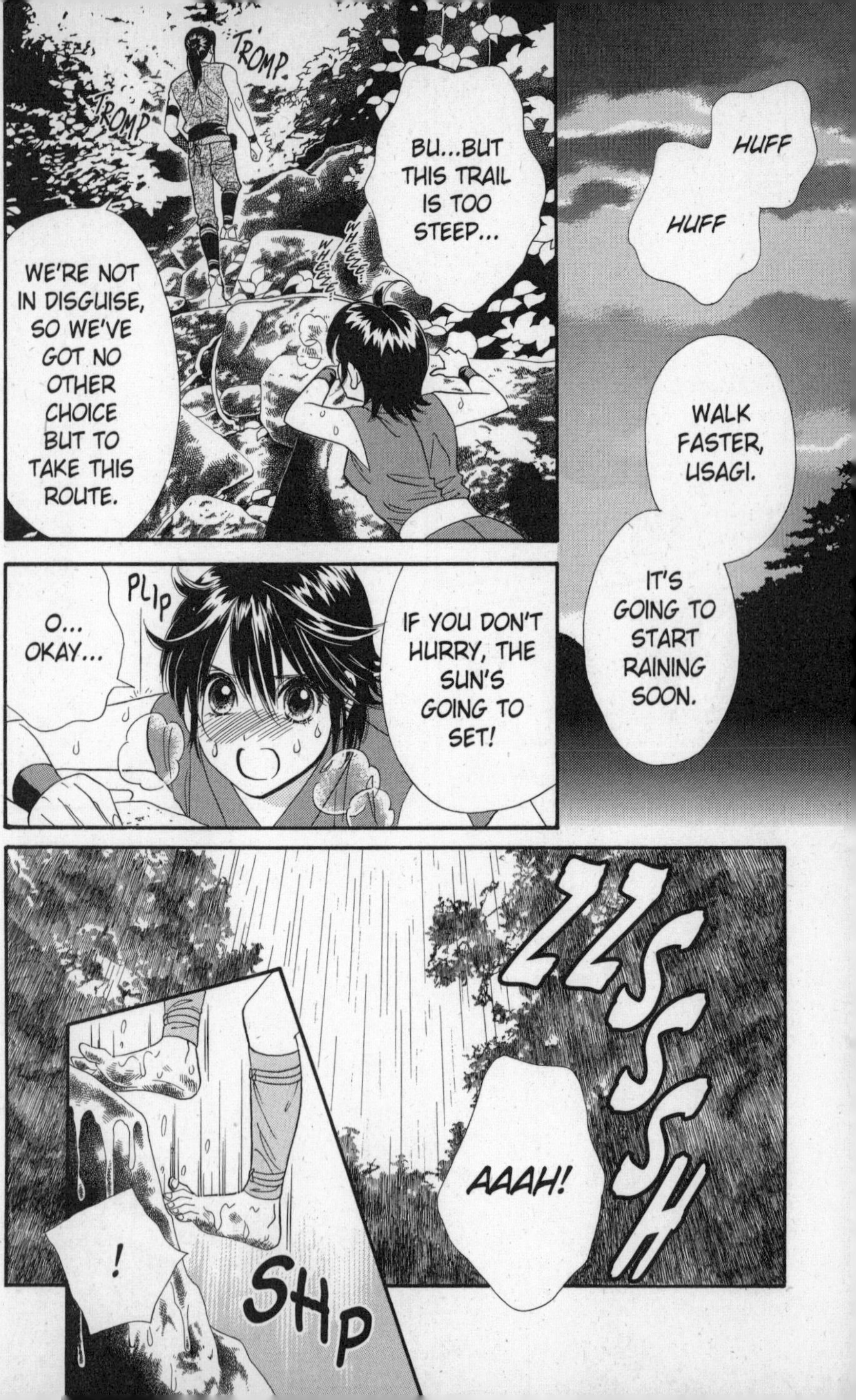
HUFF
HUFF
WALK FASTER, USAGI.
IT'S GOING TO START RAINING SOON.
TROMP
TROMP
BU...BUT THIS TRAIL IS TOO STEEP...
WHEEZE
WHEEZE
WE'RE NOT IN DISGUISE, SO WE'VE GOT NO OTHER CHOICE BUT TO TAKE THIS ROUTE.
IF YOU DON'T HURRY, THE SUN'S GOING TO SET!
PLIP
O... OKAY...
ZZSSSH
AAAH!
SHP
!

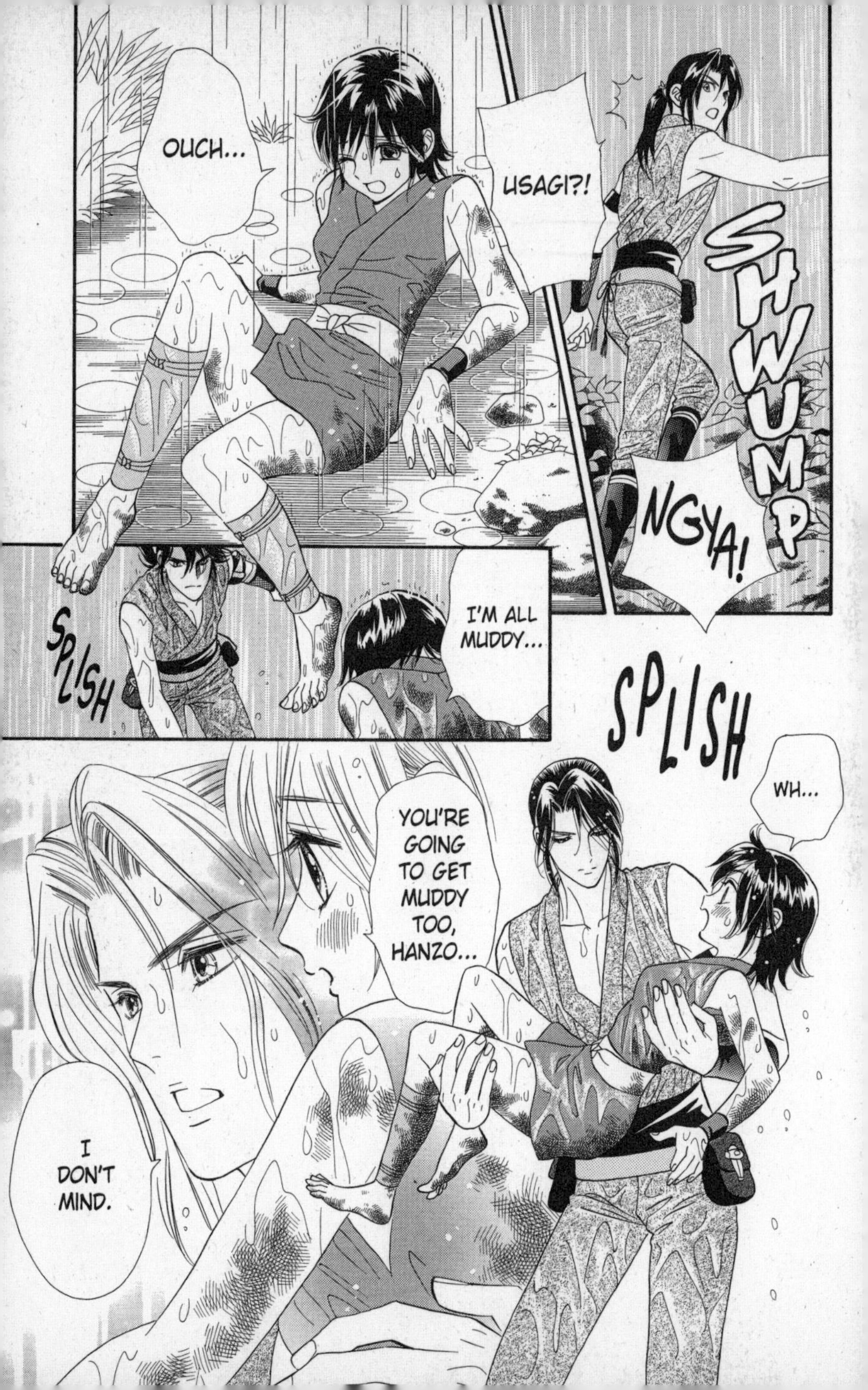
USAGI?!
SHWUMP
NGYA!
OUCH...
I'M ALL MUDDY...
SPLISH
SPLISH
WH...
YOU'RE GOING TO GET MUDDY TOO, HANZO...
I DON'T MIND.

IT'S SO COLD.
TAKE YOUR CLOTHES OFF.
HUH?
I'LL GO AND WASH THE MUD OFF IN THE RIVER.
I'll look the other way.
BUT...
JUST DO AS I SAY!!
OKAY...
RUSTLE
RUSTLE
OH...

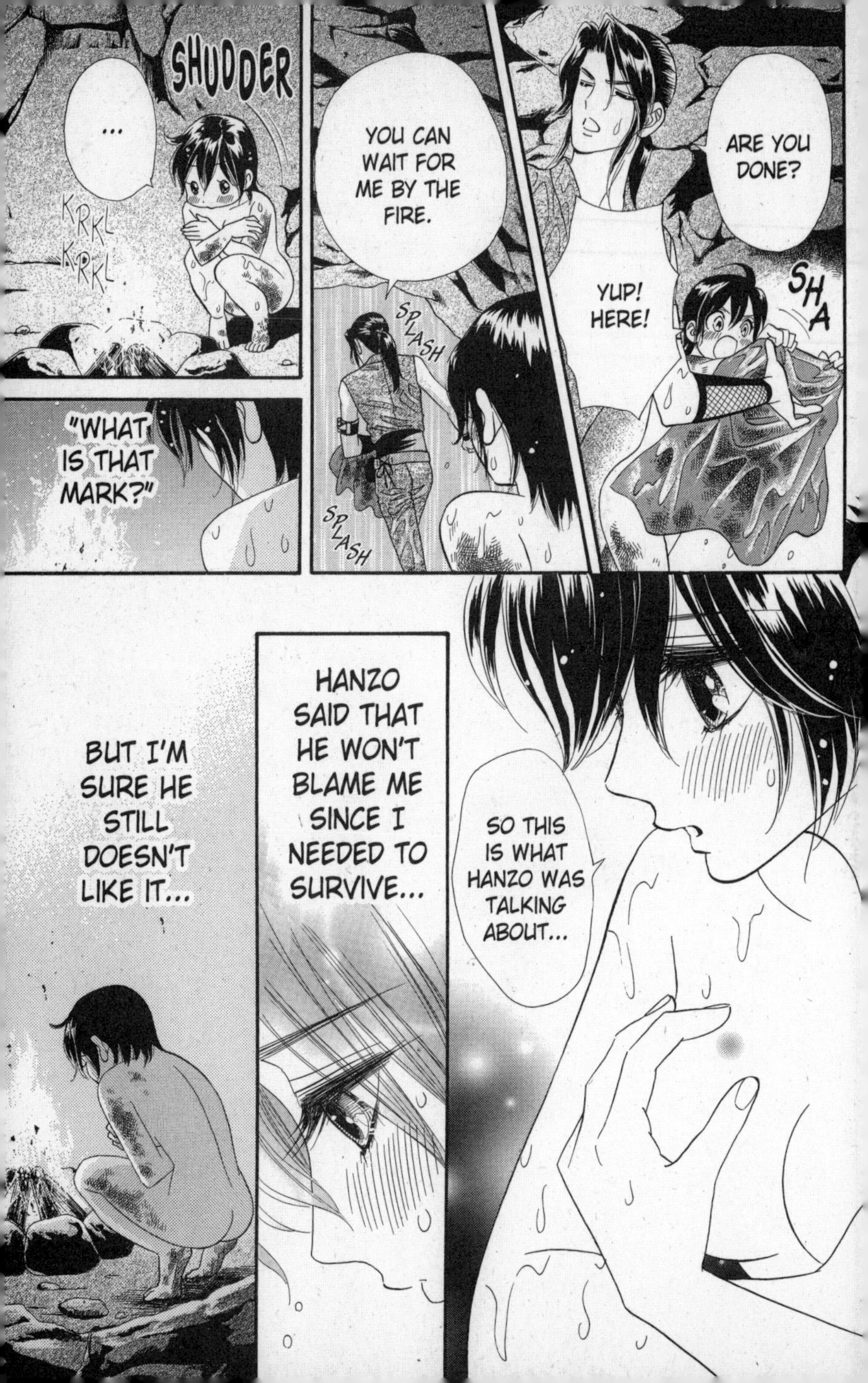
ARE YOU DONE?
SHA
YUP! HERE!
YOU CAN WAIT FOR ME BY THE FIRE.
SPLASH
SPLASH
SHUDDER
...
KRKL KRKL
"WHAT IS THAT MARK?"
SO THIS IS WHAT HANZO WAS TALKING ABOUT...
HANZO SAID THAT HE WON'T BLAME ME SINCE I NEEDED TO SURVIVE...
BUT I'M SURE HE STILL DOESN'T LIKE IT...

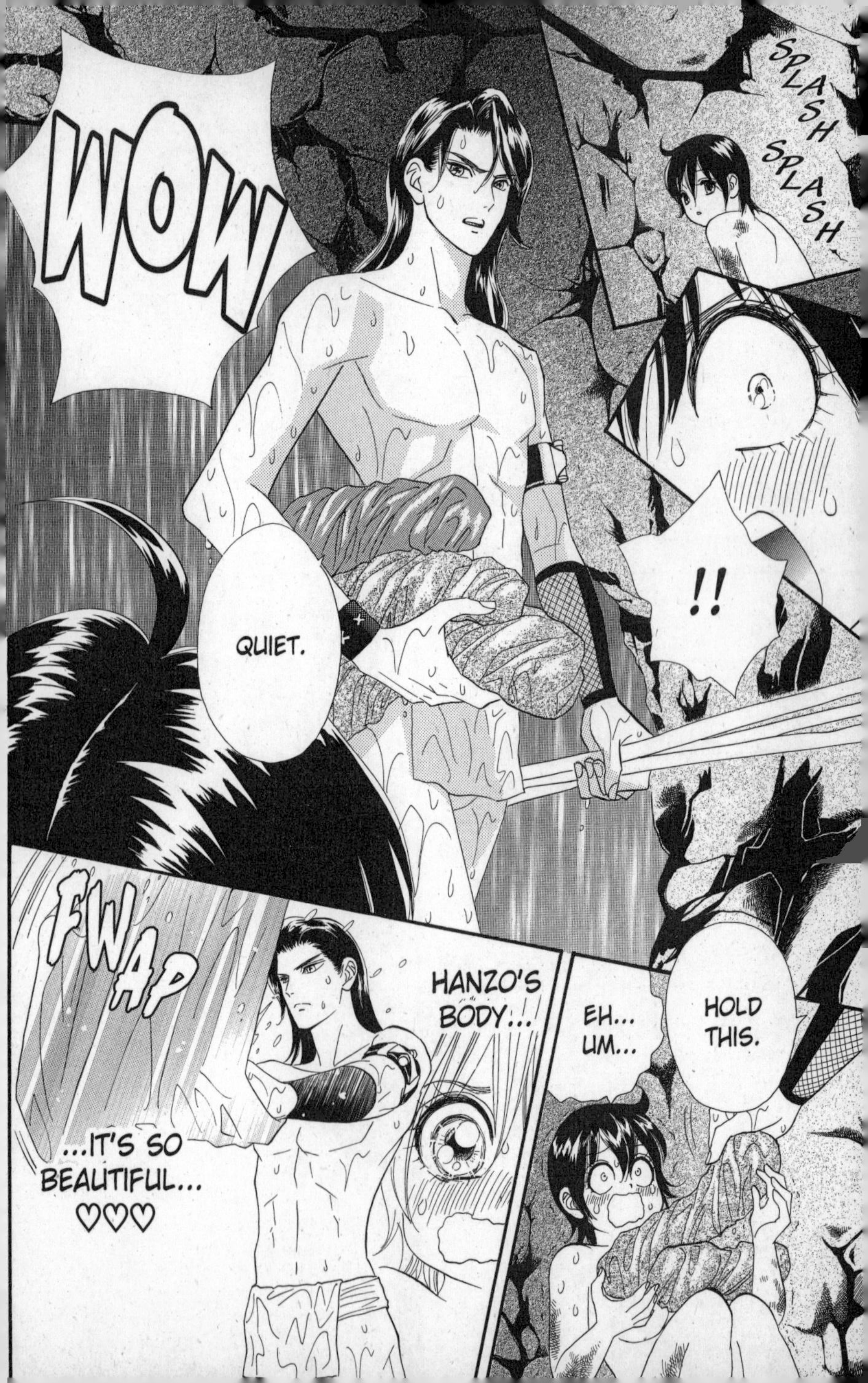
SPLASH SPLASH
!!
WOW
QUIET.
HOLD THIS.
EH... UM...
HANZO'S BODY...
...IT'S SO BEAUTIFUL... ♡♡♡
FWAP

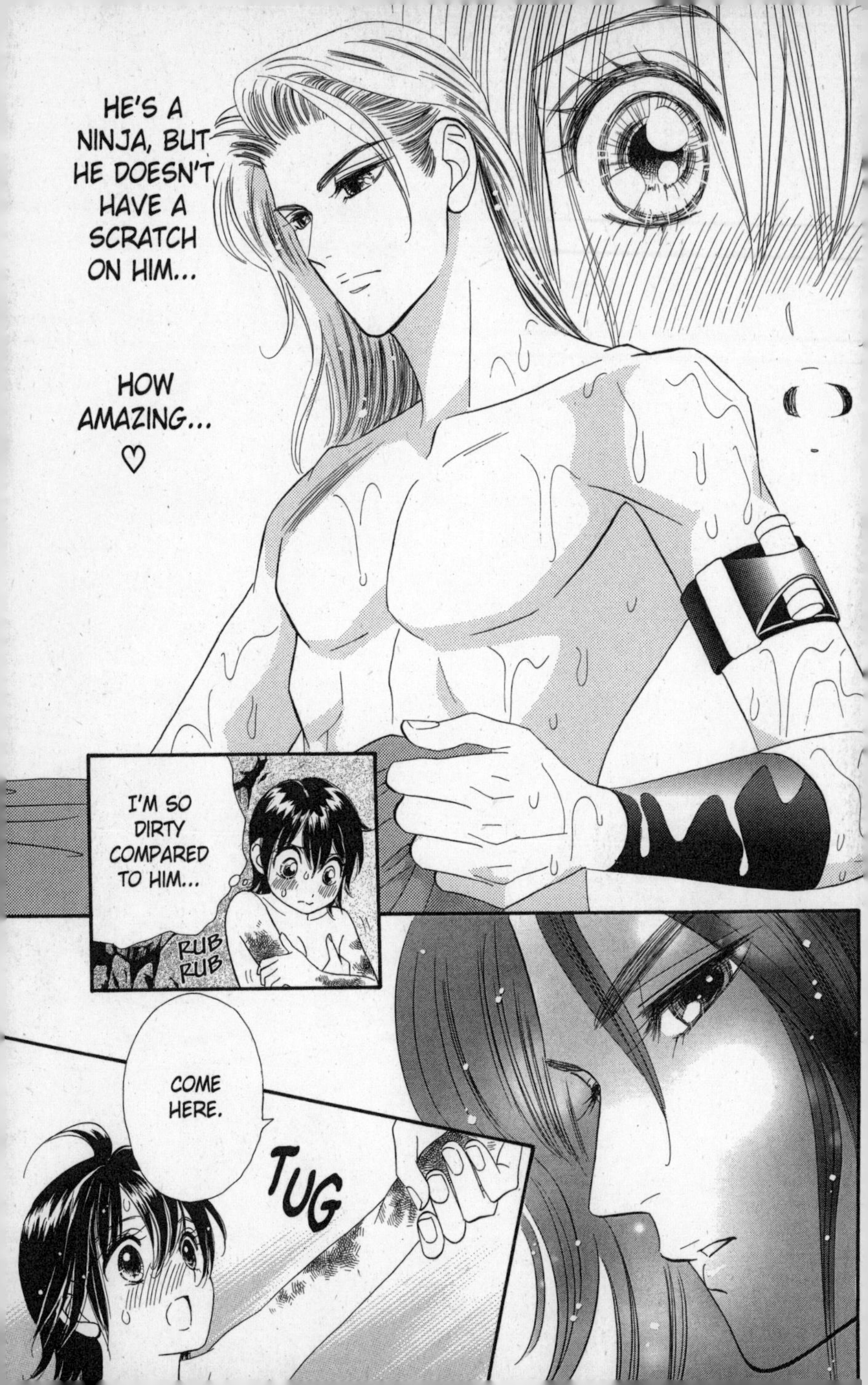
HE'S A NINJA, BUT HE DOESN'T HAVE A SCRATCH ON HIM...
HOW AMAZING... ♡
I'M SO DIRTY COMPARED TO HIM...
RUB RUB
COME HERE.
TUG

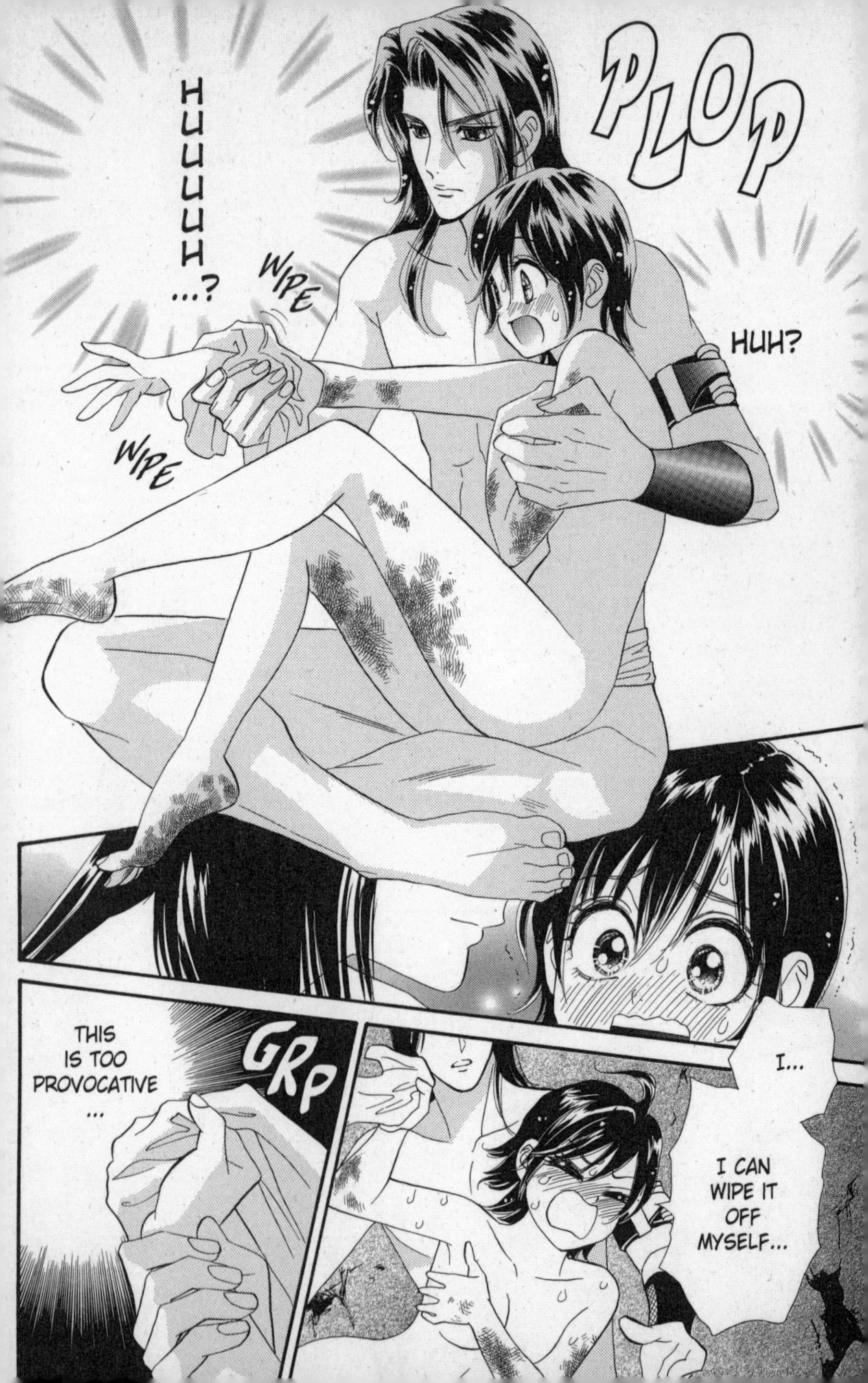
PLOP
HUH?
HUUUUUH ...?
WIPE
WIPE
I...
I CAN WIPE IT OFF MYSELF...
GRP
THIS IS TOO PROVOCATIVE ...

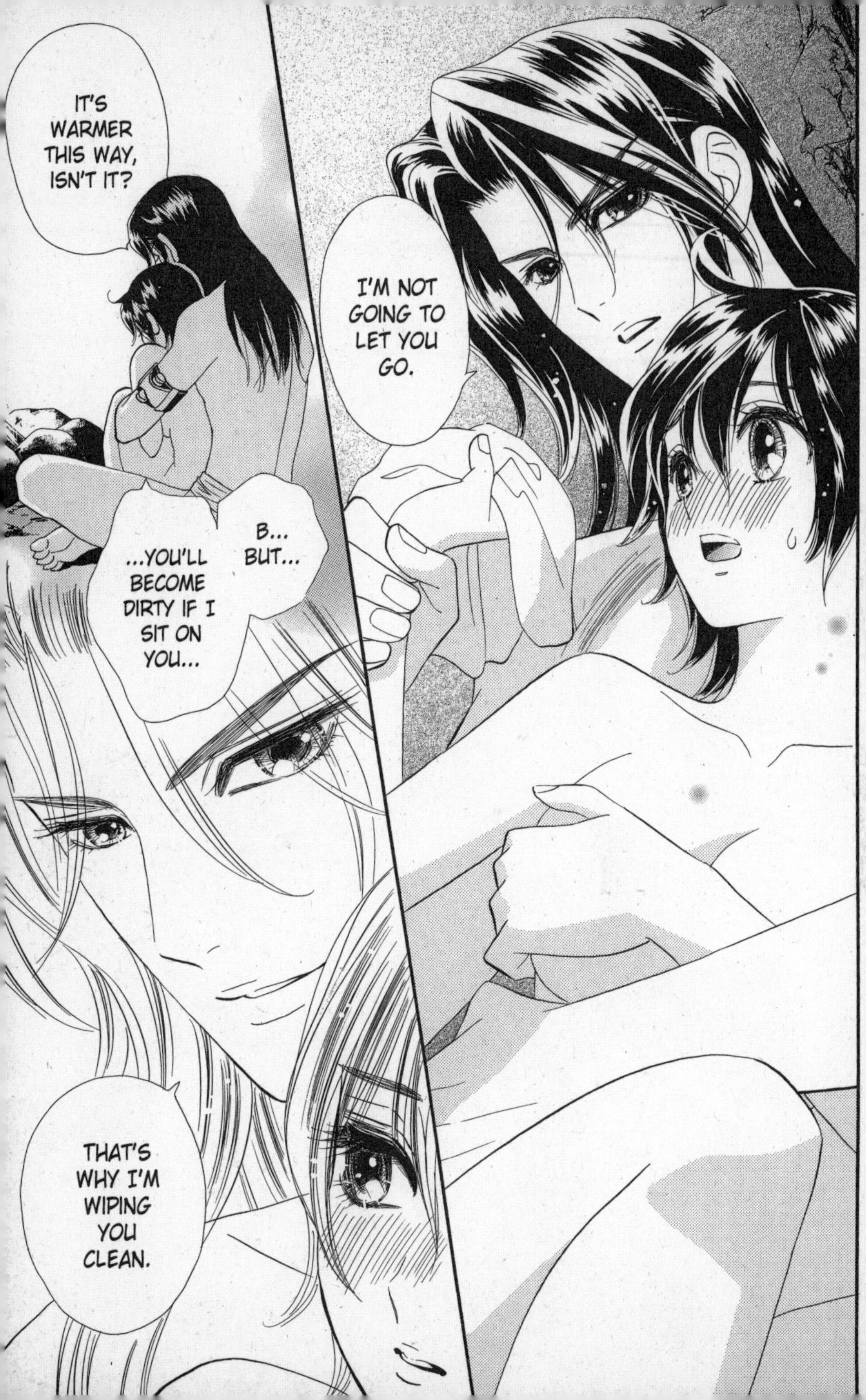
I'M NOT GOING TO LET YOU GO.
IT'S WARMER THIS WAY, ISN'T IT?
B... BUT...
...YOU'LL BECOME DIRTY IF I SIT ON YOU...
THAT'S WHY I'M WIPING YOU CLEAN.

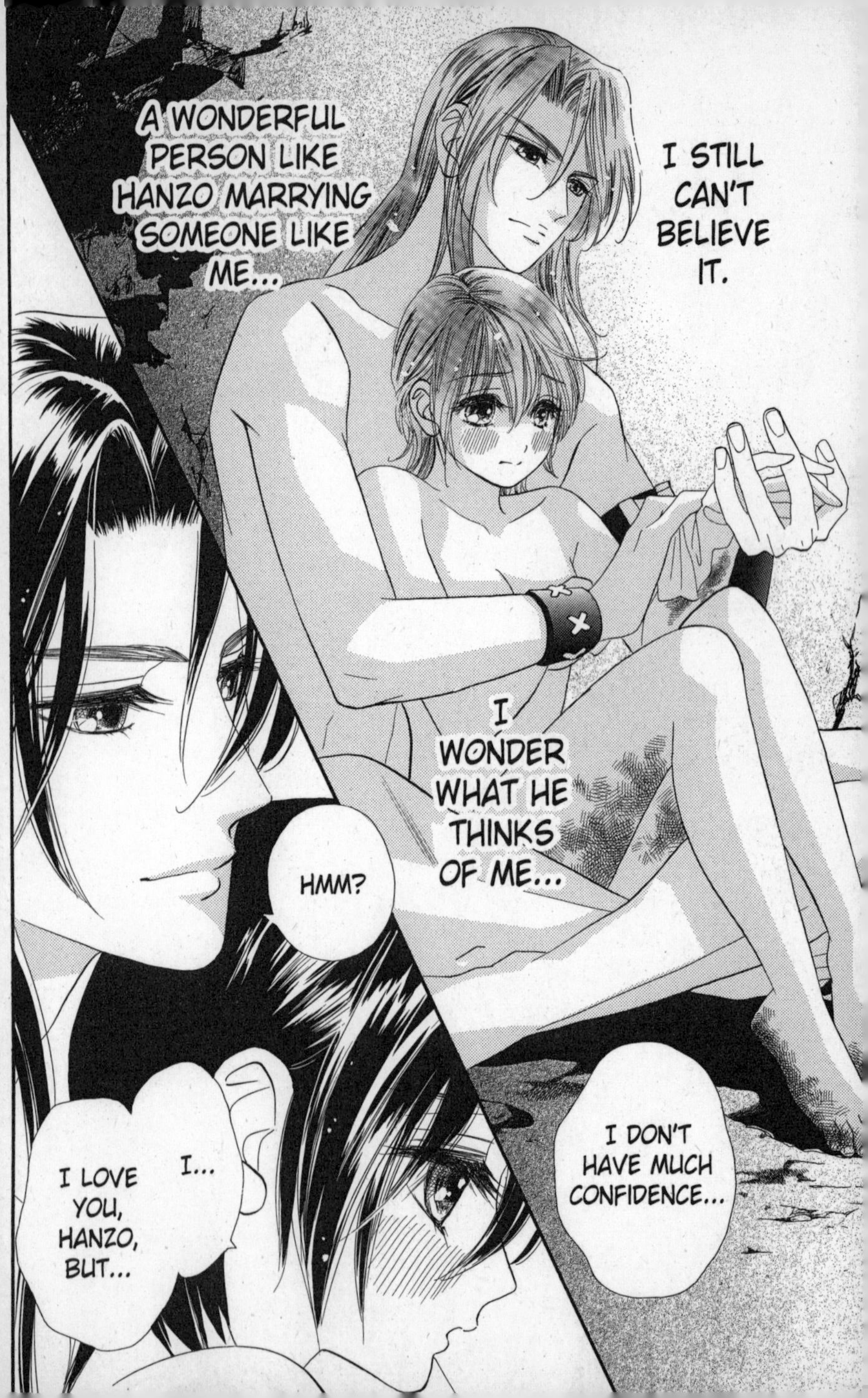

I STILL CAN'T BELIEVE IT.
A WONDERFUL PERSON LIKE HANZO MARRYING SOMEONE LIKE ME...
I WONDER WHAT HE THINKS OF ME...
HMM?
I...
I LOVE YOU, HANZO, BUT...
I DON'T HAVE MUCH CONFIDENCE...

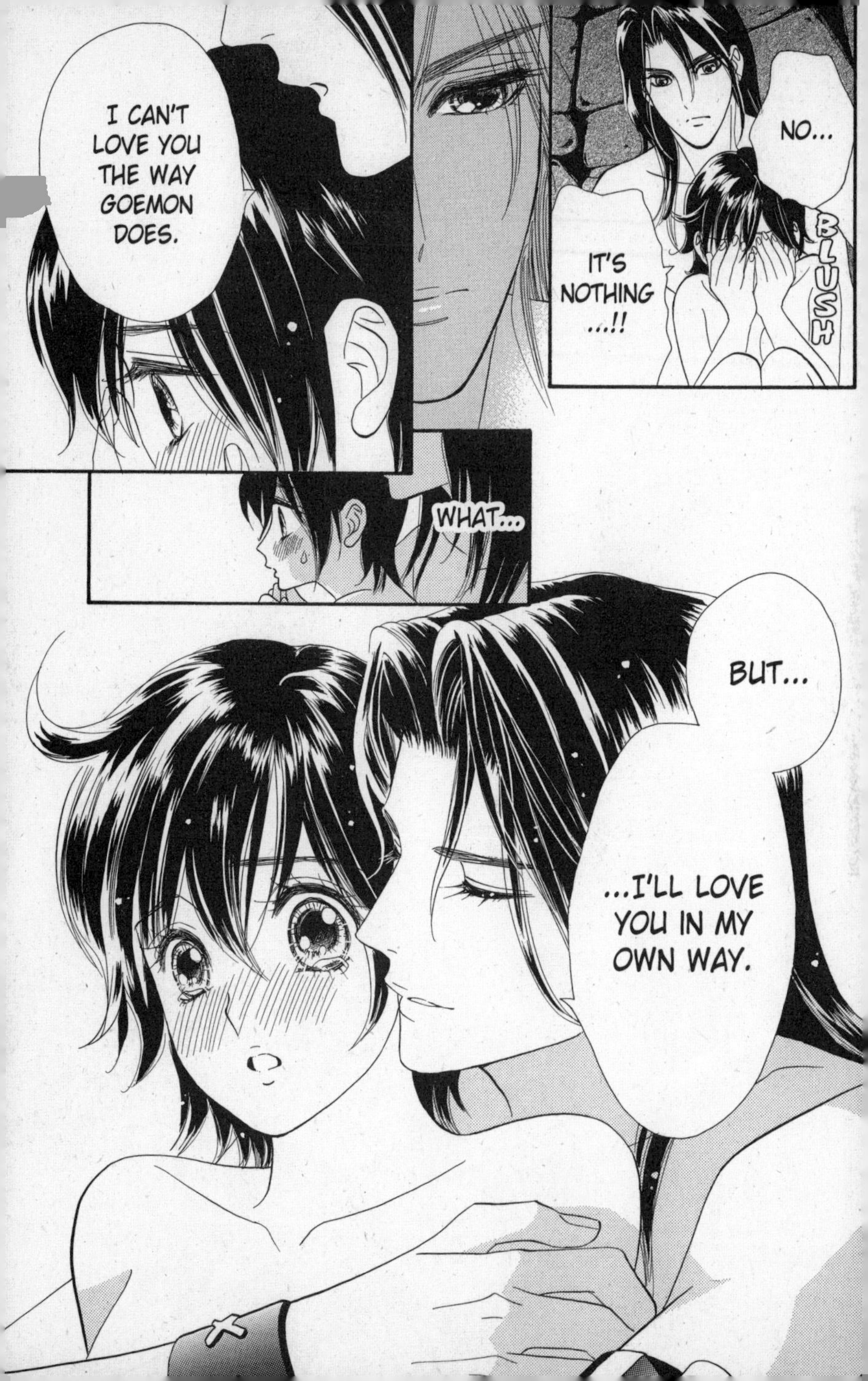
NO...
BLUSH
IT'S NOTHING ...!!
I CAN'T LOVE YOU THE WAY GOEMON DOES.
WHAT...
BUT...
...I'LL LOVE YOU IN MY OWN WAY.

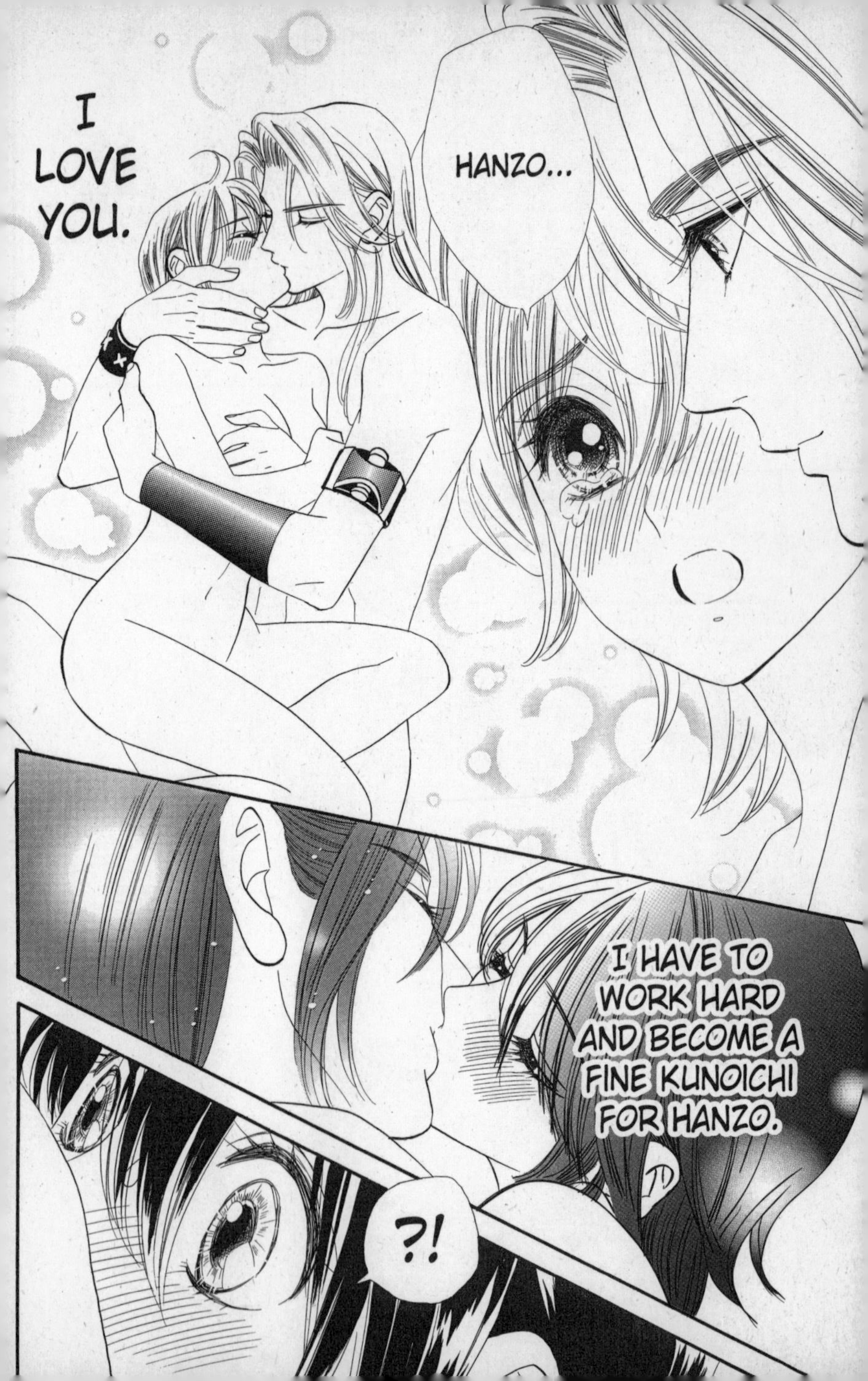
HANZO...
I LOVE YOU.
I HAVE TO WORK HARD AND BECOME A FINE KUNOICHI FOR HANZO.
?!

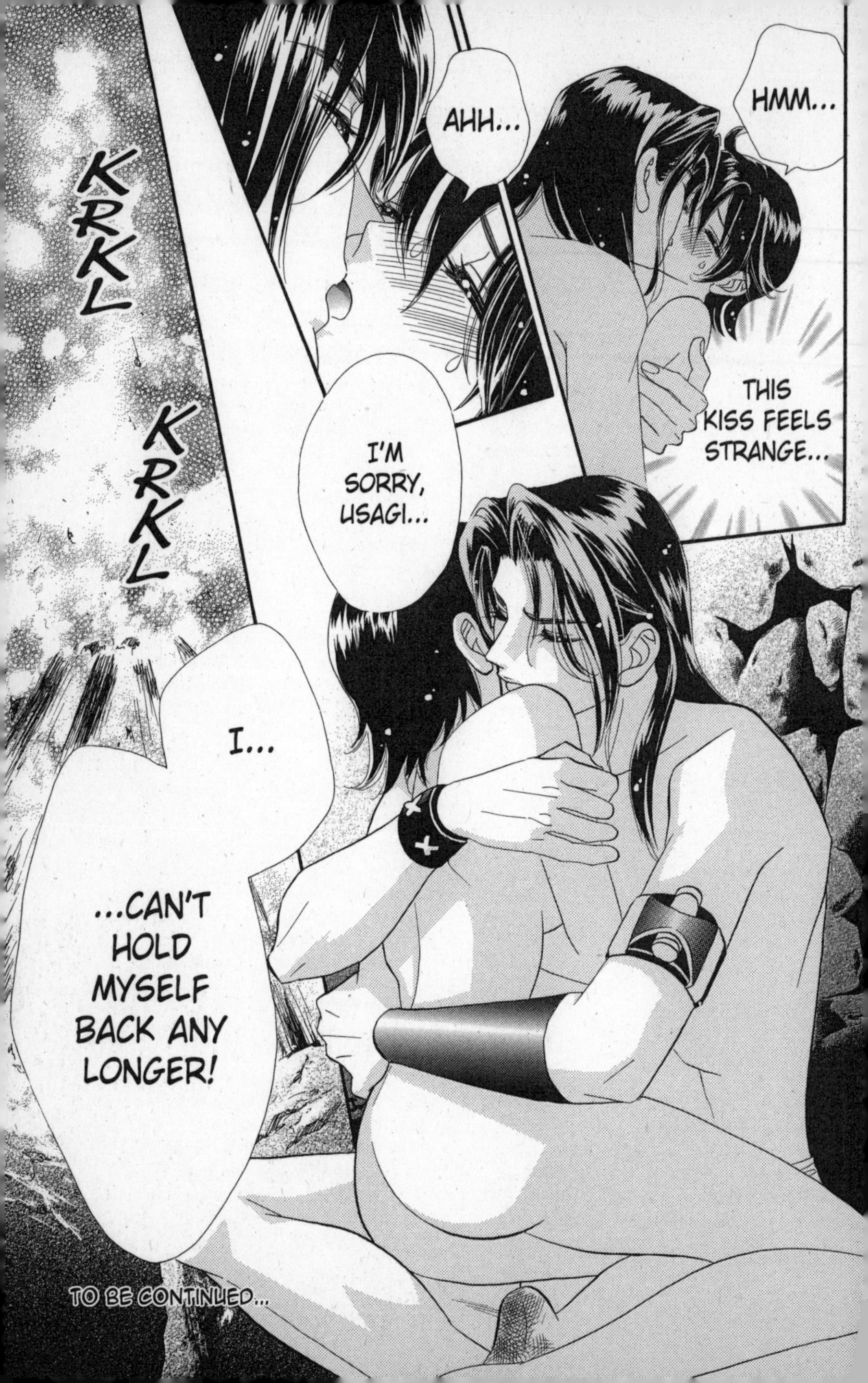
HMM...
THIS KISS FEELS STRANGE...
AHH...
I'M SORRY, USAGI...
I...
...CAN'T HOLD MYSELF BACK ANY LONGER!
KRKL
KRKL
TO BE CONTINUED...

The ways of the ninja are mysterious indeed, so here is a glossary of terms to help you navigate the intricacies of their world.

Page 17, panel 4: Sakamoto
Sakamoto is a small village in Shiga prefecture (once known as Omi province). In 1571, Mitsuhide Akechi was awarded the Sakamoto estate for serving Oda Nobunaga.

Page 21, panel 5: Margaret
Margaret is a biweekly Japanese *shojo* (girls) manga magazine published by Shueisha.

Page 22, panel 2: Oda (Nobunaga)
Oda Nobunaga lived from 1534 to 1582, and came close to unifying Japan. He is probably one of the most famous Japanese warlords. He was the first warlord to successfully incorporate the gun in battle, and is notorious for his ruthlessness.

Page 29: Mount Ikoma
Mount Ikoma is 642 meters high and located right on the border of Nara prefecture and Osaka prefecture. The top of the mountain is actually located within the Nara area.

Page 54: Shinobi
The character on Hanzo's belt is *shinobi*, which is another name for "ninja."

Page 54: "Transform"
The scarf-and-belt look Hanzo's wearing is reminiscent of Kamen Rider, a classical Japanese superhero from the '70s. The main character would utter "Transform!" and change into superhero form when he needed to fight bad guys.

Page 2: Shimo no Hanzo
Shimo no means "the Lower," and in this case refers to Hanzo's geographic location rather than social status.

Page 2: Honnoji
Honnoji is a temple in Kyoto. Oda Nobunaga often stayed here when he traveled to the capital.

Page 2: Ranmaru Mori
Ranmaru Mori is one of Nobunaga's most famous vassals. He became Oda Nobunaga's attendant at a young age and was recognized for his talent and loyalty.

Page 2: Iga
Iga is a region on the island of Honshu and also the name of the famous ninja clan that originated there. Another area famous for its ninja is Kouga, in the Shiga prefecture on Honshu. Many books claim that these two ninja clans were mortal enemies, but in reality inter-ninja relations were not as bad as stories might suggest.

Page 2: Mitsuhide Akechi
Mitsuhide Akechi became one of Oda Nobunaga's retainers after Nobunaga's conquest of Mino province (now Gifu prefecture) in 1566. He is known to have been more of an intellectual and a pacifier than a warrior.

Page 59, panel 1: Kunoichi
A term often used for female ninja. The word is spelled くノ一, and when combined, the letters form the kanji for woman, 女。

Page 106: Duke Saraie
Duke Saraie is a famous posture/walking consultant in Japan who has schools both in Japan and abroad. His "Torso Walk" (the one Hanzo is doing) is one of his most famous walking practices as it supposedly helps one's walking posture.

Page 141, panel 1: Sakai
Sakai is a city in Osaka prefecture that is one of the largest and most important seaports in Japan. Once known for samurai swords, Sakai is now famous for quality kitchen knives and other cutlery.

Page 159: Soramame
Soramame are broad beans, also known as horse beans or fava beans. *Sora* means "sky" and *mame* means "bean." *Mame* also means "often" or "spare no pains in…" Thus, while *Soramame-kun* can be translated as "Mr. Horse Bean," it also acts as a pun meaning "checking the sky diligently."

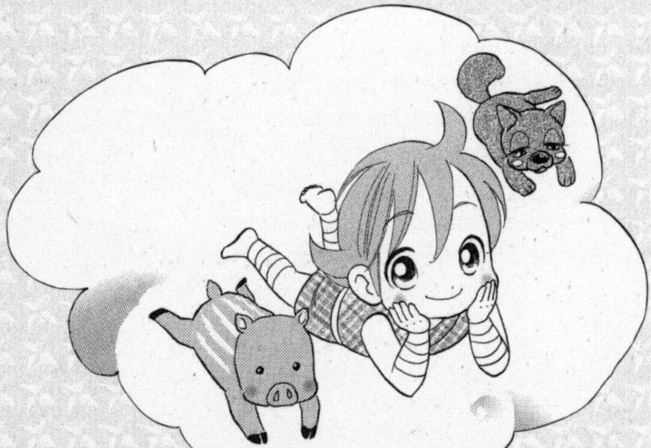

Ever since I started writing this series, I've really enjoyed drawing itsy-bitsy children. I had a lot of fun drawing little Usagi and little Kame for this volume. I also like drawing middle-aged men like Mitsuhide. Oh, and old men, and...

—Rinko Ueda

Rinko Ueda is from Nara prefecture. She enjoys listening to the radio, drama CDs, and Rakugo comedy performances. Her works include *Ryo*, a series based on the legend of Gojo Bridge, *Home*, a story about love crossing national boundaries, and *Tail of the Moon (Tsuki no Shippo)*, a romantic ninja comedy.

TAIL OF THE MOON
Vol. 10
The Shojo Beat Manga Edition

STORY & ART BY
RINKO UEDA

Translation & Adaptation/Tetsuichiro Miyaki
Touch-up Art & Lettering/Mark McMurray
Design/Izumi Hirayama
Editor/Amy Yu

VP, Production/Alvin Lu
VP, Sales & Product Marketing/Gonzalo Ferreyra
VP, Creative/Linda Espinosa
Publisher/Hyoe Narita

Printed in Canada

Published by VIZ Media, LLC
P.O. Box 77010
San Francisco, CA 94107

Shojo Beat Manga Edition
10 9 8 7 6 5 4 3 2
First Printing, April 2008
Second printing, February 2010

www.viz.com

store.viz.com

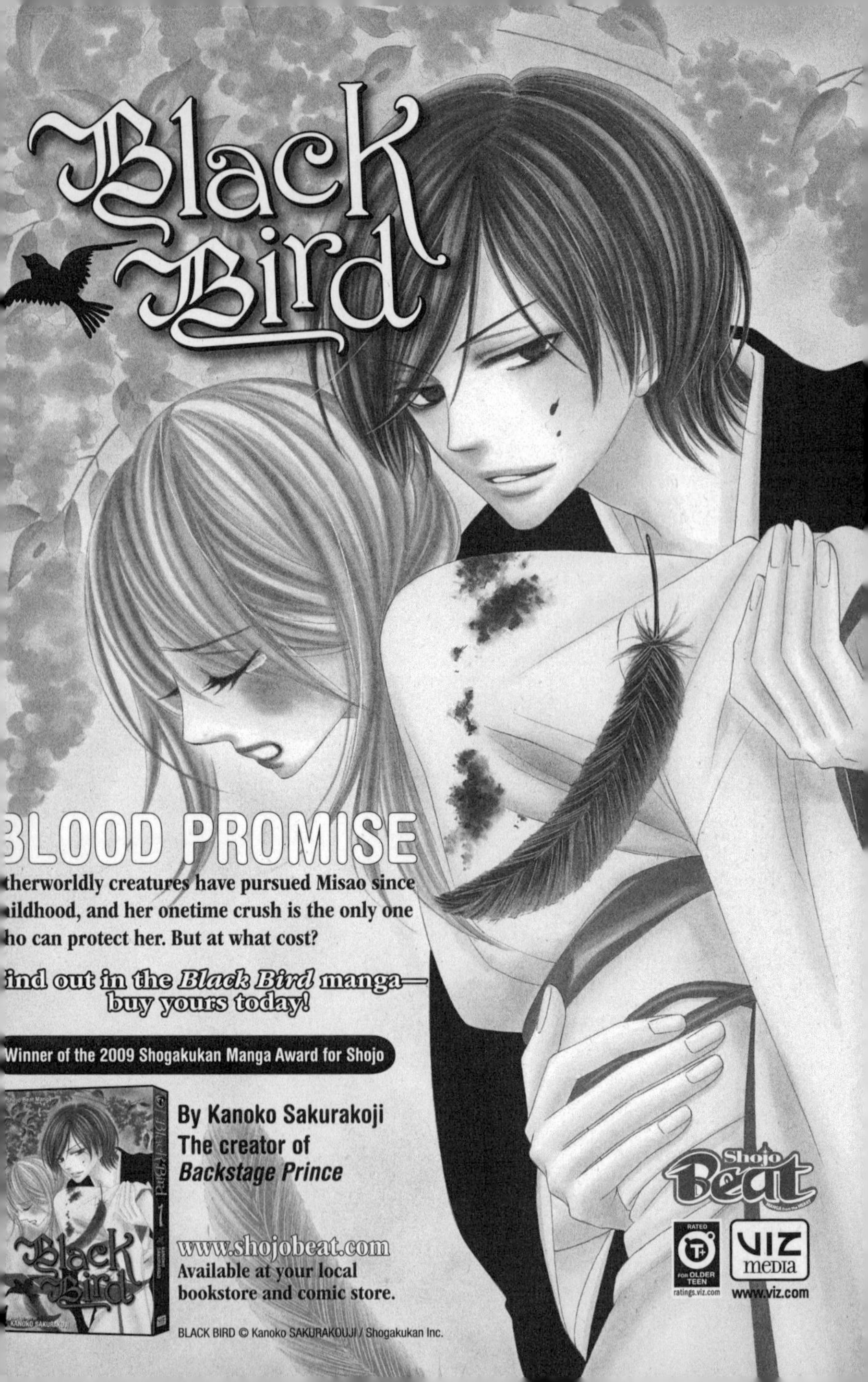

Black Bird
BLOOD PROMISE
therworldly creatures have pursued Misao since
ildhood, and her onetime crush is the only one
ho can protect her. But at what cost?
ind out in the Black Bird manga—
buy yours today!
Winner of the 2009 Shogakukan Manga Award for Shojo
By Kanoko Sakurakoji
The creator of
Backstage Prince
www.shojobeat.com
Available at your local
bookstore and comic store.
Shojo Beat
RATED T+ FOR OLDER TEEN
ratings.viz.com
VIZ media
www.viz.com
BLACK BIRD © Kanoko SAKURAKOUJI / Shogakukan Inc.

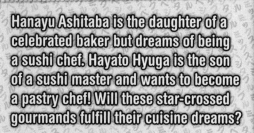

Where unrequited love is a masterpiece

13 uncut episodes on 3 discs

honey and clover
BOX 1

A story of five art school friends and two very complicated love triangles. With so much love to go around, why is everyone still single?

Original and uncut anime now available in collectible DVD box sets

On sale at honeyandclover.viz.com
and at your local DVD retailer

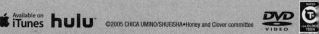

MANGA from the HEART

OTOMEN

STORY AND ART BY
AYA KANNO

VAMPIRE KNIGHT

STORY AND ART BY
MATSURI HINO

Natsume's
BOOK of FRIENDS

STORY AND ART BY
YUKI MIDORIKAWA

Want to see more of what you're looking for?

Let your voice be heard!

shojobeat.com/mangasurvey

Help us give you more manga from the heart!

www.viz.com